Exchanges of Grace

Essays in Honour of Ann Loades

Edited by
Natalie K. Watson
and
Stephen Burns

scm press

British Library Cataloguing in Publication data

A catalogue record for this book is available
from the British Library

978 0 334 04167 2

First published in 2008 by SCM Press
13–17 Long Lane,
London EC1A 9PN

www.scm-canterburypress.co.uk

SCM Press is a division of
SCM-Canterbury Press Ltd

Typeset by Regent Typesetting, London
Printed and bound in the UK by
Biddles Ltd, King's Lynn, Norfolk

Contents

A Tribute to Ann Loades

Ann Loades is undoubtedly one of Britain's most creative and engaging theologians. She has made remarkable and wide-ranging contributions to contemporary theological endeavour, and is perhaps best known as a pioneer of feminist theology in the UK and internationally. Her interests and published work also span the philosophy of religion, theological ethics, Christian spirituality and sacramental theology. She is the author or editor of over two dozen books and of hundreds of scholarly articles and chapters on topics across the range of contemporary theology.

Ann's influence has been wide across the academy. For example, for many years she was deeply involved in the Arts and Humanities Research Board, concerned with public funding for postgraduate research in theology and other disciplines; and her stature is reflected in her recent presidency of the Society for the Study of Theology. She was the first woman to be given a personal chair in the University of Durham. Her 'services to theology' were acknowledged in the bestowal of the honour 'Commander of the British Empire' (CBE) in the 2000 New Year's Honours List, among the first of its kind granted for theological work.

Beyond the academy, Ann has also served the Church, not least as a member of the Doctrine Commission of the Church of England, and as a member of the Church of England's Working Party on Women in the Episcopate. And apart from preaching, involvement in ordination training, and clergy conferences in a variety of settings, she has also shown commitment to her local congregation – as it happens, Durham Cathedral, where she was the first ever female member of the Chapter, and latterly Lay Canon, and where she has over time exercised liturgical and other ministries.

This collection honours Ann, as one of Britain's most interesting and influential theologians, well known and respected in both church and academy, and her vital contribution to contemporary Christian theology in the UK and abroad.

Essays in the volume reflect on her concerns, sometimes directly engaging with her work; several also offer revealing vignettes into Ann's refreshing style and personal verve. As editors of the collection, we wish to add to Ann's luminous list of accolades some of our own. As those who were once her students, we want to lift up her generous attention and nurture of the research students who were fortunate enough to receive her supervision. But more than that, we want to praise the way she so consistently taught and modelled the work of a theologian as one immersed in love of the Christian tradition, and at the same time 'liberal' with it, in the best sense of turning the tradition in order to work into contemporary reflection the meaning of divine mercy – a turn she makes with her characteristically fierce determination. It is her searching attention to the human implications of Christian doctrine that we have ourselves so enjoyed and appreciated in what she has taught us, and we are glad to present this work to her with congratulations and thanks, respect and affection.

We would also like to thank David Brown for his encouragement, enthusiasm and unwavering support for this project.

Stephen Burns and Natalie K. Watson

Human beings need to acknowledge the ways in which freedom and love may both honour one another and generously exchange places with each other on the ladder of ascent.

Ann Loades[1]

1 Ann Loades, 1995, 'Creativity, Embodiment and Mutuality: Dorothy L. Sayers on Dante, Love and Freedom', in Colin E. Gunton (ed.), *God and Freedom: Essays in Historical and Systematic Theology*, Edinburgh: T & T Clark, pp. 103–18, p. 118.

Contributors

Jeff Astley is Founding Director of the independent ecumenical charity, the North of England Institute for Christian Education, and Honorary Professorial Fellow in Practical Theology and Christian Education at the University of Durham. After reading Natural Sciences and Theology at Cambridge and training for the Anglican ministry in Birmingham, he has worked in parish ministry, college chaplaincy, teacher training, ministerial formation and higher education. His 1979 Durham PhD on Ian Ramsey's religious epistemology was supervised by Ann. Jeff is the author or editor of some 30 books in Christian education, practical theology or Christian studies, including academic monographs such as *The Philosophy of Christian Religious Education* (1994) and *Ordinary Theology: Looking, Listening and Learning in Theology* (2002); readers and edited collections such as *Theological Perspectives on Christian Formation* (1996) and *The Idea of a Christian University* (2004); student texts such as *Choosing Life? Christianity and Moral Problems* (2000) and *Exploring God-Talk: Using Language in Religion* (2004); and works on popular theology and spirituality such as *Beyond the Here and Now* (1996) and *Christ of the Everyday* (2007).

Tina Beattie is Reader in Christian Studies at Roehampton University, where she is also Senior Fellow of Crucible – Centre for Education in Human Rights, Social Justice and Citizenship. Her recent publications include *Eve's Pilgrimage* (2002), *God's Mother, Eve's Advocate: A Marian Narrative of Women's Salvation* (2002), *Woman* (2003), *The New Catholic Feminism: Theology and Theory* (2005), *Gender, Religion and Diversity: Cross-Cultural Perspectives*, co-edited with Ursula King (2005), and *The New Atheists: The Twilight of Reason and the War on Religion* (2007).

David W. Brown is Bishop Wardlaw Professor of Theology, Culture and Aesthetics at the University of St Andrews. He was Van Mildert Professor of Divinity, and Canon of Durham Cathedral, from 1990 to

2007, during which time he co-taught sacramental theology with Ann Loades and co-edited with her *The Sense of the Sacramental: Movement and Measure in Art and Music, Place and Time* (1995) and *Christ the Sacramental Word: Incarnation, Sacrament and Poetry* (1996). His other publications include *Tradition and Imagination: Revelation and Change* (1999), *Discipleship and Imagination: Christian Tradition and Truth* (2001), *God and Enchantment of Place: Reclaiming Human Experience* (2004), *Through the Eyes of the Saints: A Pilgrimage through History* (2005), *God and Grace of Body: Sacrament in Ordinary* (2007) and *God and Mystery in Words* (2008). He was elected a Fellow of the British Academy in 2002.

Vincent Brümmer completed a BTh and an MA in Philosophy at Stellenbosch University, South Africa, a ThM at Harvard and a ThD in Philosophy of Religion at Utrecht University (1961), after which he spent a year as research student at Mansfield College in Oxford and five years teaching philosophy in South Africa before becoming professor in the Philosophy of Religion in Utrecht (1967–1997). From 1991 until his retirement in 1997 he was founding director of the Netherlands School of Advanced Studies in Theology and Religion (NOSTER). In recognition of his academic work he received honorary doctorates in divinity from the universities of Uppsala and Durham and a knighthood in the Order of the Dutch Lion. His writings include *Transcendental Criticism and Christian Philosophy* (1961), *Theology and Philosophical Inquiry* (1981), *What Are We Doing When We Pray?* (1984), *Speaking of a Personal God* (1991), *The Model of Love* (1993), *Faith and the Modern World: Lectures and Conversations in Iran* (2004), *Atonement, Christology and the Trinity* (2005) and *Brümmer on Meaning and the Christian Faith: Collected Writings of Vincent Brümmer* (2006).

Stephen Burns is Research Fellow in Public and Contextual Theology at United Theological College, Charles Sturt University, Sydney, Australia. He was formerly Tutor in Liturgy at the Queen's Foundation for Ecumenical Theological Education, Birmingham, UK. After studying theology in Durham (being supervised by David Brown for an MA thesis and Ann Loades for a PhD) and in Cambridge, he entered ordained ministry in the Church of England and served parishes in the Diocese of Durham. He presently holds Authority to Officiate in the Diocese of Canberra and Goulburn in the Anglican Church of Australia. His publications include *Worship in Context: Liturgical Theology, Children and the City* (2006), *Liturgy*, SCM Studyguide (2006), *The*

Edge of God: New Liturgical Texts and Contexts in Conversation, co-edited with Nicola Slee and Michael N. Jagessar (2008) and *Christian Worship: Postcolonial Perspectives*, co-authored with Michael N. Jagessar (forthcoming). He is the editor of the *Renewing the Eucharist* series (2008–9).

Elizabeth C. Galbraith received her doctorate from the University of Cambridge in 1992. She is the author of *Kant and Theology: Was Kant a Closet Theologian?* (1996). In addition to continuing research in Kant Studies, preoccupation with the problem of innocent suffering led Elizabeth to research and teaching interests in Holocaust Studies. The most recent paper to result from the combination of Kantian and Holocaust studies, entitled 'Kant and "A Theodicy of Protest"', was included in *Kant and the New Philosophy of Religion* (2006). Elizabeth is currently a member of the Religion department at St Olaf College, where she is Associate Professor of Religion and teaches Christian theology, as well as Holocaust seminars for undergraduates in Religion. Over the past ten years Elizabeth has become increasingly involved in Japan and India Studies programmes and has a growing interest in Asian Christianity. Her most recent contribution to this area of studies, 'Christian Imperialism: The Case of Indian Christianity', is to be published by *Religion* in 2008.

Daniel W. Hardy died in November 2007, shortly after completing his chapter for this book. As Van Mildert Professor of Divinity at Durham University he was a colleague of Ann Loades. From Durham he moved to Princeton, New Jersey, to become Director of the Center for Theological Inquiry, before an active retirement in Cambridge, where he was involved in the Centre for Advanced Theological Studies in the Faculty of Divinity. His publications include *Finding the Church: The Dynamic Truth of Anglicanism* (2001) and *Living in Praise: Worshipping and Knowing God*, with David F. Ford (2005).

Stanley Hauerwas is Gilbert T. Rowe Professor of Theological Ethics in the Divinity School at Duke University. He is noted as being a leading voice for the recovery of the virtues in moral theology. As a theological ethicist he has written over 30 books covering issues that range from Christian non-violence to medical ethics and caring for people with mental handicaps. His most recent books continue to show his ability to cover a diverse range of topics: *Matthew*, a theological commentary (2007), *The State of the University: Academic Knowledges and the*

Knowledge of God (2007) and *Christianity, Democracy and the Radical Ordinary*, with Romand Coles (2007).

Brian Hebblethwaite read Literae Humaniores at Magdalen College, Oxford and then Theology at Magdalene College, Cambridge, before training for the Anglican priesthood at Westcott House, Cambridge. After a curacy in Lancashire he returned to Cambridge as Chaplain, then Dean of Chapel, at Queens' College and Lecturer in the Philosophy of Religion in the Faculty of Divinity. His publications earned him the higher degrees of Bachelor of Divinity in 1984 and Doctor of Divinity in 2006. Since 1980 he has been Editor for Ethics for the *Theologische Realenzyklopädie* and he was Canon Theologian of Leicester Cathedral from 1983 to 2001. A Life Fellow of Queens' College, he now lives in retirement near Ely in Cambridgeshire. His books include *The Essence of Christianity: A Fresh Look at the Nicene Creed* (1996), *Divine Action: Studies Inspired by the Philosophical Theology of Austin Farrer*, co-edited with Edward Hensderson (1998), *Ethics and Religion in a Pluralistic Age* (1999), *Philosophical Theology and Christian Doctrine* (2004), *In Defence of Christianity* (2006), and *The Human Person in God's World: Studies to Commemorate the Austin Farrer Centenary*, co-edited with Brian Hedley (2006).

John Inge is Bishop of Worcester. He is the author of *A Christian Theology of Place* (2003) and *Living Love: In Conversation with the No. 1 Ladies' Detective Agency* (2007) as well as numerous contributions to other books and articles. He is married to Denise Inge, an authority on the seventeenth-century priest and poet Thomas Traherne. They have two young daughters, a cat and three hens.

David Jasper is Professor of Literature and Theology at the University of Glasgow. He studied for his PhD at the University of Durham under Ann Loades, and was subsequently awarded a DD at Oxford and an honorary doctorate at Uppsala. He was the founding editor of the journal *Literature and Theology*. His most recent books are *The Sacred Desert: Religion, Literature, Art and Culture* (2004) and *A Short Introduction to Hermeneutics* (2004). He is co-editor of *The Oxford Handbook of English Literature and Theology* (2007).

Fergus Kerr graduated at Aberdeen University in 1953, where he was taught memorably by Donald MacKinnon. After serving in the Royal Air Force he entered the Order of Preachers and studied at Oxford, Paris and

Munich. He taught at Oxford from 1966 to 1986 and held the post of Regent at Blackfriars Hall from 1998 to 2004 when he moved to Edinburgh, where he is an Honorary Fellow in the School of Divinity at the University of Edinburgh and Honorary Professor of Modern Catholic Theology at the University of St Andrews. He is a Fellow of the Royal Society of Edinburgh. He has edited the journal *New Blackfriars* since 1995. His books include *Theology after Wittgenstein* (1986, second expanded edition 1997), *After Aquinas: Versions of Thomism* (2002), and *Twentieth-century Catholic Theologians: From Neo-scholasticism to Nuptial Mysticism* (2007).

Robert MacSwain is currently the Ramsey Fellow and Chaplain of St Chad's College, University of Durham, and a doctoral student at St Mary's College, the Divinity Faculty of the University of St Andrews. In addition to publishing articles in philosophical theology and Anglican studies, he is the co-editor with Jeffrey Stout of *Grammar and Grace: Reformulations of Aquinas and Wittgenstein* (2004), with Ann Loades of *The Truth-Seeking Heart: Austin Farrer and His Writings* (2006) and with Michael Ward of the forthcoming *Cambridge Companion to C. S. Lewis*. He is a Priest of the Oratory of the Good Shepherd.

Paul D. Murray, a married lay Roman Catholic, is Senior Lecturer in Systematic Theology at Durham University where he is also Director of the Centre for Catholic Studies. His first monograph was *Reason, Truth and Theology in Pragmatist Perspective* (2004). He is editor of *Receptive Ecumenism and the Call to Catholic Learning* (2008) and is currently working on a book, the working title of which is *Catholicism Transfigured: Conceiving Change in Contemporary Catholicism*. In June 2006 he was elected to the Board of Directors of *Concilium: International Review for Theology*.

Bridget Nichols read English and Classics at the University of Cape Town and taught briefly at the University of the Witwatersrand, before beginning research towards a PhD in Durham. She taught Liturgy in the Department of Theology in Durham and for the North East Oecumenical Course, before taking up a post as Lay Chaplain to the Bishop of Ely. Her publications include *Liturgical Hermeneutics: Interpreting Liturgical Rites in Performance* (1996) and *Literature in Christian Perspective: Becoming Faithful Readers* (2000).

George Pattison is Lady Margaret Professor of Divinity at the University of Oxford, a Canon of Christ Church Cathedral, and Director of the Oxford Centre for Theology and Modern European Thought. After a PhD at Durham on Kierkegaard's aesthetics (supervised by Ann Loades), he worked as a parish priest in Suffolk (1983–91). He was Dean of Chapel at King's College Cambridge for ten years and taught Practical Theology for two years at Aarhus University in Denmark before taking up his present post. In addition to having written a number of books on Kierkegaard (including most recently *The Philosophy of Kierkegaard* (2005)), he is a member of the editorial board of the first complete English edition of Kierkegaard's Journals and papers, and has published on such topics as theology and art, existentialism and the thought of Martin Heidegger. His latest book is *Thinking about God in an Age of Technology* (2005). His work on Dostoevsky is reflected in the collection, *Dostoevsky and the Christian Tradition*, co-edited with Diane Thompson (2001), and he is currently working on a book on Dostoevsky's Christianity.

Peter Selby is the President of the National Council for Independent Monitoring Boards for Prisons and Detention Centres, having served until retirement as Bishop of Worcester and Bishop to HM Prisons in England and Wales. He was a colleague of Ann Loades in the Theology Department at Durham while holding the William Leech Professorial Fellowship in Applied Christian Theology, and preceded her as President of the Society for the Study of Theology. He has published on the resurrection (*Look for the Living*, 1976), on tribalism in the Church (*BeLonging*, 1981), on salvation today (*Rescue*, 1997) and on debt (*Grace and Mortgage*, 1997).

Janet Martin Soskice is the University Reader in Philosophical Theology and a Fellow of Jesus College, Cambridge University. She was born in British Columbia, and studied at Cornell, Sheffield and Oxford universities. She is a past President of the Catholic Theological Association of Great Britain and the Cambridge Theological Society, and in 1997 was the McCarthy Visiting Professor at the Gregorian University in Rome. She is currently a board member of the international Catholic journal, *Concilium* and Chair of the Board of the Margaret Beaufort Institute of Theology, a Catholic house of study for women within the Cambridge Theological Federation. Her recent publications include *Feminism and Theology*, co-edited with Diana Lipton (2003), *Fields of Faith: Theology and Religious Studies for the Twenty-first Century*, co-edited with David F. Ford and Ben Quash (2005) and *The Kindness of God: Metaphor, Gender and Religious Language* (2007).

Kenneth Stevenson studied at Edinburgh and Southampton Universities before being ordained in Lincoln Cathedral in 1973. After two curacies, he was appointed Chaplain at Manchester University in 1980, where he also taught Liturgy in the Theology Faculty. In 1986 he was appointed Rector of Guildford and also served for ten years on the Church of England Liturgical Commission. In 1995 he was made Bishop of Portsmouth and also joined the Doctrine Commission. Since 1997 he has been Chair of the Anglo-Nordic-Baltic Theological Conference and became Chair of the Church of England Porvoo Panel in 1999. In 2003 he was appointed Chair of the Board of Education. He is an active member of the House of Lords. Among his publications are *Nuptial Blessing: A Study of Christian Marriage Rites* (1982), *Eucharist and Offering* (1986), *Covenant of Grace Renewed: A Vision of the Eucharist in the Seventeenth Century* (1993), *The Lord's Prayer: A Text in Tradition* (2004) and *Rooted in Detachment: Living the Transfiguration* (2007). He co-edited with Geoffrey Rowell and Rowan Williams the anthology *Love's Redeeming Work: The Anglican Quest for Holiness* (2001).

Alan Suggate lectured in the Theology Department of Durham University in Christian Social Ethics, especially European and North American but also Asian and Latin American theologies. His doctoral work on William Temple was published as *William Temple and Christian Social Ethics Today* (1987). He has explored sacramental approaches to ethics and, with Oswald Bayer, Professor of Systematic Theology in the University of Tübingen, he edited *Worship and Ethics*, comprising essays from three symposia of German Lutherans and Anglicans (1996). In Asia he focused on Japan and study visits led to *Japanese Christians and Society* (1996). He has served for nearly 40 years on the Arts and Recreation Chaplaincy board and has developed a strong interest in spirituality and creativity.

Elaine Wainwright is currently Professor of Theology and Head of the School of Theology at the University of Auckland, New Zealand. She took up this position in 2003 after 20 years in the Brisbane College of Theology and School of Theology at Griffith University. She is a New Testament scholar who specializes in gospel studies and biblical hermeneutics, with particular interest in a range of contextual and liberation approaches to scripture. Her most recent publication is

Women Healing/Healing Women: The Genderization of Healing in Early Christianity (2006) and succeeds *Shall We Look for Another? A Feminist Rereading of the Matthean Jesus* (1998) and *Toward a Feminist Critical Reading of the Gospel according to Matthew* (1991). Her scholarship is directed to the interpretation of Scripture for the transformation of Church and society toward justice and fullness of life for all.

Natalie K. Watson is a theologian, writer and publisher living in Peterborough, England. She studied theology at the Universities of Tübingen, Germany and Durham, England. From 1994 to 1997 she undertook doctoral studies with Ann Loades on the topic 'Reconsidering Ecclesiology: Feminist Perspectives'. She has published books and articles, mainly in the area of feminist theology, including *Introducing Feminist Ecclesiology* (2002) and *Feminist Theology* (2003).

Samuel Wells, a Canadian by birth, studied at Merton College, Oxford and at Edinburgh University, before coming to study with Ann Loades for his PhD in Christian Ethics at Durham University. His thesis was entitled 'How the Church Performs Jesus' Story'. He served in parish ministry in the Church of England for 14 years in Newcastle, Norwich and Cambridge. In 2005 he moved to North Carolina to become Dean of the Chapel at Duke University and Research Professor of Christian Ethics at Duke Divinity School. He has written several books on theological ethics, including *Transforming Fate into Destiny* (1998, 2004), *Improvisation: The Drama of Christian Ethics* (2004) and *God's Companions: Reimagining Christian Ethics* (2006). His book *Power and Passion: Six Characters in Search of Resurrection* was chosen by the Archbishop of Canterbury as his 2007 Lent book. He co-edited *The Blackwell Companion to Christian Ethics* with Stanley Hauerwas (2004) and *Faithfulness and Fortitude* with Mark Thiessen Nation (2000).

Isabel Wollaston is a senior lecturer in the Department of Theology and Religion, University of Birmingham, teaching and researching in the area of Holocaust studies and contemporary Jewish–Christian relations. Publications include *A War against Memory? The Future of Holocaust Remembrance*, co-edited with Kay Read (1994) and *Suffer the Little Children: Urban Violence and Sacred Space* (2001).

Introduction

DAVID W. BROWN

In this introduction to the themes adopted by other contributors in the course of this book I would like to add some thoughts of my own on Ann and her work. I have provided an intellectual biography at the end of this volume; so there is no need to introduce here a temporal aspect with different phases to Ann's thinking. Rather, I shall focus on certain recurring salient themes.

Fortunately some of my work has already been done for me by the two editors, both former research students of Ann's and therefore well acquainted with her work and with how it might be divided into appropriate categories. So I shall follow their divisions, beginning with Part 1: Searching for Lost Coins, where contributors take up or imitate Ann's interaction with the Christian tradition and, like her, seek its restoration, where appropriate.

Searching for Lost Coins: Dialoguing with the Past

Ann uses the image of lost coins to suggest not just women's hunt for their own identity as part of that tradition but also to express the more positive divine side in 'the almost obsessive quest of the Creator for the creature'.[1] Thus, in Ann's view it is not just a case of a requirement on us today to re-assess the tradition in the light of feminism and other such challenges: there is also an equal need to acknowledge in the process a God who continues to search us out through that tradition. Listening is thus just as important as challenge. So, significantly, the most substantial of Ann's works on feminism is subtitled *Voices from the Past*.[2] So far from these voices being allowed merely to echo present concerns as though their contribution were confined to being pale imitators or tame precursors of feminist issues that are now expressed more adequately, their own distinctive integrity is given full and frank acknowledgment.

Thus alongside such anticipatory elements are set other concerns that they demonstrate sit uneasily with at least some forms of contemporary feminism, and indeed present a challenge to them. So, for example, attention is drawn not just to the more obviously feminist aspects of Mary Wollstonecraft's life and thought but also to her insistence upon rearing her illegitimate child.[3] Josephine Butler's feminist reading of Scripture is set alongside her now largely forgotten concern that prostitutes be recognized as valued human beings with rights equal to the rest of society.[4] Similarly, Dorothy L. Sayers' pursuit of her own career, even though it did involve leaving the care of her child to others, is put in the context of her desire for all forms of work to be seen as creative, whether that be intellectual like her own or more narrowly practical.[5]

So not surprisingly in the contributions to this first part, the past – even where different from today – is often given significant weight. Within that framework three key themes emerge: a common human failing in the desire for control of the present, often through abuse of the past, the ambiguity inevitably involved in any attempt to retrieve the past, and the divine summons nonetheless to live in the light of some future ideal.

Control is a concern that Natalie Watson pursues in the first chapter by considering the case of bullying and the way in which some understandings of the cross, such as penal substitution, might actually contribute to manipulation of this kind, which in the end is destructive of an individual's capacity to receive or give love. The life-giving character of the Christ of the fourth Gospel provides an effective contrast. John Inge takes the Benedictine traditions of the cathedral at Durham with which Ann has long been associated, and observes how Benedict's stress on stability was not intended as a form of control. Rather, it represents an important insight into human nature that we need to recover today: from that stability can come freedom. New towns such as Stevenage were often created without thought being given to any enduring history. Local churches can help to generate that sense of stability as large communities are developed around them. Control is also a central theme in the joint contribution from Stanley Hauerwas and Sam Wells. One of Ann's favourite authors, Dorothy L. Sayers, is put in dialogue with Karl Barth on the question of how Judas' act of betrayal should be interpreted. Intriguingly, both Sayers and Barth agree that Judas should not be seen as evil in the most obvious sense of the term. His objectives may well have been good. But he wanted results only on his terms, not God's.[6] By contrast, Christian ethics should be seen as the way to abandon desire for control, with surrender now made to God alone.

George Pattison uses one of the great figures of Russian literature, Sonya in Dostoevsky's *Crime and Punishment*, to explore whether the common Christian portrayal of the woman who sacrifices herself for others (in this case through becoming a prostitute) is in the end always necessarily destructive of the valuing of women. On the one hand, Dostoevsky provides numerous hints that Sonya is intended as a Christ figure; on the other, in the final analysis her sacrifice is only of limited avail. Pattison insists that such ambiguity is not only truer to life but in part what gives the novel such power. The next contribution, from Isabel Wollaston, also focuses on ambiguities in the past, and in particular on the varied Christian response to Elie Wiesel's famous identification of God's presence at Auschwitz in a child hanging on a gallows. Whereas Jürgen Moltmann chose to elaborate that presence in terms of Christ on the cross, François Mauriac, Johann Baptist Metz and Marcel Sarot all refuse to do so, believing that any such attempt would show insufficient respect for the death's original Jewish context. But Wollaston observes that there is almost as much controversy over its interpretation among Jews themselves. Debate continues as to whether it was in fact a child involved. Equally, doubts have been expressed over the question of whether Wiesel's crisis of faith actually occurred while the incident was taking place or only once the war was over. Authoritative texts are, Wollaston suggests, precisely of this kind: ambiguously open-ended in a way that invites further exploration.

With the final three chapters in this part we move to more obviously ecclesiastical contexts. Kenneth Stevenson takes the largest body of sermons on the transfiguration from one person to survive before modern times, in the writings of the seventeenth-century bishop John Hacket. Although there is a Durham connection with Michael Ramsey (who often spoke of the transfiguration as his favourite theme), despite the frequency with which Ann has been asked to preach, it is not a topic that she herself has tackled, presumably because it is usually a theme that falls to the clergy.[7] As with Ramsey, following Luke (9.30), important links with Christ's crucifixion are made. But the real surprise is how widely Hacket ranges. Not only is classical literature freely drawn upon and shown to be relevant but the suggestion is also made that the disciples' desire to build tabernacles legitimates the beautifying of more ordinary churches. The inference may be improbable but it does demonstrate a desire to entice his diocese beyond the past into new future ideals.

Paul Murray uses his chapter to argue for the importance of an ontological understanding of the sacramental character of the Church. Such pleas can sometimes be the prelude to an essentially conservative reclaiming of the tradition, but not in this case. Murray's contention is that the Church can only function adequately as a sacramental presence to the world if it actually embodies two ideals in particular: a social concern that transcends capitalism and a consultative form of government that is neither wholly hierarchical nor crudely democratic. Finally, Peter Selby recounts the history of Christian support for the slave trade, as well as the Church's more publicized role in its abolition, in order to draw important lessons about self-deception. It is salutary to learn that even some Christian organizations (including the Society for the Propagation of the Gospel) insisted upon receiving compensation from the government for the loss of their slaves. Economic objections against change were seen as sufficient justification for the practice, and similar economic excuses continue as a counter against further change in our own day. Ideals need therefore to be set in the context of a hermeneutic of suspicion of ourselves and our own self-interested reading of both past and present.

In an image that is very much in Ann's style, Selby ends by speaking of the gospel as promising 'the dance of freed slaves'. However, as the contributors in this part amply illustrate, this can only become a reality if the Church takes seriously the critique of its past and in particular the way in which aspects of that past have so often been used, and continue to be used, as a form of control. Many other examples might have been deployed. Among those used here, the ones with which Ann will most empathize are, I suspect, those that most acknowledge the hidden power of evil in ourselves. Like Judas and the slave owner it is all too easy to presuppose in ourselves motives that are both good and right. While such realism about human nature explains why Ann is so concerned that we should not project onto Bible or tradition faults that really lie in ourselves, it is important to note that she is no less insistent that sometimes Bible or tradition is precisely where the fault lies. For Christian interaction with the past not to be counterproductive, an equal care must be exercised in Ann's view in avoiding this other danger: the desire to claim a purity for Bible or Church that denies the ambiguities of evil that also lurk within their own respective histories. The numerous strategies of control that are to be found in both offer an all too effective and sad refutation to any such simplistic view.

It is only once the reader has caught this complexity in Ann's position that she will be seen not to be pulling in two directions at once, but in fact to be consistent throughout. To return once more to the image of lost coins, God continues to search us out and know us as fallible human beings. Of course, there is prejudice against women in the Bible and in the history of the Church. But modern feminists, as they rightly seek a proper dignity for women, can be equally blind to new faults in themselves (or old ones revived). So, for example, while conceding most of Mary Daly's critique of past treatments of Mary the Mother of Jesus, Ann continues to insist on her relevance to women of today, despite her apparent lack of assertiveness.[8] Indeed, at the International Marian Congress in Rome in 2000 she resolutely defended the view that the Church of England has still not gone far enough in recovering that significance.[9]

It is the sort of careful balance that is often given short shrift nowadays. The media in particular prefer either the controversialist or at the very least someone whose views can be neatly summarized in a few lines. Balance is taken for fudge rather than a readiness to grapple with complexities. Yet, in a world where fundamentalism is as likely to afflict the liberal believer as the conservative, the atheist as much as the passionate religious, there surely has never been greater need for minds such as Ann's that resolutely refuse such simplicities. Richard Dawkins' *The God Delusion*[10] has in its few pages as many inadequately founded assertions as the dogmas of some newly established religious sect. Yet, sadly, many believers who seek to escape earlier fundamentalisms in their own lives can often end up just as dogmatic, but now on the opposite side. A telling case in point is Richard Holloway whom I first encountered in his days as a doctrinally conservative Anglo-Catholic. Over the intervening years, he has gradually moved to the fringes of Christianity.[11] While losing none of his considerable communication skills, what makes him for me an unexciting thinker is that he seems effectively to have moved from one type of fundamentalism to another. With his current attitudes a mere echo of current secular values of a particular kind, what one misses is any sense that the Christian tradition, while justly criticized, might also continue to throw up legitimate challenges of its own to contemporary society.[12] Ann is made in a quite different mould. Say one thing, and you will quickly find yourself contradicted, as Ann thinks herself into the alternative position. It is not just feminism that needs more of her ilk.

Imaginative Juxtapositions: Theology as an Integrated Discipline

In this part the various contributors interact with Ann's own understanding of the discipline or practice of theology. Suspicious of purely intellectual approaches to either doctrinal or philosophical theology, Ann has always insisted on the grounding of both in experience, especially in the experience that comes from participating in the life of the Church, its prayer and its worship. While this model could suggest a quietist, inward-looking retreat from the world, Ann's position could scarcely be further removed from any such notion. Her spiritual ideal is someone like Evelyn Underhill who consistently sought to integrate her understanding of mysticism and worship into a life of strong practical commitments.[13] Equally, Ann has repeatedly castigated her academic colleagues for not using greater integration of the various theological disciplines as a base for wider engagement with the world.

Dan Hardy (who sadly died before this volume was published) opens by finding in Ann herself a model of how the theological task should be pursued, given both the range of theological disciplines in which she took an interest while teaching and her deep commitment to worship, especially as this was mediated through the cathedral at Durham. For Hardy, it is the professionalization of theology (typified for him by the creation of the Divinity School and theology degree system at Cambridge in the 1870s) that has led to the wrong kind of perspective: system rather than insight, doctrine rather than wisdom, axioms rather than truths of the heart. Fergus Kerr illustrates how an inadequate understanding of Christian spirituality can itself sometimes be part of the problem, as he explores an important twentieth-century Catholic debate between Marie-Dominique Chenu and his former supervisor, Reginald Garrigou-Lagrange. For the latter, spirituality was essentially about subjective experience, and so not relevant to academic issues, whereas Chenu saw Aquinas' approach to spirituality, in particular contemplation, as integral to recovery of a more holistic Thomist perspective. For Garrigou-Lagrange, such considerations threatened the objectivity of the theological enterprise. But, as Kerr observes, the tide in Thomist studies is now running very much in Chenu's direction.

The next two contributions explore Ann's relationship with the theologian whom Ann herself held up as a model of such integration of 'the truth-seeking intelligence and truth-seeking heart'. Austin Farrer is as well known for the theology he developed in his sermons as in his more academic writings. While Brian Hebblethwaite finds mainly congruence between Ann and Farrer, he does note occasional reluctance on Ann's part to acknowledge the degree to which Farrer was prepared to be purely analytic or theoretical, not least on the problem of evil. It is that same problem which is addressed in Robert MacSwain's chapter, where he considers the one aspect of Farrer on the subject to which Ann has taken special objection. In an appendix to *Love Almighty and Ills Unlimited* Farrer remarks of a handicapped infant who dies shortly after birth: 'The baby smiled before it died', and asks rhetorically 'Will God bestow immortality on a smile?' Ann has responded, 'Well, why the hell not?' MacSwain, while sketching how Stanley Hauerwas' writings on the mentally handicapped can be used to reinforce Ann's objection, does end by observing that the resources for a different answer were already available within Farrer's own writings, the intellectualism of this comment nicely balanced elsewhere by stress on the corporeal character of human identity.

Theodicy continues to be the primary concern in the next contribution, from Elizabeth C. Galbraith, this time focused on the philosopher with whom Ann first engaged at the very beginning of her academic career, in her doctoral thesis. Kant is often presented as an extreme rationalist obsessed with duty and under that guise has had some surprising supporters, among them Adolf Eichmann. Galbraith develops Ann's work on Kant to suggest a rather different thinker. For Kant, 'a negative wisdom' was necessary in the face of inexplicable evil, but not pessimism, since faith urged hope for an ultimate resolution that was beyond human cognition. Thus even at the beginning of her career (whether accidentally or not) Ann had stumbled on the kind of integration she desired in a rather unexpected source. Yet, given Kant's views on worship and prayer, it is unlikely that he would have qualified as a believer in Vincent Brümmer's sense of the term. In his contribution he suggests that neither Richard Dawkins' abandonment of belief in God at 16 nor Antony Flew's acceptance of it at 82 constitute religious belief in the proper sense. Rather than following the rules of Cartesian foundationalism, this must be seen as a way of viewing the world that is founded in particular practices, metaphors and the like. One of Ann's favourite authors, Evelyn Underhill, is quoted to make the point. Even 'the most dissipated tabby on the streets' can induct people into 'the celestial quality of life', provided they refuse to be contained by existing habits of perception.

Elaine Wainwright's chapter certainly provides just such a challenge to new ways of thinking. She resorts to 'the queerer end' of biblical hermeneutics in order to interpret the story of the woman who dried Jesus' feet with her hair. Wainwright's stated aim is to open up a text-positive reading for sex workers and other sexually marginalized groups. Of all the chapters in this part this one might appear, initially at least, to stand at the furthest remove from Ann's usual way of approaching issues.[14] Yet it does illustrate well two aspects of her concern for an integrated theology that are only touched on elsewhere. First, there is Ann's resistance to specialization, her concern that biblical studies, doctrine and history all need to be integrated with one another, not treated as wholly separate disciplines. Such compartmentalization is a common tendency in much contemporary theology and Ann has publicly challenged this more than once. Anxiety about its possible consequences also helps explain her support for institutionalized connections between academic posts and the Church: regular preaching and pastoral and sacramental care constantly recall the individual to broader demands than their own possibly narrow specialism.[15] It may also possibly explain decline in graduate interest in the philosophy of religion and the move of much research in patristics to classics departments.[16] Secondly, there is Ann's desire to relate theology to the wider world, not simply by preaching to it but through recognizing it as itself also a sphere of divine activity, sacramental as it were. Although the tradition of Mary Magdalene as harlot and Josephine Butler's work with nineteenth-century prostitutes gave honour to sex workers in a rather different sense from that intended by Wainwright, there is at least this much continuity: a common acknowledgement of the capacity of those outside the Church not only to be addressed by the gospel but also to offer a challenge in their turn. It is that concern of Ann's with a world in which God is also seen as active beyond the more conventional limits of theology that is the focus of the final part.

The Dance of Grace: A Sacramental World

Part 3 opens with a chapter by Alan Suggate in which the loss of a special kind of chaplaincy work with which Ann was once involved, that to the arts in the north-east of England, is regretted not only in its own right but because of the diminution it implies in a particular attitude to theology. Suggate suggests the arts should never be seen as merely illustrative of a pre-existing theology. Rather, through helping us to discover our own creative capacities they can encourage in us a sense of awe and wonder, not only before nature and its creator but also when confronted with the work of our fellow human beings. The Spirit courses through all of us and so we are all able, in Ann's phrase, to join in the Spirit's dance. Jeff Astley is also concerned with a grace that operates outside the confines of conventional academic theology, which he has labelled 'ordinary theology'. By giving positive significance to this term he intends to plead not just for greater respect for the type of beliefs held by the great mass of ordinary religious believers but also for the distinctive ways in which such beliefs are held. Rather than formal and rational, they are conversational and intuitive, and so allow what he calls the feminine desire for connectedness that exists in all of us (both men and women) to come to the fore.[17] In a self-deprecatory phrase, Ann has frequently compared herself to a rabbit.[18] Her thinking often burrows down a hole and then comes up where others least expect it. But of course in the larger scheme of things all the rabbit's burrows are in fact connected, and so too are Ann's thoughts, as listeners discover when they persevere. Like the images and metaphors of the Christian tradition more generally, it is often those that initially appear the most disconnected that are ultimately most illuminating.

While the first two chapters in this part are concerned with giving a more central place to what might seem at the margins both of theology in general and of the sacramental in particular, David Jasper's chapter starts at the other end as it were, in a reflection on what is meant by sacramental presence in the Eucharist. Jasper suggests that, just as in the Christian sacrament there is both a presence and its deferral or absence, so exactly the same phenomenon is to be found in key literary and visual treatments of the body. The two worlds do not, therefore, stand quite as far apart as theologians sometimes suggest. Stephen Burns' discussion of the role of gesture in liturgy may be used to draw a not dissimilar conclusion. The words of the liturgy may seem to exist in a world of their own but they are communicated in part through the use of gestures (bowing, kneeling, standing, eyes open or shut, and so on) and all of these acts have meanings in the 'secular' world that condition how their religious counterparts are read. So care is necessary in their proper appropriation.

A similar stress on embodiment (a stress which is of course very much Ann's as well) is also to be found in the next chapter. Tina Beattie draws on two doctoral dissertations by female Anglican priests to underline the impact of the dearth of feminist imagery in the Christian sacraments. Particularly pertinent, she believes, is the discovery that a surprisingly large percentage of single mothers take the initiative in asking for the baptism of their newborn child, yet meet no corresponding recognition whatsoever in the traditional liturgies of the Church. However, even as early as Ephrem the Syrian, there was talk of 'the moist womb of the water' conceiving Christ himself at his baptism. One danger in revisions proposed to the liturgy in response to such a critique is that the end is now understood to be the enhancement of the self in some way. Bridget Nichols is acutely aware of such pitfalls. While stressing the importance of gesture and posture as part of training in the proper performance of liturgy, she follows Ann in insisting that the liturgy should have no intrinsic end beyond itself. Worship springs from gratitude for the gracious initiatives of God in the world's history and in our own personal lives, and so calls for no further justification.[19]

Two recurring features of these discussions of our placedness in the world, whether directly or as reflected in the liturgy, have been its bodily character and its pure particularity. Bodily expression is integral to what it is to be human and this means that we often learn indirectly and in particular ways rather than by some sort of universal system. Such an understanding challenges not only any exclusive reliance on abstract thought but also any over-simple claim to the presence of universal gestures in something such as liturgy that has encompassed such different times and cultures. Standing may mean taking responsibility for our actions but it can also indicate humility or inferiority, no less than kneeling.[20] Stick out your tongue in one cultural context and its intention is rude; in another it becomes a form of greeting. And so on. So much of the knowledge that we gain through our bodies is of this very particular kind that it also creates similar expectations elsewhere. As Janet Martin Soskice observes in the final contribution to this volume, it was a truth that Gabriel Marcel learnt while dealing with relatives' requests for information about the missing during World War One. It led him to a deep distrust of any kind of universal system, such as the Hegelianism he had earlier espoused. Yet such particularity, Soskice insists, should not lead to any diminution of hope, hope that God is at work creating a loveliness in us that means that we 'will learn in the end – to dance'.

It is entirely fitting that these should be the last words of the last contribution. For many, even for some of her former colleagues, Ann's passion for ballet and dance must have seemed quite disconnected with her other passion for theology. But closer inspection suggests otherwise. So far from being a marginal unrelated activity, it can be used to illustrate the three concerns that the editors have identified in Ann's writings in academic theology.[21] First, while some appreciation for ballet is possible without prior knowledge or training, like Scripture itself understanding is hugely enhanced the more one is immersed in traditions of interpretation and re-interpretation. Second, while some forms of dance are pure fun and others essentially intellectual exercises (even if applied), the most rewarding remain those that also have a spiritual dimension. The grace of the dancer is not just human achievement but can also convey something mysterious and transcendent. Finally, to state the obvious, dance is fully embodied and in the world, yet suggestive of so

much more. The dancer's leap hints at two worlds united more suc-
cinctly and effectively than many a more conventional theologian's
struggling pen. So however pessimistic of human nature one becomes, as
with the poet W. H. Auden optimism can remain and with it the knowledge that:

if there when Grace dances, I should dance.[22]

I began this essay by noting the double sense attached by Ann to the
notion of 'lost coins': God's search for us no less than our search for
God. It has been an important recurring aspect in her thinking. As
recently as 2005 she wrote,

a fundamental presupposition in reflecting on the relationship
between 'sacramentality' and 'spirituality' in a specifically Christian
mode is that there is a God who searches for human beings and makes
it possible for them to search for God in their turn.[23]

It is that conviction of God searching us out in the apparently most
unusual of places (including the arts) that has ensured that her concern
for the integration of the various theological disciplines has never been
introverted or inward-looking. 'Exchanges of grace' will be seen to
occur everywhere, if only we learn to expect and hope for them: not just
in the New Testament but also in liturgy no less than in the Hebrew
Scriptures, in the writings of Kant no less than in those of Barth, in
migrating birds no less than in dance.[24] It is with that largeness of vision
that the following chapters are concerned.

Notes

1 Actually a quotation from Donald MacKinnon, but also one of the reasons Ann
gives for valuing highly the work of Evelyn Underhill: 'The single most important conviction of her life was that God extends an invitation to be loved to each and every
human being.' See Ann Loades, 1997, *Evelyn Underhill*, London: Fount, p. xii.
2 Ann Loades, 2001, *Feminist Theology: Voices From the Past*, Oxford: Polity Press.
The publishers' desire for a more general main title (*Feminist Theology*) unfortunately
diverted many potential readers away from what was really a quite innovative work.
3 Loades, *Voices from the Past*, pp. 7–70, esp. pp. 22–5.
4 Loades, *Voices from the Past*, pp. 71–139.
5 Loades, *Voices from the Past*, pp. 167–92, esp. pp. 179–80. See also the relevant
extract in Ann Loades (ed.), 1993, *Dorothy L. Sayers: Spiritual Writings*, London:
SPCK, pp. 131–43.

6 As well as including Sayers' insightful comments on Judas' motives, Ann's collection of extracts from Sayers highlights a moving poem in which Judas and Jesus are envisaged meeting one another after death: Loades, *Dorothy L. Sayers*, pp. 12–15, 104–5.

7 Ramsey was Van Mildert Professor of Divinity at Durham (1940–50) and bishop of the diocese (1952–6).

8 Ann Loades, 1990, 'The Virgin Mary and the Feminist Quest', in Janet Martin Soskice (ed.), *After Eve: Women, Theology and the Christian Tradition*, pp. 156–78.

9 Reprinted as Ann Loades, 'The Position of the Anglican Communion Regarding the Trinity and Mary', *New Blackfriars* 82 (2001), 364–74.

10 Richard Dawkins, 2006, *The God Delusion*, London: Bantam Press.

11 Richard Holloway, 1997, *Dancing on the Edge: Making Sense of Faith in a Post-Christian Age*, London: Fount, was still addressed to his fellow-Christians. Two years later, in Richard Holloway, 1999, *Godless Morality: Keeping Religion Out of Ethics*, Edinburgh: Cannongate, he had, in the view of many, fallen over the edge.

12 For example, the dilemma of 'the fourteen-year-old girl in a no-hope housing estate' is used in support of the present abortion act, but no mention made of the extent to which abortion has become merely an alternative form of contraception. See Holloway, *Godless Morality*, pp. 109–30, esp. p. 123.

13 A 'mysticism active and practical', even if in retrospect she implicitly conceded by her pacifism in World War Two that her support for World War One had been somewhat naïve. See Loades, *Evelyn Underhill*, pp. 8–9, 19, 54–8.

14 It is difficult, for instance, to envisage Ann writing with ease of feet as 'phallic symbols'.

15 As successive holders of the Van Mildert canon professorship at Durham (Stephen Sykes, Dan Hardy and then myself) can vouchsafe, much was owed to Ann for her support of the principle wherever it came under challenge.

16 The suggestion of her Presidential address to the SST (Society for the Study of Theology): *Discourse* 2 (2006), 29–47, esp. p. 41ff. On the latter, for example, the classics departments at Reading and Southampton secured funding for a study of the Greek Bible in the Graeco-Roman World, and that at St Andrews for study of the history of the reception of Augustine.

17 By 'connectedness' he means what is more experiential, less confrontational and more practical.

18 The analogy was apparently first suggested to her by Stephen Sykes.

19 Defended by Ann in her Dublin essay, reprinted as Ann Loades, 'Why Worship?', *In Illo Tempore* 16 (2001), 34–42.

20 In imperial Rome emperors sat while courtiers stood, which is why in earlier church history bishops delivered their sermons seated.

21 Illustrations of all three points can be found in my own chapter (written with the aid of Ann's invaluable advice) on 'The Dancer's Leap' in David Brown, 2007, *God and Grace of Body: Sacrament in Ordinary*, Oxford: Oxford University Press, pp. 61–119.

22 Final line of his poem 'Whitsunday in Kirchstetten'.

23 Ann Loades, 2005, 'Sacramentality and Spirituality', in Philip Sheldrake (ed.), *The New SCM Dictionary of Christian Spirituality*, London: SCM Press, pp. 553–5, esp. p. 553. Her views on the topic are expounded at greater length in Ann Loades, 2005, 'Sacramentality and Christian Spirituality', in Arthur Holder (ed.), *The Blackwell Companion to Christian Spirituality*, Oxford: Blackwell, pp. 254–68.

24 For birds and theological hope, see Loades, *Evelyn Underhill*, p. 57.

PART I

Searching for Lost Coins:
Dialoguing with the Past

Chapters in this part test the vitality of the Christian tradition, resulting variously in affirmation and/or critique of its resources and relevance for contemporary life, which Ann has exemplified in her contributions to feminist theology and in particular in her concern to retrieve from the tradition crucial and durable contributions of women.

A Wider View or the Place where Love is Possible

Feminist Theology, the Cross and the Christian Tradition

NATALIE K. WATSON

Shortly after my arrival in Durham in the autumn of 1993, I was told that one of the female members of staff in the Theology Department where I was about to begin graduate study had supposedly left the Church and rejected Christianity altogether because Christianity was, in her judgement, irredeemably patriarchal. Nothing could have been further from the truth. While there are feminist thinkers such as Mary Daly and Daphne Hampson who have rejected Christianity, or at least a version of it, as irredeemably patriarchal, Ann Loades shared with me and many other students a strong sense of the importance and the joy of discovering and engaging with the Christian tradition, not merely as an intellectual exercise but essentially as the embodied continuity of worship and study, liturgy and writing.

Ann Loades was one of the pioneers of feminist theology in Britain. Although her work as a theologian, philosopher of religion and ethicist spans a much wider range of subjects, her three books in this area are landmarks that deserve much deeper appreciation and critical discussion than has hitherto been offered. *Searching for Lost Coins: Explorations in Christianity and Feminism* was published in 1987, followed by *Feminist Theology: A Reader* in 1990, and eventually, immediately before her retirement, by *Feminist Theology: Voices from the Past* in 2001. Central to all of these is engagement, the critical reading and re-reading of the Christian tradition that offers a 'wider view'.

Searching for Lost Coins is the publication of five lectures given as a response to an invitation by the Scott Holland Trust on 'theology and the significance of gender'. The Scott Holland lectures, established in 1920, are required to focus on 'the religion of the Incarnation in its bearing on the social and economic life of man [sic!]'.[1] In the first lecture, Ann Loades states:

> I write . . . with the working assumption that Christianity may still make a contribution to the perceptions of those concerned to try to shape new futures for women and men and the relationships which may obtain between them.[2]

Quoting Donald MacKinnon, she describes the search for lost coins as 'one feminine-related term for "the relentless, almost obsessive quest of the Creator for the creature"'.[3] Such a search is more than 'women's hunt for their history'. What is at stake is what Henry Scott Holland calls 'social fellowship'. Further on, she describes the Christian tradition as a 'paradoxical resource for us today'.[4] What is important here is that, in order to engage with this paradox (and aren't some of the most important aspects of Christian theology expressed in the form of mystery and paradox?), we have to widen the field of our search. Sources for theological reflection are to be found not only in the tomes of academic theologians of the past but essentially in the lives of men and women for whom their faith becomes a source for constructive and creative wrestling, not only with the texts presented to them but also with the circumstances in which they find themselves and their fellow human beings. Loades explores some features of the non-biblical tradition 'in order to find out what might still seem to be positively helpful and what has to be repudiated'.[5] She then moves on to discuss one particular development of the tradition, the 'morbid over-identification with Christ as suffering victim'.[6] Here, in an exploration of the life and work of Simone Weil, who died of self-inflicted starvation in 1943, she warns against a potentially lethal selective reading of the tradition and comments:

> It was the alliance between matter and emotion that she was unable to explore, and which might have put the elements of Christianity that she did explore into perspective, and thus discover their appropriate meaning. It is one thing to employ the metaphors of the 'imitation of Christ' as the context of love and then be sustained by it in a situation of extremity, but quite another to make the bare possibility of being in that situation a focus of attention outside the context of love. Without that context life may be eaten away by metaphor, with those who employ it literally tested to destruction by it.[7]

In 2001, Ann Loades returned to the topic of feminist theology. The contribution she seeks to make with this book is

> to enlarge feminist perspectives in a way that prevents them from being largely self-referential. As equality becomes increasingly a reality, there is a real danger that it will involve leaving some still on the margins of our attention – in some contexts, women themselves, in some others, those for whom they should have legitimate concern.[8]

Loades engages with the lives and the work of three women, Mary Wollstonecraft, Josephine Butler and Dorothy L. Sayers, and three specific issues related to their work that are still current today. These are abortion, the sexual abuse of children and the question whether gender and sexual difference are at all relevant for some aspects of Christianity. She sees as one of the strengths of the Christian faith, which all three of the women studied here share, 'its requirement to think beyond one's immediate concerns, not least in its central focusing concept of a transcendent reality'.[9] An example of this is her discussion of Mary Wollstonecraft's views on abortion. She highlights that what is at issue is not so much whether or not abortion is right or wrong, freedom or murder. Some of the views held by someone such as Mary Wollstonecraft may indeed appear rather dated now, but the task for a feminist theologian in search of lost coins is not so much to retrieve fragments of history forgotten or ignored, but to find in her work pointers towards a wider perspective that places the issues in hand in the context of what it means to be human in the image of God.

What then is this wider perspective? Is it really just the finding of her-stories alongside the official line of Church history, the unearthing of the forgotten work of women marginalized and excluded from male-dominated spaces such as the Church?

Ann Loades criticizes other writers and organizations who have engaged with the work of these three women for largely having ignored the religious faith that was so central to their lives. She notes that it may be somewhat anachronistic to describe these women as 'feminist theologians':

> Depending on what one makes of theology, a woman might wish never to claim so problematic a description as 'theologian' for herself. That said, to the extent that each of the three women described here wrote and taught theology, it is not wholly inappropriate to describe them as theologians, given that each of them supposed themselves to be talking of God in their own particular ways.[10]

The term 'feminist' can equally be applied to these women as they all worked 'for greater justice for women and children both without and within the churches'.[11]

The key to understanding Ann Loades' view on the significance of the Christian tradition for women is the theological work of Dorothy L. Sayers:

> that the Christian tradition has resources for women still to be worked out, resources that were already identified by Dorothy in the middle of the twentieth century. It is those committed to a sacramental understanding of the world whom we will find most committed to the future for women, rather than those who narrowly focus on biblical texts and attempt what at times seem implausible re-interpretations.[12]

What Ann Loades offers in *Feminist Theology* is a double critique: she challenges the shortsightedness of much modern feminist theology with regard to its history and invites a genuine theological critique of our feminist theological endeavours as genuine engagements with the Christian tradition. It is the latter on which I want to expand here.

Both the Latin *traditio* and the Greek *paradosis* hold connotations not only of that which is lost in translation but essentially also of betrayal. There are elements of the Christian tradition that have been used to distort, to betray, to interpret aspects of it in a way that means the complete and utter betrayal of those to whom it is supposed to give life. Variations of Christian theology have been used to justify slavery, homophobia, violence and incest. A recent volume of *Concilium* speaks of 'the structural betrayal of trust' with regard to sexual abuse in church institutions.[13] Women experiencing domestic violence at the hands of those whom they had trusted with their lives, and children experiencing sexual and physical abuse at the hands of priests and teachers of the faith have time and time again been told that they are to remember and imitate the suffering of Christ on the cross.

Some time ago I found myself planning a series of evening classes with a male colleague. I insisted that my colleague should teach the session on the atonement. When I expressed my strong dislike of the atonement as a theological subject, he pointed to the cross under which we were sitting, and said: 'You have to know why he is up there.' Later I realized that indeed he had a point. Although as a theologian I was able to outline the major theories of the atonement and I could speak of the limitations of substitutionary atonement and penal substitution, I had always found these rather mechanistic and an attempt to explain what was essentially beyond explanation: the complete and utter public, and yet isolated and isolating, suffering of a human being on behalf of others. Yet, I had to know 'why he is up there'. Or at least find a place in my own theology for the fact that he is.

Christian theology has found within it the resources to object to and to some extent end the kind of suffering about which women such as Mary Wollstonecraft, Josephine Butler and Dorothy L. Sayers speak. Ann Loades rightly points out that their religious faith as a source for their social advocacy is a neglected dimension of their work, conditioned though some of their views may be. We are beginning to hear the voices of survivors of sexual abuse, who seek a new theological language that moves beyond traditional male images of divine power and human submission. Yet I wonder if that in itself is enough.

While we have begun to speak theologically about issues such as domestic violence and sexual abuse, very little has so far been said from a theological point of view about the experience of being bullied, an experience of relentless emotional, psychological and sometimes physical violence that can and does lead to a fragmentation of the self that can be profoundly traumatic, yet remains up to now largely unaddressed by Christian theology.[14] Anti-bullying policies are becoming standard, but I fear little has been done to speak (theologically or otherwise) about the experiences of those who are being bullied or neglected, for whom the image of the relentless search may be a disturbing rather than a comforting one, but one that resonates with the experience they will carry with them for the rest of their lives, even when the actual bullying itself has stopped.

The experience of being bullied, be it in the school yard or at work or even in one's own home, can and frequently does lead to Post-Traumatic Stress Disorder, a medical condition also found among soldiers who return from war or victims of torture. There is now a substantial body of literature from the medical profession and in the context of counselling and therapy outlining the symptoms of this form of psychological injury.[15]

Yet as a theologian I insist that there is a wider theological question that is to be addressed. The fundamental attack of the human self, of human dignity and self-worth can lead to excessive detachment and to what is perceived to be an inability to love. The ability to love, however, is the most fundamental expression of being in the image of God. If the ability to love in a human being is marred or appears to have been destroyed, then so is the ability to receive love, the ability to make oneself vulnerable to the other, to be in a place where the whole of human life, joy and pain are allowed to exist and can be borne.

My case here is not merely that of adding another issue to the ever-growing agenda of social concerns that Christians must address, nor is it that of inviting appropriate pastoral strategies for responding to experiences that human beings might face in the modern world. My concern is a theological one: can the Christian tradition be a framework for a reading of human life that is not merely therapeutic but essentially redemptive?

In addition to being told to reflect on the suffering of Christ on the cross, women who suffer violence are often not believed, they are rendered incredible because their experiences do not fit with or disturb male privilege:

> If pastoral care and counselling pretend to help women to live their lives in a liberated and gracious way, the silencing of women by privileged men has to be taken into account. The changing of systems of privilege will cost men a lot of frustration, status, and worldly goods. There is work to be done by pastors and counsellors: work that requires a great amount of courage to see what was invisible, and to hear what cannot be said.[16]

However, this work is not merely to be done by pastors and counsellors but essentially by theologians, whose task it is explore the Christian tradition as a source of language that might enable us to articulate that which cannot be articulated, and to hear that which cannot be said.

Perhaps it is the telling and retelling of the narrative of Maundy Thursday, Good Friday, Holy Saturday and possibly Easter that will enable us maybe not to make sense of, but to hold the experience of betrayal, of the complete and utter fragmentation of the self and to allow it to exist before we rush into 'getting over it' and 'moving on'.

Much western Christian theology, even of a more modern or radical kind, is too narrowly focused on victimhood and how it can be overcome, so that there is no room for the agony of Gethsemane and the reality of the cross without which early Christianity's insistence on the reality of the incarnation remains empty and unrealistic. An example is James Alison's Girardian theology of the 'forgiving victim':

> My thesis is that Christianity is a priestly religion which understands that it is God's overcoming of our violence by substituting himself for the victim of our typical sacrifices that opens up our being able to enjoy the fullness of creation as if death were not.[17]

The canon of the New Testament chose four Gospels from the many that were extant at the time. It is John's account that I want to highlight here. The writer of the fourth Gospel does not say that Christ died for our sins: John's Christ died that we may have life, life in abundance, and as such provides a critical counter voice, a wider perspective, to those who want to reduce the suffering of Christ to penal substitution, or to any theological discourse too interested in overcoming victimhood before the reality of suffering is acknowledged. The Christ of the fourth Gospel enters into suffering knowingly, willingly, and yet triumphantly. When he breathes his last, he gives up, hands over, his spirit (*paredoken to pneuma*). Here, in John 19.31b, we find the Greek word that means 'handing over', 'passing on'. This can be, and is sometimes, read as the beginning of the life of the Church, in which God's Spirit is handed on. It is here that the life and mission of the Church begins.

The early Church discouraged those who actively sought martyrdom, although dying for one's faith was seen as the ultimate consequence of following Christ and the highest form of imitating Christ. Yet the question is whether this is true to a reading of the Christian narrative that takes into account the whole of the Christian story. The beginning of the Christian story is the incarnation, God becoming a human being, God entering the reality of human life and ultimately of human death. Perhaps asking others to imitate Christ, to suffer abuse willingly because Christ did is not the point. Christ entered our reality, bore our suffering. The cross is the place where suffering is allowed to exist, to be seen for what it is: completely and utterly meaningless and beyond what human explanation can contain. It is here, in the wider view offered from the cross, that love becomes possible, that it is possible to transcend patterns of abusing and being abused, to break the cycle of treating other human beings as objects of power, to transcend the human need to atone, where new relationships of love and care are possible.

I doubt that it is Jesus as we find him portrayed in the fourth Gospel whom those who tell abused women to think of Jesus as suffering on the cross had in mind. For the author of the fourth Gospel, the suffering and death of Jesus on the cross are life-giving, not the justification of the destruction of a human being, they are the ultimate fulfilment of the incarnation (*tetelestai*). The death of Christ is the moment of birth of the Church. Christ enters into the reality of human suffering and thereby makes life and love possible. This is the inversion, the overcoming of violence and death in the place where love is possible. John speaks of the fifth wound being the pierced side from which flow water and blood. This is an image of birth, of new creation and new life amidst suffering.

This could offer us a framework that takes us further than counselling and therapy can. Here we are not merely speaking about 'getting over a bad experience', about the need to 'move on', about survival, but about theology done with sufficient integrity to allow for the integration of the whole of human life into our reading and re-reading of the Christian narrative, about a view of human life that no longer regards the past (and the present) as what defines who we are, and a theology that speaks not merely of survival but essentially of life (although our theology of life will be meaningless if we cease to fight for the rights of those who struggle to survive).

The idea of the sacramentality of the word, for example in preaching, is not in itself a feminist one.[18] Yet in a feminist context it is not only the speaking of the word in public worship that is sacramental, but also the listening to and hearing into speech of those who have no voice, whose suffering is unspeakable.[19] Such a sacramental process of hearing and being heard can I think only take place in the gathering of women under the cross, where it is possible to gain a perspective on life that does not reduce our humanity to specific issues, where we find exchanges of grace and where, above all, love is possible.

It is here that our own attempts to atone, perhaps resulting from our own ability to explore the alliance between matter and emotion, must end. Here we can begin to imitate Christ, not by bearing meaningless suffering at the hands of those whom we trusted with our lives, but by allowing our own suffering to be entered into and borne in all its starkness and reality. It is here in the handing on of his Spirit, the inspiration of his Church, that the social action that might end violence and victimhood can begin. This would indeed be an exchange of grace. Then love, and ultimately resurrection, is possible.

Notes

1 Ann Loades, 1987, *Searching for Lost Coins*, London: SPCK, p. ix.
2 Loades, *Lost Coins*, pp. 1–2.
3 Loades, *Lost Coins*, p. 3.
4 Loades, *Lost Coins*, p. 15.
5 Loades, *Lost Coins*, p. 40.
6 Loades, *Lost Coins*, p. 41.
7 Loades, *Lost Coins*, p. 57.
8 Ann Loades, 2001, *Feminist Theology: Voices from the Past*, London: Polity Press, p. 1.
9 Loades, *Feminist Theology*, p. 3.

10 Loades, *Feminist Theology*, p. 5.

11 Loades, *Feminist Theology*, p. 5.

12 Loades, *Feminist Theology*, pp. 167-8.

13 'The Structural Betrayal of Trust', *Concilium: an International Roman Catholic Journal*, 3(2004).

14 A notable exception is Rita Nakashima Brock and Rebecca Ann Parker, 2001, *Proverbs of Ashes: Violence, Redemptive Sufferings and the Search for What Saves Us*, Boston: Beacon Press, which offers an extensive piece of narrative theology that includes reflections on the experience of institutional violence and the inadequacy of most traditional theological language to articulate and meaningfully to address such experiences.

15 See for example the work of Tim Field on bullying in the workplace, and a number of excellent websites such as www.bullyonline.org.uk.

16 Riet Bons Storm, 1996, *The Incredible Woman: Listening to Women's Silences in Pastoral Care and Counselling*, Nashville, TN: Abingdon Press, pp. 138-9.

17 James Alison, 2006, *Undergoing God: Dispatches from the Scene of a Break-In*, London: Darton, Longman and Todd, pp. 50-1. I have elsewhere asked what a feminist critique of James Alison's idea of the 'forgiving victim' would look like.

18 See for example Donald Coggan, 1988, *Preaching: The Sacrament of the Word*, New York: Crossroad, 1988.

19 See for example Natalie K. Watson, 2002, *Introducing Feminist Ecclesiology*, London: Continuum, pp. 99-100.

2

Stability and Sustainability

JOHN INGE

My doctoral work with Ann was on the theology of place. In it I argued for the importance of place, as I have done consistently since. However, Ann is the one who has remained stable in one place whereas I have lived in myriad different places over the past 30 years. She has lived in Durham for most of her adult life, engaging with both the opportunities and frustrations of attachment to one particular place. She was the first female lay member of the Cathedral Chapter at Durham, a 'New Foundation' former Benedictine cathedral. Stability lies at the heart of Benedictinism and it is that stability that I want to explore in what follows. Cathedrals like Durham manifest stability in full measure: even the break at the Reformation displayed remarkable continuity, with the dean taking the place of the prior of the monastery and the canons taking the place of the monks – quite often the first dean being the last prior and the first canons being some of the monks. A Benedictine 'flavour' is detectable in such cathedrals to this day and having served myself at Ely, another 'New Foundation' Benedictine cathedral, for several years, I have had ample opportunity to reflect upon the *stabilitas* that lies at their heart and that Ann embodies. Ann might not in all respects be much like a Benedictine but through her stability she has, arguably, been able to achieve much more than would have been possible if she had moved around. She has given an enormous amount to Durham and to the wider world through the constancy of her work based there.

Chapter 60 of the Rule of St Benedict stipulates that those who join the monastery must promise to remain in it. So crucial is stability to Benedictines that they promise it in one of their three vows, alongside obedience and *conversatio morum*, and it has been argued that the introduction of this vow 'was Benedict's most important contribution to the course of Western Monachism'.[1] The earliest extant Benedictine

Profession Book, dating from the ninth century, contains the vow in the form 'I promise obedience and stability before God and His Saints', nothing more, and since then stability is the one thing that has always been there, sometimes alone, in all the forms of the Benedictine vow.[2] As early as the thirteenth century the distinction between physical and moral stability had been introduced, thus spiritualizing the call to stability,[3] a trend that has reasserted itself in some modern commentaries on the rule. However, the great Abbot Cuthbert Butler tells us that

> it must, I believe, be held that by stability St Benedict intended that his monks should 'persevere until death', not merely in a monastery, but in the monastery of their profession. In other words, I accept what has been called 'local stability' in its most rigid and narrow sense.[4]

To him, and to countless other Benedictines, *stabilitas* thus means sticking with a particular place, a particular community, and allowing it to assist one to find wholeness as one gives oneself to it.

The English in general and Anglicans in particular have been hugely affected by their Benedictine inheritance in a whole host of ways. Benedictinism flourished in medieval England and though it was ruthlessly suppressed at the Dissolution there are again many Benedictine houses in England – in contrast to places such as Portugal, a solid Catholic country, where there is only one. The stability and moderation of the Benedictine life seems to appeal to the English temperament and is reflected in the stability that characterizes English history. Not for the Benedictine, nor the English, the rigours of the Charterhouse: they are attracted to the moderation of Benedictinism, which exalts *stabilitas* rather than self-mortification. (A Benedictine friend said to me once that 'EBC', an abbreviation for 'English Benedictine Congregation', really stood for 'every bodily comfort'.) However, England now reflects the rest of the western world in being characterized by anything but *stabilitas*: ours is, as I have reflected upon elsewhere,[5] an unprecedentedly mobile society. My experience of constant moves is the norm; Ann is the exception. Recognizing such mobility, which derives from the demands of the market, and attempting to cater for it, the Government is promoting what it calls 'sustainability', with regard to both the massive house-building programme it is requiring in the south-east and the regeneration of industrial areas in the north. Official documents wax lyrical about 'sustainable communities'.

'Sustainability' and 'sustainable development' are difficult concepts to pin down. What is surprising, as John Rodwell points out, is not only the varieties of interpretation and understanding of the terms but also 'the momentum of acceptance that they have acquired'.[6] Rodwell spent a year in the Dearne Valley looking at sustainablity and began all his interviews with the basic question 'What actually *is* sustainability?' He found that:

> The commonest key text, often adduced in organizational profiles or recalled by my interviewees, with varying degrees of accuracy, but with essentially the same sentiment, comes from the 1987 report of the World Commission on Environment and Development (Brundland for short, after its chairwoman): 'Sustainable development is development which meets the needs of the present without compromising the ability of future generations to meet their own needs.'[7] This commitment was expressed in the last UK Government report using the particularly resonant phrase 'Securing the Future'.[8]

Rodwell goes on to point out that environmental professionals, along with the other players, take it for granted that social and economic goals will have the priority. That would certainly seem to be the case as far as the influential document *Sustainable Communities: Building for the Future* launched by the Deputy Prime Minister in February 2003 is concerned. At the beginning of it were identified what were described as some of the 'key requirements of sustainable communities'. They included a flourishing local economy, strong leadership to respond positively to change, a safe and healthy environment with well-designed public and green space, high-quality private and public transport infrastructure; good, well-designed and useful buildings; a mix of home and tenures, quality public services such as education, health and so on; and a vibrant local culture. Standing on its own, however, among these key requirements, without any explanation and in inverted commas, was 'a sense of place'. It is encouraging that the importance of a sense of place is recognized but one would search in vain through the rest of the document in order to find some explanation of what is meant by this term for it is not mentioned again. The impression is given, as it is in many planning meetings I have attended, that a sense of place is important in the creation and sustenance of communities without any clear indication being given of what it might be thought constitutes such a phrase. As Wendell Berry suggests, the fact is that

> If the word community is to mean or amount to anything, it must refer to a place (in its natural integrity) and its people. It must refer to

a placed people. Since there obviously can be no cultural relationship that is uniform between a nation and a continent, 'community' must mean a people locally placed and a people, moreover, not too numerous to have a common knowledge of themselves and of their place.[9]

Sense of place is crucial to sustainable communities for, to turn things the other way around, 'to be without a place means to be detached from basic, life-supporting institutions – family, work, polity, religious community, and to be without networks of relations that sustain and support human beings'.[10] It is stability that will enable such sustainable community since, as Benedict recognized, *stabilitas* is crucial to the life of communities and they cannot thrive or be sustained when people are not committed to them. Sustaining communities when mobility reaches epidemic proportions is a huge problem: Timothy Gorringe points out that the average American stays in a place for five years and quotes Langdon who writes that

Repeated millions of times, the decision to move out robs communities of their memories and social relationships. It leaves them shallow rooted, ill equipped to provide their residents with sustenance during hard times. Sociologists have discovered that longtime residents make a disproportionately large contribution to a community; they do much to define its character and create a sense of continuity.[11]

Stable communities are formed by stable individuals and Benedict was concerned with the monks' stability of place as an essential aid to their walk with God. Why is this? Rees puts it thus:

[The] human need to be rooted in a particular locality is behind the monastic exercise of stability with reference both to material objects and to people. A tree often transplanted does not bear fruit. A man usually comes to know himself, and in that knowledge to know God, when he dwells for long periods in a stable relationship to places and persons. The sense of belonging which is generated by familiar surroundings tends to create focus for a man's awareness, so that he is able to ask himself, 'Who am I?' 'Where have I come from and where am I going?' This sense of belonging grows even more from stability of persons, from knowledge of the constancy and predictability of persons established over a long period of familiarity, and from the mutual trust, love, respect, and appreciation which come about only with time and struggle. It is part of the essence of man to be in a situation; hence he is able to receive and integrate his surroundings into himself. There is a close link between the questions 'Who am I?' and 'Where am I?' Through his incarnate situation man discovers his identity and his true relationship to God.[12]

Moving from one place to another encourages people to escape from themselves and is not conducive to psychological stability. Hundreds of years of Benedictine experience in building and sustaining communities make it clear that stability is crucial both to the community and to the individuals who constitute it. How can such stability be enabled in the face of huge changes taking place in our society? This is a question that is particularly pertinent in the east of England, the region in which I lived until recently. This region, which adds Hertfordshire and Bedfordshire to the 'old' East Anglia (Essex, Suffolk, Cambridgeshire and Norfolk), was committed by its Regional Assembly's *Plan for the East of England* in October 2004 to the building of an additional 478,000 houses between 2001 and 2021. The following month the East of England Assembly withdrew its support for the Plan that it had submitted to the Deputy Prime Minister because of what it described as the Government's grossly inadequate funding of associated transport infrastructure costs. However, following an Examination in Public, an independent panel recommended an increase in the total number of houses by 27,500 to 505,000. As I write, the Secretary of State for Communities and Local Government has published the plan so modified for consultation.

Whatever the final result, the number of new houses planned for the region is colossal and will result in a very big increase in the population deemed essential by the continuing economic growth of the area. There are important questions to be asked about whether or not such huge expansion is a good thing, with or without the spending on infrastructure that the Assembly is demanding, the increase being an example of the tyranny of the market that has produced an enormous increase in mobility in our society. However, that is not my task here, which is a much simpler one: to ask the question of whether it makes any sense to talk of sustainability in such a situation given that stability is central to sustainability. In his various works, beginning with his seminal *After Virtue*,[13] Alasdair McIntyre suggests that the development of liberalism that began during the Enlightenment period has led to the fragmentation of community and traditions essential to the creation and sustenance of a just and rational society. I have suggested elsewhere that associated with this development is the erosion of a sense of place that cannot be conducive to human flourishing: what is happening in the eastern region will produce new and unprecedented burdens upon it.

Much of the new growth will be in existing communities, which is by far the best option. The city of Ely increased in population by a third during the ten years that I lived there and this has brought strains. However, the growth has been manageable because of the sense of place and community stretching back generations, and the stability and commitment of the pre-existing population. There is, in particular, a core of people, many of them Christians, who enable the civic life of the place through voluntary work. The growth of Ely has also brought some positive changes in its wake in terms of economic prosperity and improved facilities. However, the huge number of people to be incorporated in the east of England by the Plan means that not all can be accommodated by the expansion of existing settlements. It has therefore been deemed necessary to approve the formation of at least one brand new community in Cambridgeshire and another settlement on the site of the present Cambridge airport of equivalent or greater size.

To talk of sustainability with reference to these new communities is fraught with difficulty, since they suffer in an acute form from the lack of continuity that is so crucial to stability. As Timothy Gorringe has observed:

> One of the problems of New Towns is that they have no corporate memory. When a new town was built around the small agricultural community of Stevenage, the community soon divided, the one with one set of memories, the other with memories from elsewhere which could not be simply superimposed on the new place. Memory and tradition depend on rootedness. As Simone Weil argued, early on in the Second World War, human beings do not survive without roots.[14]

It would seem from this that it is simply impossible for new communities to be sustainable without the stability that roots provide. Is there any way out of this impasse? There has been much effort put into what is called 'placemaking', something that John Sorrell, chairman of the Commission for Architecture and the Built Environment, describes as 'the architecture of everyday life'[15] and that is being enthusiastically embraced by planners. The concept has been around for some time in the United States, a seminal text being *Placemaking: The Art and Practice of Building Communities* published in 1995 by professors of architecture Lynda Schneekloth and Robert G. Shibley. They argue for the involvement of the local community as well as professionals in design and suggest that placemaking is a 'celebration of difference and an affirmation of common interest'.[16] Consultation is undoubtedly a good thing but it is not enough to create the sustainable communities that the Government requires, particularly when constructing communities from scratch. I have been heavily involved personally in consultations concerning one new community, Northstowe, a settlement of 10,000 homes to be built north-west of Cambridge, but there is a fundamental dilemma when there is no one living in a place with whom to consult.

There are very considerable difficulties here. However, the manner in which Benedictines have generally interpreted stability might be of some help. Rees tells us that Benedict did not make geographical stability an end in itself and that

> stability should not be interpreted in such a rigid way that every departure of a monk from the monastery of his profession is looked upon as a kind of apostasy. There is sufficient precedent in the lives of holy monks to indicate that a change of place or a transfer to a different community may sometimes be desirable for a monk.[17]

Peifer makes it clear that there are circumstances which would justify a change of monastery:

> St Benedict himself abandoned the community of Vicovaro when it became evident that his efforts there could bear no fruit, and many of his saintly followers, in similar circumstance, have done the same. There are sufficient precedents in the lives of Benedictine saints to show that a change of monastery may sometimes be what God wills for an individual monk.[18]

Further, and germane to the question of new towns, small groups of monks have very often left the physical location of a monastery in order to found a new one of the same congregation. When they do so it is intended that they should be 'leaven in the lump' of the new community. In this manner, at least some aspects of *stabilitas* can be transferred from one physical location to another since the memory and tradition of the community moves with the new settlers. I would suggest that it is in this manner that the potential of the contribution of the Church to new communities might best be considered and valued.[19] Given the impossibility of creating a sustainable community *ex nihilo*, some sort of sense of community can be engendered out of a bunch of new houses through the presence and witness of the Church. Where there is no corporate memory in a place, the church is able to connect it to the Christian tradition, from which so much of what is valuable in our society derives, and to serve the people who live in the place in practical ways.

The example of two new communities close to Cambridge exemplifies this point well. The churches in Cambridgeshire played a major part in the development of Bar Hill, a new community just outside Cambridge built in the 1960s and 1970s, which is the home of a vibrant Christian congregation reaching out to a large village of several thousand people. The church at Bar Hill is an ecumenical project sponsored jointly by the Church of England, the Methodist Church, the United Reformed Church, the Baptist Church and the Religious Society of Friends. From the very early days of the creation of Bar Hill the Church has been at its heart, providing worship and community services of all sorts in terms of ministry to children and young people. The original small church is now used as a base from which to provide these facilities and a larger building has been constructed adjacent to it in order to accommodate the regular worshipping congregation of some 200, as well as to enable the expansion of community work. This building is in the centre of the village adjacent to Tesco, icon of twenty-first-century Britain, providing a physical reminder of the Christian roots of our society and the fact that the Christian Church is still flourishing and making a crucial contribution to the common good.

A more recent development at Camborne, some nine miles west of Cambridge, has demonstrated how crucial to the development of community the Church can be. Though the developer's brochures showed a 'signature building' with a 'significant vertical aspect' (a politically correct manner of describing a church, we assumed), no such building was provided. Aware of this lacuna, the churches purchased a house on the development in which they housed a minister who began the work of creating a Christian community using Portacabins, named 'The Ark', placed adjacent to Morrisons, the only community facility there for some time. The Christian community was formed from Christians who had moved into Camborne, who brought with them, as do Benedictine monks moving to a new place, Christian practice and tradition as well as a commitment to serve the community. As a result, the contribution that the Church has made to Camborne is generally recognized as being immense:

> Chris runs the community youth club, and used to chair the residents association. Roger is 'Mr Fix-It' in the community and is hoping that he might retire from his Cambridge job and become the clerk of the

parish council. Both had church backgrounds in the deep past; the first now calls himself a card-carrying atheist and the second is completely de-churched. Yet both freely admit and admire that if anything good happens in the community, it probably happens at the Ark.[20]

The Ark still exists but there is now also a community centre very close by. A church school has recently opened, a move that enables the contribution of the churches to be increased, though raising sufficient funds for constructing the 'signature building' that the developers would like is an ongoing problem since the community is inevitably quite small and does not have access to significant funds.

The importance of the Church to the life and health of communities is not widely recognized: the East of England Sustainable Development Framework makes mention of faith only in listing as one of its very many objectives that of recognizing 'the value of the multi-cultural/faith diversity of the peoples in the region'.[21] However, the Joseph Rowntree Foundation has corroborated what many of us know to be the case, that

> [F]aith communities contribute substantial and distinctive bridging and linking social capital through their co-presence in urban areas, their connecting frameworks, the use of their buildings, the spaces that their associational networks open up, their engagement in governance, and their work across boundaries with others in the public domain.[22]

Meanwhile, research by the University of Cambridge commissioned by the East of England Faiths Council has confirmed the enormous contribution that faith groups make to the common good in all sorts of areas including work with homeless people, food distribution and the promotion of both formal and informal learning.[23]

What is not said in such research is that the Church puts communities in touch with the wellsprings that have nurtured its common life over centuries and provided much of what entitles our society to be called civilized. Though our society is an amnesiac one that sometimes prefers to forget the importance of its history, particularly its Christian history,[24] it is the Church that has provided one of the main ingredients of stability, sustainability and sense of place. As the report *Faithful Cities* puts it:

> faith-based organizations make a decisive and positive difference to their neighbourhoods through the values they promote, the services

they inspire and the resources they command ... The value of civic and communal commitment is unparalleled by any other agency and the church need have no embarrassment in presenting it more clearly.[25]

This sentiment is echoed in *Community Value* by Lynda Barley, whose work, according to the Bishop of London in the foreword, means that 'in future there should be no excuse for missing the significant community value of churches'.[26] There are some signs that the Government is beginning to recognize this and is looking to co-opt the Church to run services, a development with brings with it new dangers to the Church.[27] However, recognition of the crucial role that churches play in enabling all in our society to flourish is always welcome.

What is clear is that the establishment of church communities on new developments allows those who move into such developments to be connected to the Christian foundations upon which our society is built, enabling them to become more like grafts by connecting them with the Christian roots of the English culture. Often, as was the case at Camborne, there is nothing else other than retail outlets. The witness of the Church is of crucial importance to our society here as much as anywhere for, as Luke Bretherton suggests, the Church and its practices are 'the paradigmatic sign of a given culture's redemption through the sacrifice and priesthood of Jesus Christ. The church is to be a people invested with the character of the gospel, which is simultaneously to bear witness to how a given culture may be eschatologically fulfilled.'[28]

Notes

1 C. Butler, 1919, *Benedictine Monachism: Studies in Benedictine Life and Rule,* London: Longmans, Green and Co, p. 124.

2 Butler, *Benedictine Monachism*, p. 128.

3 H. Van Zeller, 1958, *The Holy Rule: Notes on St Benedict's Legislation for Monks,* London: Sheed and Ward, p. 371.

4 Butler, *Benedictine Monachism*, p. 126.

5 J. Inge, 2003, *A Christian Theology of Place*, Aldershot: Ashgate.

6 J. Rodwell, 2006, *Forgetting the Land*, unpublished Reckitt Lecture.

7 Rodwell, *Forgetting the Land*, quoting *Our Common Future*, The World Commission on Environment and Development Report, Oxford: Oxford University Press, 1987; and *The UK Government Sustainable Development Strategy*, The Department of the Environment, Food and Rural Affairs, London: HMSO, 2005.

8 Rodwell, *Forgetting the Land*.

9 W. Berry, 1992, *Sex, Economy, Freedom and Community*, New York: Pantheon, p. 168.

10 C. Pohl, 1999, *Making Room: Recovering Hospitality as a Christian Tradition*, Grand Rapids, MI: Eerdmans, p. 87.

11 P. Langdon, 1994, *A Better Place to Live*, Amherst, MA: University of Massachusetts Press, p. 76, quoted in T. Gorringe, 2002, *A Theology of the Built Environment: Justice, Empowerment, Redemption*, Cambridge: Cambridge University Press, p. 187.

12 D. Rees, 1978, *Consider Your Call: A Theology of Monastic Life for Today*, London: SPCK, p. 141.

13 A. McIntyre, 1985, *After Virtue: A Study in Moral Theory*, London: Duckworth.

14 Gorringe, *A Theology of the Built Environment*, p. 187.

15 Quoted by T. Jenkins in *The Spectator*, 5 November 2005, p. 80.

16 L. Schneekloth and R. Shibley, 1995, *Placemaking: The Art and Practice of Building Communities*, New York: John Wiley and Sons, p. 203.

17 Rees, *Consider Your Call*, p. 138.

18 C. Peifer, 1966, *Monastic Spirituality*, New York: Sheed and Ward, p. 300.

19 I am grateful to Timothy Jenkins for stimulating my thought on this and to Christopher Cocksworth and Ben Quash for their encouragement.

20 *New Housing, New Partnerships? Encounters on the Edge No. 23*, Sheffield: The Sheffield Centre/Church Army, 2004, p. 21.

21 'A Sustainable Development Framework for the East of England', East of England Regional Assembly, 2001, p. 17. Available at www.eera.gov.uk/Documents/About%20EERA/Policy/Sustainable%20Development/SDF.pdf.

22 R. Furbey *et al.*, 2006, *Faith as Social Capital*, York: The Joseph Rowntree Foundation, p. 50.

23 R. Lovatt *et al.*, 2005, *Faith in the East of England*, Cambridge: The East of England Faiths Council.

24 See J. Inge, 2007, *Living Love: In Conversation with the No. 1 Ladies Detective Agency*, Peterborough: Inspire.

25 *Faithful Cities*, The Report from the Commission on Urban Life and Faith, Peterborough: Methodist Publishing House and London: Church House Publishing, 2006, p. 76.

26 L. Barley, 2007, *Community Value*, London: Church House Publishing, p. vi.

27 L. Bretherton, 'A New Establishment? Theological Politics and the Emerging Shape of Church–State Relations', *Political Theology*, 7 (2006), 371–92.

28 L. Bretherton, 2006, *Hospitality as Holiness: Christian Witness Amid Moral Diversity*, Aldershot: Ashgate, p. 113.

3

An Apostle with Reservations

On Judas and the Vocation of Christian Ethics

STANLEY HAUERWAS AND SAMUEL WELLS

On Ann, Stanley and Sam

Ann Loades introduced Sam Wells to Stanley Hauerwas by suggesting one day in 1991 that the three, with Paula Gilbert and Duncan Forrester, take lunch together. But Sam also re-introduced Ann to Stanley, by insisting that Ann, his doctoral supervisor, read all the strange things Stanley had published in all the strange places he had published them. Sam re-introduced Stanley to Ann, because in coming to read more of what Sam had written, Stanley came to look more closely at what Ann had written. And Stanley re-introduced Ann to Sam, because in coming to understand more closely what had formed Stanley, Sam came to read more closely the sources that had formed Ann.

So Stanley and Sam are delighted to take this opportunity to celebrate Ann by putting in conversation what may appear a quite unlikely pair – Karl Barth and Dorothy L. Sayers – and, in particular, how these two contemporaries understood Judas. We are well aware that this may seem an odd way to honour Ann, but we can only ask, gentle reader, for your patience. Because Barth did theology without reserve, he loved strange conversation partners.[1] We think he would have liked Dorothy Sayers and Ann Loades very much. He would have liked them because he loved straightforward but thoughtful people who saw no reason to be apologetic about being Christian. But why Judas? Because we believe Barth's and Sayers' accounts of Judas help us see how too many of us who practise that strange discipline called 'Christian ethics' have done so 'with reservations' that belie the joy so manifest in the work of Barth, Sayers and Ann.

On Barth and Judas

In a section entitled 'The Determination of the Rejected' in *Church Dogmatics* 2/2, Karl Barth provides an extended reflection on Judas.[2] He does so because Judas illumines Barth's claim that our ability to confess our sin depends on our first having been redeemed. According to Barth, therefore, it is not surprising that the New Testament does not find the rejected at a distance, but rather in the closest proximity to Jesus. It does so because the counterpart of the elect is not the enemy without, but rather stands in closest proximity to the 'prince of this world' (pp. 459–61). Which is why, Barth stresses, it is important to recognize that Judas, even in his betrayal, remains a disciple and apostle. Judas is numbered among the twelve – requiring that he be replaced after Jesus' ascension.

Barth suggests that we should pay particular attention to the 'remarkable calm' with which the Gospels depict Judas. Judas initiates the developments that will lead to Jesus' crucifixion, but his is a paltry action that has tremendous consequences. As a result, 'Judas is *the* great sinner of the New Testament' (p. 461). He is the great sinner because he is the one for whom the presence and protection and vigilance of Jesus were in vain. This is evident at the anointing of Jesus at Bethany (John 12.1–8) when Judas protests Mary's act of anointing Jesus with precious ointment. Judas' reaction – that the oil should have been sold and the money given to the poor – is an indication that he was 'not willing that the complete devotion, which by her deed Mary had in a sense given the apostles as a pattern for their own life, should be an absolute offering to Jesus' (p. 462). For Judas, it was too small a thing that the death of Jesus should be glorified by Mary's gift.

Barth, therefore, wonderfully describes Judas as a disciple with reservations. Judas is the apostle

who ultimately regrets his own devotion and the devotion of others to Jesus, who would prefer ultimately to use the power of this devotion for something which his own judgment considers to be better: for whom Jesus is finally less important and indispensable than this better thing. He is not opposed to Jesus. He even wishes to be for Him. But he is for Him in such a way – not totally, that is to say – that actually he is against Him. He reserves to himself the right to decide for himself, in face of Jesus what the way of apostolic discipleship really involves. (p. 463)

Judas' 'reserve' means he has already decided against Jesus and become an accomplice of Jesus' enemies. For what stands between Jesus and his enemies but the claim of Jesus to total faith, absolute humility and unceasing prodigality? So it is his being the 'disciple of reserve' that means that Judas can hand Jesus over to be crucified. The thirty pieces of silver turn out to be the 'better thing' Judas wanted to maintain his independence of Jesus.

So Judas was not really opposed to Jesus. Rather he was just not for Jesus either. We should, therefore, not be surprised that Judas repented of his sin. He had refused to accept Jesus unreservedly as his Lord. He had refused to surrender himself to Jesus' death. His refusals were the necessary form his life must take because he wanted to be an apostle with reservation. That he wanted to be an apostle with reservation is the reason that Barth maintains that we cannot trust his 'repentance' – since it cannot help but be unreal and superficial (p. 467).

Judas' suicide simply confirms that he lived the life of 'reservation' to the end. Judas dies by his own hand. Barth observes:

> Obviously it is the consistent pursuit of a free choice and decision in face of Jesus – the same as led him to hand Jesus over – which now that his repentance is rejected drives him to this end, to suicide. Had he not wanted all the time to be his own judge? Well, that is what he is in this definitive way, in his death. Defying even the rejection of his repentance, he wills to take to himself that which in any case could only be given him: the final judgment, the judgment of God on his act, and therefore the restoration of the order that his act had destroyed. (p. 470)

In contrast to the death Jesus dies, Judas dies a hopeless and fruitless death. It is the death of one who is disobedient even in death because it is a death in which he continued to think himself to be his own judge. Yet that Jesus died in our place means that Judas' rejection of Jesus cannot be the last word. Judas is powerless to defy or destroy the determination and institution of his apostleship. He was chosen and called to be an apostle, not to bring Jesus under the power of humans, but humans under the power of Jesus, that is, not to deliver Jesus to sinners, but sinners to Jesus.

Barth maintains, therefore, that in one sense Judas is the most important figure in the New Testament apart from Jesus (p. 502). He was so because he alone of the apostles was actively at work in the accomplishment of God's will and what was to become the 'content' of the gospel.

37

Judas' betrayal cannot be considered an unfortunate episode, 'much less as the manifestation of a dark realm beyond the will and work of God, but in every respect as one element of the divine will and work of God' (p. 502).

Barth's account of Judas, his ability to see the humanity of Judas as well as our humanity, is a correlate of his overwhelming conviction that God is God and we are not. Many have found it odd that all things human were so compelling for this most 'theocentric' theologian. But Barth's 'humanism' reflected his ability to do theology without reservation. He was not tempted, therefore, to 'explain' Judas or to make him less or more than human. Barth's refusal to 'explain' Judas' (or our) disobedience reflects his conviction that the story of Jesus is the story of the Father's refusal of our refusal. Barth's alternative to 'explaining' Judas (or evil) is to retell the story. Accordingly, Barth is able to see Judas' 'reservation' for what it was – the all too human fear of losing control. As we will suggest below, we think it is, moreover, not accidental that, immediately after his account of Judas, Barth begins his account of the task of ethics.

On Sayers and Judas

Dorothy L. Sayers also deals with Judas by telling a story. In her twelve-play cycle of the life of Jesus, *The Man Born to be King*, she grapples with the theological, philosophical, psychological, theodical, narrative and dramatic problem of Judas. One of the most rewarding aspects of this absorbing sequence of plays is the notes that Sayers wrote to assist in the first production of the cycle on BBC Radio in 1941. Here she outlines the plot device she created to explain the circumstances of Judas' betrayal; but she also reflects extensively on the character of Judas and the nature of evil.

Sayers creates a character called Baruch, a Zealot leader who tries to gain Jesus' support at the head of an armed revolution. He enlists Judas' help to investigate whether Jesus might have any such plans, but quickly realizes that Jesus is incorruptible. Judas, on the other hand, increasingly misreads Jesus' actions and his motives, and betrays Jesus in a fit of self-deceiving hatred. 'Rather like Othello, he can only believe in innocence after he has killed it.'[3] Sayers is clear from the outset that Judas must be no simple stage villain:

One thing is certain: he cannot have been the creeping, crawling, patently worthless villain that some simple-minded people would like to make out; that would be to cast too grave a slur upon the brains or the character of Jesus. To choose an obvious crook as one's follower, in ignorance of what he was like, would be the act of the fool; and Jesus of Nazareth was no fool, and indeed St. John expressly says that 'He knew what was in Judas from the beginning'. But to choose an obvious crook for the express purpose of letting him damn himself would be the act of a devil; for a man, *a fortiori* for a God, who behaved like that, nobody – except perhaps Machiavelli – could feel any kind of respect. But also (and this is far more important for our purpose), either of these sorts of behavior would be totally irreconcilable with the rest of the character of Jesus as recorded. You might write an anti-Christian tract making Him out to be weak-minded and stupid; you might even write a theological treatise of the predestinarian sort making Him out to be beyond morality; but there is no means whatever by which you could combine either of these theories with the rest of His words and deeds *and make a play of them.* The glaring inconsistencies in the character would wreck the show; no honest dramatist could write such a part; no actor could play it; no intelligent audience could accept it. That is what I mean by saying that dramatic handling is a stern test of theology, and that the dramatist must tackle the material from his own end of the job. No; the obviously villainous Judas will not do, either dramatically or theologically – the most damnable of all sins is a subtler thing than any crude ambition or avarice. The worst evil in the world is brought about, not by the open and self-confessed vices, but by the deadly corruption of the proud virtues. (p. 15)

Sayers suggests that 'the sin of Judas was of a peculiarly over-weening loftiness' (p. 15). He sees the path opening out to crucifixion quicker than the other disciples, but 'only with his intellect and not with his heart' (p. 52). This desire to hold something back – in many respects the opposite fault to that of Peter – will prove his downfall:

Let the actor get out of his head any notion that Judas is insincere. He is passionately sincere. He means to be faithful – and he will be faithful – to the light which he sees so brilliantly. What he sees is the true light – only he does not see it directly, but only its reflection in the mirror of his own brain; and in the end that mirror will twist and distort the reflection and send it dancing away over the bog like a will o' the wisp. He has all the gifts – both the practical and imaginative; and his calculating friend the Zealot is quite right in saying that he will fall, like Adam, by the sin of spiritual pride. He could have been the greatest in the Kingdom of Heaven, but he will be the worst – the worst that is the corruption of the best. . . . [H]is intellectual pride, his jealousy, and a fundamental lack of generosity make him a ready ground for the sowing of seeds of suspicion. He can trust nobody but himself. He has grasped in the abstract the idea of purgation by suffering – he sees it; but will anybody else see it? Does Jesus really understand what it means? (pp. 100–1, 125)

Judas sees Jesus as a kind of tool – one who will carry out Judas' own model of the way of salvation. Sayers is merciless in her portrayal:

What he admired in Jesus was not really Jesus at all, but only the projection of his own ideas in another person . . . What Judas really wanted was a Jesus who would interpret Judas to the world, under his guidance and direction. (p. 199)

Once things have clearly gone astray for Judas, Sayers begins to note how easy it is to cross the fine line between suffering and cruelty. Her portrayal here is a profound venture into the ways in which human frailty can become genuinely evil.

I doubt whether Judas starts out with any clear idea about getting Jesus put to death – he probably only wants to stop his activities. But the idea of killing is now presented to him under its most attractive form – sacrificial, idealistic, flattering to his rather morbid theories about suffering, and containing just that grain of plausibility which makes a half-truth more deadly than any lie. Also, there is in Judas' masochism something which can easily invert itself and become a kind of sadism – the worship of suffering for its own sake is not very far from a desire to inflict suffering . . . The certain knowledge that Jesus sees through him hardens him into a fury of pride and hatred; gentleness and graciousness only increase his resentment (here is the sharp contrast between him and Peter), and he is now almost consciously out to hurt and destroy for sheer lust of destruction . . . Jesus has got to be guilty, to vindicate Judas. Anything else would be unbearably humiliating. It would mean that Jesus was incomparably, detestably the superior of Judas, on Judas' own ground – and that is not to be thought of. But the hidden lust of cruelty, which has masqueraded under the disguise of a masochistic love of suffering, is crawling out in its own shape. (pp. 199–200, 230, 231)

Finally, Judas takes care of his own judgement. He becomes the agent of his own damnation, holding on to pride to the last.

He goes on, down and down to the lowest pit of all, where sits the devil of pride that makes the sin unforgivable because the sinner resents and hates and refuses the forgiveness. At the bottom of that pit is only himself and his self-hatred, and here there is no place of repentance. (p. 254)

While Sayers creates the device of the Zealot leader Baruch, her description of Judas is entirely plausible within the material offered by the gospel accounts. Here, as elsewhere, the drama of *The Man Born to Be King* forces the dramatist and the audience to face up to the humanity of the characters, of the need to ponder what they were doing between appearances in the gospel text and, particularly in this case, to distinguish between the cosmological absurdity of evil and its mundane appearances in human character.

On Judas and the Vocation of Christian Ethics

Sayers' dramatic portrayal of 'the hidden lust of cruelty' and Barth's theological engagement with 'the apostle with reservations' converge in significant ways, of which four seem particularly pertinent.

First, Barth and Sayers help us see that those habits that we now identify with the 'Enlightenment' did not begin in the eighteenth century. The presumption that we can constitute ourselves through individual self-conscious and deliberate choice is not new. Judas is not going to charge in head first like Peter; he reserves the right to judge for himself. He holds back in order to make considered judgements and to understand true motives. So 'Enlightenment' is but the name that we give to the time that attempted to make the reservation we see in Judas the standard of the good.

A second characteristic, and linked closely to the first, is that Judas is a man who comes to regret his devotion to Jesus. In Barth's words, he would 'prefer ultimately to use the power of this devotion for something which his own judgment considers to be better'. Judas is not a man without passion, but he is somewhat ashamed of his passion. He is moved by

Jesus, as Sayers makes clear, but he comes to be suspicious of that in Jesus that makes disciples of people who should be thinking for themselves. As Barth points out, he is infuriated by the simplicity of Mary's devotion to Jesus at Bethany.

A third, most poignant, observation, and one most difficult to describe precisely, is that Judas' sin, which originates in pride, finally emerges as cruelty. By the time he realizes exactly what he has done, in Sayers' words

> He sees the truth about himself – the itch for suffering that was only an inverted cruelty; the refusal to believe in innocence that was rooted in the envy and hatred of innocence; the farther he goes, the more he finds hatred – he hates Caiaphas and Jesus and God and himself. (p. 254)

In short, Judas exemplifies Barth's contention that if you begin placing your hope in your own power you will end not only hating yourself but everyone else as well as God.

Finally, Judas is determined to be his own judge, even in death. His suicide, even in the face of his awareness of Jesus' redemption, is a final statement that he simply will not let Jesus have the last word. Sayers makes this absolutely clear:

> He sees the truth, not only about himself, but about sin – he sees the need for the untainted priest and the spotless sacrifice; he even knows obscurely who is the untainted Priest and Victim who could do for him what Caiaphas cannot do – but he cannot be saved because he *will* not be saved. (p. 254, emphasis in the original)

These four characteristics of Judas – the attempt to be his own creator, the sense that he regrets his own devotion, the consequences of pride and the determination to be his own judge – sound curiously familiar to us. They are so because we cannot help but recognize them in ourselves. We do so of course because, like Judas, we are all too human. But they also name habits that we find quite difficult to avoid as those who have been trained to be Christian ethicists. For in many ways Christian ethics names the attempt to practise theology with reserve.

Barth claims that a 'general conception of ethics coincides exactly with the conception of sin'.[4] For those anxious to justify the separation of theology and ethics, this notorious claim is sometimes used in order to reject Barth's claim that such a separation is a betrayal of the gospel. However, we think Barth's claim to be justified if one sees it as a continuing commentary on Judas. Barth is reminding us that those closest to Jesus, those who claim to be disciples, are too often those who are most determined to betray Jesus. For we wish to follow Jesus, but on our own terms.

For example, too often the very attempt to develop a discipline called Christian ethics separated from theology has been motivated by the concern to show that what Christians believe about morality is pretty much what any rational person would on reflection conclude.[5] That 'morality', the one that everyone believed deep down, in fact rested on the Enlightenment presumption that moral agents can only act responsibly if they are autonomous. If any notion expresses the reservation that Barth thinks characteristic of Judas, it is surely the presumption of autonomy. Sayers' Judas is absolutely determined that following Jesus should not jeopardize his autonomy.

Just to the extent that Christian ethics was determined by such notions of autonomy it could not help but provide accounts of the moral life in which Jesus could only be followed 'from a distance'. Of course there is a proper 'distance' between Jesus and ourselves. We cannot, nor should we want to be, what only Jesus was – that is, the Son of God. But because Jesus was the Son of God he made it possible for us to follow him without reserve. Yet often, in the name of being 'responsible', Christian ethicists have tried to show, particularly in matters having to do with violence, that there are times when we simply cannot follow Jesus. As a result, 'salvation' became an account of 'forgiveness' and 'eternal life' that was no longer necessarily embodied in a concrete community called Church.

Christian ethicists have come to assume that ethics must be for everybody. John Howard Yoder called this the 'Constantinian shift'. He argued that this shift was a habit of mind that continues even when the Church is no longer legally established. According to Yoder, under the influence of this shift, Christian ethicists assumed that 'morality' should be identified with questions of how we (and it is by now assumed that the Christian 'we' is identical with those who may not share our faith or have any desire to do so) are to run a society. Since thinking about morality must be tailored to fit anyone, this 'means that the heroic dimension of Christian obedience, the self-abandon and witness of nonconformity are now necessarily gone; this can't be asked of everyone'.[6]

Yet if Barth and Sayers are right then the question is never whether Christian ethics is commensurate with what everyone assumes is the right way to behave, but rather whether Christian ethics should be the study of how to behave when others will not be doing what we must do if we are to follow Jesus without reserve. Yet to follow Jesus without reserve means we must find ourselves in the company of apostles. This is not a way of life that can be done on our own. Judas may well have been, as Sayers suggests, the most intelligent of the disciples, but too often intelligence can tempt us to think that we do not need those less intelligent than ourselves. That Judas' replacement was chosen by lot is a nice indication that the Church cannot place its trust in the intelligence or personal power of those in authority.

The attempt to 'go it alone' in much of the work done in this style of Christian ethics may, we suspect, betray a disdain for the Church. At best, the Church is seen as an agent for the renewal of society; but the idea that the Church itself is constitutive of the political alternative that Christians offer the world is often thought to be irresponsible. Of course the Church often fails but, just as Judas could not determine his destiny, neither can we. The Church betrays the sin of pride if it assumes that we are so compromised by our unfaithfulness that God cannot use us. Barth is right. Judas' betrayal of Jesus is not the last word to be said about Judas nor can it ever be the last word to be said about the Church.

Behind these habits that constitute the work of Christian ethics, we believe, may lie a profound disgust in ourselves. Sayers' phrase, 'the hidden lust of cruelty' nicely describes what we fear may be an underlying anxiety in many who pursue Christian ethics. A repeated pattern is that some who become Christian ethicists come from backgrounds of profound Christian conviction – only to discover that to remain true to their roots means that they will have difficulty showing that they are a 'serious scholar or thinker'. Accordingly, they are relieved to discover that they can be a 'religious ethicist' or, perhaps even better, just an 'ethicist'. It is a terrible thing to happen to a soul to have begun wanting to follow Jesus but to be trained to do so with reserve. Such training usually means that at best you die having no more than a 'career'.

Which again is in imitation of Judas. Suicide is a strong term to use; but there is a kind of suicide associated with the death instincts of many of us who work in the field of ethics. Death is the complete absurdity in a life devoted to rationality. Hence one can fall into a collusion that assumes that we are all in the business of helping others as well as ourselves to get out of life alive – or, failing that, to have the ability to determine the meaning of our own deaths. As a result, those of us working in ethics reproduce the presumptions of a culture committed to the denial of death, namely, the attempt by a people unable to defeat death to die on our own terms.

These observations recognize the seriousness of a vocation in Christian ethics and some of the temptations and dangers involved. But then Ann has never backed away from a fight that she thought needed to be fought. So we hope that, by calling attention to Barth and Sayers' depiction of Judas, we rightly honour Ann Loades' passion, her combative spirit and most of all her fierce determination to do theology without reservation.

Notes

1 Indeed one of us even had the temerity to put Barth and Trollope in conversation. See Stanley Hauerwas, 1994, 'On Honor: By Way of a Comparison of Karl Barth and Trollope', in *Dispatches from the Front: Theological Engagements with the Secular*, Durham, NC: Duke University Press, pp. 58–79.

2 Karl Barth, 1957, *Church Dogmatics*, 2/2, translated by George Bromiley *et al.*, Edinburgh: T & T Clark. Further paginations are in the text.

3 Dorothy L. Sayers, 1943, *The Man Born To Be King: A Play-Cycle on the Life of Our Lord and Savior Jesus Christ*, New York: Harper & Brothers Publishers, p. 175. Further paginations in the text.

4 Barth, *Church Dogmatics*, 2/2, p. 518.

5 For our account of the history of the development of Christian ethics, see our chapter, 'Why Christian Ethics Was Invented', in Stanley Hauerwas and Samuel Wells (eds), 2004, *The Blackwell Companion to Christian Ethics*, Oxford, UK and Malden, MA: Blackwell Publishing, pp. 28–38.

6 John Howard Yoder, 1997, *For the Nations: Essays Public and Evangelical*, Grand Rapids, MI: Eerdmans, p. 104.

4

Abject Wisdom

Reflections on the Religious Meaning of Dostoevsky's Heroines

GEORGE PATTISON

I am sometimes surprised by the enthusiasm with which a new generation of readers seems to be taking to Dostoevsky, not least when the readers concerned are women. The reason for this surprise is simply that, from a certain point of view, Dostoevsky is so utterly out of kilter with a postmodern sensibility that has been honed by such various intellectual currents as Marxism, psychoanalysis, secularism and, not least, feminism. Even in his own lifetime, Dostoevsky consciously aligned himself with the anti-democratic and anti-modern politics of Konstantin Pobedonostsev, a leading ideologist of the Tsarist autocracy who, in the last year of Dostoevsky's life, became Procurator-General of the Holy Synod of All the Russias and thus the man responsible for ensuring the religious hegemony of the Orthodox Church, one of the central pillars of Tsarist power.[1] What point of contact can there be between a cultural horizon shaped this side of the 1970s and this most conservative (and Christian) of nineteenth-century Russian writers? I have already flagged that this question is particularly acute with regard to women, since (quite apart from the problems of his own relations to women) the representation of women in his novels is anything but unambiguous. In *Searching for Lost Coins*, Ann Loades addressed the challenge of 'why certain forms of holiness are bad for you',[2] exploring how 'a morbid over-identification with Christ as suffering victim'[3] can prove disastrous for women, with Simone Weil as one prominent, if complex, example of what she refers to, using Rudolph Bell's phrase, as 'holy anorexia'. As we shall see, several of Dostoevsky's most important female figures seem to fit this category only too well – an observation that must raise questions as to our possibilities for reading Dostoevsky (as many read him) as an important voice in modern Christian thought.

Of course, as Dostoevsky himself – and probably Pobedonostsev too – was aware, most of what proceeded from the pen of the great writer was rarely simple or direct. Since Bakhtin it has become customary to speak of the polyphonic, many-voiced, open-ended and dialogical character of Dostoevsky's novels, but if Bakhtin was the first to provide a critical apparatus for exploring this in a systematic way, it would be hard for any reader to go away from a Dostoevsky novel or story with a single, simple message. Ambiguity and ambivalence mark almost all the key characters, situations and plots of Dostoevsky's fiction, and this is as true of his depiction of women as of any other aspect of his work. This needs to be said, because, coming to Dostoevsky with assumptions that have become second nature in our contemporary cultural situation, his portrayal of women could seem especially misogynistic and well suited to illustrating what one literary rival called his 'cruel talent'.[4]

Many of Dostoevsky's female characters are developed from the stock characters of the novel – indulgent mothers, vulnerable governesses, idealistic schoolgirls, clever maidservants, black-hearted madames, poor seamstresses, good-hearted prostitutes and so on. Even here, however, Dostoevsky rings his own changes on the conventions, sometimes to the point of completely subverting them. And beyond this, Dostoevsky creates new characters from his own experience and his own time, the hysterical Katerina Ivanovna Marmeladova in *Crime and Punishment*, the independent and sexually liberated Polina Alexandrovna in *The Gambler*, the anonymous 'meek one' of the short story of that name, and many others. Yet, for all his range, Dostoevsky seems to focus disproportionately on women in situations of degradation, humiliation and abjection.[5]

Consider Katerina Ivanovna. It should be said straightaway that in this personage (probably modelled in part on the writer's own first wife[6]) Dostoevsky does not simply show a hysterically crazed woman whose behaviour is both embarrassing and absurd. He lets his readers understand why and how she has come to be like this. The decline in her social status, the appalling drunkenness of her husband, the consequent impoverishment of the whole family and her consumption – all of these go a long way to explaining her violent temper, histrionic posturing and her connivance in her daughter Sonya working the streets as a means of feeding the family and paying the rent. She is not a merely weak character. Her iron purpose is illustrated when, for example, we learn that she washes her family laundry by hand every night, hanging it up to dry by morning, because they no longer have a change of clothing – wearing herself out and doing what was 'beyond her strength' to do, as the narrator comments.[7] But her misfortunes are compounded by a vanity that is all her own, and that is not dependent on environment or circumstance. Her exaggerated view of her own erstwhile social status ('Father had the state rank of colonel and was nearly a governor by then, he only had one more step to go . . .' (CP, p. 177)) prevents her from making a more constructive response to her predicament and is constantly manifesting itself in such a way as to make life even worse than it need be. Thus she endlessly insults the German landlady by her 'haughty' behaviour and scoffs at the priest attending her husband's deathbed when he tries to speak to her of God's mercy. When she decides to hold a memorial meal for her dead husband, the narrator conjectures her primary motivation was, 'to show all these "worthless and nasty tenants" not only that she "knew how to live and how to entertain," but that she had even been brought up for an altogether different lot' (CP, p. 378). And, the narrator comments,

> Such paroxysms of pride and vanity sometimes visit the poorest and most downtrodden people, and at times turn into an irksome and irrepressible need in them. Katerina Ivanovna, moreover, was not the downtrodden sort at all; she could be utterly crushed by circumstances, but to make her morally *downtrodden* – that is, to intimidate her and break her will – was impossible (CP, pp. 378–9, emphasis in the original).

The final scene of her life, in which she leads her three youngest children out onto the street to dance and sing for money, pathetically attempting to costume them with such accessories as a broken ostrich feather that had once belonged to her grandmother and quarrelling with any passers-by who dare to comment, is a grotesque conclusion that is as revealing of her character as it is of the human effects of economic deprivation in mid nineteenth-century St Petersburg.

Such scenes as the encounter with Katerina Ivanovna and her pathetic troupe of street performers are almost pitiless, and it is hard not to sense an almost sadistic pleasure in the detail with which she and similarly 'insulted and injured' women are described.[8] They are sinned against as well as sinning, but they are nevertheless paraded before us in their moral and human nakedness as objects of curiosity, repulsion and mockery. The cumulative presence of such hysterical women in Dostoevsky's novels might just begin to suggest a systematic pattern of representing women that could, without exaggeration, be called misogynistic.

But wait. Surely we know that women also play positive, even 'redemptive', roles in Dostoevsky? Famously, the prime example of this redemptive role is found in Sonya Marmeladova, daughter of the hopeless drunkard Marmeladov and the vain, violent and hysterical Katerina Ivanovna. Yet also applicable to Sonya might be Ann Loades' words about the 'holy anorexic', when she writes that

> She can become a kind of saviour figure in her own right if she identifies herself with the suffering and dying Christ, for death becomes, so to speak, the only way forward, and death chosen freely and early is still an expression of autonomy, as well as being the only anodyne for a certain kind of pain.[9]

Such reflections problematize Sonya's 'salvific' role in the novel. Further problems arise with regard to her role as a variation on the popular figure of the good-hearted prostitute, the fallen woman who, despite her outer circumstances and the judgement of society, preserves an inner goodness and purity. In Christianity, this figure was mediated by the legend of Mary Magdalene, in which diverse elements of the biblical narrative were fused into a composite story of an adulterous and sinful woman who is saved by her pure love for Christ. The Magdalene especially fascinated the nineteenth century, and variations on the theme were prominent in the culture of the time.[10]

Of course, such a ubiquitous figure cannot be said to have a single meaning that is identical in each of its reincarnations, and it can be seen functioning both as a means of sentimentalizing (and thereby masking) the real human issues of prostitution and as a way of re-asserting the humanity of the prostitute in the face of her commodification and reification. Moreover, it is clear that Dostoevsky was very aware of the sentimental misuse of the figure of the prostitute saved by love since, in *Notes from Underground*, he mercilessly satirizes it. The second part of that short work opens with a quotation from a well-known poem by N. A. Nekrasov that tells the story of how a prostitute is saved by what Joseph Frank calls the 'ardent and unprejudiced love' of her benefactor.[11] Dostoevsky's quote, however, ends with 'etc., etc., etc.', by which, as Frank comments, 'Dostoevsky manifestly indicates that the philanthropic lucubrations of the speaker are just so much banal and conventional rhetoric'.[12] When, shortly after *Notes from Underground*, Dostoevsky returns to the theme of the possibility of a prostitute experiencing a pure and saving love, he can by no means be doing so naïvely.

In *Crime and Punishment* itself, Dostoevsky inverts Nekrasov's story, since it seems to be Sonya who saves the murderer Raskolnikov. However, this does not entirely answer the charge of authorial misogyny. For the image of the 'good' Sonya could easily be understood as functioning in a mystificatory fashion, since it abstracts her existential possibilities from the real societal obstacles placed in the way of a street-girl who might aspire to holiness. Such questions can, of course, only be addressed by turning to Sonya herself as we meet her in the pages of *Crime and Punishment*.

She is first mentioned in her father's account of his misfortunes to the ex-student Raskolnikov. The first words in which she is mentioned sum up the paradox of her existence: '"When my only-begotten daughter went out for the first time with a yellow pass..."' says Marmeladov. The 'Christological' traits of Sonya are already suggested in the appellation 'only-begotten' (in Russian as in English echoing the words of the Creed), while the yellow pass indicates her profession. When, a few pages later, we learn that she is called Sonya, we – or Dostoevsky's first Russian readers – know that this is derived from Sofia, Wisdom, and if we are still 15 years away from Soloviev's promulgation of a fully blown Sophiology,[13] the baptismal significance of this name would not be unfamiliar to Dostoevsky's theologically informed readers. Sonya, 'only-begotten' and yet a street-walker, is thus a figure of abject Wisdom, Wisdom subject to the sinfulness of the flesh. Further christological traits are soon added. When she returns from her first night's 'work', she silently lays 30 roubles on the table in an umistakable allusion to the price of Christ's betrayal. Then she goes to lie on her bed, covering herself with a large green flannel shawl.[14] Having to move out of her parents' lodging, she takes a room in the apartment of a tailor called Kapernaumov – a rather clear allusion to the Galilean town where much of Jesus' early ministry took place. The reference is underlined when we are told that not only is Kapernaumov himself both lame and tongue-tied, like many of those whom Jesus saved in the Gospels, but 'the whole of his extremely numerous family is also tongue-tied. And his wife too is tongue-tied' (CP, p. 19). When Marmeladov eventually got a job, 'Lord, it was just as though I'd moved into the Kingdom of God', he tells the student (CP, p. 20). Not least, because he 'would bring back my only-begotten daughter from dishonour into the bosom of the family' (CP, p. 21) – in the Kingdom of God, the only-begotten child will be re-united with her father after exile among the lame, the dumb and the outcasts.

Long before we meet Sonya 'in the flesh' we are thus prepared for her exceptional role. Her first entrance is when she arrives at the bedside of her dying father, at the very moment when the last rites of confession and communion are finishing. It is in her arms that her father dies, asking her forgiveness – a forgiveness 'beyond' that of the ecclesiastical ritual.

Later, Raskolnikov visits her in her room and, in a scene of extraordinary intensity (even by Dostoevskian standards), makes her read him the story of the raising of Lazarus. Their conversation at the start of the scene gives Sonya the opportunity to express her compassionate love for her mother, despite everything she has suffered at her hands: '"We're all one, we live as one"', she says of her family (CP, p. 318). When Raskolnikov asks if she prays to God, she replies '"And what would I be without God?"' (CP, p. 323). We also learn that she has been a friend to the innocent Lizaveta, murdered by Raskolnikov when she came home unexpectedly to find him standing over the body of her sister, the old pawnbroker whom he has just axed to death. It is, in fact, Lizaveta's New Testament from which Sonya reads. She hesitates to do so – her way of life and unworthiness make her an inappropriate vehicle of the Word, yet, as Raskolnikov observes,

> even though she was anguished and terribly afraid of something as she was starting out to read, she also had a tormenting desire to read, in spite of all her anguish and apprehension, and precisely *for him*, so that he would hear it, and precisely *now* . . . (CP, p. 326, emphasis in the original)

Much of the Johannine narrative is quoted verbatim as Sonya, the abject prostitute, becomes the voice that gives life to the Word who calls Lazarus from death to life. At the end of the reading, Raskolnikov declares that he has left his family to go with her.

First, however, there is the question of the murder he has committed. Later it will be to Sonya that Raskolnikov confesses his guilt. Instead of condemning him, she falls on her knees before him, embraces him and cries '"What, what have you done to yourself!"' (CP, p. 411). Then, suddenly, a new aspect of her personality is revealed:

> jumping up from her place, . . . her eyes, still full of tears, flashed. 'Stand up!' (She seized him by the shoulder; he rose, looking at her almost in amazement.) 'Go now, this minute, stand in the crossroads, bow down, and first kiss the earth you've defiled, then bow to the whole world, on all four sides, and say aloud to everyone: "I have killed!" Then God will send you life again.' (CP, p. 420)

No longer the anguished, self-accusing, abject creature of the earlier chapters, Sonya now speaks with authority, taking it upon herself to declare both the divine forgiveness and the condition for receiving it. Promising to go with him to prison and to be with him in his life sentence, she gives him the cross that Lizaveta had given her: '"We'll go to suffer together, and we'll bear the cross together!"' (CP, p. 422).

More detail could be added, but we are now in a position to see the key elements that establish Sonya as someone whose life is almost an allegory of Wisdom incarnate. She is the one who, out of the abject humiliation of her own sufferings, offers the word of forgiveness and the word of life to Raskolnikov. Yet, to the extent that she approaches allegory, we find ourselves asking whether she is still a real woman. Is such allegorization not merely another way of passing over and thus masking the reality of this 'insulted and injured' teenage prostitute. Is it not another way of saying that a women's sufferings can become acceptable if they are made the means of saving men?

A final conclusion (if a final conclusion is ever possible in Dostoevsky) would require a far more extensive analysis of Sonya than is possible here. All I shall suggest is that, if we return to the novel itself, we do not find that Sonya's allegorical role is such as to rob her of her three-dimensional humanity. There is nothing about Dostoevsky's description of her or her physical surroundings that alleviates the poverty, squalor and desperate social and psychological need of the Marmeladov family. On first visiting Sonya's room, Raskolnikov notes every squalid detail. Sonya's own uncertainties and anxieties are underlined and, when Raskolnikov departs, she 'spent the whole night in fever and delirium' (CP, p. 330). Her christological traits are, we may say, modified and humanized (though by no means normalized) by the complementary and very Russian figure of the Holy Fool – which Raskolnikov recognizes in her in this same scene (CP, p. 325). And if Sonya the prostitute is nevertheless able to become the vehicle of the divine Word, Raskolnikov the murderer is for his part, perhaps, able to tell us truths about Sonya. Hinting at his crime, he says to her

'Haven't you done the same thing? You, too, have stepped over [that is, the boundary of moral law] . . . were able to step over. You laid your hands on yourself, you destroyed a life . . . *your own* (it's all the same!)' (CP, p. 329, emphasis in the original).

For, as he goes on to explain, while readers have been encouraged to see her action as self-sacrifice for the family, it will not, in the long run, be of any use: her mother will die soon, she will not earn enough to support the other children and her sister will have to follow her to the streets. Nothing has been achieved. She has sacrificed herself for nothing. This comment is often overlooked, but it would not be the only point in the novel at which Raskolnikov is allowed to express a true or partially true insight and we should not dismiss these words as merely expressive of a bitterness that has become incapable of seeing any good for what it is.

A further important point is that Raskolnikov's 'salvation' is never finally completed in the novel. It is at best partial, and only a beginning. Sonya has no supernatural powers to shortcut the normal human processes required for a man to learn to be at peace with himself after the commission of a terrible crime. Sonya becomes a saviour to Raskolnikov: she plays the role of the divine Wisdom descending into a world of sin and desperation and opens the path of life to him. But she is at the same time a sufferer, fragile in her strength and, if she is a healer, a 'wounded healer'. Although aspects of her presentation in the novel may resemble those of the 'holy anorexic', she is in the end too life-affirming and too complex a figure to be a role model for those who might be tempted to seek that way.

Dostoevsky has brought us a long way beyond the world of nineteenth-century Romantic stereotypes. His Sonya is far more than the pure-hearted prostitute of sentimental fiction, and the story of Sonya and Raskolnikov is more than the story of a bad man saved by the love of a good woman. Both are among the insulted and injured of life, the imperfect and deeply flawed characters, sinned against and sinning, who people Dostoevskian fiction. But his interest in these characters is not simply in cruelly displaying their pitiful shortcomings and absurdities. It is rather, in the unblinking recognition of the grotesque misery of social and psychological deprivation, to explore how, even here, men and women may, through their experiences together, find a way to that Kingdom of God that eludes unambiguous earthly realization.

Notes

1 For relations between Dostoevsky and Pobedonostsev see T. Stoyanov, 2000, *Le Génie et son maître*, Paris: L'esprit des péninsules.

2 This is, in fact, the subtitle of chapter 3. See A. Loades, 1987, *Searching for Lost Coins*, London: SPCK, p. 41.

3 Loades, *Lost Coins*, p. 41.

4 N. K. Mikhailovsky. For further comment and discussion of the wider issues, see R. L. Jackson, 1993, *Dialogues with Dostoevsky: The Overwhelming Questions*, Stanford, CA: Stanford University Press, 'Introduction' and chapter 5, pp. 104–20.

5 Again, this could be seen as a particular example of his literary 'cruelty'. See especially Jackson, *Dialogues with Dostoevsky*.

6 See J. Frank, 1995, *Dostoevsky: The Miraculous Years 1865–71*, Princeton, NJ: Princeton University Press, p. 65.

7 F. M. Dostoevsky, tr. R. Pevear and L. Volokhonsky, 1993, *Crime and Punishment*, London: Vintage, p. 177. Further references are given in the main text as CP.

8 *The Insulted and the Injured* is the title of one of Dostoevsky's less read novels, dealing with child prostitution. Other characters who could be mentioned include Anastasia Filippovna (*The Idiot*), and Katerina Ivanovna (*Brothers Karamazov*).

9 Loades, *Lost Coins*, p. 44.

10 See, e.g., the works of Alexander Ivanov, Dante Gabriel Rossetti, Arnold Boecklin and Arthur Hacker – sometimes providing the artist with an excuse for soft-porn transgression of bourgeois taste, as in Jules-Jacques Lefebvre's reclining *Mary Magdalen* (exhibited at the 1876 St Petersburg salon) or Marius Vasselon's *Penitent Magdalen*. Most intriguing, however, is Jean Béraud's *Mary Magdalen in the House of the Pharisee*. This picture follows the tradition in identifying the 'sinful woman' of Luke 7 with Mary Magdalene, but has transformed the Pharisee's dinner into a gentleman's dinner in 1890s Paris. Only Jesus, at whose feet the woman lies weeping, is dressed in biblical garb. In a detail that would certainly have pleased Dostoevsky, the Pharisee is given the features of Ernest Renan, in whose *Life of Jesus* the sentimental attachment between Jesus and the Magdalene is especially emphasized. See S. Haskins, 1994, *Mary Magdalen: Myth and Metaphor*, London: HarperCollins, chapter IX, 'Magdalens'.

11 J. Frank, 1986, *Dostoevsky: The Stir of Liberation 1860–1865*, Princeton, NJ: Princeton University Press, p. 332.

12 Frank, *Dostoevsky*, p. 333.

13 See V. S. Soloviev, tr. B. Jakim, 1995, *Lectures on Divine Humanity*, New York: Lindisfarne. Dostoevsky attended these lectures and developed a personal friendship with the much younger philosopher. There are, of course, theological issues around the mutual definitions of divine Wisdom and divine Logos, yet while it is not uncontentious to see the figure of Wisdom as christologically significant, such a reading is certainly possible in imaginative and speculative terms, as the Russian sophiological tradition itself shows – even though it has never received ecclesiastical endorsement.

14 Other elements of this scene are explored in A. Johae, 2001, 'Towards an Iconography of Dostoevsky's "Crime and Punishment"', in G. Pattison and D. Thompson (eds), 2001, *Dostoevsky and the Christian Tradition*, Cambridge: Cambridge University Press, p. 179.

5

'Where He is? This is where – hanging here from this gallows.'

An Exploration of the Child-hanging Scene in Elie Wiesel's *Night**

ISABEL WOLLASTON

The choice of extracts in 'Evil, Protest, Response', Part 1 of Ann Loades' co-edited *Evil: A Reader*,[1] demonstrates that, first, the Holocaust (or 'Auschwitz') is 'the paradigm evil event to which virtually all theodicists now refer',[2] and second, the child-hanging scene in Elie Wiesel's *Night* has 'attained virtual Scriptural status in modern discussions of the-odicy',[3] alongside Dostoevsky's Ivan Karamazov. This paper explores a range of Jewish and Christian readings of this text, contrasting them to Wiesel's own observations. What is noticeable is the tendency, in many of these readings, to overlook critical discussion surrounding *Night* and relevant material elsewhere in Wiesel.

Wiesel insists he is simply a survivor-witness and teller of tales rather than a theologian.[4] He has nevertheless had a significant influence on Jewish and Christian Holocaust theologians,[5] several of whom have dedicated their books to him.[6] Richard Rubenstein describes Wiesel as 'the pre-eminent Jewish witness to the Shoah';[7] while for Tyron Inbody 'no one has articulated the biblical tradition of lament, even protest and outrage, more powerfully'.[8]

Wiesel published a Yiddish memoir *Un di velt hot Geshvign* (And the World Remained Silent) in 1956. A shorter restructured text, *La Nuit*, was published in 1958,[9] then an English translation, *Night*, in 1960.[10] *Night* charts the protagonist Eliezer's coming of age, focusing on the shattering impact that Auschwitz and Buchenwald had on his childhood faith.[11] In order to emphasize this impact, the narrative begins with Eliezer's pre-Holocaust existence in Sighet (Wiesel's hometown). For

Wiesel, Sighet represents certainty, a secure sense of one's place in the world and religious fervour; whereas Auschwitz signifies loss, dislocation and the silence of God. Arrival at Auschwitz-Birkenau marks the coming of 'night' and the abrupt end of Eliezer's childhood: 'I had become a different person. The student of Talmud, the child I was, had been consumed by the flames. All that was left was a shape that resembled me.'[12] *Night* ends with a portrait of the protagonist as an old man: three days after liberation Eliezer succumbs to food poisoning. While recovering in hospital he describes his first sight of himself since May 1944 in the ghetto: 'From the depths of the mirror, a corpse was contemplating me. The look in his eyes as he gazed at me has never left me' (p. 115).

The child-hanging scene plays a pivotal role in this stark narrative of spiritual crisis. It is the second of two public hangings recounted in quick succession. In the first 'a young boy from Warsaw' ('tall and strong, a giant compared to me') is publicly hanged at roll call for stealing during an air raid. Eliezer is moved by the defiance of the boy before the gallows, refusing a blindfold and shouting: 'Long live liberty! My curse on Germany! My curse! My–' (p. 62). The second public hanging follows a power failure at the central electrical plant in Buna, deemed to be an act of sabotage. The victims are two adults and a child. The adults die quickly, shouting their defiance. By contrast, the child (with 'the face of an angel in distress') is silent. He takes over 30 minutes to die as the prisoners file past. Overhearing someone ask 'For God's sake, where is God?' Eliezer responds 'from within me, I heard a voice answer: "Where He is? This is where – hanging here from this gallows".' After the first hanging he notes 'the soup tasted better than ever'. After the second 'the soup tasted of corpses' (pp. 63–5).

The child-hanging scene holds a particular fascination for Christian readers, attracted by its echoes of the crucifixion. Christian writers seem more intrigued by the scene than their Jewish counterparts, with discussion of the text often becoming an intra-Christian dispute. The first Christian reading of the text was by the French Catholic novelist, François Mauriac, who helped Wiesel find a publisher for *La Nuit*, then provided a Foreword. Instead of seeing Wiesel as a witness to, or author of, the child-hanging scene, Mauriac identifies him with all child victims of the Holocaust and one in particular, noting that his 'dark eyes still held the reflection of the angelic sadness that had appeared one day on the face of a hanged child'.[13] Mauriac wonders whether he should speak to Wiesel of that which both separates and links them, that is that other Jew, this crucified brother who perhaps resembled him and whose cross conquered the world? Did I explain to him that what had been a stumbling block for his faith had become a cornerstone for mine?

He decides to say nothing: 'all I could do was embrace him and weep' (p. xxi).

If Mauriac was the first Christian to comment publicly on Wiesel's text, the most controversial response is that of Jürgen Moltmann. Whereas Mauriac opted for a mute gesture of compassion, Moltmann elects to speak. He interprets the child-hanging scene as 'a shattering expression of the *theologia crucis*'. Responding to Wiesel's 'Where He is? This is where – hanging here from this gallows', he comments that 'any other answer would be blasphemy. There cannot be any other Christian answer to the question of this torment.'[14] He then ruminates on 'the fullness of life in the trinitarian history of God', concluding

it is true in a real, transferred sense, that God himself hung on the gallows, as E. Wiesel was able to say. If that is taken seriously, it must also be said that, like the cross of Christ, even Auschwitz is in God himself.[15]

While some follow Moltmann's lead in meditating on the text in the light of Christian understandings of the cross and (divine) suffering, others accuse him of appropriating it in a manner that is at best insensitive and at worst offensive.

The controversy surrounding Moltmann's remarks suggests that the child-hanging scene functions as a litmus test of what constitutes an appropriate Christian response to the Holocaust. He is accused of displacing or substituting Wiesel's voice with his own. His critics are quick to assume the moral high ground, often claiming to do so in the name of those who died. Marcel Sarot accuses Moltmann of presenting 'a gross caricature' of Wiesel's story.[16] Roy Eckardt, Moltmann's harshest critic, asks 'why has the word "Christian" been inserted here? The sufferer was a Jew. Further, the voice giving the answer is that of a Jew', adding 'we plead only for respect for the dead children, women, and men who could never accept such propositions'.[17] Contra Eckardt, Moltmann's insertion of the word 'Christian' is significant precisely because it suggests that he is fully aware of the difference between Wiesel's text and his own reading of it, which, he believes, is true 'in a real, transferred sense' (as opposed to a literal one?).

Pointing to Christianity's long history of anti-Judaism and anti-semitism, Moltmann's critics believe that Christians ought to be particularly sensitive when commenting on the Holocaust. Judged on these terms, they find Moltmann's approach wanting. Wiesel's text is interpreted as a judgement challenging Christians to take 'responsibility in shame and penitence, for the centuries of Christian antisemitism which made it possible for Auschwitz to become a reality'.[18] Echoing Mauriac, they suggest that the most appropriate Christian response is silence. Johann Baptist Metz insists that

> no Christian-theological identification of God is possible. If at all, this can be done only by the Jew imprisoned together with his God in the abyss . . . Only he, I think, can alone speak of a 'God on the gallows' not we Christians outside of Auschwitz who sent the Jew into such a pit of despair or at least left him in it.[19]

Silence, however, is not the final word. Christian speech is still possible, but only if it is 'ruptured' by its encounter with texts such as Wiesel's. Dorothee Sölle maintains that a Christian reading *is* justified, but only if 'it clarifies what the story from Auschwitz contains'.[20] Such responses may take the form of eradicating all traces of anti-Judaism and antisemitism from Christian thought and practice, and/or a radically reformulated theology that responds to the encounter with the irredeemable elements of human history (encapsulated in the child-hanging scene) by emphasizing the need for solidarity with those who suffer and reflecting on divine silence and/or absence.[21] The problem is that Moltmann might well endorse such a position and claim, in all good faith, that his theological reading of the child-hanging scene meets these criteria.

There are fewer Jewish commentaries on the child-hanging scene. The majority interpret it as the climactic point in Wiesel's crisis of faith. Michael Berenbaum suggests that it 'vividly describes the transition from belief to disillusionment'[22] as Eliezer realizes that 'God is implicated in the death of the innocent, or perhaps God, in his omnipotent innocence, struggles between life and death'.[23] For Rubenstein, it marks the collapse of Wiesel's 'symbolic universe', even though he continues to believe in God as the all-powerful Lord of History.[24] For Alfred Kazin, 'the pain of this sudden loss of faith by an intensely religious young Jew, still a boy' is what sets *Night* apart from all other Holocaust memoirs.[25]

Jewish commentators note that Wiesel's spiritual crisis does not mark the 'death' of God or lead to atheism but is firmly rooted in the Jewish tradition of contention with God.[26] Kazin praises Wiesel's ability to capture

> something at the heart of the age-old Jewish experience: an intimacy with God so deep rooted and familiar that it could rail against Him in a bitterness more eloquent of faith than all ritual practice of faith.[27]

For David Blumenthal, Wiesel is the 'paradigmatic survivor', the voice of protest par excellence.[28] He grants the child-hanging scene authoritative status by including it within 'Text-ing', a grouped field of commentaries on four Psalms – 128, 44, 109 and 27 – that form the heart of his book *Facing the Abusing God*.[29]

Some Jewish readings interpret the child-hanging scene as a parody of the crucifixion, designed to emphasize the gulf between Auschwitz and Calvary, Judaism and Christianity. Lawrence Langer describes it as a 'kind of second crucifixion' with the crucial difference that is 'ungraced by the possibility of resurrection'.[30] In using crucifixion imagery to represent Jewish suffering, Wiesel stands within an established tradition, other examples being Marc Chagall's *The White Crucifixion* (1938) and Chaim Potok's *My Name Is Asher Lev* (1972).[31]

If we consider why the scene is read as a rewriting of the crucifixion, the answer appears to lie with first the reference to 'three gallows' (p. 64); second, Wiesel's allusion to God 'hanging here on this gallows'; and third, an identification of the young boy with the crucified Christ. Yet Wiesel never says that the young boy died flanked by the two adults, or suggests that these adults are anything but 'innocent' victims (unlike the thieves on Calvary). Raul Hilberg, a historian, maintains that the description of the third victim as a child is dramatic licence on Wiesel's part because he was in reality an adult. Hilberg cites a written statement by Zygfryd Halbreich listing 'the names of the three hanged men who had attempted an escape'.[32] In a 1989 essay, Kazin recalls his growing disillusionment with Wiesel:

> the more I learned about him, the more I pursued the vast literature about Auschwitz, the less surprised I would have been to learn that the episode of the boy struggling on the rope had never happened.[33]

This querying of the scene's factual accuracy is generally absent from Christian readings, but resurfaced in 2006 following Oprah Winfrey's choice of *Night* for her Book Club. The Israeli newspaper *Haaretz* published an interview with Auschwitz survivor Rabbi Dov Edelstein, who insisted that Wiesel's account was accurate: 'I remember the exact details. There is no doubt about this. I am a living eyewitness.'[34]

Wiesel claims that he left the child-hanging scene 'ambiguous on purpose',[35] so that any attempt to determine his intended meaning might seem misguided. Yet he goes out of his way to reject any suggestion that the scene is fictional or that he claims God died on the gallows. Incensed by Kazin's 'outrageous statement', Wiesel vented his feelings in a public lecture: 'how dare he, an American Jew, who discovered the tragedy of our people very late, from other people's testimony, deny the validity of a survivor's testimony'.[36] He compared Kazin to a Holocaust denier and named two Auschwitz survivors as witnesses (Yaakov Hendeli and Freddy Diamond), as well as the three victims: Nathan Weissman, Yanek Grossfeld and Leo Yehuda (younger brother of Freddy Diamond).[37]

Wiesel's second complaint is more complex. He insists that his protest is an expression of faith: 'had I lost it I would not rail against Heaven. It is because I still believe in God that I argue with Him.'[38] However, he admits that the child-hanging scene is 'the only time when I spoke about the absence of God, the God who kills and therefore can kill himself'.[39] He complicates matters further by pointing out that it was a 'voice' within him that spoke, introducing an element of distance between himself and the statement about God hanging on the gallows: 'whose voice was it? I did not say it was mine. And what if it was God's?'[40] He later tries to clarify his position suggesting that 'it is God Himself that the killer is determined to murder'.[41]

Commentators often read *Night* as a factual account, yet there are questions as to when Wiesel had his crisis of faith. *Night* locates this in Auschwitz, but Wiesel seems to tell a different story in his memoirs:

I said my prayers every day. On Saturday I hummed shabbat songs at work, in part, no doubt to please my father, to show him I was determined to remain a Jew even in the accursed kingdom. My doubts and my revolt gripped me only later,[42]

adding

I had neither the strength nor the time for theological meditation or metaphysical speculation about the attributes of the Master of the Universe. The daily bread ration was the centre of our concerns.[43]

Wiesel then suggests that he began questioning God in 1948–9. Whereas *Night* emphasizes discontinuity and rupture, stressing the shattering impact that the Holocaust had on Eliezer's childhood faith, the memoirs suggest more continuity between Wiesel's accounts. Does Wiesel insert a post-war religious crisis into his account of Auschwitz? Alternatively, his memoirs can be interpreted as a rewriting of *Night*, one reflecting his later recovery of more traditional faith. While far from coming full circle, the later Wiesel is closer to his childhood faith than the author of *Night* (and possibly Wiesel in Auschwitz). He comes closest to resolving this seeming contradiction in an interview with Carol Rittner. Discussing *Night* he admits 'it is true I said that God was "murdered"', but immediately qualifies this:

> I can say that it was true for that moment, that it may be true for certain moments, but it is no longer true for my entire life. We have to believe in the Deity, that God is alive because we are alive and our lives are entwined.[44]

With hindsight, he suggests that the sense of crisis permeating *Night* reflected his position at a particular point in time, one he recognizes and owns, but has now moved beyond. He fails to say whether this 'moment' was his experience in Auschwitz or the period when he wrote *Night*.

Wiesel's use of symbolism is significant in understanding his intended meaning. He consistently draws on biblical motifs. *Night* is structured as both a reversal of the Exodus (in which the Jews are driven from freedom into slavery and the Angel of Death smites Jewish children rather than those of the 'Egyptians') and as a rewriting of the *Akedah* (Genesis 22) where the son survives and the father is killed. The fractured relationships between fathers and sons form a constant thread, as sons abandon or kill their fathers. Wiesel does not spare himself. Eliezer prays he will never abandon his father but admits to failing this test. After his father dies in Buchenwald, he comments, 'if I could have searched the recesses of my feeble conscience, I might have found something like: free at last!' (pp. 91, 107, 112). An intentional inversion of crucifixion imagery is consistent with this approach. By employing the central Christian image in this particular context, Wiesel communicates his belief that, while the cross is 'a symbol of love and compassion' for Christians, it has also 'symbolised, even incarnated, suffering and terror' inflicted *by Christians*.[45]

Children play a central role in Wiesel's symbolic universe. The presence of a particular child, the 'sad eyed angel', set the second public hanging apart (pp. 63–4). What, then, does this child signify for Wiesel? He identifies childhood with innocence and the religious fervour of his

own childhood. For Wiesel, the death of a child represents the irretrievable loss of a particular future as well as 'the death of innocence, the
death of God in the heart of man'.[46] He claims that in Jewish tradition
'a child always suggests the presence of God' because 'God appears to us
not only as innocent but as vulnerable as a child'.[47] Wiesel consistently
mourns the 'death' and irretrievable loss of the child he was, from
whom he is separated by 'an abyss'.[48] He seeks to bridge this gulf in a
vain attempt to recapture his lost fervour. Children (often accompanied
by old men and/or madmen) appear throughout his work, as does
Sighet, the template for every village. Wiesel desperately seeks to recover
what has been lost. Yet the impact of the Holocaust is such that 'I don't
recognise myself in the child who studies there with fervour, who says
his prayers'.[49]

This brief discussion of Jewish and Christian readings of the child-
hanging scene suggests that John Roth was correct when he described it
as 'an enigma. Its meaning is neither single nor announced directly.'[50]
However, it is perhaps not quite as 'ambiguous' as Wiesel claims: both
he and a number of commentators on the text are adamant that some
readings are simply unacceptable. This paper has raised a number of
questions about how we should read such a text, who (if anyone) 'owns'
it, and whether there are criteria by which we can judge some readings
as more authoritative or transgressive than others. However, the complexity of the text, and its author, is such that even Wiesel at times seems
unsure about how to answer such questions. Commenting on the controversy over *Night*'s factual accuracy, Ruth Franklin suggests that 'the
purpose of a commentary is to explicate – but also to invite discussion,
argument, more commentary'.[51] The ever growing number of commentaries on the child-hanging scene, including those by Wiesel, and the
ongoing controversy over how we should interpret it, suggest that it has
attained 'scriptural status' in more ways than one.

Notes

* When I was a postgraduate at Durham, Ann gave me my first taste of university
teaching when she invited me to teach a class on the controversy surrounding how we
interpret the child-hanging scene for her course 'Philosophy and the Christian
Religion'. It therefore seemed appropriate to revisit the topic in this essay. I am grateful to Ann for her support and encouragement. She provided me, and many other
aspiring lecturers, with a challenging model of what an academic could and should be.

1 Jeff Astley, Ann Loades, David Brown (eds), 2003, *Evil: A Reader*, *Problems in Theology* 2, London: T & T Clark. They include the child-hanging scene, and edited responses to it by Moltmann, Eckardt, Sölle and Metz.

2 Stephen Davis (ed.), 2001, *Encountering Evil: Live Options in Theodicy*, new edn, Louisville, KY: Westminster John Knox Press, p. xiii. Astley, Loades and Brown agree, observing that, whereas in the past, the 'paradigm of evil, a test case for theodicy', was the Lisbon Earthquake, an example of natural evil, '*our* question centres on such human evils as the Holocaust and Hiroshima' (*Evil: A Reader*, p. 5).

3 Richard Bauckham, 'Theodicy from Ivan Karamazov to Moltmann', *Modern Theology* 4 (1987), 83–97, p. 83. He suggests that Camus' account of the death of a young boy in *The Plague* has attained similar status.

4 See my '"Telling the Tale": The Self-Representation and Reception of Elie Wiesel', in Edward Kessler and Melanie Wight (eds), 2005, *Themes in Jewish–Christian Relations*, Cambridge: Orchard Academic, pp. 151–69.

5 See Irving Greenberg and Alvin Rosenfeld (eds), 1979, *Confronting the Holocaust: The Impact of Elie Wiesel*, Bloomington, IN: Indiana University Press, and Carol Rittner (ed.), 1990, *Elie Wiesel: Between Memory and Hope*, New York: New York University Press.

6 Holocaust theologians who have dedicated books to Wiesel include Harry James Cargas, 1992, *Conversations with Elie Wiesel*, South Bend, IN: Justice Books; Emil Fackenheim, 1970, *God's Presence in History*, New York: New York University Press; and John Roth, 1979, *A Consuming Fire: Encounters with Elie Wiesel and the Holocaust*, Atlanta, GA: John Knox Press. Wiesel also has his critics, e.g. Norman Finkelstein, 2000, *The Holocaust Industry*, London: Verso.

7 Richard Rubenstein, 1995, 'Elie Wiesel and Primo Levi', in James Pacy and Alan Wertheimer (eds), *Perspectives on the Holocaust: Essays in Honor of Raul Hilberg*, Boulder, CO: Westview Press, p. 162.

8 Tyron Inbody, 1997, *The Transforming God: An Interpretation of Suffering and Evil*, Louisville, KY: Westminster John Knox Press, p. 112.

9 Elie Wiesel, 1958, *La Nuit*, Paris: Les Éditions de Minuit.

10 The first English translation was by Stella Rodway. A new English translation by Wiesel's wife Marion appeared in 2006. *Night* had little impact at first. By contrast, the 2006 translation shot straight to the top of the bestsellers' lists in the United States after being chosen by Oprah Winfrey as the fifty-fifth entry in her Book Club.

11 In the 1960 English translation there are a number of inconsistencies that suggest that Eliezer is not identical with Wiesel, e.g. Eliezer is not quite 15 when he arrives at Auschwitz, whereas Wiesel would have been 15 in May 1944. This inconsistency is corrected in the 2006 translation.

12 Wiesel, 2006, *Night*, London: Penguin Books, p. 37. All subsequent page numbers for references to *Night* are given in the main body of the chapter.

13 François Mauriac, 'Foreword', in Wiesel, *Night*, p. xxi. Wiesel dedicated his first novel, *Dawn* (1960), to Mauriac. He describes their initial meeting in 'An Interview Unlike Any Other', in *A Jew Today*, New York: Vintage, pp. 17–23, and *All Rivers Run to the Sea: Memoirs*, New York: Alfred A Knopf, pp. 265–72.

14 Jürgen Moltmann, 1974, *The Crucified God: The Cross of Christ as the Foundation and Criticism of Christian Theology*, London: SCM Press, pp. 273–4.

15 Moltmann, *The Crucified God*, pp. 274–8, p. 278.

16 Marcel Sarot, 'Auschwitz, Morality and the Suffering of God', *Modern Theology* 7 (1991), 135–52, p. 137.

17 A. Roy Eckardt, 'Jürgen Moltmann, the Jewish People and the Holocaust', *Journal of the American Academy of Religion* 44 (1976), 675–91, pp. 683–4.

18 Kenneth Surin, 1986, *Theology and the Problem of Evil*, Oxford: Basil Blackwell, pp. 123–4. See also Karl Plank, 1994, *Mother of the Wire Fence: Inside and Outside the Holocaust*, Louisville, KY: Westminster John Knox Press, pp. 145–6.

19 Johann Baptist Metz, 1984, 'Facing the Jews: Christian Theology after Auschwitz', in Elisabeth Schüssler Fiorenza and David Tracy (eds), *The Holocaust as Interruption*, *Concilium: an International Roman Catholic Journal* 175, pp. 26–33, pp. 29–30.

20 Dorothee Sölle, 1975, *Suffering*, London: Darton Longman & Todd, pp. 146–7. See also Plank, *Mother of the Wire Fence*, p. 147; Sarot, 'Auschwitz', p. 136.

21 See, for example, Flora Keshgegian, 2003, 'Witnessing Trauma: Dorothee Soelle's Theology of Suffering in a World of Victimization', in Sarah Pinnock (ed.), *The Theology of Dorothee Soelle*, Harrisburg, PA: Trinity Press International, pp. 93–108; Plank, *Mother of the Wire Fence*, p. 147.

22 Michael Berenbaum, 1979, *The Vision on the Void: Theological Reflections on the Works of Elie Wiesel*, Middletown, CT: Wesleyan University Press, p. 10.

23 Berenbaum, *The Vision on the Void*, p. 45.

24 This insistence on remaining loyal to the God of History is where Rubenstein and Wiesel differ. Rubenstein recalls going through 'a period of impatience' with Wiesel's 'convoluted and tortuous efforts to maintain some kind of relationship with his God' ('Elie Wiesel and Primo Levi', p. 150).

25 Alfred Kazin, 1989, 'My Debt to Elie Wiesel and Primo Levi', in David Rosenberg (ed.), *Testimony: Contemporary Writers Make the Holocaust Personal*, New York: Times Books, pp. 115–28, p. 120.

26 See Anson Laytner, 1990, *Arguing with God: A Jewish Tradition*, Northvale, NJ: Jason Aronson.

27 Kazin, 'My Debt', p. 119.

28 David Blumenthal, 1993, *Facing the Abusing God: A Theology of Protest*, Louisville, KY: Westminster John Knox Press, p. 250. The attention given to Wiesel in 'Evil, Protest, Response' suggests that Astley, Brown and Loades agree with Blumenthal on this point.

29 Blumenthal insists that in theology 'plurivocity and ambiguity, not uniformity and consistency' should be the norm (p. 61). Text-ing therefore consists of four commentaries: *Words* (focusing on exegesis), *Sparks* (spiritual readings), *Affections* (the voice of 'the abused person who has moved towards a righteous anger and moral outrage' (p. 134)) and *Con-verses* (the voice of 'the abused person who is walled in by silence' and turns their rage inward (p. 134)). Intriguingly, Blumenthal includes the child-hanging scene in Con-verses rather than Affections.

30 Lawrence Langer, 1975, *The Holocaust and the Literary Imagination*, New Haven, CT: Yale University Press, pp. 76, 85.

31 See Ziva Amishai-Maisels, 1993, *Depiction and Interpretation: The Influence of the Holocaust on the Visual Arts*, Oxford: Pergamon Press, pp. 178–97; and David Roskies, 1984, *Against the Apocalypse: Jewish Responses to Catastrophe*, Cambridge, MA: Harvard University Press, pp. 258–310.

32 Raul Hilberg, 2001, *Sources of Holocaust Research*, Chicago: Ivan R Dee, p. 176, n. 84.

33 Kazin, 'My Debt', p. 123

34 Shahar Ilan, 'I am a Living Eyewitness', *Haaretz*, 12 July 2006. Edelstein does, however, question the plausibility of a Rosh Hashanah service attended by 10,000 Jews in Buna (*Night*, pp. 66–8): 'I wonder what could have happened to Wiesel that he would write such a thing. It's simply hallucinatory. He must have been dreaming.'

35 Elie Wiesel, 1985, 'Questions and Answers at Brandeis-Bardin, 1978', in Irving Abrahamson (ed.), *Against Silence: The Voice and Vision of Elie* Wiesel, New York: Holocaust Library, vol. 3, pp. 246–52, p. 246.

36 Elie Wiesel, 1999, 'Looking Back', in Peter Hayes (ed.), 1999, *Lessons and Legacies, Volume III: Memory, Memorialization, and Denial*, Evanston, IL: Northwestern University Press, pp. 7–19, p. 15; and *All Rivers*, pp. 335–36.

37 See Wiesel, 'Looking Back', p. 15 and *All Rivers*, p. 336.

38 Elie Wiesel, 2000, *And the Sea is Never Full: Memoirs, 1969-*, London: HarperCollins, p. 70.

39 Wiesel in Cargas, *Conversations*, p. 103.

40 Wiesel, 'Questions and Answers', p. 246.

41 Wiesel, *And the Sea*, p. 70.

42 Wiesel, *All Rivers*, p. 82.

43 Wiesel, *All Rivers*, p. 83.

44 Carol Rittner, 'Interview with Elie Wiesel', in Rittner, *Elie Wiesel*, p. 32.

45 Elie Wiesel in Ekkehard Schuster and Reinhold Boschert-Kimmig, 1999, *Hope against Hope: Johann Baptist Metz and Elie Wiesel Speak Out on the Holocaust*, New York, Paulist Press, 1999, p. 66.

46 Elie Wiesel, 1989, *A Beggar in Jerusalem*, New York: Schocken Books, p. 99.

47 Wiesel in Cargas, *Conversations*, p. 103.

48 Elie Wiesel, 1995, 'Passover', in *From the Kingdom of Memory: Reminiscences*, New York: Summit Books, pp. 147–54, p. 148.

49 Wiesel, 'Making the Ghosts Speak', in *From the Kingdom of Memory*, p. 137.

50 Roth, *A Consuming Fire*, p. 63.

51 Ruth Franklin, 'A Thousand Darknesses', *New Republic* (20 and 27 March 2006), pp. 28–33, p. 33.

'In all supernatural works, we rather draw back than help on'

The Seven Transfiguration Sermons of John Hacket (1592–1670)[1]

KENNETH STEVENSON

Although a layperson, Ann has, I know, gained something of a reputation as a preacher. Not only has her presence graced numerous college chapels, she has also delivered sermons at St Paul's, Canterbury and St Giles' Cathedrals, as well as the University Sermons at both Oxford and Cambridge. A number have also been published. This leads me to hope that what follows is a suitable tribute because it examines a key collection of sermons from an earlier age.

Who was John Hacket?

The seventeenth-century theological scene is awash with big names such as Lancelot Andrewes, Richard Baxter and Jeremy Taylor. But lesser known figures can be equally absorbing. By accident, I came across John Hacket while working on some research on the history of the interpretation of the transfiguration. He came at me with something of a welcome surprise, partly because I had never heard of him before, and partly because no one else has preached anything like so much specifically on the transfiguration – which is something of a feat for Anglican seventeenth-century studies.

Much of what we know about Hacket comes from a memoir written by his old friend Thomas Plume (1630–1704), which was published in 1675 as a prelude to a collection of 100 of his sermons, which were bequeathed to Plume on Hacket's death.[2] The overall tone is approving and at times adulatory, but Plume does not overlook the vagaries of

Hacket's personality: he was a small man, with sharp eyes (as the engraving at the head of the book shows), who suffered from impatience with slower minds. He was born on 1 September 1592, in the Strand, London. His father was a Senior Burgess of Westminster, and the young lad attended Westminster School, along with the future priest-poet, George Herbert. Andrewes was Dean of Westminster at the time and took an interest in Hacket, encouraging him in his studies, and even paying for some of his books when he went on to Trinity College, Cambridge as a student in 1608. Ordained in 1618 by John King (1559?–1621), Bishop of London, Hacket was blessed with a depth of scholarship, and what we would nowadays call powers of communication, that attracted the attention of notable figures, including John Williams (1582–1650), Lord Keeper of the Seal and Bishop of Lincoln, who secured for him the influential parish of St Andrew's, Holborn in 1624.[3] Like many clergy at the time, he was a pluralist and held the living of Cheam from the same year onwards. This enabled him to preach in London during 'the season', with a congregation gathered from the legal and other professions, and then spend the summer months in the more healthy, rural atmosphere of Cheam, as it then was, and enjoy for a short time being not too far from Plume, who was made Vicar of Greenwich in 1658. Hacket was already (from 1621) a Royal Chaplain, and in 1631 he was made Archdeacon of Bedford.

But the tide was turning against Hacket and his ilk. Moderate Laudian that he was – he tried to discourage Archbishop Laud from some of his more enthusiastic ecclesiastical astringencies – he was unable to survive at Holborn after 1645. The Parliamentarians moved in on him, taking the opportunity of snaffling the money that Hacket had raised over the years for the rebuilding of St Andrew's. But he held onto Cheam, and was among the small but steady band of clergymen, like Simon Patrick (1626–1707) at Battersea, who kept using parts of the Prayer Book in public worship, even though the full services were officially proscribed.[4] At the Restoration, his fortunes took a turn for the better. He took an active part in the wider discussion about the re-introduction of the Prayer Book and, at the time of the Savoy Conference, he is said to have seen through Baxter's attempt to distance himself 'from the Old Reformation way'.[5] He could have returned to Holborn, but his heart was not in it. He turned down the Bishopric of Gloucester, but accepted Coventry and Lichfield (as it then was) in 1661. His episcopate was noted for a number of achievements: he did his best to woo Nonconformist clergy into the Establishment; he preached regularly in ordinary parish churches (not all bishops bothered to do this to such an extent); he was generous to the poor, as he had been at Holborn; and he rebuilt Lichfield Cathedral – a magnificent medieval building that had suffered during the Civil War. He died on 28 October 1670.

The 'Century of Sermons'

As Peter McCullough has suggested, the '96 sermons' of Lancelot Andrewes edited by William Laud and John Buckeridge (1562–1631) were, among other things, an attempt to place the great preacher in the same league as Pope Leo the Great – whom we associate with a similar surviving number of preachments.[6] A 'century' seems by comparison a more ordinary figure, even if slightly greater![7] Of what do they consist? Apart from occasional sermons, such as those preached at Court in Hacket's early years before King James I and King Charles I, the bulk are made up of clusters on specific subjects, many of them on sequential verses of scripture.[8] Thus, the opening 15 are on the incarnation, the first 8 based on Luke 2.7–14. There follow 6 on the baptism of Christ, based on Matthew 3.13–17. No fewer than 21 on the temptations in the wilderness come next, based on Matthew 4.1–11. Then follow the 7 transfiguration sermons, on Luke 9.28–36. A group of 5 on the passion comes next, followed by 9 on the resurrection (neither of these sets uses sequential biblical texts). A small collection on the descent of the Holy Spirit (Whitsun) goes through Acts 2.1–4 (the last is on Acts 2.12–13). The next groupings are the 'occasional' sermons, including two before King James I on Gunpowder Day (5 November). The last two are for All Saints' Day, on Revelation 6.9–10.

The arrangement of these sermons is instructive. There is a kind of pattern that travels through the liturgical year, stepping out for a chunk of civic and royal sermons, and then concluding with All Saints. The puzzle, however, concerns where the transfiguration sermons are placed. Plume positions them between the temptation set and the passion, perhaps reflecting ancient precedent by connecting them with Lent, rather than the 6 August festival. A word of explanation about this is perhaps needed. The feast of the transfiguration was abolished at the English Reformation, though it reappeared, in the Calendar only (but without any collect or readings), in the Restoration Prayer Book of 1662. However, as Hacket himself explains near the start of his first sermon on the transfiguration, he is well aware of both the old Latin tradition of reading it on the Second Saturday of Lent, and of the (much later) August festival. Yet his own view is that transfiguration belongs to Eastertide, thus giving the whole series a resurrection flavour, the transfiguration of his hearers now.[9] In practical terms, this probably means that the sermons were delivered as a course over seven Sundays. If he started the course on the Sunday after Easter, this would mean ending on Whitsunday, which Hacket with his strong liturgical sense would have avoided. My own suggestion, for what it is worth, is that these sermons were delivered at Evensong, in those days an afternoon service, and that he began on Easter Day itself, and therefore concluded on the Sunday after the Ascension.

What of the actual texts of the sermons themselves, whether of the transfiguration sermons or of the others? Editors are not unknown to 'edit'! These sermons, however, show signs of having been delivered much as they are in their present condition. Of course, like all good preachers of his time, Hacket would have delivered them from memory (preachers who did otherwise, especially in prominent positions, were generally laughed at). But there are indications, particularly when he admits to running out of time (from the pagination he seems to have a standard length of around ten pages), that what has come down to us may well be a fair and accurate reflection of what he actually preached. They are from the two volumes of manuscript notes that Hacket left to Plume when he died.

General Characteristics of the Sermons

The two most striking characteristics of the sermons are that they are scripturally based, but backed up by a whole range of scholarship and illustration that combines, at least to the contemporary reader, both the practical exposition of the Bible and a strong sense of the history of interpretation. What scholars of all shapes and sizes wrote about the Bible in the centuries before Hacket mattered to him a great deal. In this he was by no means unique – it is more a question of the sheer extent of his scholarship. As I have indicated already, and as we shall see in more detail with the transfiguration sermons, he likes moving from one verse to another, probing, questing, admiring, and ready to face uncertainties over interpretation. But when it comes to illustration, he is quite ready to use Aesop's fables, animals and all, to contrast the moral of the tale with the grace and power of the gospel. In this, like other seventeenth-century preachers, but unlike more serious figures such as Lancelot Andrewes, he is following in the footsteps of the popular preachers of the late Middle Ages.[10] As one reads these parts of the sermons, a wry smile begins to appear. One gets the impression of a vivid mind at work in the business of sermon construction which always includes the need for embedding ideas and concepts in the minds of his hearers. And like other preachers of the time, he is also not afraid to quote ancient pagan texts, such as Virgil, which, like the fables, would have been familiar territory for many people in his congregation.

But what is most striking of all is the sheer range of theological reading that lies behind these sermons, and it comes from the whole of the Christian repertoire. Hacket is known to have made theological reading a priority throughout his life, and within days of his death at Lichfield had books on order in London from Plume that included non-English material. The margin notes of these sermons give clear citations to the authors, whether they are alluded to or actually quoted. These include patristic figures such as Origen, John Chrysostom, Basil the Great and Augustine of Hippo, as well as medievals, such as Bernard of Clairvaux and Thomas Aquinas, and late Byzantine biblical scholars like those remarkable twelfth-century exegetes Euthymius Zigabenus and Theophylact, to say nothing of Reformation figures such as Martin Luther and John Calvin. He cites or quotes far more freely than many other figures, Andrewes included, but his overall style is plainer and more accessible.

The Transfiguration Sermons in Context

While quantity is by no means the same as quality, Hacket is indeed unique in offering more sermons on the transfiguration than anyone else in the Christian tradition thus far. Augustine managed three – and the second and third are very short indeed. Nearly every other figure, the influential John Chrysostom included, produced only one.[11] Only in the later Byzantine-Medieval era do we encounter preachers who provide us with two: Gregory Palamas, enthusiast for the Byzantine feast, and Peter of Celle (1115–83), who was preaching at a time when the August festival was only partially observed in the West, mainly by religious communities.[12] It was not official for the western Church until the time of Pope Callixtus in 1457.[13] Nevertheless, however biblically based the transfiguration manifestly is, the fact that the festival was in so many ways a recent innovation would have been a strong argument for its abolition at the Reformation.

The other unusual feature is that he chooses to base his sermons on the Lucan narrative: the opening words of the first sermon are 'because St. Luke doth more completely narrate all the circumstances of Our Saviour's Transfiguration than the other Evangelists; therefore I have chosen to entreat out of his words that glorious miracle'.[14] Three observations need to be made about such a choice. One is that in his other sermons, Hacket shows no such 'Lucan bias': for example, the baptism and temptations sermons are based on Matthew's Gospel (the latter case probably explained by the fact that Matt. 4.1–11 is the Gospel for the First Sunday in Lent); with a less familiar narrative, Hacket evidently thought he had a free hand. Second, it is very unusual indeed to encounter sermons on anything other than Matthew's narrative before this date, because Matthew was the standard liturgical reading, whether in early Lent or for the August festival. The exceptions are all early and date from a time when lectionaries were less formed than they later became. In the West, we have a sermon on Mark's narrative as part of a course on the Gospel by Jerome. In the East, there are three, all on Luke's Gospel: Cyril of Alexandria and Proclus of Constantinople in the fifth, and Timothy of Jerusalem in the sixth century.[15] All the others – without exception – are Matthew-based, however much the preachers (as Hacket does from his Lucan base) drew important variants from the other evangelists in the course of dealing with the narrative. Third, in picking Luke, Hacket expresses what becomes something of an Anglican trait. The only other seventeenth-century transfiguration sermon that has come down to us is from Mark Frank (c.1612–64), which in all likelihood dates from a later time than Hacket; it too is based on Luke's narrative, specifically on Peter's enthusiasm to build the three tabernacles (Luke 9.33).[16] When it comes to the re-introduction of the provision of a collect and readings for the feast in Anglican service books from the nineteenth century onwards, it is increasingly the case that the Lucan narrative is chosen in preference to Matthew, the more traditional lection. The seal appears to be placed on such a move in the great little book by Michael Ramsey on the transfiguration, which gives special space to Luke's approach.[17] This is reflected in Anglican adaptation of the new Sunday Lectionary. For everyone else, Roman Catholics included, there is the best of all worlds: a three-year synoptic scheme both in connection with Lent and for the August festival. The difference is that Anglican service books stick with the synoptic scheme for the former but use Luke only for the latter.[18]

Five Lucan Variants

As biblical scholars have eloquently told us over the years, the three synoptic accounts differ in a number of important details. Luke's account provides us with significant examples, all of which Hacket takes care to discuss.

The first concerns the fact that the purpose of the mountain trek was to *pray* (Luke 9.28). In the first sermon, Hacket brings this home in a number of ways. Having set the scene by describing it 'as a glorious miracle', he goes on to assert that the mountain of transfiguration is 'holy because the Sacred Trinity did open itself in that place'.[19] But most interesting of all is the typology he uses in relation to the worship of the people of Israel: the golden candlestick (Ex. 25.31) corresponds to the light of preaching; the table of shewbread (Ex. 25.30) is the Eucharist; and the altar of incense (Ex. 30.1) is prayer.[20]

The second concerns the 'change in appearance' (Luke 9.29), not the more complicated 'transfigured' of the other two evangelists (Matt. 17.2; Mark 9.3). Here Hacket interprets Luke's plainer language in terms of deliberately understating what cannot be overstated:

> St. Luke neither compares him to the sun above (cf. Mt 17.2) or to the snow beneath (cf. Mk 9.3), but says enough to make us conceive, that positively it was the greatest splendour that could be likened to any created thing,[21]

which leads him back to a favourite transfiguration theme, that of spiritual ascent.

The third is about the 'exodus at Jerusalem' (Luke 9.30), which he discusses in the third sermon. In this case, Hacket skims over the difference, by going straight for the essential difference between Jesus' 'metamorphosis' (the Greek word used in Matthew and Mark) and the various changes of *form* in ancient pagan literature (for example, Ovid), where there is no relation between what the god or goddess turns into and what they were before. By contrast, Jesus retains his human body, because he is yet to die and be raised from the dead – a truth Hacket applies to the disciples, who 'did win the crown of life', and were 'indeed fit to preach of Christ's cross'.[22] There is no doubt in Hacket's mind of what the exodus of Jerusalem is about – the cross, and (by implication) what we would nowadays call the cost of discipleship.

The fourth variant, seldom discussed, is about who 'they' are who enter the cloud when the disciples are filled with fear (Luke 9.34).

Because there are so few commentaries on Luke's Gospel in the patristic and medieval East and West, and because there were so few sermons specifically on the Luke narrative, and because this is such an easily overlooked (and even obscure) issue, the question is not definitively dealt with until the twelfth century, with Euthymius Zigabenus, a Byzantine biblical scholar who comments on all three Gospels, and pronounces here that only Moses and Elijah entered the cloud, and not the three disciples as well. Hacket follows Euthymius at this point in the sixth sermon, naming him in the process;[23] and he proceeds with an interesting series of observations about the suspicious nature of clouds, doubtless in part reflecting the experience of damp, foggy life at certain times of the year in seventeenth-century London.

Finally we have the decision by the three disciples themselves (Luke 9.36), rather than the command of Jesus (Matt. 17.9; Mark 8.9), not to say anything about what has happened. This Hacket uses as a springboard for some comments about the need for reticence in the life of the Church at the time. What holds Hacket's attention particularly is what to do at a time of theological and religious controversy, of which he would have been more than conscious as a London incumbent in the 1630s and 1640s.

> When a discord is unfortunately raised between party and party, among Members of the same Church, so that the factions grow stiff and rigid on both sides, the best way is to command silence to all, that the fire of strife and emulation may go out for want of combustible matter.[24]

Other Special Features

Many other observations could be made about these sermons but a few in particular stand out. Near the start of the first sermon, once he has declared his hand for Luke, Hacket has to face up to another difference between Luke, who places the transfiguration 'after eight days' (Luke 9.28), and the other two, who reckon after six (Matt. 17.1; Mark 9.12). Biblical scholars have toiled over these differences and their possible symbolism. Here, as elsewhere, Hacket faces these variants (and even enjoys them) without trying to harmonize them. He comes out with a pearl of wisdom:

> when outwardly there seems to be some disagreement between the text of one Evangelist and another, these difficulties do whet our

industry to study the book of God: there must be knots and mysteries hard to be understood . . . that man may always learn, and God may always teach onto the end of the world.[25]

Then there is the place of Peter in the whole narrative. When he is discussing the choice of the three disciples, Hacket acknowledges the three as an inner cabinet but 'it is well to take off all claim of supremacy by this instance, that John and James were in the company'.[26] This expresses a common Reformation agenda, understandable in mid seventeenth-century England. Later on, when it comes to Peter's enthusiasm for building tabernacles, he follows a long tradition in both East and West of addressing Peter direct, but he does so in his own way. Transfigured Christ may have been, but 'Thou Peter shalt not think it good to be with Him, but run away and deny Him'. And as if to rub the point home, 'no other Tabernacle shall be built for Him, but a cross of Malediction'.[27]

There are other contrasting features that spring to mind. Hacket is happy to indulge in allegory on a number of occasions, and one example is the whiteness of Christ's clothing (Luke 9.29). Here he provides three interpretations, all of which are applied to us. It is the baptismal robe – a view first put forward, with reference to Galatians 3.27 (being clothed with Christ), by Bede (c.673–735), whom Hacket read but does not cite here.[28] It is also the robe of justification, 'clothed with the merits of Jesus Christ', a robe that needs to cover the whole body. And it is the 'robe of glory', for eternal life in the resurrection. By drawing these distinctions, Hacket provides a sacramental, theological and eschatological focus.

Hacket is on less secure ground when he moves from discussing the three tabernacles (Luke 9.33) to the question of proper church buildings. Yes, Peter got it wrong, and to try to hold the moment of transfiguration in history and delay the outworking of salvation is folly. But worship still has to be offered in a fit manner and in a building in good repair. As the future rebuilder of Lichfield Cathedral, who was thwarted in his plans to do the same with St Andrew's, Holborn (where, admittedly, the need may not have been so great), Hacket's strictures can nonetheless earn some of our sympathy.

Can any heart be so hardened to suffer that Table to be unfurnisht with Ornaments, at which we have often been fed with the Bread of Life, and the Cup of Benediction? I charge not this place with any such neglect, but I commend and pronounce them blessed especially, who have been liberal, that God's honour might be set out among us in the beauty of holiness; and I lament it where it is otherwise; for it is a mournful sight methinks to see any place excel the Church in preeminence and magnificence; not as I thought the Lord did favour us for fair walls and roofs without a fair inside: but first it signifies the almightiness, when we honour him with the best and chiefest of all outward things: and secondly it makes our seal shine before men, that we love our Heavenly Father better than all the wealth of the Earth; and the Lord loveth a cheerful giver.[29]

Hacket's musings on the centrality of worship and the importance of worthy places in which it is to be offered could not be plainer.

Conclusion

It is sometimes said that a sermon is out of date the moment it is preached. There is no way in which Hacket's seven transfiguration sermons could be preached today except, perhaps, in some reconstructed heritage liturgy – which would be the very last thing that he himself would have wanted. Theologically, he draws together different parts of Christian tradition, principally the old Lenten focus of glory before the cross and the joyous 'miracle' of the August feast, to produce a striking synthesis. Such a synthesis is one of exegesis, illustration, reception-history and practical application. One point of comparison is, perhaps, Henry King (1592–1669), son of John King, who ended his ministry as Bishop of Chichester.[30] But deeply learned as his sermons are, and even though they share similar traits, King is more Calvinist in tone, and there is nothing like the range of historical sources, nor the secular illustrations. For Hacket the whole repertoire of the history of interpretation of the Bible matters, and matters a great deal – which mixes well with our own age, when sermons might not be as complex as they were in his day but reception-history has a prominent place in biblical studies.

Hacket does not stand in the sparkling, premier league of seventeenth-century preachers. But he brings us slightly nearer the ground, albeit Holborn rather than, say, a Norfolk village. In style we are still in the learned legacy of the earlier part of the century, but this is no sophisticated metaphysical homiletic. There is a more relaxed air about these sermons as well as an engaging, circumspect mixture of affection and demand, of accessibility and mystery. Hacket's God is the God of grace and glory, who embraces the problematic present, with all the religious and political tensions that made up his part of the seventeenth century.

Hacket represents the unity of so many different facets of talent, from Aesop's fables to the eastern and western Fathers. And all the time he is the subtle master of his own very disparate material. What comes through in these seven sermons is the juxtaposition of the transfiguration experience, distant and wonderful as it is, with frail human nature, which by instinct is more ready to 'hold back' when imaginative encouragement can help us 'draw on' – in the Easter faith.

Notes

1 Thomas Plume, 1675, *A Century of Sermons upon several remarkable subjects by The Right Reverend Father in God John Hacket, Late Lord Bishop of Coventry and Lichfield*, London: Robert Scott, p. 415 (Sermon 1); hereafter referred to as *A Century of Sermons*.

2 See *A Century of Sermons*, pp. i–liv; they were reprinted in 1865. What follows about Hacket's life is taken from the 'Memoir', as well as from articles on Hacket and Plume in the *New Dictionary of National Biography*. Plume became Archdeacon of Rochester in 1679 and founded a Professorial Chair in Astronomy at Cambridge.

3 Williams went on to become Archbishop of York in 1641.

4 See, for example, John Spurr, 1991, *The Restoration Church of England: 1646–1689*, New Haven, CT and London: Yale University Press, p. 7.

5 See Robert Bosher, 1957, *The Making of the Restoration Settlement: 1649–1662*, London: Dacre, pp. 227–8.

6 See Peter McCullough, 'Making Dead Men Speak: Laudianism, Print and the Works of Lancelot Andrewes, 1626–1642', *Historical Journal*, 41(1998), 401–24.

7 A similar 'century' of sermons by Thomas Wilson (1663–1775), Bishop of Sodor and Man, exists, for which see *The Works of Thomas Wilson: II: Sermons*, Bath: Crutwell, 1775. Plume had a similar 'century' of his sermons published after his death.

8 See index at the start of *A Century of Sermons*.

9 *A Century of Sermons*, pp. 411–12 (Sermon 1). For a discussion of the evolution and development of the feast, see Kenneth Stevenson, 'From Origen to Palamas: Greek Expositions of the Transfiguration', in Bollettino della Badia Greca di Grottaferrata (Tertia Seria) 4 (2007), pp. 197–212, and 'From Hilary of Poitiers to Peter of Blois: A Transfiguration Journey of Biblical Interpretation', *Scottish Journal of Theology* 61.3 (2008), pp. 288–306.

10 See the classic study, G. R. Owst, 1933, *Literature and Pulpit in Medieval England*, Oxford: Blackwell, pp. 149–209.

11 For Augustine, see Edmund Hill (tr.), 1991, *The Works of St. Augustine: Sermons III/3*, New York: New City Press, pp. 340–4 (Sermon 78), 345–6 (Sermon 79), 347–9 (Sermon 79A); for John Chrysostom, see *The Nicene and Post-Nicene Fathers*, Second Series, vol. 10, Edinburgh: T & T Clark, 1991, pp. 345–51 (Homily 56 on Matthew).

12 For Palamas, see Greek texts in Migne, *Patrologia Graeca* 151.423–36 (Homily 34), 435–50 (Homily 35); for Peter of Celle, see Migne, *Patrologia Latina* 202.840–3 (Sermon 65), 843–8 (Sermon 66). Peter was abbot of La Celle from 1150, abbot of St Remigius, Reims, from 1162 and Bishop of Chartres from 1181.

13 See R. W. Pfaff, 1970, *New Liturgical Feasts in Later Medieval England*, Oxford: Clarendon Press, pp. 12–39.

14 *A Century of Sermons*, p. 411 (Sermon 1).

15 For Jerome, see Sister Marie Liger Weald, IHM (tr.), 1965, *The Homilies of St. Jerome II*, Fathers of the Church 57, Washington, DC: Catholic University of America Press, pp. 159–68; for Cyril, see R. M. Tonneau (ed.), 1953, *Sancti Cyrilli Commentarii in Lucam: Pars Prior*, Corpus Scriptorum Christianorum 140: Scriptores Syri 70, Louvain: Dubecq, pp. 119–23; for Proclus, see Migne, *Patrologia Graeca* 65.763–72 (Sermon 8); for Timothy of Jerusalem, see Migne, *Patrologia Graeca* 86.255–66.

16 See *Sermons by Mark Frank II*, Library of Anglo-Catholic Theology, Oxford: Parker, 1849, pp. 318–55.

17 See Arthur Michael Ramsey, 1949, *The Glory of God and the Transfiguration of Christ*, London: Longmans.

18 See Kenneth Stevenson, '"Rooted in Detachment": Transfiguration as Narrative, Worship and Community of Faith', *Ecclesiology* 1 (2005), 13–26, pp. 21–2.

19 *A Century of Sermons*, p. 414 (Sermon 1).

20 *A Century of Sermons*, p. 417 (Sermon 1).

21 *A Century of Sermons*, p. 422 (Sermon 2).

22 *A Century of Sermons*, p. 434 (Sermon 3).

23 See Euthymius Zigabenus' Commentary on St Luke, Migne, *Patrologia Graeca* 129, pp. 949–50; while Jerome's Latin is unambiguous in its implication that only Moses and Elijah enter the cloud, the Greek texts are not so clear.

24 *A Century of Sermons*, p. 476 (Sermon 7).

25 *A Century of Sermons*, p. 413 (Sermon 1).

26 *A Century of Sermons*, p. 414 (Sermon 1).

27 *A Century of Sermons*, p. 445 (Sermon 4).

28 Bede, Homily 1.24 on The Gospels, in Lawrence T. Martin and David Hurst OSB (trans.), 1991, *Bede the Venerable: Homilies on the Gospels: Advent to Lent*, Cistercian Series 110, Kalamazoo: Cistercian Publications, p. 238; he also makes this connection in his commentaries on Mark and Luke, see Migne, *Patrologia Latina* 92, pp. 247 and 454.

29 *A Century of Sermons*, p. 453 (Sermon 5).

30 See Mary Hobbs, 1992, *The Sermons of Henry King (1592–1669)*, Rutherford, NJ/Madison, WI/Teaneck, NJ: Fairleigh Dickinson University Press/Scolar Press.

7

Redeeming Catholicity for a Globalizing Age

The Sacramentality of the Church

PAUL D. MURRAY

Introduction

As has already been noted at earlier points in this volume, Ann Loades'
theological interests range broadly, stretching from her early deep
immersion in Kant and theodicy to encompass feminist theology, the
retrieval and broadening of the category of the sacramental, engagement with spiritual and mystical theology, and a lifetime of holding
theology and the arts in intimate conversation, coming to clearest
expression in her original treatment of Dorothy L. Sayers as a theologian. In holding these interests together, Ann's writings reflect a common dual conviction variously at work in a wide range of contemporary
theology to the effect that, first, truth is something done, something
lived, as much as something thought and said; and second, the demon-
stration of the reasonableness and appeal of Christian faith is ultimately
more a matter of performance, of practice, than of reasoned argument
and conceptual re-articulation.[1] In a sense, this holding of cognitive and
practical concerns in conversation can be traced back to Ann's early
work on Kant – although typically operating in a more integrated
fashion than Kant's own division of labour would suggest – and has,
perhaps fittingly, been most clearly shown in the texts she has written in
the lives of many others through her teaching and characteristically
generous encouragement.

Reflecting both this widespread dual conviction concerning the inter-
weaving of the analytical and practical poles of theological work and the
combined interests of someone working on the ecclesial-organizational
realities of Roman Catholicism[2] with a more amateurish wing in the

sociopolitical dimension of the Church's mission,[3] this chapter probes two key questions: first, what is the appropriate character of Christian sociopolitical engagement, given the context of global capitalism? Second, quite what does it mean in practice to claim that the distinctive being and practice of the Church constitutes its primary mode of political theology? These explorations are held together through common recourse to the notion of the sacramentality of the Church (thus taking up one of Ann's own privileged categories but in a more explicitly ecclesiological direction than she tends to do); or, in language that might resonate more among the Protestant traditions, the anticipatory witness of the Church. The integrating argument is that, prior to any specific teaching or action, the very life of the Church – discussed here under the category of catholicity – should be sacramental of a globalization for the good.

There are four stages to the chapter. First, the challenge posed to Christian sociopolitical engagement by the emergence of a genuinely global capitalist economy is briefly identified. Second, via reflection on Christian hope, the authentically sacramental character of Christian activism and ecclesial existence more generally is identified and illustrated. Third, the concept of catholicity is probed in relation to that of the sacramentality of the Church. Fourth, attention is given to the ways in which a redeemed performance of the catholicity of the Church – explored here specifically in relation to Roman Catholicism – might disclose afresh what it means to exist as a global communion, the health of which presupposes the health of all its parts.

Global Capitalism and the Gospel of Justice

While accepting that globalization *per se* is not a recent phenomenon, the collapse of Soviet Communism in 1989 and the subsequent truly global spread of a deregulated capitalist system is rightly viewed as having posed distinctive new challenges to Christian political theology and practice. Whatever concerns there were about the state-sponsored atheism and repression intrinsic to the soviet system, when viewed in directly socioeconomic rather than more generally political, cultural or religious terms, it did at least represent a genuine alternative to the dominant liberal capitalism of the then-called First World. As such and as was exemplified by classical Latin American liberation theology and their associated programmes of conscientization and societal reconstruction, the communist alternative lent a certain legitimacy to calls not just for the amelioration of capitalism's worst effects but for a more radical denunciation and transformation of the entire system.[4]

In contrast, all such moves have become considerably more ambiguous and difficult to press now that global capitalism holds sway as the only game in town. Short of committing to the fomenting of either violent or anarchic modes of global crisis and revolution – with Al-Qaida being the clearest manifestation of the former and elements of the anti-globalization movement representing the latter – the options appear to have narrowed to two different modes of transformative engagement from within the system itself. I will refer to these as the 'strategic radical' and the 'modest reformer' respectively. Where the 'strategic radical' envisions a long process of incremental change that will finally serve to transform neo-liberal capitalism beyond all recognition (through, for example, the sustained application of imagination, analysis and strategic pressure to the workings of the World Trade Organization),[5] the modest reformer is basically convinced that the current system represents the best and only option while nevertheless seeking for the curtailing of its worst consequences and the refining of its general workings.[6]

In practice, strategic radicals and modest reformers will frequently find themselves sharing very similar short-term strategic aims. Given that there is no existing alternative system to which ready appeal can be made, each must work from within the current system for its betterment. With this, up to a point at least, the required practical steps in any situation will be similar whether one seeks capitalism's fundamental transformation over the long haul or simply its more immediate and more modest refining. The difference is largely one of scale.

Indeed, the respective instincts of the strategic radical and the modest reformer may even require to be held in tension. Where the idealism of the strategic radical prevents her from becoming complacently accommodated, in the way that the modest reformer might, to the adequacy of *what is* and so keeps her moving towards *what might be*, the pragmatism of the modest reformer keeps things focused on the only place where action can actually be effective – within the contingencies of present circumstance. Borrowing a phrase coined by Nicholas Rescher in relation to a different, although not entirely unrelated, context we might refer to the emphases of the modest reformer and the strategic radical as jointly contributing to a stance of 'pragmatic-idealism'.[7]

In this purview, the Christian vocation for justice appears multi-dimensional, ranging from, first, the compassionate recognition of suffering and the focusing of attention and resource on its immediate alleviation, through, second, the recognition that such suffering can be causally intertwined with systemic weaknesses, which require analysis so as to enable both more effective prediction and ameliorative redress and clear focus for prophetic denunciation, to, third, the application of imagination and further analysis to the exploration of alternative modes of proceeding that might overcome key aspects of current systemic weakness, through to, fourth, the application of effective strategic pressure in support of the realization of such alternative possibilities.

Each of these dimensions of Christian sociopolitical involvement is crucial and capable of bearing witness to the healing, redeeming work of God in Christ and the Spirit. Yet none is capable of doing so adequately except in relation to the other three. Similarly, such bearing of witness in the round exceeds the capacities of any one individual at any one time and requires the conjoined witness of the whole. In this regard, it is notable that all four dimensions of concern are indeed exemplified in the work of many of the Christian social justice agencies – in the UK context, one thinks particularly of CAFOD, Christian Aid and Progressio (formerly the Catholic Institute for International Relations). Indeed, given the sophistication that characterizes their work of analysis, re-imagining and strategic advocacy, combined with continual direct responsive engagement with the tragic complexities of particular situations, it is fair to say that the Christian social justice agencies are the locus of some of the most significant political theology currently being pursued. But *does* all of this internal pragmatic response, analysis, imagining and strategizing exhaust the range of Christian hope? Alongside such modes of responsible action from within, is there any place for and possibility of a prophetic stretching of imaginations beyond the standard logic?

Hope-filled Leanings and the Sacramentality of the Church

If the respective stances of the strategic radical and the moderate reformer each have their own virtue, their own contribution to make, they each also have their own potential vice, their own potential failure of hope. Where an extreme intrinsicist version of the latter might over-optimistically regard globalization as the vehicle of the Spirit's moving us interminably towards a more equitable distribution of the world's resources and opportunities,[8] the former might tend towards an extrinsicist, overly pessimistic denunciation of the reality of God's transforming presence in this order and a correlative assertion of an unqualified self-willed activism as lying at the heart of the sociopolitical dimension of the Christian vocation. But, as Nicholas Lash recognizes, authentic Christian hope discounts both any ungrounded optimism regarding *our* ability to construct the Kingdom according to our own timescale and any unqualified pessimism regarding the in-principle impossibility of its realization.[9] The Christian task might not be to assert and to construct the Kingdom, but it is to lean into its coming; to be shaped and formed in accordance with it so as to become channels for its anticipatory realization and showing in the world.

Alongside, then, and transfusing the earlier-identified four dimensions of pragmatic Christian sociopolitical action, it is vital also to recover an authentic sense of hope as both transcending the current logic of things and as being capable of coming to prophetic sacramental expression, or anticipatory witness, in ways that stretch beyond immanent progress. Alongside the need for imaginative, expertly informed attempts to develop from within the practices, regulations and structures necessary to make globalization work more strongly for the good of all, there is need also for dramatic prophetic initiatives capable of attractively disclosing richer possibilities than the prevailing logic can imagine.

One of the most significant examples here is the Focolare 'Economy of Communion' project, involving over 800 businesses worldwide that are run on self-sustaining, profit-making principles but bound by a common core commitment to divide profits between direct aid to those in need, wider promotion of the 'culture of giving' (through training, education and the establishment of new projects) and growth of the business itself.[10] Another example is provided by the Shared Interest co-operative lending society wherein lending members commit to receiving a rate of interest below commercially available rates in order to provide seed-fund loans for fair-trade business initiatives in areas of need throughout the world. Originally established by Traidcraft in 1990, but now enjoying independent viability with over 8,400 investing members and a total shared investment in excess of £20 million, Shared Interest is an established going concern, albeit in a relatively modest way.[11]

Contrary to the internalist strategies outlined earlier, such initiatives do not represent potentially realizable short-to-medium-term strategic aims for the wider public realm. Rather, they are best viewed as relatively ad hoc prophetic-sacramental performances, anticipatory showings, of the alterity of the gospel and the eschatological reality of the Church, which transcend the possibilities of strategic internal reform by working from a different centre of gravity, capable of bringing an interrupting and genuinely transformative vision to bear. Their value should be measured not in terms of the achieving of wholesale societal transformation but in their ability to out-think standard logic with illuminating possibilities that transcend standard imaginative limits, capable of moving our desires and wills more deeply in accordance with their originating impulse, abiding sustenance and true orientation in the life of God.

More basic than any such specific performances of the sacramentality of the Church, however, is the claim variously voiced by Stanley Hauerwas, John Milbank and William Cavanaugh that the being and life of the Church more generally represents the true form of Christian political theology in as much as here is found the authentic story of human sociality well told, well performed.[12] The assumption here is that, before any specific initiatives *ad extra*, whether of a more directly pragmatic or a more intentionally sacramental/anticipatory character, the life of the Church well lived is itself already missionary, already sacramental of possibilities that transcend the conventional; and this in small, local and modest ways as well as in the more dramatic.[13]

In this vision, being, we might say, takes a certain qualified precedence over doing – qualified because there can be no artificial distinction between being and doing; our being is in an important sense what we live, what we become. Indeed, in God who is pure act, unqualified being simply *is* fully actualized doing. The qualified precedence of ecclesial being over doing that is spoken of here intends to suggest that our ecclesial doing is, at its most authentic, not simply a matter of disparate, insignificant acts needing to be imposed on reality as on a blank sheet of paper. Rather, such doing is both the expression of a prior given – the given of existing from, within and towards the being in act of God – and the means of deeper appropriation of that given. As Rahner would put it, freedom and dependence on God exist in direct not inverse relation.[14] This is a dependence, a 'leaning in', that frees and energizes; a 'leaning in' that sets us on our feet.

This qualified precedence of being over doing is in evidence more generally within Catholic theology. It lies behind the common sense of the inadequacy of purely functional rather than ontological understandings of the sacramentality of ordained ministry. Again, presupposed in the practice of infant baptism is the recognition that the most important things in life – starting with life itself, about which we are most conspicuously not consulted – are given rather than chosen; or, perhaps better, given before they are chosen. We might refer to this recognition of a prior givenness – of an act of being that precedes and opens our own particular being and from which and into which we live; of an act of being that is prior to all, present to all and promised to all – as the contemplative heart of Catholicism.

In this regard, the emphasis of Hauerwas, Milbank and Cavanaugh on the primary sacramentality of the life and being of the Church *ad intra* ahead of any specific initiatives *ad extra* represents, in itself, a welcome return of the Church to the centre of political theological discussion. Equally, it must be acknowledged that, if this fruitful perspective is not to collapse into a form of ecclesiological idealism – the charge that has oft been laid at its door[15] – then it needs to have integrated within it a critical ecclesiology, a political theology of the actual lived practice and organizational reality of the Church that views ecclesial reality both as potentially sacramental of the Kingdom and as in need of continual conversion and renewal if it is to fulfil, even partially, this calling.[16] Given the growing body of literature exploring possible relationships between catholicity and globalization, the issues here identified as pertaining to the sacramentality of the Church can be usefully tested out through an exploration of the potential for the catholicity of the Church, duly retrieved, reconceived and freshly performed, to figure something of the potential redeeming of globalization.[17]

In Search of Catholicity

Even etymologically there is resonance between 'catholicity' and globalization. The 'according to the whole', the *kath'holou*, of catholicity might well first have been used to emphasize the importance of holding to the whole truth of Christ as lived within the church catholic in distinction from the partial truths of heresy. But even on these christological grounds it is entirely appropriate that catholicity came to be extended in the direction of the spatio-temporal category of universality. The point is that, as variously written into the deep fabric of creation and as variously lived by the particular churches around the world, the whole truth of God in Christ and the Spirit requires the elusive, ever-renewed gathering of the whole in configured communion for anything approaching its adequate showing in the world.

At the heart of Catholicism, then, is a concern for both universality and particularity; for a universality, indeed, that is the holding of the diverse localities, the diverse particular centres of Catholicism in relationship. Catholicism, we might say, exists between its Petrine and its Pauline instincts – between the centripetal and the centrifugal forces of the Spirit's activity in the world; between the embracing arms of Bernini's colonnades in St Peter's Square and the outward-facing stance of the basilica of St Paul Outside the Walls. Of course, von Balthasar would rightly encourage us to extend this tension-laden force field of Catholicism further to include also its Marian pole, symbolizing the need always to attend, as explored earlier, with active contemplative openness to the prior givenness of the call and being of the Church and the consequent question as to how this might be appropriately deepened and intensified.[18]

All of this both could be and needs to be significantly extended and tested through successive close engagement with the various constructive readings of the catholicity of the Church that have been pressed in modern theology, both within Roman Catholicism and across the Christian traditions more broadly, perhaps starting with Johann Adam Möhler's groundbreaking early work.[19] That acknowledged, theological vision alone is incapable of realizing the potential that catholicity has to act as a transformative sacramental witness to a globalization for the good, wherein the health of each requires the health of all and the health of the whole the health of each part. Such transformative sacramental witness is a matter of practice rather than theory. Alongside vision and advocacy it requires therapeutic analysis of Catholicism's dysfunctions and disabilities, its pathologies and paralyses. It is a work not simply of celebration and proclamation, nor even simply of inspiration and encouragement but of healing, repair and redemption, oriented upon asking in love and prayerful attentiveness how the Church is called to be more fully, more clearly, more convincingly what it already is given to be. Accordingly, the remainder of this chapter briefly explores just one such possible dimension of Roman Catholicism's current dysfunction and needed repair.

Redeeming Catholicity for a Globalizing Age

It is widely acknowledged that *the* core dysfunction of contemporary Roman Catholicism relates to an imbalance between its centralizing pole on the one hand and the far-flung particular local churches on the other. Although this imbalance has thus far secured the visible unity of Roman Catholicism amid the pressures of postmodernism, it has done so at the cost of a significant diminishing and disempowering of the legitimate local diversity of Roman Catholicism. Clearly this broad issue relates both to matters of inculturation and of lay participation but most directly, perhaps, to the need for a reworking of the relationship between Petrine primacy and the College of Bishops. In this regard, Lash, refining a related suggestion of Archbishop John Quinn, advocates a reforming process leading to the establishment of a 'standing synod' of bishops as a corrective balance to Petrine presidency.[20] His hope is that this might promote a cascade of subsidiarity whereby all with appropriate expertise and experience might be drawn into the Church's decision-making processes. While fully in sympathy with this proposal and hope, I suggest that the corrective to the balance of power that it represents needs to be taken further in the direction of papal–episcopal reciprocity while preserving the appropriate conserving role of the Bishop of Rome.

In essence, the suggestion here is that the initiating role of the Bishop of Rome, in all matters of significance beyond the Archdiocese of Rome, should be made clearly subject to formal agreement by the College of Bishops, or its elected representatives. The dual purpose of this would be to contain the initiating role of the centre (and so limit the dysfunction of the centre's stifling over-definition of the diverse locality of Catholicism) and to promote far greater initiating action and responsibility *in* the localities. In turn, the Bishop of Rome would retain the role of ratifying any initiatives in the localities of significance beyond the internal workings of a given diocese. A direct implication of this proposed strategy is that the appointment of bishops would revert, as in ancient practice, genuinely to being a matter for the local church (subject to ratification by the Bishop of Rome), thus serving also to correct a further dimension of the dysfunction associated with the current imbalance of power wherein the process of episcopal appointment stands as a highly effective means of both exerting centrist control over the localities and promoting a culture of general subservience in these localities.

The developments proposed here would preserve the appropriately discerning, conserving, communion-holding role of the Bishop of Rome – making the College collectively and the localities individually accountable to the Bishop of Rome – while making the initiating dimension of the Bishop of Rome's own ministry much more clearly accountable to the College. Further, to avoid any possibility of the Bishop of Rome holding the College and the localities to ransom by refusing to endorse any desired initiatives, it is possible to imagine a mechanism whereby the College, perhaps on behalf of an individual bishop, could require that any given issue be re-opened as live for up to, say, three times within a given papacy, after which the Pope could rule a disputed matter out of court for the remaining duration of his papacy but not automatically beyond that. This would, in effect, serve to introduce a mechanism into Catholicism for dealing with disputed, unresolved issues and for ensuring that definitive judgement is only passed when full consideration has run its course and real consensus has been reached.[21]

Now clearly such developments alone would not be sufficient to repair the current dysfunction in relationship between the centre and its localities. For this we would need something along the lines of the cascading subsidiarity imagined by Lash and the development of other appropriate analogous structures and institutional spaces to support this. More specifically, it would require that the kind of developments here proposed in the structural relationship between Rome and the local churches be in turn mirrored by similar developments in the structural relations between bishops and the local church (both clergy and laity) and between priests and people in parochial contexts. This would accord the entire body of the Church a role in discernment and decision-making beyond the merely consultative, while preserving the appropriately conserving and executive roles of the hierarchy.

Further, along with such structural changes, the transition to whole-body Catholicism would also require related developments at the level of process, ethos and virtue. At the process level it would require recognition that appropriately discerned decisions take time to mature and emerge into clear view and so require space for trial, testing and due consideration. Similarly, as regards ethos and virtue, it would require development from a situation in which holding conversation is a relatively alien phenomenon within Catholicism to one in which Catholics both individually and collectively became habituated in the virtues of good Christian conversation. At the core of such conversation, as befits any genuine discerning *kath'holou* ('according to the whole'), should be the recognition that the responsibility to speak clearly the truth as one sees it needs always to be balanced by, indeed made subject to, the corresponding responsibility to attend to the truth as perceived by other participants. The aim is to discern the good of the whole rather than just one's own perceived good or that of factions within the whole. It goes without saying that Catholicism has an immense amount to learn here from the alternative ecclesial experiences of other traditions; and this not just as a conceptual, textual exercise but through close study of their actual practices.

But is not this all just dreamy, delusional distraction therapy – another form of potential ecclesiological idealism – that may serve to lessen the sense of pain caused by the significant dissonance between reality and desire but which remains powerless to effect any real change? What does it mean to love the Church, to live by faith and to proceed here in hope?

At one level it means, I suggest, to seek wherever possible to open and nurture creative spaces for experiments in good practice: whether in the parochial or diocesan contexts, within the academy, within national and international movements, or in informal groups outside the formal structures of the Church. Such spaces are not simply important for the individuals who participate in them and are sustained in hope by them. They are vital to the Church collectively in nurturing, learning and modelling the kind of virtues of mutual accountability, collective discernment and clear conversation into which Roman Catholicism must grow for the sake of its own catholicity and, thereby, for the sake of its sacramentality and sign-value for the world. They provide both an invaluable resource bank for future potential learning – music stored in the ecclesial piano stool – and have value in their own right as creative performances of Catholicism: sacramental enactments of the Church seeking to discern what it means to live according to the whole truth in Christ.[22]

At another level, seeking here to live by faith, hope and love involves the focused analysis in particular contexts of the factors militating against Catholicism being an effective learning community and how they might most effectively be tended. Further, given that many of these factors will be of a non-explicitly theological character – cultural, psychological, organizational, anthropological and so on – it is necessary for this diagnostic-therapeutic analytical framework to be multi-stranded. The implication is that, while retaining systematic rigour, ecclesiology must cease to be a purely conceptual, theoretical affair – what Nicholas M. Healy pejoratively refers to as 'blueprint ecclesiology'[23] – by becoming much more directly engaged with the particularities of lived practice.

But what about those aspects of ecclesial culture and institution that are persistently resistant to change? Perhaps, at one level, we are not to worry unduly about this. As Susan K. Wood recognizes, intrinsic to the very notion of the sacramentality of the Church is the recognition that the signifier, the Church, is not in any straightforward, unqualified or necessarily constant sense to be identified with the reality that is signified and disclosed (at least in part and on occasion).[24] Again, following Cavanaugh,[25] might we not say that the sacramentality of the Church consists, ironically, not in its adequacy but precisely in its penitential sinfulness as a particular showing of the great drama of redemption? But lest such points – doubtlessly true though they are – should descend into a complacent acceptance of any of the Church's specific failings, do we not need also to sustain due focus on and hope in the possible gracious renewal of the Church?

Perhaps here a helpful analogy exists in what *can* happen in dysfunctional situations in the natural order, for example chronic alcoholism or significant marital difficulties. While those in such situations can indeed remain doggedly resistant to change to the point of self-destruction, they can also make very surprising turnings around. Crisis can intensify to the point that resistance and denial is broken open and the combined instinct for survival and concern not to destroy utterly what one loves moves to metanoia. Of course, in Christian perspective such turnings around are never simply a purely natural movement but a movement of grace in our hearts. Similarly, on account of Christ's promise that the Church would never be allowed to fall into total and irredeemable frustration – a relatively minimal promise it has to be said – trust is fittingly evoked that this will be all the more the case in relation to the Church.

Finally, let us take this to its sharpest point and ask what it might mean to live by faith, hope and love even if one's options appear to be reduced to passive endurance. It would mean, I suggest, to embrace even this: to make action of endurance and attentiveness, sustained by the memory that it is in Christ's making action of passion that the waters of the New Jerusalem flowed from his side and sustained also by leaning into the promise that the Spirit will similarly provide in our own weakness.

Notes

1 See Paul D. Murray, 2004, *Reason, Truth and Theology in Pragmatist Perspective*, Leuven: Peeters, pp. 1–22, 131–61.

2 See Paul D. Murray, 2007, 'On Valuing Truth in Practice: Rome's Postmodern Challenge', in Laurence Paul Hemming and Susan Frank Parsons (eds), 2008, *Redeeming Truth: Considering Faith and Reason*, London: SCM, pp. 184–206; also Paul D. Murray (ed.), 2008, *Receptive Ecumenism and the Call to Catholic Learning*, Oxford: Oxford University Press.

3 See *Political Theology*, 3 (2000), for papers from the May 1999 Newman College, Birmingham conference on 'Proclaiming the Gospel of Justice in a World of Global Capitalism: The Future of Political Theology?'; *Studies in Christian Ethics*, 15 (2002), for papers from the July 2001 Ushaw College, Durham conference on 'Global Capitalism and the Gospel of Justice: Politics, Economics and the UK Churches'.

4 For the contested charge, from an otherwise sympathetic Christian socialist perspective, that liberation theology represents an insufficiently critical adoption of Marxist categories in such a fashion as embeds anti-theological norms into liberation theology's very basis and so occludes the yet more radical vision of human society authentic to the Christian tradition, see John Milbank, 1990, *Theology and Social Theory: Beyond Secular Reason*, Oxford: Blackwell, pp. 206–55.

5 See the work of the Malaysian economist, Martin Khor, 2001, *Rethinking Globalisation: Critical Issues and Popular Choices*, London: Zed Books.

6 See George Soros, 1998, *The Crisis of Global Capitalism: Open Society Endangered*, London: Little, Brown & Co.

7 See Nicholas Rescher, 1992–4, *A System of Pragmatic Idealism*, vols 1–3, Princeton, NJ: Princeton University Press; also Murray, *Reason, Truth and Theology*, pp. 91–130.

8 See Nicholas M. Boyle, 1998, *Who Are We Now? Christian Humanism and the Global Market from Hegel to Heaney*, Edinburgh: T & T Clark; 'The Hiddenness of the Spirit: The Disappearance of God from the English Cultural Framework', *New Blackfriars*, 85 (2004), 195–211.

9 See Nicholas Lash, 1981, *Matter of Hope: Theologian's Reflections on the Thoughts of Karl Marx*, London: Darton, Longman & Todd, pp. 250–80; 'All Shall Be Well: Christian and Marxist Hope', in *Theology on the Way to Emmaus*, London: SCM, 1986, pp. 202–15; 'Hoping Against Hope, or Abraham's Dilemma', in *The Beginning and the End of 'Religion'*, Cambridge: Cambridge University Press, 1996, pp. 199–218; also Paul D. Murray, 2007, 'Theology "Under the Lash": Theology as Idolatry Critique in the Work of Nicholas Lash', in S. C. Barton (ed.), *Idolatry*, London: Continuum, pp. 247–66.

10 See www.edc-online.org/uk/_idea.htm; also Lorna Gold, 2004, *The Sharing Economy: Solidarity Networks Transforming Globalisation*, Aldershot: Ashgate.

11 See www.shared-interest.com.

12 See Stanley Hauerwas, 1974, *Vision and Virtue: Essays in Christian Ethical Reflection*, Notre Dame: Fides, p. 221; *The Peaceable Kingdom*, Notre Dame: University of Notre Dame Press, 1983, p. 99; *In Good Company: The Church as Polis*, Notre Dame: University of Notre Dame Press, 1995; Milbank, *Theology and Social Theory*, p. 380–438; William Cavanaugh, 'The World in a Wafer: A Geography of the Eucharist as Resistance to Globalization', *Modern Theology*, 15 (1999), 181–96.

13 See Milbank, 'Stale Expressions: The Management-Shaped Church', *Studies in Christian Ethics*, 21 (2008), pp. 117–128.

14 See Karl Rahner, 'Current Problems in Christology', *Theological Investigations*, 1 (1965), London: Darton, Longman & Todd, pp. 149–200, p. 162.

15 E.g., Theo Hobson, 'Against Hauerwas', *New Blackfriars*, 88 (2007), 300–12.

16 For the classic expression of the Church's own continual 'need of being purified', see Vatican II, '*Lumen Gentium*, The Dogmatic Constitution on the Church', *Vatican Council II: The Conciliar and Post Conciliar Documents*, Austin Flannery OP (ed.), Leominster: Fowler Wright, 1980 [1975], pp. 350–423, p. 358. Notable here is that Cavanaugh, in an as yet unpublished paper, appeals precisely to 'A Penitential Account of Local Practices and Church Unity' (presented to Leuven Encounters in Systematic Theology VI, 9 November 2007) to counter the charge of 'ecclesiological Monophysitism'.

17 See Richard Marzheuser, 'Globalization and Catholicity: Two Expressions of One Ecclesiology?', *Journal of Ecumenical Studies*, 32 (1995), 179–93; Robert J. Schreiter, 1997, *The New Catholicity: Theology Between the Global and the Local*, Maryknoll, NY: Orbis; Avery Dulles, 'The Catholicity of the Church and Globalization', *Seminarium*, 40 (2000), 259–68; Peter De Mey, 'Is the Connection of "Catholicity" and "Globalization" Fruitful? An Assessment of Recent Reflections on the Notion of Catholicity', *Bulletin ET*, 13 (2002), 169–81, to which essay I am grateful for the Dulles reference; Gerard Mannion, 'What's in a Name? Hermeneutical Questions on "Globalization", Catholicity and Ecumenism', *New Blackfriars* 86 (2005), 204–15.

18 See Hans Urs von Balthasar, 1986, *The Office of Peter and the Structure of the Church*, San Francisco, CA: Ignatius Press, pp. 183–212.

19 See Johann Adam Möhler, 1996 [1825], *Unity in the Church, or, The Principle*

of Catholicism, Presented in the Spirit of the Church Fathers of the First Three Centuries, ed. and trans. Peter C. Erb, Washington, DC: Catholic University of America Press.

20 Nicholas Lash, 2003, 'Vatican II: Of Happy Memory – and Hope?', in Austin Ivereigh (ed.), *Unfinished Journey*, London: Continuum, pp. 13–31, pp. 28–30; compare John Quinn, 2000, *The Reform of the Papacy: The Costly Call to Christian Unity*, New York: Crossroad, pp. 176–7.

21 See Murray, 'On Valuing Truth', pp. 190–1, 197, 203.

22 An invaluable contribution is made by Bradford Hinze, 2006, *Practices of Dialogue in the Roman Catholic Church*, New York: Continuum. Hinze analyses various structures of decision-making within recent Catholicism and assesses how effectively they promote relevant ecclesial virtues; for review see Murray in *Ecclesiology*, 4 (2008), forthcoming.

23 See Nicholas M. Healy, 2000, *Church, World and the Christian Life: Practical Prophetic Ecclesiology*, Cambridge: Cambridge University Press, pp. 25–51.

24 See Susan K. Wood, 2004, 'Jesus and Perspectives in Roman Catholic Ecclesiology Today', in Carl E. Braaten and Robert W. Jensen (eds), *The Ecumenical Future*, Grand Rapids: Eerdmans, pp. 126–37.

25 See note 16 above.

8

Freedom from the Body of Death

Celebrating the Bicentenary of the Act to Abolish the Slave Trade

PETER SELBY

The grieving women seemed to be bowing and reaching into the distance. Such was the image of which I read many years ago in an account of a visit by an anthropologist to Sierra Leone. They grieved, but the gesture was strange to her eyes. In the course of her time there, this anthropologist attended a number of funerals and was struck by some of the ways in which grief was manifested. We tend to think that everybody throughout the world grieves in the same way but, of course, that is not true. Different cultures and communities grieve in different ways. What this anthropologist noticed were people grieving with gestures that looked strangely like people bowing and reaching forward into the distance, and she set herself to discover what this gesture had come from and why it was associated with grief. She found people quite reluctant to talk about it, and it took her quite a time to investigate the matter and come to some sense of what the gesture was about. What she discovered was that these grieving gestures had originated in the experience of people standing on the seashore, watching their loved ones transported out of sight across the ocean as slaves, and more than 200 years later they were still grieving that way.

Honoured as I am by the invitation to contribute to a *Festschrift* for Ann Loades, a friend and colleague of many years, I find myself reflecting that, alongside her varied interests as a theologian, and in particular her remarkable and radical holding together of contemporary issues and parts of the theological tradition often much neglected, for as long as I have known her Ann has also practised as a dance teacher. It seems appropriate therefore to begin this reflection with the physical, with a dance of grief, and to bring together, following the recent celebration of the bicentenary of the Act of Parliament that abolished the slave trade in the British Empire, the slave trade in its historical and present manifestations as a *bodily* phenomenon: slavery was above all else a trade in bodies, and the Sierra Leonese dance of grief was clearly a bodily response. Much of Ann's writing and thinking is, as well as radical and traditional, also physical, aware of the sheer physicality of the dynamics of oppression and liberation, and for that reason if for no other I hope that this entry into the topic may respect her awareness of that bodiliness in history, tradition and present-day reality.

For it is the case that remembrance is something too often considered as an activity of the mind, but this Sierra Leonese dance illustrates the point that grieving happens in the *body*, and in this case not just in the outpouring of tears and sobs. For if you grieve by making use of a gesture that has that particular history to it, then as you grieve – perhaps for a loved grandparent or relative, granted that will be for somebody who has definitely never known slavery in her time – you keep alive the meaning of that gesture because you enact it in your body. And even if you could not personally describe what the gesture meant as you did it, and that would have been true for many people, you would nonetheless be keeping alive in your body the memory of that terrible transportation. It is calculated that some 10 to 12 million African people were transported across the Atlantic, and that, over the two- to three-hundred-year period of the slave trade that I am discussing, probably one and a quarter million died. Captains of ships would face considerable punishment if they did not carry out this duty and sometimes slaves were thrown over the side into the sea to drown if it was thought that they were going to be allowed to escape. How many thousands upon thousands will have danced the dance of grief we shall never know. When we speak of the slave trade, we are, in short, talking about another holocaust of human bodies, and a holocaust carried out over a long period of time.

It was my privilege for some seven years to be a close colleague of a Barbadian bishop, the then Bishop of Croydon, Wilfred Wood. Occasionally he would bare his soul and say that, while of course he thought that what we call the Holocaust, the murder of 6 million Jews, together with gypsies, gay people, trade unionists and communists by the State during the Third Reich, was a profound outrage, he could not but admit to some feeling that that particular outrage had usurped all others from people's memories and that they really had forgotten that there was more than one holocaust in human history. Slavery in all its manifestations is a truly outrageous history, a history of terrible human cruelty, of activities that we now would call sexual abuse but then were regarded not in that way but simply as the assertion of the white person's natural right to gratification. We are talking about the terrorizing of people, and ultimately about the objectification, the commodification of human beings, a terrible trade in bodies.

The slave trade that was abolished in the British Empire by the Act of 1807 is a piece of our history from before the industrial revolution and it is clear that slaves were regarded pretty much as machines are – indeed machines are often treated more kindly. So if a machine does not work, you kick it, and if it still does not work you do worse than that. The slave trade whose end we were invited to celebrate in 2007 was in fact something absolutely horrendous. The question must therefore be, is it really proper to celebrate the end of something so horrendous without some note of responsibility or apology or reparation to the descendants of people who still bear the marks of that history?

In the preparations to celebrate the bicentenary much emerged into the public consciousness that had lain hidden before. A radio broadcast, designed to bring to light the extent to which many of our most important institutions still gain from the profits of the slave trade, began in the Codrington Library at All Souls', Oxford, named after the same benefactor whose money came from the exploitation of slaves, the same Codrington who endowed the Caribbean Theological College. In that radio programme, the Archbishop of Canterbury, Rowan Williams, was confronted with a letter from one of his predecessors to a bishop asking for more 'supplies', and asked for his reaction. He indicated that he was deeply shocked, but perhaps not as shocked as when he encountered in the minutes of the Society for the Propagation of the Gospel the record of a discussion of the need to find solutions to the problem of 'refuse' slaves. When human beings become 'supplies' and elderly or injured human beings become 'refuse', we know ourselves transported into a world where human beings have ceased to be persons and become mere assets, designated 'refuse' when they cease to be of any value as such. They were traded as bodies for their labour or their sex, and when useless for that became part of the body of death. The dance of grief is the enactment in advance of a bereavement that the slave trade actually represented for those being transported: the slaves died before they died, members in life of the body of death.

The marks of the slave trade continue in many ways and the Sierra Leone example mentioned above is but one such, and not the worst. The trafficking of human beings for sex has rightly attracted attention during the celebration as perhaps the most palpable current example of the continuation of a slave trade into our time. What makes it a slave trade is precisely that objectification of human persons, their transformation from person to mere asset, which slavery puts into practice. But it is not the only one, even if it is now widely reported.

A further experience may illustrate the way in which the marks of the slave trade continue: some years ago, I was invited to take part in one of what were then quite common, namely Partners in Mission Consultations, in which people from different parts of the Anglican Communion visited a particular Province, and offered insights and reflections on what they saw. It was a hugely educational activity, in my case to the Province of the Indian Ocean, which is the Seychelles, Mauritius and Madagascar, an absolutely fascinating area. One of the things that they are struggling with is what they refer to, in a word that we might feel is utterly quaint to the point of being unusable, as 'concubinage', that is to say, people in a relationship who are not married, a rather common experience for us. For the people of the Seychelles, if you were in concubinage, you were excluded from the sacraments. In a fascinating discussion with the then Archbishop of the Indian Ocean, who was Bishop of the Seychelles, French Chang Him, he revealed that he really found this excommunication the deepest possible embarrassment. For the historical fact had been that slaves were not allowed to marry, because if they married they were of course less easily disposable when it came to selling them or moving them on. They would then be encumbered; so to prevent that they were not allowed to marry. In those circumstances, if there was to be any stability of relationship, what came to be known as concubinage was the only possibility. There is in effect therefore a double cruelty which still survives: slaves' right to marry was interfered with, and they were punished then for having the only kind of stable relationship that the ban on marriage left to them, punished by the Church in the name of the Church for a circumstance that was in fact a highly honourable way of living in the context of the oppression of slavery.

The invitation to celebrate the passing of a statute to end this horror in the British Empire was therefore always going to be ambiguous. We were to celebrate the ending of something that should never have begun, and the success of a political campaign that, on any reckoning, took far too long and should never have been necessary in the first place. That good and wise Christian people campaigned as they did against the slave trade is a matter for thankfulness: it is proper to be thankful that we are united with them in the communion of the saints, who in every generation have hungered and thirsted for righteousness and now live where the righteousness of God governs all things in the realm where Jesus reigns supreme. And yet to look at those old posters offering human beings for sale as slaves, let alone to read the terrible accounts of the conditions they endured on the slave ships that transported millions – and drowned a large number – is to be torn between thankfulness that this trade was outlawed 200 years ago last year, and horror that it happened at all.

And when we have been seared and sickened by the detailed remembrances of the past, then we have to allow our minds to ponder this most difficult of questions about the slave trade: how could human beings, not exceptional human beings, have watched and consented to such things? It is the central theological question about this body of death, that it could be seen and accepted by so many who were in their own minds committed to the journey of life. For these were not monsters who did this, but (for the most part) worthy men and women, Christians many of them, who would gather as we in our time gather to hear the same Scriptures and taste the same sacraments. They believed they too were hungry and thirsty for righteousness, and they found that on the whole they were satisfied with at least some of their achievements in that direction. It was ordinary people, not to mention respectable people, as ordinary and respectable as those whom we meet each day, who knew this and consented to it. Perhaps they too, like us in our day, had qualms about what they heard about some of the excesses, but imagined (as we often do) that these were exceptional hard cases, to be weighed against other stories that no doubt also circulated about good slave owners who were kind and gentle to their slaves.

For after the searing memories, and yet perhaps before we decide what apologies or reparations may be appropriate, the reflections should burden us with this question: how could such persons watch and consent to such things? It is *the* question, because only that question will lead us in our day to that depth of reflection that will ensure that we notice what we are watching and consenting to, and, like those whose wisdom, foresight, courage and persistence we celebrate today, withdraw our consent, refuse to collude, hunger and thirst enough, till the trade in human lives in our time – the trafficking, the sex trade and all its other gross manifestations – are brought to an end. No doubt the question goes wider even than the analogies and continuations that bear most resemblance to the slave trade: it must extend to the search for other manifestations of the body of death, the attitudes to other members of the created order, to its resources, to the stability of its climate or to the majestic variety of its species, where our tolerance or our looking away will raise for successive generations the same question: how and why did they consent to such things while at the same time professing an obedience to the call of life? Whence comes this consent to the power of the body of death, and how are we to be delivered from it?

The gentle reasoning that sustains the body of death, and shields our eyes from its consequences in any generation, comes from the economic realities that move us more deeply and operate at a level of routine that prevents their even surfacing into the realm of consciousness. That reasoning led to the quite general belief among those who resisted the call for the emancipation of the slaves that it could quite simply not be afforded, that the economy could not sustain giving the liberty and dignity due to those who worked the plantations, and they therefore continued to opt for slavery instead. And the evidence that it was an economic doctrine that gained supremacy over ethical considerations and enabled the slave trade to persist is that, over the three decades when emancipation came to be debated in the years following the ending of the slave trade, the final resolution of the matter had to include payments to slave owners, including ecclesiastical corporations such as the Society for the Propagation of the Gospel, in 'compensation' for the freeing of their slaves. The freedom of slaves had its price, and finally it was a price that had to be paid for the democratic assent of Parliament. The iron shackles so vividly described by the Archbishop of York, John Sentamu, in a recent visit to Tanzania reflect a shackling of the heart by doctrines and aspirations that are at root economic: the body of death is sustained in the lives of people by the belief that ethical decisions are dependent on economic doctrines.

It is of course very hard to believe that prosperity follows justice, and not the other way round, because when we are presented with a social issue, whatever it is, the opposite view constantly presents itself. The message our courageous forebears understood in the heat of their campaign to abolish the slave trade was that, if you really wanted to prosper, to enjoy the benefits of a free society, you would have to set all free, and if you did not do so it would be a sure sign that you were not free yourself. The orthodoxies of economic thinking are but the intellectual working out of the conviction that there are hungers and thirsts to be satisfied before the hunger and thirst for righteousness can be. The fettering of our hearts and minds with such thinking is something we do because it suits us, and once fettered we are brilliant at justifying the place at which we have arrived. What the abolitionists recognized was the need for different economic thinking – Henry Thornton was their economist, who along with those of different gifts – Wilberforce,

Clarkson, the freed slave Equiano – broke those innocent-looking shackles of the soul that declared that slavery could not end because its end could not be afforded. Put with some bitter irony by William Cowper,

> I own I am shock'd by the purchase of slaves
> And fear those who buy them and sell them are knaves.
> What I hear of their hardships, their torture, their groans
> Is almost enough to draw pity from stones.
> I pity them greatly, but I must be mum,
> For how could we do without sugar and rum?[1]

Such words present the central issue, albeit in a tone full of cynicism. The implication is that slavery was perpetuated, and its modern-day equivalents are perpetuated because we cannot imagine how we could afford to do otherwise.

And to the central theological question, the question how people could consent to this economic shackling of the soul, there is a clear and simple biblical answer. That answer is backed by the centuries of the Church's history where Christians have allowed their discipleship to be guided by wise counsellors. As an answer it is simple, but at this time also deeply paradoxical. For the Bible's answer to the question why we watch and consent to the enslavement of peoples and all the other manifestations of the body of death is that human beings have a deep propensity to prefer slavery to freedom, and so consent to shackle the hands and feet of innocent and helpless men, women and children because we have allowed our hearts and minds to be shackled. Women and men with free hearts and minds do not fetter the lives of others.

And in what consists this fettering of the heart? Surely it comes from the hungers and thirsts that are not for righteousness but for the things that we think we cannot do without. If we were truly able to celebrate this bicentenary, we have to recall not just the brutality but also the gentle reasoning that said change was impossible because it could not be afforded, that if the economy was strong enough we could help people more. Is that old reasoning – or new? Was the infamous comment of Margaret Thatcher that the Good Samaritan was only able to help someone because he had money in his pocket the source of so much disdain because it expressed precisely the slave-making assumption that economics precedes ethics as the determinant of human behaviour – and except for the saints and heroes of the human race it has to.

The economy – in our time the globalized capitalist economy – is the theoretical foundation of the body of death whatever form that takes. Whether it is the emancipation of slaves or the reduction of carbon emissions, the first instinct is to declare them impossible on the simple grounds that it would make life too expensive, erode profit margins and (much as we assert we want to) would put our economic survival in jeopardy.

Yet there is no doctrine less supported by history: the unaffordable has become affordable under the political pressure that meant that it had to be so. More than that: the economic doctrine yields to experience, and what was impossible becomes necessity. As the horizon that is at one point declared to mark the limit of our vision comes closer we see beyond it, and we know that the horizon of human history makes emancipation from the body of death not just an invitation but the only hope.

The problem, if there is one, is that this recurring process is one that we choose not to remember as such. We recall the heroic examples of the abolitionists without noticing the reasoning that they needed to subvert, a reasoning that we now take for granted: who would now defend slavery on economic grounds? The choreography of freedom is one that involves a remembering – in heart and body – of the constant cycle that teaches that declaring something economically impossible is simply to repeat the slave owners' chant. The reality is that we afford what we choose, and we are called to the choice of life. The Christian movement is the dance of freed slaves who recall in their bodies the exchange of grace that transforms the grief dance of the women of Sierra Leone into the liberty song of the Easter people. They remember that the body of death will yield to the living body, and that pretending otherwise is to make humanity repeat a story that we know from experience to be untrue, that freedom cannot be afforded. In reality, it is the only thing that can be.

Notes

1 William Cowper, 1788, 'Pity for Poor Africans', *Northampton Mercury*, 9 August 1788, reproduced in William Cowper, *The Poetical Works of William Cowper*, Edinburgh: William P. Nimmo, 1863, pp. 418–19.

PART 2

Imaginative Juxtapositions:
Theology as an Integrated Discipline

Chapters in this part appreciate the manifold interconnections between Christian spirituality and Christian theology, which mark so much of Ann's writing. They combine the celebration of the Christian tradition and the forgotten voices in it with developing new and imaginative ways of both critical reading and creative appropriation. The result has been a repeatedly voiced concern on Ann's part to avoid artificial divisions in theology, a concern that is taken up by a number of contributors to this part.

9

Theology and Spirituality
A Tribute to Ann Loades

DANIEL W. HARDY

A large view is needed if we are fully to appreciate the range of the contribution of Ann Loades to theology, to the Church and to the academy. From my first acquaintance with her when I arrived in Durham in the 1980s, I recall so many times, some in her office at the top of Abbey House, many in passing, others during meetings and conferences, when she spoke vigorously and to the point. Her contributions were never trivial, and they were often decisive for the matter at hand; 'mild' or 'ineffectual' are not words one could associate with her. At the same time I know well the enormous and constructive impact her teaching and supervision have had on those fortunate enough to work with her, and the fair-mindedness with which she examined. Only at worship in the Cathedral was the strength of her presence subdued; but even there she had plenty to say afterwards about what still needed to be done to bring that ancient institution up to date!

In her, one finds a remarkable combination of intellect, passion, integrity and dedication. Even more, she is one of those whose life and work show the interpenetration of Christian spirituality, theology, ethics and realism, both in academy and Church. That is why in what follows, by way of doing her honour, I return to the question of what is needed to make this interpenetration effective.

Introduction

In the vast attention now given to 'spirituality', its natural association with theology is often forgotten. Through the ages the two have been at least somewhat differentiated, but they have also been held in what has usually been a fruitful tension from which both have benefited. 'Lived spirituality' has been differentiated from what is normative for Christian faith but the one has also been informed by the other. And the same has held in the reverse direction: the coherent presentation of Christian faith has been distinguished from lived spirituality but has also been significantly enriched by it. Although it is seldom acknowledged as such, there has been a significant relocation of the relation of theology and spirituality.

By now, however, a major change has occurred in this relationship of distinction and mutual enrichment. The reasons lie deep within changes both in conceptions and practices of human life and also in notions of what is proper to Christian faith, as well as in how these are established. But the overall result has been that human life has tended to become self-referential, whether narrowly or broadly conceived, while Christian faith – as such or in its ecclesial embodiment – has become self-referential in its own terms, either narrowly or broadly. So the two – life and faith – have tended to break apart and follow separate courses.

An additional complication now is that life today may or may not be seen in 'spiritual' terms. Is there such a 'thing' as the 'self', or a spiritual 'core' or 'integrity' or 'dynamic' of which the living of life is an expression, or not? On the one hand, perhaps living is just a question of 'getting on with things', in which one does not need reflexivity about the 'centre' of this activity. If so, all this talk about 'spirituality' may serve as a mask for the unwillingness to acknowledge that there is no enduring self. On the other hand, even if there is a spiritual centre of some kind, perhaps there are no inherent constraints that limit the kind of living in which it may engage; maybe it is unencumbered by any sense of a 'rightness' about the way to live life. Such ideas – that there is no enduring self, or no such thing as a right way for living – have wide currency today, whether explicitly recognized or not.

Yet it is undeniable that there is a remarkable upsurge of concern with spirituality, outside and within the churches. Outside religious institutions, 'spirituality' often provides a focus different from the convergence of scientific, technological and commercial interests in human affairs today; and 'spirituality' has provided leverage for counter-movements: environmental, liberation, peace, feminist, gay, for example. Within religious institutions, when it is recognized that spirituality shapes the ordinary life of lay Christians (as distinct from what they are told is normative by those who control the churches), it serves as an important focus of concern. It is in fact a new form of the priesthood of all believers and, like that, a counter-force to hierarchical ecclesial control. Hence both post-Vatican II Roman Catholicism and the World Council of

Churches have been strongly interested in spirituality. Not that all spirituality is to be found in either the counter-movements or the churches: much of it comes from elsewhere: from indigenous local traditions of different kinds, or as a more personal pursuit among individuals seeking meaning and purpose for lives lacking satisfying depth otherwise.

The surge in 'spirituality' is made more complex by global awareness. As if it were not already a very varied phenomenon, the self-sameness of 'spirituality' in the West is challenged by the recognition of other long-standing spiritual traditions of the world and of localized indigenous expressions (pagan, aboriginal or North American Indian, for example). Nowadays these are presented as intrinsically valuable, with no concern for their correlation with what has been more 'natural' in western traditions. In the new marketplace of spiritualities, the results are confusing and uncertain: what then is spirituality? What relation, if any, do these different forms of spirituality have?

There are counterparts to such problems in the changes that have occurred in, and the questions now confronting, Christian theology. There is, of course, renewed awareness of the variegation of what some thought was a simple, and simply learned, faith, a variegation by tradition, history and context that touches every aspect of faith. And nowadays there are widespread disagreements as to whether there is truth in the normative assertions of Christian faith, whether they do indeed refer to a real God or not, or are actually rationalizations – backings – for the choice by some groups of particular ways of thinking and living. These questions are reinforced by the presence of other great religious traditions with claims that appear to rival Christian ones, and by those who conclude – often quite stridently – that all religious assertions are to be relativized by reference to a transcendent focus common to them all ('pluralism') or as culturally variant forms of the phenomenon called 'religion' or of 'spirituality'.

Such difficult questions are often side-stepped by those concerned simply to 'get on with' – or attract other people to – Christian belief and practice, and their prevalence in the 'secular' climate of today is not faced. Then there is a growing awareness of important theological differences in worldwide Christianity, which tends to polarize Christians into two camps: those who focus – and in doing so often harden – the traditional norms of Christian faith as a way of enforcing them, and those who soften them in order to attract more people. Just this polarization is found in most of the interaction of Christians with public dilemmas, for example the current befuddlement about whether homosexuality should have a legitimate place in Christian life.

The dislocation of the relationship of spirituality and theology presents a serious challenge to both, and very serious questions appear:

1 Can spirituality without theology have the coherence and depth of truth – and the sense of 'rightness' – needed for fully human life? There are, of course, significant attempts to provide these for spirituality without privileging theology but the question remains whether they are sufficient to provide what is needed.

2 Can theology without spirituality fully understand the work of God in the Holy Spirit and integrate it with the dynamics of human life as lived? Again, theological programmes – even the best – commonly claim that they do, but on closer examination they often generalize about the human condition without engaging with the full depths of particular human lives.

3 Can spirituality and theology be related only through some kind of 'bridging' of their concerns external to what each aspires to provide, through some notion or relation extrinsic to each of them: would that be sufficient to enable each to enrich the other without compromising it? There is a very serious issue here. If each of the terms spirituality and theology is already constituted and precedes and determines the interrelating of the two, the interrelating can only realize possibilities already implicit in the two and 'you can rearrange the furniture, even move it to a new location, but you still have the same old furniture'.[1] If instead we reckon with the relation of the two as having an ontological status of its own, then we can have a relation through which both spirituality and theology may change through their relating. Since our survey of the two shows that each is already changing, by causes internal and external to each, a notion of the relation between them – as important in its own right – allows simultaneous, mutual change with the possibility of greater coherence between the two.

The question we now face is what can be – and should be – done about all this?

The Distinctive Dynamics of Spirituality

Looked at from the viewpoint of Christianity, at least in the Anglican tradition, spirituality and theology are actually distinct but integrated. Spirituality is said to be the most personal and intimate aspect of the life of faith, how we live in the Spirit. It is what is sometimes called 'intentional discipleship', and has to do with the shape and texture of a Christian lifestyle. It is also said to be contrasted with theology, at least theology taken in a narrow sense, with 'what we believe and how we believe it'. The contrast that is usually assumed is that between what is personal and what is less than personal, even if theology affirms the personhood of God, or that between the practical, performative or lived and the theoretical or cognitively known.

As a first approximation, despite the danger of borrowing a 'mechanical' image from the world of computers, we may take it that spirituality as now understood refers to something like the 'operating system' of life, by which human beings co-ordinate their existence in the world. As such, this 'operating system' necessarily coincides with the (in the case of computers, mathematical) conditions that make it possible[2] – a computer operating system manifests such conditions in its code (which is why such codes are guarded so jealously) – and itself sets the conditions for other forms of life with which it is to be compatible and interact, as an operating system establishes conditions for the forms of software that may be used with it and enables their use. In that sense, the 'spiritual' in human beings may be taken both to embody basic conditions of human life and to provide conditions for being and action, but as actually operative in human life in the world. In such a case, there is no sharp distinction between the conditions and the activity that they generate. It seems to me that such a conception is found in the Book of Deuteronomy:

> Surely, this commandment that I am commanding you today is not too hard for you, nor is it too far away. It is not in heaven, that you should say, 'Who will go up to heaven for us, and get it for us so that we may hear it and observe it?' Neither is it beyond the sea, that you should say, 'Who will cross to the other side of the sea for us, and get it for us so that we may hear it and observe it?' No, the word is very near to you; it is in your mouth and in your heart for you to observe. (Deut. 30.11–13, NRSV)

Here, the word of the Lord is so near to human beings as to motivate them in observing it.

A similar view is found in the long tradition of 'spiritual philosophy' that receives expression in Samuel Taylor Coleridge's very influential *Aids to Reflection* (1825/31):

> Hooker distinguishes Spirit from Soul; and as far as I understand him, forms the same conception of Spirit as I have done in the Aids to

Reflection – namely, as a focal energy from the union of the Will and the Reason – i.e. the *practical* Reason, the source of Ideas as ultimate Ends. – Ah! If Hooker had initiated & as it were matriculated his philosophy with the *prodocimastic* Logic – or previous examination of the *Weights & Measures* in use! S.T.C.[3]

If we compare this with the computer-code notion, what Coleridge does is to see God as imaged in the human Spirit (like the 'conditions' manifested in the 'code'), where the Spirit focuses and combines the Reason ('a direct aspect of truth, an inward beholding'[4]) and the Will (compare the code governing the operation of software) in the energizing of practice toward 'ultimate ends'.

What is found in the active human spirit, furthermore, is an 'all-present power' (comparable to the 'eternal' mathematics on which the computer is indirectly based) deriving from the Triune God, which forms the spirit inwardly.

Whenever, therefore, the Man is determined (i.e. impelled and directed) to act in harmony of inter-communion must not something be attributed to this allpresent power as acting *in* the Will? and by what fitter names can we call this than the LAW, as empowering; THE WORD, as informing; and THE SPIRIT, as actuating.[5]

Hence it follows for Coleridge that 'Christianity is not a theory, or a speculation; but a life; – not a philosophy of life, but a life and a living process.'[6] And there, in the operative life of faith, its conditions are actively appropriated. By such lively faith its own operative conditions are actively appropriated as a 'higher gift', by which human beings are elevated beyond lesser forms of reason (and willing) to a divinely infused 'power' of life.

As must already be evident, however, this is no easy path, but one that requires putting other things in their place: writing a code that maximizes its own conditions, and is operatively satisfactory, requires 'training'. In the case of the formation of the spirit through the ages, this 'training' has taken the form of disciplined 'spiritual exercise':

As excessive eating or drinking both makes the body sickly or lazy, fit for nothing but sleep, and besots the mind, as it clogs up with crudities the way through which the spirits should pass, bemiring them, and making them move heavily, as a coach in a deep way; thus doth all immoderate use of the world and its delights wrong the soul in its spiritual condition, makes it sickly and feeble, full of spiritual distempers and inactivity, benumbs the graces of the Spirit, and fills the soul with sleepy vapors, makes it grow secure and heavy in spiritual exercises, and obstructs the way and motion of the Spirit of God, in the soul.[7]

The 'spirit' is always focused through a way by which it may be made most intensively present, 'spiritual exercise'. This is what we might call a 'way of intensity' that is reasoned but simultaneously highly practical – a 'living wisdom' by which the human being is formed in such a way as not to be trapped by lesser instincts and goals, but to be formed in the good. 'Philosophy did not mean abstract technical theories produced by professionals but the living wisdom of a life led according to reason.'[8]

But we saw earlier that notions of spirituality such as these are seriously affected by modern circumstances: first, for some people they are modified by, for others they are challenged by practices of spirituality from other religious traditions and local indigenous forms of life; second, for many more, they are contradicted by strident claims that there is no such 'thing' as the 'self', or a spiritual 'core' or 'integrity' or 'dynamic' of which the living of life is an expression. A few words about these very large issues must suffice.

In response to the first effect, in the form in which we have been examining it so far, spirituality is an emphasis of most – if not all – the great and local religious traditions, though not necessarily in precisely similar ways. Insofar as I understand Islam, full integrity of self-subsistence is attributable only to Allah and only derivatively to human beings: 'whoever strives hard, he strives only for his own soul; most surely Allah is self-sufficient, above (need of) the worlds'.[9] The conditions for the living of life are given by the Holy Spirit: 'The Holy Spirit has revealed it from your Lord with the truth, that it may establish those who believe and as a guidance and good news for those who submit.'[10] But if we look elsewhere, outside the 'religions of the book', there is no such ready attribution of human integrity to divine gift.

Yet, primarily in the West, there are sharply antithetical claims – the second effect noted above. Often they are directed against one particular, quite long-standing, conception of the self, as substantial:

Like the surface of the Earth, the brain is pretty much mapped. There are no secret compartments inaccessible to the surgeon's knife or the magnetic gaze of the brain scanner; no mysterious humours pervading the cerebral ventricles, no soul in the pineal gland, no vital spark, no spirits in the tangled wood. There is nothing you can't touch or squeeze, weigh and measure, as we might the physical properties of other objects. So you will search in vain for any semblance of a self within the structures of the brain: there is no ghost in the machine. It is time to grow up and accept this fact. But, somehow, we are the product of the operation of this machinery and its progress through the physical and social world. [It constructs a model of the organism of which it is a part and, beyond this, a representation of that organism's place in relation to other, similar, organisms: people. As part of this process it assembles a 'self', which can be thought of as the device we humans employ as a means of negotiating the social environment.]

Minds emerge from process and interaction, not substance. In a sense, we inhabit the spaces between things. We subsist in emptiness. A beautiful, liberating thought; and nothing to be afraid of. The notion of a tethered soul is crude by comparison.[11]

In a sense, therefore, the self is less a substance than a logical 'third' operator, whose ontological status is that of 'orchestrator of adaptive interaction between the organism and the world'. But as part of this performative process it builds a story of itself – a 'narrative self' – fictionalized from momentary impressions. What is lacking in this account, however, is any notion of a received self, or one whose pathway or dynamic is derived from a source other than its own construction. It appears not to need to embody reference to such a source. It is not far from notions of spirituality that have emerged recently. As Robert Wuthnow finds in the USA,

I argue that a traditional spirituality of inhabiting sacred places has given way to a new spirituality of seeking – that people have been losing faith in a metaphysic that can make them feel at home in the universe and that they increasingly negotiate among competing glimpses of the sacred, seeking partial knowledge and practical wisdom.[12]

In this 'spirituality of negotiation', people search among complex and confusing meanings for the fleeting moments that convince them that there is anything beyond everyday life that gives meaning.

Yet very important issues – from opposite directions as it were – appear in these two accounts. The one refers the self and its integrity explicitly to the divine gift, the other explicitly to the position of a device employed in the process of interactions. They serve to remind us of the dilemmas of theology and spirituality to which we pointed before: first,

can spirituality – in this case the notion of a self built through its operations – without theology have the coherence and depth of truth (and the
sense of 'rightness') needed for fully human life? Second, can a theology
without spirituality – in this case a spirituality entirely received by the
gift of God – fully understand the work of God in the Holy Spirit and
integrate it with the deepest dynamics of human life as lived? Third, how
can the two – spirituality and theology – be related dynamically,
through a relation by which they may grow with each other?

The Distinctive Dynamics of Theology

We have seen a triangulation of issues in spirituality: a distinctive western tradition now finding itself alongside other great religious traditions, and also strongly challenged by antithetical claims about the self
in which it disappears, as it were, into its operations. We have found
that the triangulation leaves significant problems in its wake. We need
now to look more carefully at theology.

There is an interesting description of theology in the compilation of
Anglican spirituality, *Love's Redeeming Work: The Anglican Quest for
Holiness*. Speaking of the spiritual writing of the Anglican tradition, the
compilers say:

> [T]hey all did their theology less by the systematic examining of doc-
> trinal structures than by reflecting on the shape of Christian life . . .
> This should not be taken to suggest that the doctrinal structures were
> of no importance to them, let alone that their language for Christian
> living and understanding could be preserved unchanged if the funda-
> mental doctrines were different or absent. That is a typically modern
> misreading. But it is true that the coherence of their Christian world-
> views depends less on system than on a sense of what a human life
> looks like when it is in the process of being transformed by God in
> Christ . . . For them, thinking about God was closely bound up with
> thinking about how human beings became holy, came to show in
> their lives the grace and glory of God . . . It would be accurate to say
> that the great doctrinal themes are a steady backdrop, sensed and
> believed but not pulled centre-stage for debate and explanation; an
> inhabited landscape rather than on Ordnance Survey map.[13]

If this is an accurate description of the position of theology in this
tradition, a great deal has happened to change it. To compress a long

story which cannot be recounted here, theology itself has had to face a concatenation of factors. Above all, perhaps, theology in the West has heard the steady drumbeat of the European Enlightenment and has sought to preserve its truth-telling by Enlightenment methods, chiefly by unremitting pursuit of the objectivity in faith. It has been a pursuit through which lived spirituality has been marginalized, if not ignored altogether. This has been accompanied by a professionalization of Christian life, by which universities (from the 1870s, when the Old Divinity School in St John's Street, Cambridge was built by public subscription and the first degrees in theology were awarded) and theological colleges were understood to be places – with the appropriate professional standards – of training for those who were to be 'professionals' in control of the life of the Church.[14] It was at this point, it seems to me, that the integration of theology and spirituality, the one as 'landscape' for the 'journeys' of the other – which were as much possible for the laity as for anyone – gave way to 'controlled' education in the disciplines, appropriate to equip the professional to teach others. And the disciplines – under the pressure of emergent norms of education – treated 'objectivity' as paramount. At the same time, the focuses of Christian life as lived (worship, sacraments, church, ministry, practical life, for example) tended to disappear from education. Surprisingly, in a fashion similar to the pressures on spirituality, a further problem came from other factors within and beyond church life: first, the rapidly increasing variegation of forms of life and culture that confronted the churches, such a variation as to outstrip the usual forms of church life and leadership; and second, the early onset of what we now call globalization in the form of attempts to spread Christian belief into an expanding empire, which brought disagreements about what was appropriate in such a venture of faith among other indigenous forms of religion and life.

To be sure, there were – and (because these problems are still with us) are – vigorous attempts to respond. But most usually they required theology to close in on itself, and to insist ever more strongly that there were – are – only some ways in which it is appropriate for Christians to believe, and that Christian faith is the entrance point into this 'pre-givenness' of belief for cognition. Such suppositions are commonplace in doctrinal theology. And it is widely supposed that the only available alternative is to 'loosen' such expectations: 'but that I cannot believe!' So we are met with unhappy possibilities: either believe (where belief is cognitive, with little room for the personal or social internalization characteristic of spirituality); or believe with strong qualifications (in which case there is a steady erosion of the 'inhabited landscape' of spirituality). Most of today's struggles in theology seem to take place within this set of alternatives.

Practical Ideals in Relating Spirituality and Theology

Given the present situation in both spirituality and theology it seems that we need to find new ways of relating the two. Before moving on to directly spiritual/theological matters, I would like to note some practical desiderata for the outcome.

If these 'ways of relating' the two are to satisfy the needs of each, they need to be capable of engaging each at its deepest level. For example, for each there needs to be a combination of the 'intensity' appropriate to it with the 'extensity' that is also found in it. Theological examples of such a combination of intensity and extensity are found in the triunity of the Godhead and also in the Trinitarian character of humanity or of the economy of salvation of humanity. It makes a good deal of difference how these are elucidated, whether in substantial or dynamic terms for example, and whether they are traced as fully in human personal and social identity to the degree – or in the dynamic terms – they need to be if they are to be of any help in spirituality; that elucidation is largely missing from theology today. A question that would be quite important is: can we have a Spirit-led notion of the divine Trinity that might cast light on psycho-dynamics? Conversely, what does the journey of human beings tell us about the dynamics of the Creator?

Next, we need developed notions of how the affinity between the Lord and human being/salvation actually happens. The dictum that has been so important in modern Trinitarian theology, 'the immanent Trinity is the economic Trinity', conceals a highly important issue: how the copula 'is' operates, for the Lord or for human identity in its individual and social forms or for their active interrelation. Is this simply a 'given' 'affinity' of some objective kind or is it always active in the interaction of the Lord and human life, just as the relating of two human beings (not to mention the complexities of one-to-many relationships) is always changing. How is there 'intermediation' between the Lord and the dynamics of individual or social relationships? I need not say how important the development of 'intermediation' will be, if theology and spirituality are to grow together.

One can survey all theology and spirituality in these terms: *intensity, extensity, affinity* and *intermediation*. But the basic question for a discussion of the relation of theology and spirituality is whether they can be not only congruent but interdynamic in such matters. It seems to me that the capacity of the understanding of the Lord (the deepest awareness of the identity of the Lord) to have an affinity with the understanding of human spirituality (the deepest concerns of people) has been strikingly limited since the beauty and nearness of God to people – evident in the eighteenth-century revivals – was displaced by the modern supposition that God is a vague, distant condition for – but not otherwise related to – life in the world. On just this ground, some would argue that the very form of theology has to change – from doctrine to wisdom – because only such a theology is capable of being God-, self-, humanity-, community- and world-involving.

The implications of what we have been saying just now are that theology must attend to the intensity of *God* in God's extensity in its mediation within *our* intensity and extensity. Likewise, spirituality must attend to the deeper possibilities – our intensity in our extensity – within each of us and all of us together. By working out of the same set of categories, we may discover the ways in which theology is mediated within spirituality and vice versa, how there is actually affinity between the ways of God and the ways of human beings in the world.

Putting all this slightly differently, in specifically Christian terms, the issue is how the 'logic' of the Lord in the Lord's presence within the formation of the human spirit happens through the operation of human spirit. If put in these terms, the goal of learning will be to bring human reason and agency to participate fully in the 'inner reason' of the triune God, through an unfathomable transformation of us by the Spirit of Christ, by which we are conformed to the mind of Christ. That 'sanctified' or 'spiritual' reason is the vehicle for 'spirituality'.

The Dynamics of Divine and Human Identity

From these formal considerations, through which we have identified the main desiderata for bringing theology and spirituality into a dynamic relationship, we must turn finally to fleshing these out.

If theology is to be rendered suitable for spirituality, what is central is the realization that God's identity is not a straightforward 'given' that is simply to be acknowledged and its implications traced out in the reading of Scripture, in doctrines and in ways of life whose precepts are then to be obeyed. It is more like an infinitely intense identity evident in the Scriptures that reaches beyond any conception of identity that we have, and yet an identity that in itself – in the concentrated form designated by the Trinity of God – is infinitely extensive. This is of such a kind – and we will have more to say of this in a moment – that it also extends into the identity of everything else, giving each 'thing' the intensity of its own particular identity. Look at the way in which this is shown in a key passage in the Book of Exodus.

> God said to Moses, 'I AM WHO I AM.' He said further, 'Thus you shall say to the Israelites, "I AM has sent me to you."' God also said to Moses, 'Thus you shall say to the Israelites, "The LORD, the God of your ancestors, the God of Abraham, the God of Isaac, and the God of Jacob, has sent me to you":
> This is my name forever,
> and this my title for all generations. (NRSV, Ex. 3.14–15)

There are three layers to notice in this.

1 'I AM WHO I AM.' The infinite intensity of the identity of the Lord is of an 'I am' identified by a deeper 'I am', itself implicitly identified by a still deeper 'I am', and so on. It calls to mind the story of a Hindu asked about what holds the world up. 'Why,' he said, 'it rests on the back of a turtle.' 'And what holds the turtle up,' he was asked. 'It rests on the back of another turtle,' he said. 'And what of that turtle?' 'Well, you see, sir, it's turtles all the way down!' I don't suggest that the 'I am' of the Lord is quite that sort of thing, even if you might say that the 'I am' is based on another 'I am', and that too is based on 'I am', and so on. Instead, we have here a pathway into a mystery that grows greater and greater, leading us more and more deeply into the greater and greater intensity of the Lord's identity, into the deepest purity of identity. It is rather dangerous to stop this process of signification somewhere along the way, which is what we do when we say 'God' in order to provide ourselves with an axiom or starting point for conclusions to be drawn: that objectifies what cannot be objectified.[15]

2 How does this 'infinitely intensive identity' relate to us? It is because it is antecedently bent on such a relation.

   i That infinitely intense identity, the deepest purity of intention, takes a very special form: 'I will be with you . . . This is my name forever, and this my title for all generations.' The infinitely intense identity of the Lord is already infinitely extensive, eternal; it is everywhere and always, for all generations. In itself, that 'narrow' 'infinitely intensive identity' is also 'broadly' and dynamically intensive, which is what we mean when we talk of the Trinity immanent in the Lord.

ii As such it is implicated in everything, whether or not we recognize it. So we find that the Lord – I AM WHO I AM – is an infinite depth of identity, a permanently mysterious core of identity that is also extensive, and thus implicated in the identity and coherence of everything as its source and goal. The identity of the Lord is infinitely intense as it is implicated in everything else. In Christian faith, this is 'God with us', Emmanuel, through whom all things were created for their end.

3 The identity of the Lord is, both in itself and for all else, also highly dynamic: it propels creation into existence and impels people through time; it 'spirits' them to become a history (it is sometimes suggested that this is the genesis of the very notion of history). This dynamic identity that reaches everywhere and always is the God who has been the God of the ancestors of this people, who calls them together, who brings them out of their misery and who always gives them hope. It is from this that a continuous history and life for these people arises, as the same intense identity had moved and guided those who had gone before.

i Just what is the character of this dynamic? It seems clear that its primary character is self-giving. In other words, the intensive identity of the Lord becomes extensive through self-giving, the 'giving over' of itself – even the intensity of itself – into 'the other'. So when it propels people, it impels them to engage with each other and together toward the future. That has two interesting consequences:

ii It means that the primary act of creation is an act of self-giving by the Lord and the continuance of creation has no other source: 'I will be with you until the end of time.'

iii Such self-giving is always disequilibrating: we should not look for balance, equality and equipoise in God or in human spirituality; we should expect these always to be surpassed in self-giving.

That is the kind of theology needed for spirituality. In the identity of the Lord, we need to look for neither a set of conditions for the world as we find it, nor a 'sky-god' (as one 'spiritual' person said recently on the BBC). There in the Lord is the dynamic intensity that we associate with the Spirit, the infinite identity we find in the Son, and the intensity of that same identity – its deep and abiding faithfulness – that we associate with the Father, all three implicated in each other.

And by the way, this is what makes it possible to rejoice in the depths of the Lord as interwoven in everything else. And if the Lord whom we address is the infinitely intensive identity implicated in everything at every time, we can rejoice in the steadiness this provides, enjoy the Lord and enjoy everything in the Lord. By comparison, I find habits of 'halting' the process of signification appropriate to the Lord and 'labelling' the Lord, or using 'God' as an axiom on which to build great systems of doctrine and practice, unhelpful – even unworthy of the Lord of whom we have been speaking.

If spirituality is to be rendered suitable for theology, we need to realize how closely the identity of the Lord is bound up with its implications for us, the divine condition with the human condition. It touches us in our inmost depths, in our spirit. (The reason 'labelling' the Lord is unhelpful is that it blocks us not only from the identity of the Lord but also from the full depth of its implications for us.) In T. S. Eliot's words, the 'condition of absolute simplicity' does 'cost not less than everything'.[16] Knowing the truth of the identity of the Lord requires the intensification of heart and life for which we all yearn, and their transformation. It is the deep source from which our identity comes and the intensity of the 'I' that I am derives from that. In that sense, it is the heart of true spirituality. If we are to grasp our own significance, or the significance of what happens to us, we need to measure them by the intensity of the Lord's identity as it extends fully into who we are: conceptions of the Lord meet our conception of who we are. Poor conceptions of the Lord beget poor conceptions of human life in the world, while poor notions of human life cause distorted views of the Lord. Life today abounds with such distortions: people too sure of their very limited understanding of the Lord also do terrible damage to others.

If we are to move beyond such encumbrances, we need first to learn how the infinitely intensive identity of the Lord is actually *mapped* onto our lives. This is what is shown in the familiar beginning of the Gospel of John: 'in the beginning was the λογος, and the λογος was with God, and the λογος was God . . . and in him was life, and the life was the light of all people'. In Proverbs 8, Wisdom is first in God's work, 'before the beginning of the earth'. Wisdom, it seems, is the inner pattern of God's work: it is what differentiates things, the heavens, the deep, the skies, the earth, the inhabited world, the human race. And that is what calls everything into being, differentiates it from others, directs it to its proper shape, always embracing it in the good pleasure of the Lord. Everything we are and do derives its shape and life from its configuration by the Lord, that is from Wisdom.

What this means is that, as we look deeply into the infinitely intense identity of the Lord, we find that it is ordered in such a way that everything that is is imprinted with its own pattern, the pattern that we can find both through the study we undertake and through the right kinds of relationship with others with whom we share the task. Although the habits of modern academic study lead us no further than concentrating on the patterns and finding them for ourselves, reading them more deeply may trace them – and our common study – to their source in the inner pattern of the Lord. Reading them that way is where the excitement really begins and therein, ultimately, we find the delight of the Lord, the One in whom the Lord delights and through whom the Lord rejoices in 'his inhabited world and delight[s] in the human race' (Prov. 8.31), and who (in turn) rejoices in the Lord. Always, the issue is one of finding in us the One through whom the Lord gives all things their shape. We are to 'examine [ourselves] to see whether [we] are living in [this One]' (1 Cor. 13.5). That is the standard of our truth and our 'rightness', and it is not somehow outside us: the issue for us is whether we become strong *in* the One through whom the Lord gives us our shape.

Conclusion: Intermediation in Theology and Spirituality

What of the 'intermediation' by which the affinity of theology and spirituality is established? As we have found a form of theology suited to the redevelopment of its relation to spirituality, and a form of spirituality appropriate to this, we have been employing the 'intermediation' we earlier found to be desirable, if not necessary, through which can be established the affinity of the truth sought in theology with the deepest human needs sought in spirituality. It is one that seeks to maximize the accessibility of each to the other. It is not an 'external' addition to each of the two, not a 'bridge' extrinsic to the two, but located profoundly within each. And, as I suggested much earlier, it is one that itself changes as they change and promotes further change in them as it does so. For the process of finding the implicated-ness of the infinite identity of the Lord (and, in Emmanuel, the Lord with us) in the proximate depths of human identity is in fact the work of the Holy Spirit. And it never finishes until all things are fulfilled in the Lord.

Notes

1 Brian Massumi, 2002, *Parables for the Virtual: Movement, Affect, Sensation*, Durham, NC: Duke University Press, p. 70.

2 Computer operating systems are based on mathematical structures (the Mandelbrot set) produced by a simple mathematical rule, 'structures which are there no matter who does it, who puts it on their computer, no matter what computer you use'. Stephen Penrose in *Science and Spirit*, March–April 2003, p. 37.

3 S. T. Coleridge, 1990, *The Notebooks of Samuel Taylor Coleridge*, ed. Kathleen Coburn and Merton Christensen, Princeton, NJ: Princeton University Press, vol. 4 (Text), p. 5443/97, emphasis in original.

4 S. T. Coleridge, 1993, *Aids to Reflection*, ed. J. Beer, London: Routledge, p. 224.

5 Coleridge, *Aids to Reflection*, p. 77, emphasis in original.

6 Coleridge, *Aids to Reflection*, p. 202.

7 Coleridge, *Aids to Reflection*, p. 99.

8 Douglas Hedley, 2000, *Coleridge, Philosophy and Religion: Aids to Reflection and the Mirror of the Spirit*, Cambridge: Cambridge University Press, p. 97.

9 Qur'an 29.6.

10 Qur'an 16.102.

11 Paul Broks, 2003, *Into the Silent Land*, New York: Atlantic Monthly Press, excerpted in *Science and Spirit*, January–February 2004, pp. 56–7.

12 Robert Wuthnow, 2000, *After Heaven: Spirituality in America since the 1950s*, Berkeley, CA: University of California Press, p. 3.

13 Geoffrey Rowell, Kenneth Stevenson and Rowan Williams (eds), 2001, *Love's Redeeming Work: The Anglican Quest for Holiness*, Oxford: Oxford University Press, pp. xxiv–xxv.

14 See Anthony Russell, 1980, *The Clerical Profession*, London: SPCK, pp. 239ff.

15 John Deely, 2001, *Four Ages of Understanding*, Toronto: University of Toronto Press, p. 431.

16 T. S. Eliot, 'Little Gidding', v, 41, in T. S. Eliot, *The Complete Poems and Plays of T. S. Eliot*, London: Faber & Faber, 1969, p. 198.

10

Theology as Spirituality

Conflicting Views

FERGUS KERR

No one has done more than Ann Loades to show that 'spirituality' need not – indeed cannot – be regarded as an entirely separate matter from the practice of serious Christian theology. This, however, is not an insight that has always seemed a platitude. One of the nastiest disputes in twentieth-century Roman Catholic theology brought into open conflict two of the most eminent friars of the Order of Preachers in recent times, precisely over the relationship between theology and spirituality: Marie-Dominique Chenu (1895–1990) and his older confrère Réginald Garrigou-Lagrange (1877–1964).

The dissertation that Chenu wrote at the Dominican University in Rome was supervised by Garrigou-Lagrange.[1] An exegetical study of Thomas Aquinas on contemplation, the dissertation also sets out to challenge the assumption allegedly then in place, that spirituality has to do introvertedly with a person's soul and its progress in overcoming sin, rather than with one's contemplative surrender to the objectivity of God. Young Chenu's construal of Aquinas on contemplation was designed to retrieve a radically theocentric conception of Christian spirituality over against late nineteenth-century piety, at least in French Catholic circles, with its putative focus on the subjective experience of the individual.[2]

Chenu's first course, when he began teaching at the French Dominican college at Le Saulchoir, was on the patristic sources of the thought of Aquinas. In 1936–7, he lectured on Bonaventure's *Itinerarium mentis in Deum*, not only contrasting Aquinas with his great Franciscan contemporary but also implying that, in its own way, the *Summa Theologiae* could and should be read as a kind of 'journey of the mind into the divine mystery'. Just as challengingly, Chenu lectured in 1938–9 on 'Augustine and Denys: The Two Platonisms of St Thomas'. In these and several other ways he began to edge out the standard way of expounding Aquinas – then, and in some places still!

In 1937, Chenu, newly appointed head of the college, issued a manifesto: *Une école de théologie: Le Saulchoir*.[3] The result was a summons to Rome to be interrogated by a handful of his fellow Dominicans, headed by Garrigou-Lagrange. In 1942, in German-occupied Paris, Chenu heard on the radio that the book was now on the Index of Prohibited Books. Another colleague, Thomas Philippe, was dispatched from Rome to dismiss Chenu from his post.[4]

Chenu's 'unsound', not to say near-'heretical', thoughts were to be found in passages such as this:

> Theological systems are only the expression of spiritualities . . . The greatness and the truth of Bonaventuran or Scotist Augustinianism are entirely in the spiritual experience of Saint Francis which became the soul in his sons; the grandeur and the truth of Molinism are in the spiritual experience of Saint Ignatius' *Exercises* . . . A theology worthy of the name is a spirituality, which finds the rational instruments adequate to its religious experience. It is not the luck of history that Saint Thomas entered the Order of Saint Dominic; and it is not by some desultory grace that the Order of Saint Dominic received Saint Thomas Aquinas. The institution and the doctrine are closely allied with one another, in the inspiration that carried the one and the other into a new age, and in the contemplation, which, goal of both, guarantees the fervour, the method, the purity, and the freedom of their spirit.[5]

Unbelievable as this may seem to us now, such claims were held to reduce theology to spirituality.

Chenu on Aquinas

In his finest book, *Introduction à l'étude de S. Thomas d'Aquin* (1950)[6] – still one of the best introductions, half a century later – Chenu contends that we cannot understand Aquinas without detailed study of the historical context to which he belonged, and of the historical conditions under which he worked: the Dominican Order, the University of Paris, the academic institutions and literary forms of the day, the legacy of Augustine, Denys and the Neo-Platonist tradition and so on, as well as his engagement with the recently discovered works of Aristotle. The

Summa Theologiae could no longer be treated, credibly, as a self-standing system transcending all history and time. On the contrary, like any classic it is precisely as belonging to the setting in which it is composed that it continues to disclose how permanently interesting it is.

Chenu combats the then standard way of expounding the *Summa Theologiae*. Far from reflecting a decision to complete what may be demonstrated about God by reason before considering what may be said solely in virtue of revelation, the fact that Aquinas deals with the questions *de Deo uno* before going on to those *de Deo trino*, 'results from an option characteristic of Latin theology, which implies a spiritual itinerary towards the God of revelation'.[7] Moreover, however pervaded with metaphysics, the questions *de Deo uno* deal with the God of the Book of Genesis, not the god of Aristotle's *Physics*: the God of Abraham, Isaac and Jacob, who points us towards Christ. We have to retain the religious character of this text, Chenu insists, never reducing it to a 'deist' theodicy.

For all the importance of Aristotle, Chenu insists, Aquinas should not be read as if he repudiated his inheritance from Augustine. Though references to the *platonici* are usually critical, this should not occlude how much he takes for granted from the Neo-Platonist tradition. He cites Denys as much as Aristotle. We need to remember the twelfth-century Renaissance, the presence of Islamic culture, the evangelism of the Friars and much else that students of Thomas Aquinas now, decades later, regard as an essential part of understanding his work.

The best access to Chenu's distinctive approach to Thomas is to be found in a recently translated book, in which, by reconstructing the historical context, he brings out Aquinas' evangelical intention and its actuality for today.[8] As for his legacy, it may be traced in the work of many theologians now. In particular, the second volume of Jean-Pierre Torrell's *magnum opus* presents Aquinas as 'spiritual master' – his theology as clearly oriented towards contemplation as his spirituality expresses itself in his theology.[9]

Garrigou on Aquinas

Réginald Garrigou-Lagrange studied and taught at Le Saulchoir before moving to Rome, where he lectured from 1909 until 1960.[10] Chenu was not the only student whose research he directed: 30 years later he supervised the future Pope John Paul II. He had a great influence on Jacques and Raïssa Maritain.[11] Among the greatest spiritual directors of his day, he published several major works, the most widely respected being *The Three Ages of the Interior Life*, an extraordinary synthesis of Aquinas' speculative and John of the Cross' mystical theologies. In all his teaching Garrigou-Lagrange insisted that contemplative prayer was open to every Christian, not confined to a devout elite.

He was a controversial figure, much admired but also often caricatured, even demonized. His big book on God, for example, is not as dreadful as some have asserted: 'the God of the Bible and the Gospel has been reduced to a *caput mortuum* of frozen abstractions . . . overwhelmingly boring . . . nothing but a gigantic and futile exercise in tautology'.[12]

For Garrigou-Lagrange, however, Aquinas' work – chiefly the *Summa Theologiae* – was an unsurpassed (and unsurpassable) achievement in systematic theology. He saw no point in studying how Aquinas' thought interacted with that of his contemporaries (obviously lesser men), or how it was shaped by his inheritance from earlier Christian thinkers (let alone Jewish and Muslim ones) – anything good these ever had to say was absorbed in Aquinas' synthesis. On the other hand, serious students needed to work on Aristotle and Aquinas' commentaries on Aristotle. Otherwise, knowing nothing of his metaphysics, they would misunderstand Aquinas completely.

In the key text, *La Synthèse thomiste* (1946), we can see Garrigou-Lagrange at his most characteristic.[13] In Aristotle, Aquinas discovered the 'natural metaphysics of human intelligence'. As this argument unfolds it delivers a philosophy of being, differing entirely from philosophies of appearance (phenomenalism), of becoming (evolutionism) and of the ego (psychologism). Phenomenalism is still on the market, the others we might be inclined to relabel as process thought and subjectivism; but the main aim of philosophical studies for neophyte theologians had to be to establish for themselves a moderate form of metaphysical, epistemological and moral realism. It is, of course, not a silly idea that would-be theologians should examine their philosophical presuppositions.

Anyway, what goes wrong when Catholic theologians lose their skill at metaphysics? Lip service was, of course, paid to Thomas Aquinas, Garrigou-Lagrange says, with his typical sarcasm: in those days Catholic theologians had at least to pretend to be Thomists. Yet, he asks rhetorically, how Thomist are you if, while accepting the dogmas expounded in the *Summa*, you follow Descartes on the spiritual life – privatizing your relationship with God? The truths of common sense may be a sufficient foundation for theology, you may say – yes indeed, Garrigou-Lagrange replies, warming to his theme, but the problem is that the student's grip on common sense is often weakened by modern subjectivist theorizings: phenomenalism, idealism, positivism, pragmatism and so forth.

When theologians choose history of doctrine as their specialism and abandon metaphysics (which he seems to regard as the unavoidable corollary), then relativism creeps in. Recently, for example, Garrigou-Lagrange reports, one theologian asserted that, while speculative theology no doubt produced beautiful systems in the Middle Ages, it no longer has a role: serious work is now all in positive theology – historical scholarship, that is to say – rather than in metaphysical system-building (naming no names but thinking probably of Jean Daniélou). Another would return to what he holds to be the true position of the Greek Fathers before the time of Augustine (perhaps Henri de Lubac) – as if the labours of Thomas Aquinas and seven centuries of Thomists were of no value!

Pragmatism is the great temptation: 'A doctrine according to which truth is a relation, entirely immanent to human experience, whereby knowledge is subordinated to activity, and the truth of a proposition consists in its utility and satisfactoriness'.[14] Is the dogma of the incarnation affirming that Jesus is God a statement of fact or a pious exhortation, that we must act towards Jesus 'as if' he were God? Is Christ really present in the Eucharist, or do we only act 'as if'? Succumbing to the allurements of pragmatism, he fears, Catholic theologians forget how to understand dogmas as true, immutable and as conforming to the extramental reality that they express. Above all, what dogmas express is *not* our religious experience – that is Garrigou-Lagrange's reiterated refrain.

With rough humour, he asks sardonically, 'Who can claim to *experience* the hypostatic union?'[15] We may experience, not the mystery itself, but its effects in us – if you like: 'The Spirit Himself giveth testimony to our spirit, that we are the sons of God' (Rom. 8.16, Douay-Rheims Bible). Thomas Aquinas would agree to that, no doubt allowing that the Spirit evokes in us a filial affection, which – if you like – you may say you 'experience'. Yet even this 'experience', Garrigou-Lagrange says deflatingly, would be difficult to distinguish from mere sentimental affection.

Worse still, another theologian claims that theology is at bottom a spirituality that has found concepts adequate to its religious experience. This position comes from the German Romantic Tübingen School and especially from Johann Adam Möhler. Here, clearly, Garrigou-Lagrange is attacking Chenu. Thomist theology would be the expression of Dominican spirituality, Scotism that of Franciscan spirituality, Molinism that of Ignatian spirituality and so on. These three schools of spirituality, it would be said, are tolerated in the Catholic Church and so the 'theologies', which are their conceptual expressions, each being in conformity with a particular religious 'experience', would all be equally 'true'. Often, however, Garrigou-Lagrange protests, these theologies contradict one another – what is to be said about this?

This 'spiritualization' of theology, reducing it to the conceptual articulation of a religious experience, deprives it of all 'scientific' objectivity. This is what happens if we abandon the notion of truth as conformity with objective reality, proposing rather to define truth as conformity with constantly developing experience, moral and religious: 'The enthusiasm of hope and charity, if it is not to remain a beautiful dream of religious emotion, must rest on a faith which is in conformity with reality, not merely with the exigencies of our inner life, or even with our best intentions.'[16]

Williams on Aquinas

Things have changed. Aquinas should be read as 'a mystical thinker', according to Herbert McCabe, meaning by this that

> he was centrally concerned with the unknown and, in one sense, ineffable mystery of God . . . in what is sometimes misunderstood as his dryly rational approach, even in his arguments for the existence of God, he is in fact engaged in, and inviting the reader to be engaged in, a mystical exploration which is not at all the same thing as a mystical experience.[17]

This reading of Aquinas as a mystical theologian, the pedagogue of a theological initiation that is simultaneously a spiritual formation, has been worked out in convincing detail by A. N. Williams, quite independently of McCabe but not without saluting Chenu's claim about the 'mystical import' of the *Summa Theologiae*. For Williams, Aquinas, in the *Summa*, was writing a theology 'concerned with the conditions of the possibility of union with God'.[18]

Mystical experiences might be a by-product but Aquinas' 'mystical theology' is concerned with the union of God and the man or woman created in God's image. This union with God takes place not by spiritual feats on our part – not in the first place because of anything we human beings do – but because of who God is. The *Summa* (so often regarded as an objective and impersonal exposition of Christian dogma in as systematic and syllogistic a manner as possible) is, rather, an invitation into discovering the conditions for union with the God who is intent on union with humanity – already anticipated in the incarnation.

Deliberately rejecting other theological projects familiar in his day – projects that start from the history of salvation, from the Christ mystery as present in the Church and so forth – Aquinas focuses on God.[19] For him, theology is primarily concerned with God – not with history or human experience, or rather history and human experience are treated as the way of achieving that perfect knowledge of God that is eternal beatitude, everlasting bliss.

The impetus to understand God, as Williams puts it, is part of the larger process by which God draws human beings towards himself – the gracing of nature that we may come to glory. Throughout the *Summa* (she contends) Aquinas drew on the basic Augustinian insight: know-ledge necessarily precedes love, you cannot love what or who you do not know – our fulfilment is not to be found in ourselves, in any of the good things of this world, it lies outside ourselves – in attaching ourselves, or being attached, to something that is not us.

For Aquinas, Williams insists, theological activity is a form of union with God, an anticipation of the beatific vision. Of course this will be fulfilled only in heaven but in some form this contemplative union with God is available here and now: in heaven the human mind will be united to God by one continual everlasting activity; but in the present life, in so far as we fall short of the unity and continuity of this activity, so of course we fall short of perfect beatitude.

However, isn't this contemplation simply a form of prayer? This is a question that we are inevitably going to ask, Williams allows; but this is where she brings theology and spirituality together. Beatitude, for Aquinas, is an operation of the mind by which the mind is united to God in knowing God. This knowing might of course be a direct appre-hension of God in prayer but Aquinas says nothing to suggest that he means only that. Surely he includes and even focuses on theological reflection, Williams argues. Moreover, his notion that contemplative activity is a matter of our using our minds does not imply some objec-tionable intellectualism or reveal disdain of the emotions. Rather, for Aquinas, our highest activity must be one that engages our highest powers and their highest object: contemplation is the mind's absorption in God, which means that this highest of activities is necessarily intellec-tual – a conclusion, as Williams says, decidedly at odds with modern notions of bliss as well as of 'spirituality' and indeed of what we human beings are.

Aquinas does not equate happiness with human satisfaction *per se*, not even with intellectual satisfaction. For him spirituality is a matter, not of personal fulfilment, but of God's bringing a person into an anticipation of the beatific union. Theology, like prayer, the practice of the virtues and so on, is a theocentric activity, if you like an eccentric activity – a way in which people are drawn towards God and drawn beyond themselves.

Aquinas differs from many writers who might be respectable authorities on the spiritual life. This is the heart of Williams' argument. It is not reflection on one's own experience of God's goodness or intense awareness of God's presence (or absence) that motivates unitive love, she says, for Aquinas: it is meditation on God's nature. The painstakingly technical consideration of the divine nature that unfolds in the opening questions of the *Summa* – considering divine simplicity, goodness, transcendence, immanence and so on – needs to be approached (so she argues) as a form of meditation, designed to incite the love that leads to union. Far from being an impersonal exposition of a metaphysical theology of the First Cause or whatever, so A. N. Williams suggests, the questions on God in the *Summa* are in their own way an *itinerarium mentis in Deum*: an invitation to readers to exercise their minds with whatever depth and clarity may be attainable when the created contemplates the Uncreated, so that the created is drawn into the life of the Uncreated.

A. N. Williams focuses on the question in which Aquinas considers how the created mind comes into the light: the light of reason, the light of grace and the light of glory.[20] The more light there is in the mind the more perfectly the mind sees God and those who have greater love have more light. This loving contemplation is clearly started here and now. However, as Williams insists again, contemplation for Thomas Aquinas is not some particular method or form of prayer – rather it is the activity by which our attention is drawn to God and into the beatific vision. We are creatures with minds[21] – creatures who can be fulfilled only by knowing the highest object, the richest other that our minds can entertain – God.

What Williams invites readers to realize is that Thomas Aquinas' theology is dominated by God but that means by beatitude and by beatific vision. Aquinas' God is never aloof or indifferent or detached and separated from creatures, as critics often think. On the contrary, union with God has been the plan all along. Whatever else the famous Five Ways are intended to do, Williams says in her most daring proposal, each in its own way suggests not only God's connection to the world but also a divine desire to be connected with the world. The First

Mover moves something towards itself; the efficient cause causes something other than itself; awareness of contingency induces the thought of a necessary being who freely gives being to all else that exists; the degrees of being imply the highest being's sharing of goodness and perfection with others; and the divine mind's ordering of the universe towards its divinely ordained destiny presumes the desire to do some such thing.

The God of the Five Ways is the source and end of all because Aquinas begins by looking at creation for signs of the creator. Yet the heat of debates over the use of 'natural theology' means that the Five Ways have been overlooked as each in its own way a description of God (so to speak), as the one who desires to attract and unite all things to himself. Similarly, when Aquinas considers the question of divine goodness, he at once goes on to divine goodness as *communicated*; so also with perfection and so on. Aquinas says nothing of God, so Williams argues, that does not simultaneously refer to that which is not God.

In retrospect, of course, we can appreciate what troubled Garrigou-Lagrange: a great exponent of classical spirituality as well as a much admired exponent of Aquinas' theology, he could conceive of 'experience' only as something that escaped rational control. He was too marked – wounded even – by the Modernist crisis that afflicted the Roman Catholic Church in the decade before 1914. Whether A. N. Williams will persuade students of the *Summa Theologiae* to allow the text to function as their own 'journey into God' remains to be seen. No one now would study or teach the work of Thomas Aquinas without the kind of contextual-historical introduction that Chenu provided. For a thirteenth-century theological text to act as an initiation into a contemplative life is perhaps beyond most of us now. But the principle that theology and spirituality need not conflict with one another, but that, on the contrary, theology may be engaged in contemplatively, has surely been established in our day – something for us to celebrate!

Notes

1 '"De contemplatione" (Angelicum 1920), La Thèse inédite du P. M.-D. Chenu', ed. Carmelo Giuseppe Conticello, *Revue des Sciences Philosophiques et Théologiques* 75 (1991), 363–422.

2 See Christophe F. Potworowski, 2001, *Contemplation and Incarnation: The Theology of Marie-Dominique Chenu*, Montreal and Kingston: McGill-Queen's University Press.

3 M.-D. Chenu, 1985, *Une Ecole de théologie: Le Saulchoir*, Paris: Cerf.

4 Thomas Philippe (1905–93), later chaplain to Jean Vanier, founder of L'Arche.

5 Chenu, *Une Ecole de théologie*, pp. 148–9.

6 *Towards Understanding Saint Thomas*, trans. A.-M. Landry and D. Hughes, with authorized corrections and bibliographical additions, Chicago, IL: Henry Regnery, 1964.

7 Chenu, *Towards Understanding St Thomas*, p. 321.

8 Originally published in 1959, recently translated with introduction by Paul J. Philibert OP: see *Aquinas and His Role in Theology*, Collegeville, MN: The Liturgical Press, 2002.

9 Jean-Pierre Torrell OP, 2003, *Saint Thomas Aquinas*, volume 2: *Spiritual Master*, Washington DC: Catholic University of America Press.

10 Cf. Richard Peddicord, 2005, *The Sacred Monster of Thomism: An Introduction to the Life and Legacy of Reginald Garrigou-Lagrange, OP*, South Bend, IN: St Austin's Press.

11 Cf. Ralph McInerny, 2003, *The Very Rich Hours of Jacques Maritain: A Spiritual Life*, Notre Dame, IN: University of Notre Dame Press.

12 Thus Louis Bouyer (1913–2004), formerly a Lutheran pastor, priest of the French Oratory and himself a major theologian, Newman scholar and liturgist: see *The Invisible Father: Approaches to the Mystery of the Divinity*, Edinburgh: T & T Clark, 1999, p. 248.

13 *Reality: A Synthesis of Thomistic Thought*, St Louis, MO: Herder, 1952.

14 Garrigou-Lagrange, *Reality*, para. 1367.

15 Garrigou-Lagrange, *Reality*, para. 1384, emphasis in original.

16 Garrigou-Lagrange, *Reality*, para. 1392.

17 Herbert McCabe, 'The Logic of Mysticism', in Martin Warner (ed.), 1992, *Religion and Philosophy*, Cambridge: Cambridge University Press, pp. 45–59.

18 A. N. Williams, 'Mystical theology redux: the pattern of Aquinas's *Summa Theologiae*', *Modern Theology* 13 (1997), pp. 53–74.

19 Cf. *Summa Theologiae* I, 1, 7.

20 *Summa Theologiae* I, 12.

21 'Minds are what we are', as Donald MacKinnon used to say in the moral philosophy classroom at Aberdeen in 1950, going on to cite Hopkins: 'O the mind, mind has mountains . . .'.

11

Ann Loades and Austin Farrer

BRIAN HEBBLETHWAITE

Ann Loades has been a stalwart participant in the series of International Conferences on the Theology of Austin Farrer that began in my own college (Queens' College Cambridge) back in 1977 and ended with two conferences in 2004, marking the centenary of Farrer's birth. She gave a paper, 'Austin Farrer on *Love Almighty*', at the second Farrer conference, held at Princeton Theological Seminary in 1981, and co-edited with Jeffrey Eaton the book, *For God and Clarity*, that came out of that conference.[1] I shall be considering her theodicy essay in that book shortly.

Together with Charles Conti, Ann organized the third Farrer conference, held in 1983 at Keble College, Oxford, where Farrer had ended his days as Warden; and, together with David Jasper, she was in charge of the British end of the fourth Farrer conference, held in 1986 at Louisiana State University, Baton Rouge, under the auspices of Edward Henderson.[2] She chaired a discussion there.

The fifth Farrer conference was held, in conjunction with the Centre for the Study of Literature and Theology, at Hatfield College, Durham in 1989. The organization of this conference was shared by the Centre's Director, David Jasper, and Ann, who chaired most of the sessions. She co-edited, together with Michael McLain, the book that came out of that conference.[3]

I rather think Ann missed out on the sixth Farrer conference, held in 1992, at Berkeley, California;[4] but in the centenary year, 2004, she was fully engaged in the Farrer celebrations. In the commemorative volume, *Captured by the Crucified*, she has an essay, 'The Vitality of Tradition: Austin Farrer and Friends'.[5] At the Austin Farrer Centenary Conference in Oriel College, Oxford, a conference chaired by its *fons et origo*, Basil Mitchell, Ann was a very visible presence, chairing David Brown's paper on 'Analogy and the Use of Images', and proposing a vote of thanks to Basil Mitchell at the Conference Dinner.[6] Later the same year, a second celebratory conference was held at the St James Center for Spiritual Formation in Baton Rouge, Louisiana, again under the auspices of Edward Henderson, at which Ann read a paper on Dorothy Sayers, one of Farrer's contemporaries whom she had discussed in her essay in *Captured by the Crucified*.

Then, in 2006, together with her co-editor Robert MacSwain, Ann published a splendid book of readings from Austin Farrer's writings, entitled *The Truth-Seeking Heart*, a title which, as I shall be observing later in this chapter, sums up the spirit not only of Farrer's work but also of her own.[7]

Clearly Farrer has been a figure of seminal significance for Ann Loades' own theology and spirituality. What I want to do in this tribute to her is to look briefly at five subject areas with which she has been engaged and ask to what extent there can be discerned some influence from, or relation to, the work of Austin Farrer. The five subject areas are theodicy, ethics, sacramental spirituality, literature and music, and feminist theology. Once again, it can certainly be said at the outset that the 'passion for God and clarity' that Jeffrey Eaton and Ann, in their introductory remarks to the Princeton volume, ascribed to Farrer's work 'on nearly every page'[8] can equally be ascribed to her own.

Theodicy

The influence of Farrer on Ann's book *Kant and Job's Comforters*[9] is slight but discernible. The English translation of Leibniz's *Theodicy* used by Ann in connection with Part II of her book was the one edited by Farrer,[10] and Farrer's 40-page Introduction was clearly on her mind. She quotes, from this Introduction, the passage in which Farrer remarks on the minimal role played by the Christian scheme of redemption in Leibniz's rational theodicy.[11] And, in connection with Kant's reaction against Leibniz and indeed against any theoretical theodicy, Ann refers to Farrer's comment, in *Faith and Speculation*, about Kant's preference for the field of action and for a moral foundation for theistic belief. She goes on to note Farrer's reservations about this: 'Farrer himself did not suppose that the kind of "contextual encouragement" Kant offered would take the weight of religious belief.'[12] I am reminded of the footnote in Farrer's very first book, *Finite and Infinite*, where, having observed that 'a balance of scientific and moral passion makes the typical metaphysician', he remarks: 'If in Kant the two were liable to come unstuck, that is an index of his ill-success.'[13]

Preliminary studies towards *Kant and Job's Comforters* were published by Ann between the years 1975 and 1983, the very years of her involvement with the early Farrer conferences and of her own Princeton paper, later published in *For God and Clarity*. That paper, entitled 'Austin Farrer on *Love Almighty*', considers Farrer's own theodicy book[14] in relation to two deeply moving published accounts: first of the death of a young woman of 25 and of her parents' reactions, and second of 'the abject creature lurking in each one of us' exemplified by the forced execution of a victim of the Nazis and the excuses made by those made to carry out the deed. Certainly no theodicy that fails to confront 'horrendous evils'[15] of this kind can be deemed morally credible. For Ann it is Austin Farrer's stress on the incarnation and on Christ's cross and resurrection that enables him to face up to such horrors and carries the main weight of his theodicy. For Farrer – and for Ann – what justifies God's action in creation is God's own identification of himself with his creatures out of pure redemptive love. Ann refers to Donald MacKinnon in this connection and anyone who recalls MacKinnon's profound wrestling with the problem of evil in his lectures and writings might suppose there to be more in common between Ann and that massive Scottish philosopher than between Ann and the demure Warden of Keble. Indeed, I observe that MacKinnon's name occurs more frequently than Farrer's in *Kant and Job's Comforters*. On the other hand, MacKinnon was one of Farrer's friends discussed by Ann in *Captured by the Crucified* and I recall MacKinnon's great admiration for Farrer, expressed, most notably for me, on the day after Farrer's death, when he cancelled the topic of a graduate seminar and devoted the whole hour and a half to a tribute to Austin Farrer. And there is no doubt that Ann found in Farrer's own theodicy much of the same depth and sensitivity that she found in MacKinnon's work.

It needs to be stressed, however, that we can find in Farrer's writings, as well as that depth and sensitivity and as well as that emphasis on incarnation and redemption, rather more theoretical theodicy in the style of Leibniz than there is to be found in Kant, MacKinnon or Ann herself at that stage. I tried to spell out this aspect of Farrer's theodicy in my own contribution to the centenary conference at Oriel.[16] And in that same centenary year, Ann herself acknowledges as much in what she says about Farrer's criticism of C. S. Lewis' *The Problem of Pain*:

> Lewis had not sufficiently allowed for the requirements of the vast physical system that God as Creator is committed to uphold. In such a world, pain is better understood as 'the sting of death, the foretaste

and ultimately the experience of sheer destruction', which cannot be related to the will of God as an evil wholly turned into a moral instrument. Rather, he argued, pain is 'the bitter savour of that mortality out of which it is the unimaginable mercy of God to rescue us'.[17]

But I note that the selection chosen from Farrer's theodicy book in *The Truth-Seeking Heart* is the final chapter of *Love Almighty and Ills Unlimited*, 'Griefs and Consolations', not the more Leibnizian chapter on 'Physical Accident'.

Ethics

Ann's concern with theodicy, like Farrer's and MacKinnon's, already manifests a profound concern with morality and practice. The centenary volume, *Captured by the Crucified*, is subtitled 'The Practical Theology of Austin Farrer'; and Ann's contribution to that book, 'The Vitality of Tradition: Austin Farrer and Friends', brings out, among other things, the influence on Farrer of Christian ethicists such as MacKinnon, George Bell and Helen Oppenheimer. And while Evelyn Underhill's writings were primarily concerned with mysticism, her interest in the saints and her conviction that the heart of Christianity is to be discerned in the life of sacrificial love are emphases equally shared by Farrer and by Ann herself.

I propose, in this section, to concentrate on Ann's writing on the subject of abortion, an ethical problem about which Farrer admittedly had little to say; but I shall conclude the section by speculating on how Farrer might have reacted to what Ann writes about this subject.

In the mid 1990s, in my capacity as editor for ethics for the German encyclopaedia, the *Theologische Realenzyklopädie,* I commissioned Ann to write an article on *Schwangerschaftsabbruch* (abortion). Her article appeared, duly translated into German, in volume 30 of that encyclopaedia in 1999. Ann worked up the same material into a more extended piece as her contribution to the book *Faithfulness and Fortitude*, a book of essays engaging with the work of Stanley Hauerwas, one of the most significant contemporary exponents of Christian theological ethics.[18] In this detailed and searching exploration of the historical background and the contemporary dilemmas in relation to which the ethics of abortion has to be discussed, Ann is particularly concerned to argue that unless Christian communities can persuasively foster women's full dignity, whether or not women are mothers, it seems unlikely that women will inevitably want to appropriate the 'grace' of pregnancy and childbirth, as a biblically-based but Christian theologically-developed ethic might propose.[19]

In commenting on Ann's essay, Hauerwas, not surprisingly, expresses complete agreement with this communitarian emphasis: 'We both think that abortion should not be an issue for Christians because we should be a community in which abortion just does not come up.'[20]

The only reference to abortion in Farrer's writings that I have found is in the Appendix on 'Imperfect Lives' at the end of *Love Almighty and Ills Unlimited*, in connection with the problem of what the tradition has called 'ensoulment'. Ann's reaction to this Appendix is addressed elsewhere in this *Festschrift* by Robert MacSwain, and I forbear consideration of the topic here. I simply note that Farrer himself concentrates attention on the individual person bearing the divine image rather than on the community into which a child is born. The same might be thought to be true of the few sermons in which Farrer tackles specifically moral issues, such as the one on 'Conscience'[21] and the one on 'Chastity'.[22] In the latter, his pretty conservative advice on sexual ethics is based on respect for the personal integrity of the human person, body, heart and spirit. On the other hand, he does make the following categorical affirmation:

> Primarily Christians are members of Christ's body, secondarily they are members of one another in Christ; and the very special bodily bond of sexual union must fit into the system of relationships within the body of Christ.[23]

So the communitarian emphasis is there in Farrer after all, and I do not think he would have disagreed with Ann or with Hauerwas over this aspect of their treatment of the issue of abortion. What his attitude would have been to the perspective of feminist theology I consider in the final section of this essay.

Sacramental Spirituality

All commentators on the genius of Austin Farrer stress the way in which he combined philosophical acuity, theological perspicacity and spirituality. Farrer's own spirituality is not only evident from his devotional addresses at the Eucharist[24] and his suggestions for turning the Creed into prayer[25] but also in his work on doctrine and philosophical theology generally. It is entirely appropriate that *The Truth-Seeking Heart* should appear in the series 'Canterbury Studies in Spiritual Theology'. In their Preface to that Reader, Robert MacSwain and Ann refer to 'Austin Farrer's profound integration of the truth-seeking intelligence and the truth-seeking heart'.[26] Indeed we have no reason at all to complain about the fact that Farrer's phrase 'the truth-seeking intelligence' becomes 'the truth-seeking heart' in the title of Ann and Robert's Reader.

The connection between doctrine and spirituality in Farrer's work was stressed by Stephen Platten in his paper at the third Farrer conference and by Diogenes Allen in his contribution to *Captured by the Crucified*.[27] But Allen brings out a further connection between Farrer's spirituality and his practical theology. For Farrer, prayer and spirituality are not simply contemplative but concerned with the formation of the mind and will.

These connections, between philosophy, doctrine and spirituality, and between spirituality and practice, are equally true of Ann herself and no doubt reflect both the attraction and the influence of Farrer on Ann's work over the years. Where spirituality is concerned, one might mention Ann's involvement as Lay Canon of Durham Cathedral, the series of addresses on sacramental spirituality organized by David Brown and Ann to celebrate the nine-hundredth anniversary of Durham Cathedral, her participation in the St James Center for Spiritual Formation in Baton Rouge and her contribution, 'Sacramentality and Christian Spirituality', in *The Blackwell Companion to Christian Spirituality*.[28] Out of the Durham series of addresses came the book, *Christ: The Sacramental Word*, edited by David Brown and Ann.[29] Although Farrer is not mentioned in the editors' introduction, which is entitled 'Introduction: The Divine Poet', I would imagine that Farrer would wholeheartedly share their conviction that words can and do function sacramentally. One of the pieces in this volume, the one by John Riches on 'Balthasar's Sacramental Spirituality and Hopkins' Poetry of Nature: the Sacrifice Imprinted upon Nature',[30] opens up another dimension of sacramental spirituality that would surely have appealed to Austin Farrer. I have myself carried out a comparative study of Farrer and Balthasar on the subject of finite and infinite freedom,[31] and would very much like to see a similar comparative study of Farrer and Balthasar on sacramental spirituality.

Ann's concern with spirituality and ethics may be seen not only in her essay for the Hauerwas volume but also in her involvement in many committees and conferences and in such projects as CHASTE (Churches Alert to Sex Trafficking across Europe), an ecumenical charity devoted to combating this evil and aiding its victims. Clearly Ann has gone way beyond Farrer in such practical involvements but the principles behind such work are his and hers alike.

The twofold reference to poetry in what was said above about *Christ: The Sacramental Word* points forward to the fourth subject area of mutual concern for Ann Loades and Austin Farrer.

Literature and Music

Farrer's love of literature is apparent from his sermons and occasional writings.[32] He was himself a poet, and the literary, even poetic, quality of his own writing has often been noted. It was entirely appropriate that the fifth Farrer conference should have been held in conjunction with the Durham Centre for the Study of Literature and Theology. At that conference, Hans Hauge read a paper entitled 'The Theologian as Literary Critic, and the Literary Critic as Theologian: Austin Farrer, Helen Gardner and Frank Kermode'.[33]

Ann's involvement in that conference has already been mentioned and there is no doubt that she has responded to, and shares, Farrer's conviction of the importance for theology of the literary imagination. I perceive that *Christ: The Sacramental Word* is given the subtitle, on the cover if not on the title page, 'Incarnation, Sacrament and Poetry'. And its companion volume, also edited by David Brown and Ann, is entitled *The Sense of the Sacramental: Movement and Measure in Art and Music, Place and Time*.[34] Of course the question raised by this latter book is whether the extension of theological interest from the verbal to the visual and the oral takes us beyond Farrer.

In his essay in *The Human Person in God's World*, David Brown observes of Farrer, 'We know that he had no interest in music'.[35] The only evidence provided for this claim comes in a footnote referring us to Stephen Platten's paper from the third Farrer conference, in which Platten reports, on the basis of a personal interview with a lifelong friend of the Farrer family, that Farrer 'appeared not to understand music'.[36] Platten remarks that this may account for the paucity of musical allusions in Farrer's writings. This can hardly be described as irrefutable evidence and I must confess to finding it rather hard to believe. Certainly there are not many musical allusions in Farrer's writings, but there are at least five sermons – 'David Danced Mightily',[37] 'The Bells of Heaven',[38] 'The New Song',[39] 'Praises of the Creator' (preached at the dedication of the new organ in Trinity Chapel)[40] and 'Into the Hands'[41] – that might well lead us to question the categorical claim that Farrer had no interest in music. The last of these five sermons is especially noteworthy in that, in speaking of our pictures of heaven, Farrer observes 'some of us, for brief periods, can find in music a little heaven on earth'.[42]

Be that as it may, it remains true that music did not feature very prominently in Farrer's sense of the sacramental. This is indeed a dimension where Ann has extended the range of sacramental theology into wider aesthetic domains. I refer here to the essay that she did me the honour of contributing to my own *Festschrift*.[43] Her essay there is entitled 'On Music's Grace: Trying to Think Theologically about Music'. In it she argues powerfully for the place of music in worship, moreover for recognizing music as itself a means of grace. She does not restrict this sacramental understanding of music to sacred music. And she draws attention to the corporate and physical aspects of music-making, as in a quartet or an orchestra or in jazz. 'An identifiably "incarnational" understanding of music', she concludes, 'must needs attend to its sheer physicality through corporeality in time.'[44] In her final section, she gives examples of the way in which music can still enable praise to be given even in circumstances of horrendous evil. Here we are reminded of her writing on theodicy, discussed in my first section above. But she ends with a reference to music making worship possible not only in relation to the depths of grief and rage, but also in relation to conviviality and companionship, not least in the form of dance. But who preached the sermon, 'David Danced Mightily'? Austin Farrer. So perhaps the link between Ann Loades and Austin Farrer is still to be discerned at this point after all.

Feminist Theology

However, when we turn to the final subject area – feminist theology – we might well suppose that the link is definitely broken. Ann's major contribution to this movement in modern theology is discussed elsewhere in this *Festschrift*, and I restrict myself here to the rather unlikely quest for a residual, perhaps more than residual, relation between Ann's feminist theology and Austin Farrer.

Farrer himself lived and wrote before the rise of feminist theology and, spending nearly all of his working life in men's colleges in Oxford, he was not confronted by issues of justice for women much of the time. On the other hand we must not forget his family and friends, and Ann herself, in her essay in *Captured by the Crucified,* draws our attention to a number of women thinkers who will surely have had some influence upon him. Among them, Helen Waddell and Dorothy Sayers are regarded by Ann, in her book *Searching for Lost Coins,*[45] as something in the nature of proto-feminists. It is interesting, too, to read of Iris Murdoch's presence at early meetings of the *Metaphysicals*, a group of mainly High Anglican theologians and philosophers concerned to challenge the anti-metaphysical bias of contemporary linguistic philosophy in Oxford. Austin Farrer was a leading member of the *Metaphysicals*. I cannot resist quoting Iris Murdoch's biographer, Peter Conradi, at this point. In describing the *Metaphysicals*, he refers to 'elfin, occasionally waspish Farrer, leading Oxford theologian, Warden of Keble and mystic who in his exceeding shyness and brilliance recalled [to Denis Nineham, apparently] "a sort of male Iris"'.[46] Two much more pertinent quotations from Ann herself may serve to indicate possible links between Farrer and feminist theology. For the second edition of David Ford's *The Modern Theologians*, Ann revised and updated her article on 'Feminist Theology' and in it we find the following remarks:

> Feminist theologians are notably preoccupied with the impact of theological convictions on the lives of women, and this gives feminist theology a very wide agenda. Feminist theology seeks a reintegration of areas of theological discipline too often kept apart, such as liturgy, pastoral practice, ethics, and spirituality as well as with theology construed as doctrine.[47]

At least the second of these two sentences recalls very strongly what has been said about Farrer's agenda. And then, at the beginning of her chapter on abortion in *Faithfulness and Fortitude* to which I have already alluded, Ann writes:

> By 'feminist' I mean someone committed to seeking greater justice for women, and I take it that men as well as women may be feminist and that Stanley Hauerwas is as much a feminist as I am.[48]

Could she, I wonder, say the same about Austin Farrer? Not, I suppose, if it is a question of explicit commitments, in word and deed, to seeking greater justice for women. Given his time and place, this was hardly on Farrer's explicit agenda. But when we think of all Farrer said and wrote about the integrity of the human person, its implications for the just treatment of both women and men are quite clear and I do not think that Farrer, had he had the opportunity to read *Searching for Lost Coins*, would have said anything other than *Amen*.

In conclusion, I would simply like to reiterate my conviction that Austin Farrer's 'passion for God and clarity' and his 'profound integration of the truth-seeking intelligence and the truth-seeking heart' are equally reflected in the life and work of Ann Loades.

Notes

1 Jeffrey C. Eaton and Ann Loades (eds), 1983, *For God and Clarity: New Essays in Honor of Austin Farrer*, Allison Park, PA: Pickwick Publications.

2 Papers from this conference were published in Brian Hebblethwaite and Edward Henderson (eds), 1990, *Divine Action: Essays Inspired by the Philosophical Theology of Austin Farrer*, Edinburgh: T & T Clark.

3 Ann Loades and Michael McLain (eds), 1992, *Hermeneutics, the Bible and Literary Criticism*, Basingstoke: Macmillan Press.

4 Papers from this conference were published in F. Michael McLain and W. Mark Richardson (eds), 1999, *Human and Divine Agency: Anglican, Catholic, and Lutheran Perspectives*, Lanham, MD: University Press of America.

5 David Hein and Edward Hugh Henderson (eds), 2004, *Captured by the Crucified: The Practical Theology of Austin Farrer*, New York: T & T Clark International.

6 Papers from this conference were published in Brian Hebblethwaite and Douglas Hedley (eds), 2006, *The Human Person in God's World: Studies to Commemorate the Austin Farrer Centenary*, London: SCM Press.

7 Ann Loades and Robert MacSwain, 2006, *The Truth-Seeking Heart: An Austin Farrer Reader*, Norwich: Canterbury Press.

8 Eaton and Loades, *For God and Clarity*, p. xiii.

9 A. L. Loades, 1985, *Kant and Job's Comforters*, Newcastle upon Tyne: Avero Publications Ltd.

10 G. W. Leibniz, 1951, *Theodicy: Essays on the Goodness of God, the Freedom of Man and the Origin of Evil*, trans. E. M. Huggard, edited with an Introduction by Austin Farrer, London: Routledge & Kegan Paul Ltd.

11 Leibniz, *Theodicy*, p. 74f.

12 *Kant and Job's Comforters*, p. 136. The Farrer reference is to Austin Farrer, 1967, *Faith and Speculation: An Essay in Philosophical Theology*, London: Adam & Charles Black, p. 74f.

13 Austin Farrer, 1959, *Finite and Infinite: A Philosophical Essay*, 2nd edn London: Dacre Press, p. 87.

14 Austin Farrer, 1962, *Love Almighty and Ills Unlimited: An Essay on Providence and Evil*, London: Collins.

15 See Marilyn McCord Adams, 1999, *Horrendous Evils and the Goodness of*

God, Ithaca, NY and London: Cornell University Press.

16 See Brian Hebblethwaite, 2006, 'God and the World as Known to Science', in Hebblethwaite and Hedley (eds), *The Human Person in God's World*, pp. 70–7.

17 See Hein and Henderson, *Captured by the Crucified*, p. 35. The quotation from Farrer comes from 'The Christian Apologist', in Jocelyn Gibb (ed.), *Light on C. S. Lewis*, London: Bles, 1965, p. 41.

18 Mark Thiessen Nation and Samuel Wells (eds), 2000, *Faithfulness and Fortitude: In Conversation with the Theological Ethics of Stanley Hauerwas*, Edinburgh: T. & T. Clark.

19 Nation and Wells, *Faithfulness and Fortitude*, p. 255.

20 Nation and Wells, *Faithfulness and Fortitude*, p. 329.

21 Austin Farrer, 1973, *The End of Man*, London: SPCK, pp. 77–80.

22 Austin Farrer, 1960, *Said or Sung*, London: The Faith Press, pp. 178–83.

23 Farrer, *Said or Sung*, p. 178f.

24 Austin Farrer, 1952, *The Crown of the Year: Weekly Paragraphs for the Holy Sacrament*, London: Dacre Press: A. & C. Black Ltd.

25 Austin Farrer, 1955, *Lord I Believe: Suggestions for Turning the Creed into Prayer*, London: The Faith Press Ltd.

26 Ann Loades and Robert MacSwain (eds), 2006, *The Truth-Seeking Heart: Austin Farrer and his Writings*, London: Canterbury Press, p. viii.

27 See Stephen Platten, 'Diaphonous Thought: Spirituality and Theology in the Work of Austin Farrer', *Anglican Theological Review* 69 (1987), 30–50, and Diogenes Allen, 2004, 'Farrer's Spirituality', in Hein and Henderson, *Captured by the Crucified*, pp. 47–65.

28 Arthur Holder (ed.), 2005, *The Blackwell Companion to Christian Spirituality*, Oxford: Blackwell, pp. 254–68.

29 David Brown and Ann Loades (eds), 1996, *Christ: The Sacramental Word*, London: SPCK.

30 Brown and Loades, *Christ*, pp. 168–80.

31 Brian Hebblethwaite, 1999, 'Finite and Infinite Freedom in Farrer and von Balthasar', in F. Michael McLain and W. Mark Richardson (eds), 1999, *Human and Divine Agency: Anglican, Catholic, and Lutheran Perspectives*, Lanham, MD: University Press of America, pp. 83–96.

32 See, for example, 'Poetic Truth', in Austin Farrer, 1972, *Reflective Faith*, London: SPCK, pp. 24–38, and 'Inspiration: Poetical and Divine', in Austin Farrer, 1976, *Interpretation and Belief*, London: SPCK, pp. 39–53.

33 Hans Haugh, 1992, 'The Sin of Reading: Austin Farrer, Helen Gardner and Frank Kermode on the Poetry of St. Mark', in Loades and McLain, *Hermeneutics*, pp. 113–28.

34 David Brown and Ann Loades (eds), 1995, *The Sense of the Sacramental: Movement and Measure in Art and Music, Place and Time*, London: SPCK.

35 Hebblethwaite and Healey, *The Human Person in God's World*, p. 86.

36 Platten, 'Diaphonous Thought', n. 84.

37 Farrer, *Said or Sung*, pp. 184–9.

38 Austin Farrer, 1970, *A Celebration of Faith*, London: Hodder and Stoughton, pp. 188–92.

39 Austin Farrer, 1976, *The Brink of Mystery*, London: SPCK, pp. 107–8.

40 Farrer, *The Brink of Mystery*, pp. 41–4.

41 Farrer, *A Celebration of Faith*, pp. 112–16.

42 Farrer, *A Celebration of Faith*, p. 115.

43 In Julius J. Lipner (ed.), 2005, *Truth, Religious Dialogue and Dynamic Orthodoxy: Essays in Honour of Brian Hebblethwaite*, London: SCM Press, pp. 25–38.

44 Lipner, *Truth*, p. 35.

45 Ann Loades, 1987, *Searching for Lost Coins: Explorations in Christianity and Feminism*, London: SPCK.

46 Peter J. Conradi, 2001, *Iris Murdoch: A Life*, London: HarperCollins, p. 305.

47 David Ford (ed.), 1997, *The Modern Theologians: An Introduction to Christian Theology in the Twentieth Century*, 2nd edn, Oxford: Blackwell, p. 575.

48 Nation and Wells, *Faithfulness and Fortitude*, p. 233.

12

Imperfect Lives and Perfect Love

Austin Farrer, Stanley Hauerwas and the Reach of Divine Redemption

ROBERT MACSWAIN

Ann Loades and Austin Farrer

As Brian Hebblethwaite demonstrates in the preceding chapter, for 25 years Ann Loades has been one of the leading scholars associated with the legacy of Austin Farrer (1904–68).[1] In a number of books and articles, Ann expresses her deep appreciation for Farrer's creative fusion of philosophy, theology, biblical interpretation and sacramental spirituality as held within the matrix of a firm commitment to Anglican Christianity. Typically, however, appreciation does not blunt her critical edge. This became abundantly clear to me in 2004 at the Farrer centenary conference in Baton Rouge, Louisiana. During this conference Ann summarized Farrer's life and work for an audience of respectful Americans. In the midst of a primarily positive assessment she paused to consider the brief Appendix – 'Imperfect Lives' – to his book on the problem of evil, *Love Almighty and Ills Unlimited*.[2] Here Farrer engages in some pessimistic speculation regarding God's capacity to 'immortalize' those whose mental faculties are below what some might consider 'human': namely infants and the severely mentally handicapped. Speaking of an infant who dies soon after birth, Farrer writes, 'The baby smiled before it died. Will God bestow immortality on a smile?' (p. 190). Ann quoted this passage, then suddenly looked up from her notes, glared at us defiantly and asked, 'Well, why the hell not?'

I take this anecdote as my point of departure for two reasons. First, it is 'pure Ann', and nicely captures her distinctive combination of intellectual energy, vigorous engagement, keen compassion and moral sensitivity. Ann may deeply appreciate Austin Farrer but she does not defer to him – or anyone – uncritically. Second, and more significantly, Farrer does indeed seem to have thought himself into a corner in this Appendix, and in the remainder of this chapter I'd like to see if he can be helped out of it. I thus offer this chapter to celebrate Ann's own engagement with Farrer, express some of what I have learned from her, and acknowledge her concern about 'Imperfect Lives'. To this end I will also look to another theologian mentioned by Hebblethwaite in connection with Ann's work, who has also contributed a chapter to this volume, namely Stanley Hauerwas. In short, Hauerwas' arguments about the place of the mentally handicapped in the life of the Church challenges the intellectualism expressed in 'Imperfect Lives' and in so doing points us back to another, more helpful element in Farrer's own theology: that is, his belief that our salvation is 'bodily'. Accentuating this aspect of Farrer's thought allows us to include the deaths of infants and the severely mentally handicapped within the reach of divine grace. Imperfect lives, including our own, may still be redeemed by perfect love.

'Imperfect Lives'

Ann is not the only Farrer scholar worried by this Appendix. Brian Hebblethwaite says that 'one could imagine Farrer's arguments being called upon to justify not only abortion but also infanticide', although he adds (rightly) that 'Farrer himself certainly would not have approved of that'.[3] And Robert Boak Slocum complains that Farrer's conclusions here are 'strikingly disappointing and inconsistent with his other positions'.[4] But what exactly does Farrer say?

He begins the Appendix with the observation that one of the 'commonly reckoned evils of human life is the death of speechless infants, before they reach the stature of humanity; another is the survival of imbeciles, who are incapable of ever reaching it' (p. 189). These are obviously controversial and disturbing claims, and they will be considered extensively below.[5] But, having made this observation, Farrer continues by saying that the *theological* problem

> specially posed by these disorders is not that they should be permitted to befall our kind, but that we do not know how we should relate to the mercy of God beings who never enjoy a glimmer of reason. Are they capable of eternal salvation, or are they not? (p. 189)

One can already see the danger lurking in Farrer's restriction of 'human' status to those of us capable of speech and reason, but his justification for this is complex and will be considered in a moment. Meanwhile, he immediately moves to block the threat of infanticide or euthanasia: 'Out of natural piety, and a respect for the divine image in man, we treat [such individuals] as human. We do not kill our imbeciles; we baptise dying infants and give them Christian burial' (p. 189). So, as Hebblethwaite argues, while Farrer's theory may be disturbing, his practice is sound. Tradition provides moral guidance where speculative reason is confounded. But this agnosticism, we may feel, is neither a safe nor satisfactory state of affairs. Thus we want to determine why Farrer's theory seems to have fallen out of sync with his practice and to bring the two back into harmony.

Farrer proceeds to make an uncomfortable but defensible point. In regard to such individuals, he says

> We are inclined to think of a rational person walled up, as it were, in their bodies, and bricked in with stupid flesh; he is cruelly treated in being denied light, air, and utterance. This, at least, is a fallacy of sentiment; the rational person is not there. (p. 189)

In taking this uncomfortable position, however, Farrer is in complete agreement with much contemporary thinking – even much contemporary Christian thinking – about human nature. If we abandon a Platonic or Cartesian substance dualism that identifies our rational selves with an essentially immaterial, immortal soul, then in what does our rationality, humanity or personhood subsist? More specifically, how do we think – and with what?[6]

Farrer's description of the supposedly rational person 'denied utterance' by being 'walled up' in 'stupid flesh' recalls Wittgenstein probing Augustine's account of his speechless yet supposedly thoughtful infancy, struggling to find the words to express his already developed concepts.[7] Like Wittgenstein, Farrer turns this common story upside down and identifies reason with speech. We do not first think and then learn to talk; rather, we first talk and then learn to think. And we learn to talk by being talked to by others. Thinking is internalized talking. Mentality is not primarily individual and internal but social and cultural. For those with Wittgensteinian sympathies, in making these various claims Farrer is on good, solid ground.[8]

But he then goes on to associate the achievement of speech–reason–mentality with personhood. Earlier in *Love Almighty and Ills Unlimited*, in the chapter 'Man Redeemed', he spells this out very clearly:

Man, in being man, is both a body and a beast . . . But if he is a beast, he is a talking beast, and in his speech lies his reason. Through reason he shares, however faintly, that truth which is the mind of God, and becomes a copy or reflection of the divine likeness: in short, a person. (pp. 106–7)

This linkage of reason and personhood is, of course, a very common move in contemporary ethical thought and I will come back to it in a moment. For now, however, note Farrer's *theological* application of this move:

the rational person offers an opening to God's mercy which humbler creatures do not . . . Man is not first an immortal soul; he is an animal on whom the capacity for everlasting life has been conferred. For he has been enabled to talk, and in acquiring speech has acquired the rudiments of reason. (p. 107)

Thus Farrer identifies reason with speech, links the achievement of speech and reason with the status of personhood and humanity, and further argues that – unlike 'humbler creatures' – such rational beings provide a unique 'opening to God's mercy'. That is, only such speaking, reasoning, human persons have the 'capacity for everlasting life'.

Returning to 'Imperfect Lives', this general argument is then further developed and specifically applied to 'speechless infants [and] imbeciles'. Farrer asserts that if 'there ever was a speaking and loving person, there is a creature for God to immortalize' (p. 190). He then sets up the rhetorical question that Ann finds so vexing: 'But if the reasoning person never developed, what are we to think? The baby smiled, before it died. Will God bestow immortality on a smile?' (p. 190). After this question, Farrer raises the further complication of both natural and medical abortions, the many millions of embryos – indeed the vast majority – that fail to survive the womb or even the earliest stages of gestation. Are they bound for an immortal existence? And he makes things even more difficult for himself by stating that, even if we grant 'the origin of an immortal soul with the attainment of speech and reason', we may still be driven to ask, 'What degree of reason?' (p. 190). Mental handicap comes in various stages. Is there a cut-off point beneath which God does not have sufficient material with which to build an immortal soul? What IQ level is required for heaven? Farrer's conclusion is both bleak but hopeful, granting his assumptions:

We do not know where to draw the line; that is to say, we do not know where God draws it. But we may be sure that he loves and saves whatever there is to be saved or loved; if his love or power does not act, it is because there is nothing for it to act upon. He makes no arbitrary discrimination. (p. 190)

In short, within the broader context of *Love Almighty and Ills Unlimited*, Farrer's argument in 'Imperfect Lives' may be expressed as follows:

1 'Man is not first an immortal soul; he is an animal on whom the capacity for everlasting life has been conferred. For he has been enabled to talk, and in acquiring speech has acquired the rudiments of reason' (p. 107).
2 Thus, in failing to acquire both speech and reason, 'speechless infants' and 'imbeciles' do not 'reach the stature of [either] humanity' or personhood (p. 189).
3 We 'do not know how we should relate to the mercy of God beings who never enjoy a glimmer of reason' (p. 189), but if 'there ever was a speaking and loving person, there is a creature for God to immortalize' (p. 190).
4 Indeed, God 'loves and saves whatever there is to be saved or loved' (p. 190).
5 Therefore, although we 'do not know where to draw the line', we know that God 'makes no arbitrary discrimination' (p. 190).

The conclusion of the argument – (5) – is thus an expression of agnosticism regarding the eternal fate of those described in (2) rather than a confident dismissal of such individuals from the halls of heaven. Still, given their apparent lack of an immortal soul, the vexing question lingers: 'Will God bestow immortality on a smile?'

It is important not to dismiss Farrer's line of reasoning too quickly but rather to identify where it seems to go wrong. While I cannot speak for Ann, I am happy to consider (1), (4) and (5). But (2) is ethically repugnant in its limitation of the set of 'humans' or 'persons' to those with speech and reason, and the theological problem is most obvious in (3). Rather than immediately address these various difficulties, however, I now wish to bring 'Imperfect Lives' into conversation with the very different thought of Stanley Hauerwas on the place of the mentally handicapped in human society generally and the Church in particular.

Stanley Hauerwas, the Mentally Handicapped and the Church

What makes Hauerwas such an interesting contrast with Farrer here is that they both agree on (1) above. Like Farrer – and at least partly under his influence – Hauerwas accepts a basically post-Wittgensteinian, non-dualistic understanding of human nature. Like Farrer, Hauerwas does not assume that infants, the mentally handicapped or indeed any of us are born with an immortal soul 'in addition to' our bodies that essentially qualifies us for 'personhood' and automatically destines us for eternal life with God. In fact, Hauerwas' position on the relation between body and soul, on the unity and stability of the 'self', is arguably more radical and further removed from conventional dualistic conceptions than Farrer's. But where Hauerwas decisively parts company with Farrer is in the conclusions he draws from their mutual starting point.[9]

In short, Hauerwas consistently inverts our standard assumptions – assumptions prevalent in both philosophical *and* theological anthropology – that privilege 'normal' adult reasoning capacities as the criteria for either humanity or personhood. Indeed, he regards the latter term as a dangerously ambiguous and elusive concept best to be avoided. By contrast, inspired by the work of Jean Vanier and his L'Arche communities, Hauerwas lifts up those described by our contemporary culture as 'mentally handicapped' (Farrer's 'imbeciles') and argues that both they and those who care for them in fact provide for us an icon of *true humanity* – and, indeed, even an icon of true divinity. While not necessarily to be desired, the birth of a mentally handicapped child is also not an evil to be deplored but rather a gift to his or her family and to the wider community – a gift to be welcomed, cherished and benefited from. In other words, Hauerwas offers a radical transposition of values regarding what constitutes both human nature and society and divine nature and society. By dispensing with our normative assumptions about such matters, he clears a space for the mentally handicapped to survive and even flourish, and further invites us to consider the challenging possibility that such a space is actually more 'human' and thus more conducive to our own flourishing as well – that is, those of us who do not have learning disabilities.

Professor John Swinton of the University of Aberdeen has recently collected ten of Hauerwas' most important and influential essays on the mentally handicapped and invited various other scholars and practitioners to interact critically with this body of work. In response to these critics, friendly and otherwise, Hauerwas writes:

One of the most frustrating aspects of my work, for friend and foe alike, is I have always tried to do theology by indirection. By indirection I mean I have tried to resist the temptation to make theology another set of ideas that can be considered in and of themselves. For example, anyone concerned to discover what 'my' doctrine of God might be or what my 'theological anthropology' entails will look in vain for any essay or book on those theological topics. But that does not mean I do not think about questions classically associated with the doctrine of God or theological anthropology; I try to write about such issues in relation to material practices that exemplify what is at stake.[10]

Having revealed his method, Hauerwas then says, with admirable candour:

My reflections on the challenge the mentally handicapped present to some of our most cherished conceits about ourselves is best understood as my attempt to develop a theological anthropology. In brief, I 'use' the mentally handicapped to try to help us understand what it means for us to be creatures of a gracious God. For I think it a profound mistake to assume that a strong distinction can be drawn between those who are mentally handicapped and those who are not mentally handicapped once it is acknowledged that we are equally creatures of a God, who as Augustine observed, created us without us, but who refuses to save us without us.[11]

And Hauerwas rounds out his position by making an additional crucial, liturgical, ecclesial move:

The mentally handicapped remind us that the 'us' that is saved is the body constituted through Christian baptism that is anything but an individual. If we take seriously practices of the church such as baptism, we are all, mentally handicapped and the non-mentally handicapped, creatures drawn into a kingdom of patience making possible our friendship with God and one another.[12]

Near the end of the response, Hauerwas offers some striking reflections on the human capacity for communication through gesture and body that bear directly on Farrer's emphasis on speech and reason as outlined above. He argues that 'the language of gesture' can be as cognitive as speech, indeed may even be 'the most determinative cognitive claims we can make', given that they 'cannot be abstracted from the ones making the claim'. Even those who cannot speak may still communicate with their bodies. Such gestures remind us of 'the significance of the body whose silence often tells us what we most need to know to be with one another'.[13]

Finally, he concludes the essay with a vision of the Church that he has articulated and defended for three decades, namely as a community that includes, values, celebrates and cares for mentally handicapped lives:

> here we see a people who believe that there is nothing more significant to be done in a world of such deep injustice than to take the time to be friends with the handicapped. I know of no better vision of peace.[14]

Earlier in the essay, Hauerwas goes so far as to describe the Church as 'a community that is constituted by our sharing our lives with the mentally handicapped'.[15] If this is what truly *constitutes* the Church, then one may say that Hauerwas has made such mutual sharing the *bene esse* – or even the *esse* – of the Church, rather than other, more familiar candidates (such as bishops!).

'The Body of Christ'

As stated at the conclusion of my second section, rather than deal directly with the problematic elements of Farrer's 'Imperfect Lives', I first wished to contrast Farrer's position on the mentally handicapped with that of Stanley Hauerwas. While I must resist the temptation to develop these points in detail, it is clear that they agree on (1) above, and perhaps also (4) and (5), but that they radically disagree on (2) and (3). As for (2), despite – or perhaps because of? – his Wittgensteinian credentials, Hauerwas rejects Farrer's linkage of speech and reason with humanity and personhood.[16] Characteristically, Hauerwas reverses the onus of proof and requires the non-mentally handicapped to prove *their* humanity by their treatment of those with such disabilities.[17]

But, readers may object, how can I maintain that Hauerwas rejects (3) – that is, that we 'do not know how we should relate to the mercy of God beings who never enjoy a glimmer of reason', but if 'there ever was a speaking and loving person, there is a creature for God to immortalize' – when Hauerwas is and has been and remains conspicuously silent on the topic of eschatology, whether individual, corporate or cosmic? That is, does Hauerwas really even address Farrer's *theological* concern in (3), or does he simply deal with the *ethical* issue of (2)? And, while Hauerwas has certainly written extensively about the mentally handicapped, what about Farrer's other problem in 'Imperfect Lives', the death of infants?

It is true that Hauerwas has rarely discussed the traditional topics of Christian eschatology[18] – but remember his comments above regarding his method of theological indirection. Through this method, he has spent his career trying to demolish the distinction between theology and ethics. Thus I would argue that if his writing on the mentally handicapped is his way of developing a theological anthropology 'in relation to material practices that exemplify what is at stake',[19] then such anthropological conclusions have eschatological implications. Likewise, his ecclesial conclusions have eschatological implications. Hauerwas does not need to tell us explicitly that the mentally handicapped are 'going to heaven', because once you see *and practice* his understanding of their central place in the Church, the Body of Christ, the question answers itself. 'The way to solve the problem you see in life is to live in a way that will make what is problematic disappear.'[20] If the Church, the Body of Christ, is constituted by the mentally handicapped and those who share life with them in mutual friendship, then to ask whether God is able to 'immortalize' people with such disabilities is nonsense. If the mentally handicapped are, as Hauerwas argues, 'a prophetic sign of our true nature as creatures destined to need God and, thus, one another',[21] then our salvation is inextricably linked with – and perhaps more precarious than – theirs. And if, as Hauerwas says,

> we take seriously practices of the church such as baptism, we are all, mentally handicapped and the non-mentally handicapped [which thus includes, let us add, mentally handicapped and non-mentally handicapped *infants*], creatures drawn into a kingdom of patience making possible our friendship with God and one another.[22]

This mention of baptism reminds us of Hauerwas' strong emphasis on the body and its significance – but it also sends us back to Farrer, albeit to a different text than 'Imperfect Lives'. Nine years before *Love Almighty and Ills Unlimited*, Farrer published a remarkable essay titled 'The Body of Christ'.[23] Beginning with a consideration of Christ's presence in the Eucharist, he then discusses the incorporation of Christians into the Body of Christ through baptism. In a deeply lyrical and suggestive passage, he writes:

Our bodies are to extend the body of Christ, his body is to annexe our bodies to itself – our bodies, not our bare souls. Body is the foundation, we start from body. My thoughts and actions lift themselves out of my body, play around it, alter and pass; my body remains. By virtue of my body I am founded in time and place, through it I am inserted in my environment. Jesus, conceived by the Holy Ghost in the womb of Mary, established in the world a body joined uniquely to the life of God, and our bodies are to be united with his body in one extended body, the mystical Church. Our state of redemption, like our existence, like his incarnate existence, is to begin with the body. (p. 119)

The method by which we become part of this body is also bodily: the links between its members

are not merely mental, Christ will not have them to be so. He will have us all grafted into his body by baptism. Here is a physical fact: each of us has either been baptised, or he has not; the baptismal water has either flowed upon us, or it has not. (p. 119)

The Eucharist is likewise physical: 'actual bread, actually blessed and consecrated by the one apostolic priesthood. Here is bodily fact once more, a fact constantly repeated, through which Christ renews, actualizes and reveals his mystical body on earth.' In short, through baptism and Eucharist, Christ has instituted 'a web of bodily relations binding our bodies together' (p. 119). And this web of bodily relations is not purposeless, but rather exists for our salvation:

It is the mercy of Christ to begin my salvation with my body. This me, the mere opaque bodily fact, the me which is there before my will, and whether I will or no, and which I can only remove by self-destruction, by the insane pretence to dispose of what is not mine either to create or to destroy . . . Christ takes this me, and annexes it to himself by bodily bonds, without waiting for the sanctification of its acts and uses. He takes it, and presents it as a part of himself that it may be sanctified. (p. 122)

In reading these passages, particularly in the context of Hauerwas' work, one recognizes the radically physicalist nature of Farrer's soteriology here. True, he immediately follows the preceding quote by adding, 'Meanwhile he acknowledges [my body] for his, his body and blood, *so long as I have faith*, and repent my deadly sins' (p. 121, emphasis added).

But this is the only subjective, mentalistic note in an overwhelmingly objective, physicalistic score. Clearly, Christ's choice and action precedes – or 'prevents' – ours both onto-logically and chrono-logically. Thus, even our faith is a mere – though literal – afterthought.

In other words, nine years before he wrote 'Imperfect Lives', Farrer already had all the pieces in place to solve his own problem. Our redemption is not mental but bodily. 'Speechless infants' and 'imbeciles' are as 'capable of eternal salvation' as any of us and for precisely the same reason: not that we have speech and rationality and so are persons, but because we have bodies and so are creatures. Farrer got into a muddle in 'Imperfect Lives' because he did not follow through with the full implications of his insights in 'The Body of Christ'. Or, put differently, in 'Imperfect Lives' he reverted to a *structural* dualism, albeit a linguistic dualism rather than a substance dualism, with a linguistic soul rather than a substantial one. Instead of the bodily nature of salvation so beautifully described in 'The Body of Christ', it again becomes a matter of rational ability. Even in 'Imperfect Lives', however, Farrer remembers Catholic practice: 'We do not kill our imbeciles; we baptise dying infants and give them Christian burial' (p. 189). But rather than bring his theory back in line with his practices, he wonders why the practices don't seem to make sense – and so inadvertently opens the door for the practices to be abandoned.[24]

By contrast, Hauerwas' theology may be seen as a relentlessly consistent attempt to bring Christian theory into line with Christian practices, rather than vice versa. Thus, instead of wondering how God could possibly redeem the mentally handicapped, Hauerwas concludes that such individuals are 'reminders that before God none of us are whole; but God makes possible the joining of our bodies through which we become whole'.[25] Thus we cannot contrast 'imperfect' lives with 'perfect' ones because we are all imperfect. But we are also all redeemable, as the bodily, created objects of a perfect love.[26]

Notes

1 In addition to the various works mentioned by Hebblethwaite one could include Ann's entry on Farrer in Alister McGrath (ed.), 1998, *The SPCK Handbook of Anglican Theologians*, London: SPCK, pp. 120–3.

2 Austin Farrer, 1962, *Love Almighty and Ills Unlimited*, London: Collins. 'Imperfect Lives' covers pages 189–91. Further citations to this volume will be provided parenthetically within the main text.

3 Brian Hebblethwaite, 2006, 'God and the World as Known to Science', in Brian Hebblethwaite and Douglas Hedley (eds), *The Human Person in God's World: Studies to Commemorate the Austin Farrer Centenary*, London: SCM Press, pp. 72–3.

4 Robert Boak Slocum, 2007, *Light in a Burning-Glass: A Systematic Presentation of Austin Farrer's Theology*, Columbia, SC: University of South Carolina Press, p. 48.

5 Farrer wrote this book in 1961 when the term 'imbecile' was still in common usage. Throughout this chapter I follow Hauerwas in using the still controversial term 'mental handicap' to cover perhaps a wider range of ability and disability than Farrer may intend in this Appendix. In addition, as will be discussed further in the course of the chapter, one may certainly question the three assumptions expressed if not explicitly defended by Farrer: first that infants have not yet reached 'the stature of humanity'; second that the (severely) mentally handicapped are incapable of ever attaining such status; and third that the birth and survival of such individuals is an 'evil' (i.e. a misfortune) to be regretted.

6 These questions are of course hugely controversial and complicated and cannot be settled here. While currently on the defensive, substance dualism is still a viable position in both philosophy and theology and it would be a mistake to simply assume its falsity or defeat. For a brief discussion within the context of a larger argument, see pages 123–7 of David Brown, 2000, *Discipleship and Imagination: Christian Tradition and Truth*, Oxford: Oxford University Press. And, indeed, Farrer's own precise position on the nature of soul and its relation to body cannot be determined simply from *Love Almighty and Ills Unlimited*; rather, a full account would need to take in his major philosophical volumes (*Finite and Infinite*, Westminster: Dacre Press, 1943 and *The Freedom of the Will*, London: A & C Black, 1958), as well as other writings. For the sake of argument and brevity, however, I will in the remainder of this chapter adopt a 'Wittgensteinian' reading of Farrer.

7 See Augustine's *Confessions*, Book I, chapters 6–8, and Ludwig Wittgenstein's *Philosophical Investigations*, Part I, Paragraphs 1–3, 32 and 206. For a good discussion of Wittgenstein's understanding of Augustine in these passages, see Fergus Kerr, 1997, *Theology after Wittgenstein*, London: SPCK, pp. 38–42.

8 Among several other passages expressing this Wittgensteinian view, see Farrer's sermon 'Thinking the Trinity', reprinted in Ann Loades and Robert MacSwain (eds), 2006, *The Truth-Seeking Heart: An Austin Farrer Reader*, Norwich: Canterbury Press, p. 157; and Farrer, *Love Almighty*, p. 114.

9 See 'The Sanctified Body: Why Perfection Does Not Require a "Self"', in Stanley Hauerwas, 1998, *Sanctify Them in the Truth: Holiness Exemplified*, Edinburgh: T & T Clark, pp. 77–91, especially pp. 78, 86 and 90, n. 15. For the record, Farrer was an important influence on Hauerwas' early thinking on the topics of character, selfhood and agency: see Stanley Hauerwas, 1975, *Character and the Christian Life: A Study in Theological Ethics*, San Antonio, TX: Trinity University Press, p. 27, n. 41 and p. 87, n. 6. Although I will not develop the contrast further in this chapter, it should also be noted that Hauerwas' general approach to the problem of evil is very different from Farrer's in *Love Almighty and Ills Unlimited*, being less abstractly theoretic and more thickly narrative. See Stanley Hauerwas, 1990, *Naming the Silences: God, Medicine, and the Problem of Suffering*, Grand Rapids, MI: William B. Eerdmans Publishing. This book is, incidentally, based on lectures delivered at the University of Durham in 1989.

10 Stanley Hauerwas, 'Reflection on Dependency: A Response to Responses to My Essays on Disability', in John Swinton (ed.), 2004, *Critical Reflections on Stanley Hauerwas' Theology of Disability: Disabling Society, Enabling Theology*, Bingham-

ton, NY: The Haworth Press, pp. 192–3. Subsequent references to Hauerwas' essays will be from this volume, which was also published as *Journal of Religion, Disability, and Health*, 8, 3 and 4, 2004.

11 Hauerwas, 'Reflection on Dependency', p. 193.

12 Hauerwas, 'Reflection on Dependency', p. 193. I have presented Hauerwas' position here in three block quotations from a single piece of writing because in this recent essay he condenses 30 years of groundbreaking thought on the relation between Christian doctrine, the mentally handicapped and the Church. There is much that could be drawn from these compact statements but I will instead point interested readers toward the volume as a whole.

13 Hauerwas, 'Reflection on Dependency', p. 197.

14 Hauerwas, 'Reflection on Dependency', p. 197.

15 Hauerwas, 'Reflection on Dependency', p. 195.

16 See especially Hauerwas' critique of Joseph Fletcher in 'The Retarded and the Criteria for the Human' (Swinton, *Critical Reflections*, pp. 127–34). Fletcher holds that 'any individual who falls below the I.Q. 40 mark in a Stanford-Binet test is "questionably a person", and if you score 20 or below you are not a person' (p. 131). Transposed into theology, this exactly parallels Farrer's concern about intellectual capacity and eternal redemption: if such individuals are not persons, then how can they be saved?

17 Hauerwas, 'The Retarded', p. 132.

18 A possible exception would be his brief, passing comment in *Naming the Silences* that, in contrast to the heroine of *Charlotte's Web*, a child's fate is not that of a spider (p. 148).

19 Hauerwas, 'Reflection on Dependency', p. 193.

20 Ludwig Wittgenstein, 1980, *Culture and Value*, Chicago, IL: University of Chicago Press, p. 27e.

21 Hauerwas, 'Suffering the Retarded: Should We Prevent Retardation?', p. 105.

22 Hauerwas, 'Reflection on Dependency', p. 197.

23 Originally published in *The Crown of the Year: Weekly Paragraphs for the Holy Sacrament* (Westminster: Dacre Press, 1952), reprinted in Loades and MacSwain (eds), *The Truth-Seeking Heart*, pp. 117–24. Subsequent references to this essay will be from this volume, in parentheses in the main text.

24 Of course, one may ask whether Farrer's view in 'The Body of Christ' entails the traditional position that only the baptized can be saved. I cannot argue this point here, but I would contend that even in this text the primary category is the body that is baptized rather than baptism itself. Human bodies, including infants and the mentally handicapped, may be saved not because they have or have not been baptized but because they are *baptizable*.

25 Hauerwas, 'Reflection on Dependency', p. 197.

26 I am grateful to David Brown, Stephen Burns, Joe Cassidy, Ed Henderson, Stanley Hauerwas and Natalie K. Watson for comments on an earlier version of this chapter, and I am especially grateful to Ann Loades for inspiring it.

13

Kant, Job's Comforters and Adolf Eichmann

ELIZABETH C. GALBRAITH

In her doctoral thesis, later published as *Kant and Job's Comforters*, Ann Loades traced with precision the evolution of Kant's philosophical theodicy from its pre-critical Leibnizian phase evidenced by essays such as *'Nova Dilucidatio'* and 'Some Reflections on Optimism' to the critical position best characterized by Kant's oft-neglected 1791 essay, 'On the Failure of All Attempted Philosophical Theodicies'.[1] According to Loades, 'before his so-called critical revolution, Kant on the whole wrote about theodicy in the manner of a Leibnizian',[2] exuding Leibnizian optimism that God had indeed created the 'best of all possible worlds' and assuming divine permission of, in particular, natural evils.[3] In part III of *Kant and Job's Comforters*,[4] Loades offered a nuanced analysis of what she named Kant's pre-1781 'contemplative optimism' in order to better illumine the *self*-critical nature of Kant's post-1781 writings. Hume seems likely to be the one who awoke Kant from his dogmatic slumbers concerning theodicy, as well as on the bounds and capacities of reason. By the time he wrote his three great *Critiques*,[5] Kant had become skeptical of the assumption that the wisdom of God could be defended by theoretical reasoning from the natural world. Such scepticism is reflected in his 1791 essay on theodicy, which Kant begins by dismantling classical defences of the justice and righteousness of God in light of the problem of evil and concludes the opening section with the claim that

> no theodicy proposed so far has kept its promise; none has managed to justify the moral wisdom at work in the government of the world against the doubts which arise out of our experience of the world. (KW VI, p. 129; FT, p. 263).

No longer able to assert that this is the best of all possible worlds,[6] Kant sets himself on the path of restricting knowledge in the realm of theodicy.

In *Kant and Job's Comforters*, Loades stressed the consistency between the 1791 rejection of philosophical theodicies and the cognitive limitations that Kant had placed upon all philosophical investigation (including his own) from the *Critique of Pure Reason* onwards. However, as Loades pointed out in Part IV of *Kant and Job's Comforters*, Kant's rejection of philosophical theodicies is not the end of the story. Having dismissed what he considers the most traditional defences of God given in theodicies, Kant could quite easily have ended his essay. Instead, however, he informs the reader, 'we are capable at least of a negative wisdom' (KW VI, p. 130; FT, p. 263). In large part such negative wisdom entails acknowledging 'the necessary limits of our reflections on the subjects which are beyond our reach' (KW VI, p. 130; FT, p. 263) – a refrain familiar to anyone acquainted with the three *Critiques*. But it also entails what Kant refers to as 'authentic theodicy' (KW VI, p. 131; FT, p. 264), and, according to Kant, 'such an authentic interpretation I find expressed allegorically in an old scripture' (KW VI, p. 131; FT, p. 264). The old scripture Kant has in mind is the book of Job.

The biblical character Job is the model for Kant's response to the good person confronted by evil. According to Loades, the Job of Kant's essay, less the patient sufferer than the exemplar of veracity at all costs, exemplified what had been for Kant a watershed in his own theological presuppositions, and yet at the same time revealed a dimension of Kant's preoccupation with theodicy that survived into his critical phase, namely a resilient faith in divine providence. Kant's treatment of Job provides sufficient evidence that his own pre-critical 'contemplative optimism' has been replaced by a more cautious cognitively restricted and yet still authentically hopeful theodicy. It is therefore appropriate that I commence this paper with a review of those sections of 'On the Failure of All Attempted Philosophical Theodicies' that elucidate Kant's 'authentic theodicy', thus providing a window into Kant's most sincere post-1781 religious reflections.

After briefly introducing Job as the pious and fortunate believer who undergoes a terrible fate sent to try him (KW VI, p. 132; FT, p. 264), Kant turns to his main concern, namely the dispute that takes place between Job and his friends:

Each side proposed his own theodicy for the moral explanation of his bad luck, each according to his own opinion (or rather according to his station). The friends of Job accepted the doctrine that explains all woes in the world by reference to divine justice; they are punishments for crimes committed. Although they were not able to name any crime with which to charge the unfortunate man, they nevertheless believed they could judge a priori that Job must have committed such a crime, or else divine justice would not have allowed him to become so unhappy. (KW VI, p. 132; FT, p. 265)

In contrast, 'Job confidently asserted that the conscience of all his life did not reproach him' (KW VI, p. 132; FT, p. 265). And, for Kant, the arguments proposed by either side are not of ultimate importance. Rather, 'the character which the men exhibited while they reasoned' is more worthy of attention (KW VI, p. 132; FT, p. 265):

Job spoke as he thought, as he felt, and as every man in his position would feel. His friends, however, spoke as if they were overheard by the Almighty whose behavior they were judging, and as if they cared more for winning his favors by passing the right judgment than for saying the truth. The dishonesty with which they affirmed things of which they should have confessed that they had no knowledge and with which they feigned convictions which in fact they did not have, contrasts with Job's free and sincere outspokenness, which is so removed from lying flattery that it almost borders on temerity . . . 'Do you want', asked Job, 'to defend God with unjust arguments?' (KW VI, p. 132; FT, pp. 265–6)

Kant's sympathies clearly lie with Job, a man who has the courage to stand by his convictions in the midst of the most trying circumstances. His calling God to account, his refusal to retreat into self-blame and his confident resistance to the accusations of his so-called friends, who, Kant implies, are lying flatterers of God, afford him Kant's admiration. Most significantly, Kant emphasizes Job's retort, accusing his friends of defending God with unjust arguments. Kant also reminds his reader that, in the conclusion to the biblical account, 'God made the condemnation fall upon his friends, because, considered from the standpoint of conscience, they had not spoken of God as well as his servant Job did' (KW VI, p. 133; FT, pp. 265–6). And the reasons why Job is justified by God could not be clearer to Kant:

Only the uprightness of the heart, not the merit of one's insights, the sincere and undisguised confession of one's doubts, and the avoidance of feigned convictions which one does not really feel (especially before God where dissemblance would never work), these are the qualities which caused the upright man Job to be preferred in the eyes of the divine judge to the pious flatterers. (KW VI, p. 133; FT, pp. 266–7)

A refusal to give answers that do not match the facts characterizes Job's response to his own suffering in contrast to the responses of his friends. Kant, like Job, took it to be 'a sin to flatter God and make inner confessions, perhaps forced out by fear, that fail to agree with what we really think'.[7] What Kant perhaps most admires is Job's exposure of the inadequacy of traditional theodicies (which not only claim more knowledge of the workings of the divine than is warranted but also tend to vindicate God while falsely accusing the innocent sufferer) in combination with his ultimately vindicated veracity, even in the expression of the most profound doubts about God's treatment of him.[8]

In *Kant and Job's Comforters* Loades imaginatively juxtaposed Kant with Job's comforters so as to highlight his own critical rejection of traditional theodicies. At the same time, however, she argued that Kant's authentic theodicy entailed not only veracity at all costs but also an equally authentic trust in divine providence, a trust that had survived the transition from the pre-critical to Kant's critical phase. Such trust in divine providence is also revealed in Kant's 1791 essay through his account of the divine theophany. According to Kant, God reveals to Job the ambiguity of the created world, with aspects that seem to affirm and others that seem to deny divine providence. This, Kant tells us, *is*[9] the work of a wise Creator: 'God showed Job an ordering of the whole which manifests a wise Creator', but 'his ways remain inscrutable for us, already in the physical ordering of things but even more in the connection between this order and the moral one (which is even more unfathomable to our reason)' (KW VI, p. 133; FT, p. 266).

In response to the theophany of God,

> Job confessed not that he had spoken sacrilegiously for he was sure of his good faith, but only that he had spoken unwisely about things that were above his reach and which he did not understand (KW VI, p. 133; FT, p. 266).

The point for Kant is that human reason simply cannot fathom the paradox of how a morally ambiguous world is also the result of a providential Creator. It is for precisely this reason that traditional theodicies fail. But, just as in the *Critique of Pure Reason*, where Kant is willing to 'deny knowledge in order to make room for faith',[10] so in his essay on theodicy, Kant finds it necessary to deny knowledge in order to safe-guard faith in divine providence when he tells us that 'theodicy is not a task of science but is a matter of faith' (KW VI, p. 134; FT, p. 267). Such faith for Kant means 'the moral attitude of reason in its assurance of the truth of what is beyond the reach of theoretical knowledge'.[11] Concerning Job's faith, Kant tells us:

> The faith which arose out of such unusual answers to his doubts, that is, which arose simply out of the conviction of his ignorance, could arise only in the soul of a man who in the midst of his most serious doubts could say, 'Until the hour of my death, I will hold fast to my piety' [Job 27.5–6]. (KW VI, p. 134; FT, p. 267)

Kant commends the sincere man of faith, who refuses to accept expla-nations that do not meet with the facts (no matter how pious they may appear to be), who is willing to acknowledge his cognitive limitations and who, in the midst of the most serious doubts, 'holds fast' to his piety. Kant concludes his treatment of Job with the critical assertion:

> With this resolution Job proved that he did not base his morality on his faith but his faith upon his morality. In this case, faith, however weak it may become, is a truer and purer one; this kind of faith is not found in a religion that cultivates self-interest and seeks favors, but a religion of good behavior. (KW VI, p. 134; FT, p. 267)

For religious critics of Kant's philosophy, the notion that Job 'based his faith upon his morality' and not vice versa typically proves problem-atic, as does the idea of 'a religion of good behavior'. Such claims, thought to be typical of Kant's critical reduction of religion to morality, do, however, hint at the most crucial moral underpinning to Job's resilient faith. We will now turn from Kant's essay on theodicy to his more specifically moral philosophy, and to the fatal reduction of that philosophy in the service of genocide, in order to elucidate the relevance and ultimate value for the theodicy project of 'basing one's faith on morality'.

More than any other philosopher, Kant emphasized the way in which the moral life is centred on duty. In the *Groundwork of the Metaphysic of Morals*,[12] Kant's aim was 'to seek out and establish the supreme prin-ciple of morality' (KW IV, p. 248; G, p. 60) and his starting point was the conception of the 'good will': 'it is impossible to conceive anything at all in the world, or even out of it, which can be taken as good without qualification, except a good will' (KW IV, p. 249; G, p. 61). A 'good will', he goes on to argue, 'is not good because of what it effects or accomplishes . . . it is good through its willing alone' (KW IV, p. 250; G, p. 62). And what should guide the will in action is the strictest sense of duty: actions have moral worth when done 'not from inclination but from duty' (KW IV, p. 255; G, p. 66). Thus, for Kant, a good will is a will always to do one's duty regardless of one's inclinations, or feelings for others. What counts as ethical is our will to do our duty and the disinterested application of our reason in support of that will (KW IV, p. 270; G, p. 80). For this reason, 'duty for duty's sake' has become the ethical mantra in connection with Kant's concept of duty. Furthermore, an action done from duty has its moral worth, according to Kant, not in the purpose to be attained by it but in the maxim in accordance with which it is decided upon (KW IV, p. 256; G, p. 68). The only appropriate maxim is 'to act out of reverence for the law' (KW IV, p. 256; G, p. 68), and by 'law' Kant means a universal law, valid for all. In other words, a person is morally good when they seek to obey a law valid for all persons according to an objective standard not determined by individual desires. According to the first formulation of the categorical imperative: 'I ought never to act except in such a way *that I can also will that my maxim should become a universal law*' (KW IV, p. 258; G, p. 70, emphasis in original). Thus, the early modern era's most renowned moral philosopher provided a blueprint for ethical action.

How can it be then, that, as noted by the late Emil Fackenheim in *To Mend the World*, 'the man who probably will go down in history as its greatest organizer of mass murder knew, believed, and occasionally practiced bits of the teaching of Immanuel Kant'?[13] Adolf Eichmann, who belonged to the highest ranks of the Nazi government, was the person primarily responsible for organizing the transportation of millions of Jews to their deaths. Though initially escaping prosecution for war crimes, in 1961 he was captured in Buenos Aires and brought to Israel for trial. In her landmark work, *Eichmann in Jerusalem*, Hannah Arendt documents the moment when, during the trial, Eichmann 'suddenly declared with great emphasis that he had lived his whole life according to Kant's moral precepts, and especially according to a Kantian definition of duty'.[14] One of the judges, 'either out of curiosity or out of indignation at Eichmann's having dared to invoke Kant's name in connection with his crimes', decided to question the accused. And, to the surprise of everybody, Eichmann came up with an approximately correct definition of the categorical imperative: 'I meant by my remark about Kant that the principle of my will must always be such that it can become the principle of general laws'.[15]

Upon further questioning, Eichmann added that he 'had read Kant's *Critique of Practical Reason*'.[16]

Although Eichmann then proceeded to explain that he had ceased to live by Kantian principles from the moment he was charged with carrying out the Final Solution, Arendt suggests that he had instead 'distorted' the Kantian formula along the lines of Hans Frank's formulation of 'the categorical imperative in the Third Reich' in *Die Technik des Staates*: 'Act in such a way that the Führer, if he knew your action, would approve it.'[17] Further, Arendt suggests, 'there is not the slightest doubt that in one respect Eichmann did indeed follow Kant's precepts: a law was a law, there could be no exceptions'.[18] Eichmann took his duty of obeying the law of the Führer to such an extreme that when Himmler, contrary to the Führer's command, ordered the dismantling of the extermination facilities in Auschwitz in 1944, Eichmann objected.

In Fackenheim's view, Arendt was right: Eichmann did obey the Kantian principle of 'duty for duty's sake'. He was, Fackenheim notes, 'a dutiful, idealistic mass-murderer, not merely a sadistic or opportunistic one'.[19] The horror is increased, Fackenheim suggests, by the fact that Eichmann also sought to fulfil the formulation of the categorical imperative referred to above: 'for there is no doubt that the "maxim" of his acting was to make through his own will the Führer's will into universal law'.[20] Thus, through the most unseemly juxtaposition of Kant and Eichmann, the Hitlerization of Kant's categorical imperative[21] was made possible.

Yet, and crucially for Fackenheim (for whom, according to Zachary Braiterman in *God After Auschwitz*, the philosophy of Kant was the authoritative bar before which Jewish thought was justified[22]), Kant's ethical blueprint could only become an accessory to the Nazi genocide by the reduction of his formula to its kernel, while divorcing that kernel from its core and thus from the very 'heart and soul of Kant's categorical imperative'.[23] When Kant formulated his categorical imperative, he took it for granted that every human being is entitled to respect, as is clear from its second formulation, according to which one should

> act in such a way that you always treat humanity, whether in their own person or in the person of any other, never simply as a means, but always at the same time as an end. (KW IV, p. 287; G, p. 96)

'Every rational being', Kant tells us, 'exists as an end in himself, *not merely as a means* for arbitrary use by this or that will' (KW IV, p. 286; G, p. 95, emphasis in original). Moreover,

> man is not a thing – not something to be used merely as a means: he must always in all his actions be regarded as an end in himself. Hence I cannot dispose of man in my person by maiming, spoiling, or killing. (KW IV, p. 288; G, p. 97)

Morality is, according to Kant, the only condition under which a rational being can be called an end in himself (KW IV, p. 293; G, p. 102), and for this reason 'morality, and humanity so far as it is capable of morality, is the only thing which has dignity' (KW IV, p. 293; G, p. 102). Moreover, 'that which constitutes the sole condition under which anything can be an end in itself has not merely a relative value – that is, a price – but has an intrinsic value – that is, dignity' (KW IV, p. 293; G, p. 102). And this dignity is above all price, with which it cannot be brought into reckoning or comparison without as it were a 'profanation of its sanctity' (KW IV, p. 294; G, p. 103).

It was precisely human dignity that was targeted for destruction in the Holocaust, and only through a perversion of the categorical imperative did Kant's ethical philosophy become an accessory to that crime. According to Fackenheim, whereas Kant had offered the second formulation of the categorical imperative on behalf of human dignity, the Eichmanns of the Third Reich invoked the first formulation of that imperative on behalf of a destruction of that very same human dignity.[24] The logic of the death camps entailed the extermination of the Jews and included the annihilation of their human dignity as the precursor to murder, through the practice of all kinds of humiliation and torture.

According to the late D. M. MacKinnon,

> the good will, the treatment of ourselves and our fellows as ends and not as means, these things are not butterflies which we can capture and pin like so many moral prizes in a glass case.[25]

They are, however, principles that should ground our concern for ourselves and our respect for the dignity of our fellow human beings; and they should make us all the more aware of our obligations toward each other. In *Kant and Job's Comforters*, Loades noted that 'Kant comes to realize that it is human wickedness rather than human experience of "natural evil" that is central for theodicy'. And when he does so, 'trust in divine justice becomes the crucial feature of his theodicy'.[26] In the light of an Eichmann, Kant's most profound conviction (rendered in all its significance by Loades), that the kind of life we lead 'must make a difference',[27] seems less the precarious reduction of religion to morality than an immensely faithful hope for divine justice:

> It could never be that the issue is all alike, whether a man has acted fairly or falsely, with envy or with violence, albeit to his life's end, as far at least as human eye can see, his virtues have brought him no reward, his transgressions no punishment.[28]

And, of course, for such divine justice to be realizable, intimations of immortality must ensue:

> We know nothing of the future, and we ought not to seek to know more than what is rationally bound up with the incentives of morality and their end. Here belongs the belief that there are no good actions which will not, in the next world, have their good consequences for him who performs them; that, therefore, however reprehensible a man may find himself at the end of his life, he must not on that account refrain from doing at least one more good deed which is in his power.[29]

Ann Loades recognized the religious import of these morally founded intimations on Kant's part. His stubbornly persisting faith that ultimately justice, both divine and human, must prevail makes Kant's 'authentic theodicy' as relevant in a post-Holocaust world as it was in his own enlightened one.

Notes

1 Immanuel Kant, *Über das Misslingen aller philosophischen Versuche in der Theodicee*, 1791, in *Immanuel Kants Werke, Band I–XI*, Heidsheim, Berlin: Verlag Dr H. A. Gestenberg, 1973, vol. VI (hereafter KW). 'On the Failure of All Theodicies', trans. Michel Despland, in *Kant on History and Religion*, Montreal: McGill-Queen's University Press, 1973 (hereafter FT).

2 Ann Loades, 1985, *Kant and Job's Comforters*, Newcastle-upon-Tyne: Avero, p. v.

3 Loades, *Kant and Job's Comforters*, p. 109. Natural disasters result from laws implanted in nature by the deity.

4 Loades, *Kant and Job's Comforters*, pp. 101–32.

5 *Kritik der Reinen Vernunft* (*Critique of Pure Reason*), *Kritik der Praktischen Vernunft* (*Critique of Practical Reason*) and *Kritik der Urteilskraft* (*Critique of Judgment*).

6 See Loades, *Kant and Job's Comforters*, p. 143.

7 KW IX, p. 139. Immanuel Kant, 1967, *Philosophical Correspondence, 1759–1799*, ed. and trans. Arnulf Zweig, Chicago: University of Chicago Press, p. 80 (Letter to Lavater, 28 April 1775).

8 It is worth noting that at the time of writing 'On the Failure of All Attempted Philosophical Theodicies', Kant himself was preoccupied with the repressive policies imposed by Frederick William II, who had recently acceded to the throne in Prussia, and may have been facing certain pressures to compromise his own veracity.

9 My emphasis.

10 KW III, p. 125. Immanuel Kant, *Critique of Pure Reason*, trans. N. Kemp Smith, 1964, London: Macmillan.

11 Quoted in Loades, *Kant and Job's Comforters*, p. 146.

12 Immanuel Kant, *Grundlegung zur Metaphysik der Sitten*, KW IV. *The Moral Law, or Kant's Groundwork of the Metaphysics of Morals*, trans. H. J. Paton, 1956, Hutchinson's University Library (hereafter G).

13 Emil Fackenheim, 1994, *To Mend the World*, Bloomington, IN: Indiana University Press, p. xxxvi.

14 Hannah Arendt, 1963, *Eichmann in Jerusalem*, London: The Viking Press, p. 120.

15 Arendt, *Eichmann in Jerusalem*, p. 121.

16 Arendt, *Eichmann in Jerusalem*, p. 121.

17 Quoted in Arendt, *Eichmann in Jerusalem*, p. 121.

18 Arendt, *Eichmann in Jerusalem*, p. 122.

19 Fackenheim, *To Mend the World*, p. 270.

20 Fackenheim, *To Mend the World*, p. 270.

21 Fackenheim, *To Mend the World*, p. xl.

22 Zachary Braiterman, *God After Auschwitz*, Princeton, NJ: Princeton University Press, 1998, p. 137.

23 Fackenheim, *To Mend the World*, p. 272.

24 Fackenheim, *To Mend the World*, p. 273

25 D. M. MacKinnon, 'Kant's Agnosticism', *Blackfriars*, 28 (1947), 256–63, p. 261. Quoted in Loades, *Kant and Job's Comforters*, p. 142.

26 Loades, *Kant and Job's Comforters*, p. 121. Loades also noted that 'In the 1750's [Kant] relied on the goodness of the deity almost without hesitation', by the 1790s 'divine goodness is the presupposition of divine justice, and it is divine justice on which he comes to rely in the first instance'. See Loades, *Kant and Job's Comforters*, p. 109.

27 Loades, *Kant and Job's Comforters*, p. 148.

28 Quoted in Loades, *Kant and Job's Comforters*, p. 148.

29 Quoted in Loades, *Kant and Job's Comforters*, pp. 148–9.

14

Religious Belief and 'the Dissipated Tabby'

VINCENT BRÜMMER

Recently I heard the atheist Richard Dawkins state in a BBC interview that he had believed in God until he was 16. He then came to the conclusion that the theory of evolution provided a more satisfactory explanation for the way things go in the world. At that point, for him belief in God became an outdated theory.

Dawkins' fellow atheist Antony Flew took leave of belief in God when he was 15 years old. For him, the main difficulty was the problem of evil. He could not believe in the existence of a God who allows so much evil to occur in the world. During his career as a philosopher, Flew became one of the most significant contemporary defenders of atheism. In his many writings, Flew defended a 'negative atheism' based on the 'presumption of atheism', that is the claim that atheism is true until it is proven false.[1] For him, the burden of proof lies with the theist who has to show, first, that the concept of God is coherent and, second, that there are sufficient reasons to believe that this concept is instantiated in reality. In his writings, Flew tried to show that up to now nobody has succeeded in providing a satisfactory response to these two demands. All traditional attempts to demonstrate the coherence and truth of belief in the existence of God have failed. The existence of God is therefore an unsubstantiated theory.

Recently, however, Flew seems to have become 'converted' to belief in God.[2] After the discovery of the double helix structure of DNA, Flew now claims, it has become 'inordinately difficult even to begin to think about constructing a naturalistic theory' explaining the emergence of living organisms from lifeless matter or the way in which such organisms gained the ability to reproduce genetically. In chapter 14 of *The Origin of Species*, Charles Darwin argues that 'all the organic beings that have lived on earth have descended from one primordial form, into which life was first breathed'.[3] Thus Darwin seems to have believed that life was somehow miraculously 'breathed into' the first living beings by God. Darwin's theory of evolution therefore explains the origin of species from one primordial living being but not the origin of that primordial being itself. Flew considers it unlikely that life somehow originated from a complex primordial chemical 'soup'. On the contrary, the incredible complexity of life makes it likely that 'a form of intelligence' is somehow involved in its origin. For this reason, Flew now believes that the argument for Intelligent Design is 'enormously stronger' than when he first met it. Belief in God is therefore not contrary to the theory of evolution but rather an important supplement to it. For Flew, such belief is no longer an outdated theory.

This does not mean, however, that Flew now believes in the personal loving God of Christian revelation. For him, the fact of evil still excludes this view. His 'theistic' supplement to the theory of evolution requires no more than 'an Aristotelian God who has the characteristics of power and intelligence' and not the God of revelatory theology. Flew characterizes his belief as 'minimal deism' and refers to the kind of deism defended by Thomas Jefferson, who

> believed that, while reason, mainly in the form of the argument from design, assures us that there is a God, there is no room either for any supernatural revelation of that God or for any transactions between that God and individual beings.[4]

In spite of these qualifications, many evangelical Christians in America looked on Flew's 'conversion' as a significant confirmation of their faith over against the claims of atheists, whereas many atheists disqualified Flew's 'conversion' as the misguided view of an 82-year-old man who has failed to keep up with recent scientific literature.

I suggest that both these reactions are misguided since they uncritically assume that religious belief is a kind of explanatory theory analogous to scientific theories, a theory that can be either outdated or not and that is or is not a useful supplement to the theory of evolution. This is the view assumed by both Dawkins and Flew. I suggest that Dawkins is mistaken in thinking that he believed in God until he was 16. He had merely accepted a disputed (if not scientifically doubtful) hypothesis and then exchanged this for the theory of evolution. Similarly, Flew's 'conversion' is not his coming to believe in God but rather his coming to accept an explanatory hypothesis that he had previously rejected. Apart from the question whether Flew's 'minimal deism' is a satisfactory scientific hypothesis explaining the origin of organic life, it is obviously not belief in the God in whose personal fellowship believers find their ultimate happiness.

The view on the nature of religious belief assumed by the likes of Dawkins and Flew has become obvious to many people today because they are captivated by a dominant picture in modernity. Descartes' Enlightenment project to find firm foundations for all our knowledge has had a determining influence on modernity.[5] On the one hand it has led to an unparalleled flowering of science. By constructing explanatory theories from which hypotheses can be derived that in turn are open to empirical testing, scientists have extended our knowledge and control of our physical environment in an unprecedented way. The success of science has, however, had the effect that the search for knowledge has become the paradigmatic model for all thinking. Many intuitively assume that *all* thinking is aimed at extending our knowledge, that human beings are mere knowing subjects and that reality is merely the object of knowledge. This dominant picture has made many of us blind to the multiplicity of our forms of thought or 'language games'. The effect of this for the way religious belief is understood in modernity has been disastrous. People like Dawkins and Flew as well as their opponents and supporters tend intuitively to consider religious belief as an explanatory hypothesis analogous to hypotheses in science. As such, religious belief is judged to be unsatisfactory and unjustified.

What is needed here is that we are freed from bewitchment by modernity's paradigmatic picture of thinking. Belief in God should not be understood as an explanatory hypothesis but as a way in which believers make sense of their lives and experience in the light of their search for personal fellowship with God. It is a way of looking on life and experience with the eyes of faith. This understanding of the nature of religious belief is well illustrated in Ann Loades' little book on Evelyn Underhill. Ann points out that when Evelyn Underhill

> embarks on the task of commending what she argues to those immersed in the practicalities of life . . . she wants them to see the world differently . . . 'Look with the eyes of contemplation on the most dissipated tabby of the streets, and you will discern the celestial quality of life set in an aureole about his tattered ears.' . . . She wants us to see ourselves as parts of the whole in which, like the tabby, we are also immersed, our 'arrogant personality' sunk into the stream of life, so that our senses enable us to 'savour' the world.[6]

In this chapter, I try to analyse this view on the nature of religious belief. Briefly, I suggest that belief in God is a way of understanding or looking on life and the world of experience in the light of the heritage of metaphors and narratives, moral principles, assumptions and spiritual practices handed down to the community of believers in a religious tradition such as Christianity. This understanding bestows meaning and significance on our lives and our experience of the world and thus determines the attitudes and actions that are appropriate in relation to life and the world in which we live.

Let us briefly reflect on the various elements in this definition.

Metaphors and Narratives

In trying to understand something we ask: 'What is it like?' In other words we understand things by comparing them to other things. In this way our thinking is fundamentally metaphorical.[7] Sallie McFague defines metaphor as

> seeing one thing *as* something else, pretending 'this' is 'that' because we do not know how to think or talk about 'this', so we use 'that' as a way of saying something about it. Thinking metaphorically means spotting a thread of similarity between two dissimilar objects, events, or whatever, one of which is better-known than the other, and using the better-known one as a way of speaking about the lesser known.[8]

McFague stresses that the things we compare metaphorically are not only similar in some respects but also dissimilar in others. Thus the range of our generalizing metaphors is always limited and it is essential that we should not overlook these limits. Metaphorical statements 'always contain the whisper, "it is *and it is not*"'.[9]

In modern Greek, the word 'metaphor' is used for a city bus as a vehicle for transferring people from point A to point B. In an analogous way, we might say that metaphor is a 'vehicle' used to transfer meaning from context A to context B. Terms with which we usually say something in one context (for example, to talk about other people) are used to say something in another context (for example, to talk about God). This transfer of meaning is based on the analogy between what we do with our words in one context and what we do with the same words in a very different context. Clearly this analogy is not identity. God is not like other people. Because of the difference between the contexts only part of the penumbra of meanings and implications that the term has in the one context is transferred to its use in the other context. Only those implications are transferred that are relevant and applicable in the context to which the transfer is made. Thus in the case of religious language the implications for the meaning and significance of life and experience are the ones that are primarily relevant.

For this reason, religious metaphors are always 'existential' or 'self-involving'[10] in the sense that they express the meaning and significance of life and experience and the actions and attitudes to which this commits us. When we call God a rock, we do so to say that he is trustworthy and dependable and not that he is made of silica! When we talk about the all-seeing eye of God, we confess that we cannot hide from God since God is aware of everything that happens, not only in the world but also in the hearts and minds of all of us: 'Almighty God, unto whom all hearts are open, all desires known, and from whom no secrets are hidden . . .'. However, as Wittgenstein points out, it would transgress the 'logical limits' of the metaphor within the context of the religious form of life to ask after the eyebrows of God.[11] For this reason, all the metaphors employed in God-talk are primarily relational: they are intended to express the ways in which believers ought to relate to God in their actions and attitudes. Since these are varied and complex and in fact comprise the whole way of life of believers, a large variety of complementary and mutually supportive metaphors is needed in order to express all the various aspects of this relation. The heritage of a religious tradition therefore presents believers with an extensive fund of metaphors by which they can express their understanding of (the way they are to relate to) God and what this entails for the meaning and significance of their lives and experience.

Often these metaphors take the form of stories or narratives depicting situations or events in terms of which believers can understand the meaning or significance of situations and events they encounter in their own lives. The Bible presents believers with a large fund of such narratives. In varying degrees some (but not all) of these have a historical basis. The parables of Jesus, for example, are stories that obviously are not intended to be understood as historical accounts. Although theologians do sometimes speculate about the time and place where Job lived, it is clear that the religious use of the book of Job as a narrative metaphor does not require us to interpret it as a historical account. The same applies to the first chapters of the Book of Genesis. Other biblical narratives, such as the narrative of the Exodus or the gospel narratives, clearly do have some historical basis but have obviously been imaginatively extended in order to enhance the metaphorical understanding of the meaning of our lives and experience expressed in them. They are neither mere historical accounts nor mere mythical expressions of religious understanding and it is not always clear where the one ends and the other begins. However this may be, the 'mythical' extensions are essential for the meaning of the narratives as religious metaphors. All attempts to 'demythologize' these narratives in order to eliminate the myth and reconstruct the history merely reduce their function as religious metaphors. This is comparable to the way in which Flew's 'minimal deism' eliminates the religious meaning of full-blown Christian belief in God. It may (or may not) be a satisfactory explanatory hypothesis supplementing the theory of evolution but it is by no means the expression of the meaning of life and experience presented by the Christian message.

Moral Principles

It is clear that understanding life and experience in terms of the metaphors and narratives handed down in a religious tradition commits believers to a comprehensive way of life. In this sense we could say that the metaphors and narratives of a religious tradition express a comprehensive policy for life. Often such a policy is also expressed in terms of a code of moral principles.[12] Such principles are moral rules or precepts in which some specific form of behaviour is described and the circumstances specified under which this behaviour is appropriate. Thus, for example, whenever circumstances C obtain (for instance, one is confronted by someone in need) one should always adopt form of behaviour B (for instance, offer assistance). A moral code consists of a coherent system of such principles, which together express a policy for living. Moral discourse in terms of metaphors and narratives is more basic than that in terms of principles. We do not *add* our metaphors and narratives as embellishments to our principles but rather *abstract* our principles from our metaphors and narratives. Nevertheless, we cannot do without this form of abstraction. We need discourse in terms of principles for various reasons, the two most important of which are the following.

First, we need general moral principles for the sake of moral instruction.

We thus have to reduce the extreme complexity of the Christian life of love to relatively few principles, in much the same way as we have to reduce the complexity of English . . . composition to a few grammatical and syntactical principles when we want to teach someone. We need the moral law in something of the same way as we need grammar books. We formulate schematized and condensed sets of rules, because these can be taught to pupils fairly readily, and only when the pupil has mastered these can he develop the finer points of style. And just as we are careful to point out that to write grammatical English is not to have a good English style, so we also insist that to keep the commandments is not to live the Christian life. A man can keep all the rules of grammar, and yet write woodenly, and a man can keep the whole of the moral law and yet live a deadly life.[13]

Second, it is necessary in any society that people co-operate in common action even when they differ in the religious or ideological commitments expressed in the differing sets of metaphors and narratives by which they make sense of their lives and experience. In order to achieve consensus on such common action, they need to abstract what is common in what they do and argue about the advisability of that. We therefore need common moral principles even when we differ in the religious or ideological metaphors and narrative by which we live. Thus a communist, a Christian and a humanist could only reach agreement about whether they should feed the refugees if they stick to shared moral principles and avoid arguing about whether they should build the classless society, do the will of God or strive for the advancement of humanity.

Assumptions

We have seen that understanding life and experience in terms of religious metaphors and narratives entails commitments: by understanding our lives and experience of the world thus, we commit ourselves to the religious form of life expressed by them. Do they also entail truth claims about reality? Does the language game of religion also require us to claim that these metaphors are in some way factually true or 'reality depicting'?[14] Some philosophers deny this. Thus R. B. Braithwaite argued that religious beliefs are merely stories in which we express our moral commitments and which inspire us to a moral way of life.[15] For this purpose it is not necessary to claim that the stories are in some way factually true. They are merely useful and meaningful fictions. They do not refer to a real God and his relations with us. On the contrary, they refer only to us and our moral life in the world and God exists only as one of the characters in the story.

According to Wittgenstein, language games are embedded in forms of life. Thus religious belief is necessarily embedded in the religious form of life. However, language games, like religious belief, are also constituted by 'tacit presuppositions' about reality. It would be logically incoherent to participate in the language game and at the same time to deny the tacit presuppositions that constitute it. In this way a language game like religious belief does indeed entail truth claims about reality. Wittgenstein introduces the term 'tacit presupposition' in the context of some remarks on behaviourism.[16] He makes use of the following example: If a doctor hears the groaning of a patient, he *tacitly assumes* that the groaning is an expression of pain. However, he cannot feel the patient's pain himself. A behaviourist might reject this tacit presupposition as being empirically unverifiable and would therefore look on the patient merely as an object exhibiting groan-behaviour. This behaviour could be terminated by treating the patient with analgesic. In rejecting the tacit assumption, however, the behaviourist takes leave of the form of life of personal relations, since the assumption that you have feelings, emotions and so on, even though I cannot myself experience them, is logically constitutive for my treating you as a person rather than as an object.

Treating somebody else as a person also assumes that the other is a free agent in the sense of being the initiator of his or her own actions and hence having the ability to have done other than he or she did. Since this is a counterfactual presupposition, it is also not verifiable empirically: I can only observe what you do in fact and not that you could have acted differently from the way in which you acted in fact. The determinist who rejects this counterfactual presupposition also takes leave of the form of life of personal relations, since the presupposition is logically constitutive for this form of life and for the language game embedded in it. Since such tacit presuppositions are in this way *logically constitutive* for the language game, they cannot be doubted or denied *within* the language game itself. Doubting or denying them would entail doubting or denying the language game as such.[17]

Similarly the assumption that God exists as a personal being who relates to the world can be understood as a constitutive presupposition of the form of life in terms of which believers make sense of life and experience, and of the language game in which this is expressed. Within the language game this assumption cannot be doubted or denied since denying it would entail taking leave of the language game itself and the religious form of life in which it is embedded. This is well illustrated by the following example:

> If I say 'The Lord is my strength and shield,' and if I am a believer, I may experience feelings of exultation and be confirmed in an attitude of quiet confidence. If, however, I tell myself that the arousal of such feelings and confirming of attitude is *the* function of the sentence, that despite appearances it does not refer to a state of affairs, then the more I reflect on this the less I shall exalt and the less appropriate my attitude will seem. For there was no magic in the sentence by virtue of which it mediated feelings and confirmed attitudes: these were *responses* to the kind of Being to whom, I trusted, the sentence referred: and the response is possible only so long as that exists to which or to whom the response is made.[18]

Clearly then, understanding the meaning of life and the world in terms of religious metaphors and narratives entails assumptions about the existence and nature of God and the way in which he relates to the world. Such metaphors fail to provide the understanding sought for in religion if they are taken to be merely useful fictions and not in some sense 'reality depicting'.

Realism-claims with reference to the existence and nature of God differ in two important respects from realism-claims with reference to the empirical world. First, they are not empirical hypotheses that are open to empirical verification or falsification. It is here that Dawkins and Flew misinterpret the nature of religious claims. Second, they are 'existential' in the sense that they cannot be divorced from the religious form of life for which they are constitutive. For believers, the claim that God really exists is internally connected with the form of life to which they are committed and that bestows meaning on their lives and experience of the world. It follows that belief in the real existence of God stands or falls with commitment to this form of life. The justification of the belief follows necessarily from the justification of the commitment. Doubting or denying the existence of God, or looking on it as a conjecture of which the relative likelihood or unlikelihood could somehow be established independently, would be quite absurd within the language game of religious belief. Such doubt or denial is only possible if at the same time we were to reject the language game as such. In these ways, the real existence of God differs from that of the empirical world. The whole penumbra of meanings and implications that the term 'really exist' has with reference to the empirical world does not carry over to the claims that believers make with reference to God.[19]

Spiritual Practices

Apart from metaphors and narratives, moral principles and assumptions, the heritage of a religious tradition also includes a variety of spiritual practices such as liturgy and prayer. In such practices, believers establish, restore and acknowledge their fellowship with God.[20] In asking things of God we acknowledge our dependence on God and this acknowledgement is a necessary condition for establishing personal fellowship with God. Confessing our sins and asking God's forgiveness is a necessary condition for restoring the fellowship damaged through our sins. In prayers of thanksgiving and praise we acknowledge the fact that God in his mercy wants to maintain a relationship of fellowship with us. I can therefore agree with Calvin in defining prayer as an 'exercise of faith'. The same applies to the 'form of life' of the believer. This life is the realization of the same fellowship. In their lives, believers relate to the world in fellowship with God, and in their prayers they seek the fellowship with God in which they relate to the world.

Because of this connection between prayer and the life of faith, they have often been identified in some way or other. Thus Origen interpreted the life of the believer as itself a kind of prayer: 'the whole life of the saint is one mighty integrated prayer'[21] and Ian Ramsey suggests that a time of prayer can be like the believer's life in miniature.[22] Or one might say that prayer is an explicit expression of what is implicit in the whole of the believer's life.

If the whole life of the believer is a life of fellowship with God, why is it necessary in praying to repeat this whole in miniature? Why is it necessary to make explicit what is implicitly present in any case in the life of the believer? One might respond by referring to human imperfection. One might say that prayer would be unnecessary in heaven, since there all life will naturally be fellowship with God. However, in this life we need continual training in order to live our lives in this way. Sanctification requires special effort. It does not come naturally to us. Thus O. C. Quick writes that

> prayer represents the dedication of all human activity to God. It is the special part cut off, as it were, from our total activity in order that therein the dedication of the whole may be made self-conscious and thereby more complete.[23]

There is much truth in this view. The ability to see oneself and the world with the eyes of faith requires training, and prayer and liturgy are ways in which we train ourselves in this. Thus Alhonsaari points out that

> when praying, the believer is . . . repeatedly making himself see the world in a certain way in which everyday experiences are fitted into what he thinks is the proper reality; he is repeatedly bending his emotional life and his behaviour to conform to this reality.[24]

Prayer becomes what John Drury calls 'the school of seeing'.[25] In prayer and liturgy we are trained to see our lives and the world in terms of our faith and to live our lives in accordance with this way of seeing. In different forms of prayer believers consciously face up to various aspects of their lives in fellowship with God, and in this way train themselves for this life of fellowship. Thus in petition believers face up to their own dependence on God; in intercession they face up to their own concern (or lack of concern) for the needs of others before God; in penitence they face up to their own faults as sins in which their fellowship with God is being damaged; in dedication they face up to their own commitment (or lack of commitment) to doing God's will; in praise they face up to looking on the world as an expression of God's goodness, holiness and glory; in thanksgiving believers face up to looking on their own capacities and opportunities and the fulfilment of their needs as gracious gifts from God. In this sense, prayer is indeed a form of meditation in which believers consciously face up to the way in which they relate to God, to themselves, to the world and to other people in their actions and attitudes. Thus, in prayer believers make the dedication of their whole life to the fellowship of God, in the words quoted from Quick, 'self-conscious and thereby more complete'.

Although this is true, it is also one-sided. Although prayer does further the life of faith, its significance goes further than merely being a means to this end. In their prayers, as in their lives, believers are *practising* their fellowship with God, and not merely *practising for* it. The practice of prayer is not like practising swimming strokes without going into the water. In praying, believers aim at *really* establishing, restoring and acknowledging their fellowship with God. Although this fellowship does result in acts, these are the effects and not the purpose of praying. William Temple is right in emphasizing that 'the proper relation in thought between prayer and conduct is not that conduct is supremely important and prayer may help it, but that prayer is supremely important and conduct tests it'.[26] Prayer and the life of fellowship with God are impossible without each other. It would be absurd to think that we could enter through prayer into fellowship with God if this is not manifested in the life we live. On the other hand it is impossible to live a life of fellowship with God if this fellowship is not established and re-established again and again, and this fact acknowledged in praise and thanksgiving.

Notes

1 Antony Flew, 1976, *The Presumption of Atheism, and Other Philosophical Essays on God, Freedom and Immortality*, London: Elek for Pemberton, chapter 1.

2 See Antony Flew and Gary R. Habermas, 2004, 'My pilgrimage from atheism to theism: an exclusive interview with former British atheist professor Antony Flew', www.biola.edu/antonyflew/flew-interview.pdf. See also Peter S. Williams, 2004, 'A change of mind for Antony Flew', www.arn.org/docs/williams/pw_antonyflew.htm, and Flew's letter on 'Darwinism and Theology' *Philosophy Now* 47 (2004), www.philosophynow.org/issue47/47flew.htm.

3 Quoted by Flew in his letter on 'Darwinism and Theology'.

4 See Flew and Habermas, 'My pilgrimage'.

5 On this point, see my paper on 'Modernity, Post-modernity and Religious Belief', in *Brümmer on Meaning and the Christian Faith: Collected Writings of Vincent Brümmer*, Aldershot: Ashgate, 2006.

6 Ann Loades, 1997, *Evelyn Underhill*, London: Fount, pp. 27–8.

7 On this point, see my paper on 'Metaphorical Thinking', in *Brümmer on Meaning*, and chapter 1 of my *Atonement, Christology and the Trinity: Making Sense of Christian Doctrine*, Aldershot: Ashgate, 2005.

8 Sallie McFague, 1993, *Metaphorical Theology: Models of God in Religious Language*, London: SCM Press, p. 15, emphasis in original.

9 McFague, *Metaphorical Theology*, p. 13.

10 See Donald Evans, 1963, *The Logic of Self-Involvement: A Philosophical Study of Everyday Language with Special Reference to God as Creator*, London: SCM Press.

11 Ludwig Wittgenstein, 1966, *Lectures and Conversations on Aesthetics, Psychology and Religious Belief*, compiled from notes taken by Yorick Symthies, Rush Rhees and James Taylor, ed. Cyril Barrett, Oxford: Blackwell, p. 71.

12 For an extended analysis of the relation between religious metaphors and moral principles, see my paper on 'Religious Models and Moral Principles', in *Brümmer on Meaning*.

13 J. R. Lucas, 1976, *Freedom and Grace*, London: SPCK, p. 100.

14 For this term, see chapter 7 of Janet Martin Soskice, 1985, *Metaphor and Religious Language*, Oxford: Clarendon Press. See also my paper on 'Metaphorical Thinking' in *Brümmer on Meaning*.

15 R. B. Braithwaite, 1971, 'An Empiricist's View on the Nature of Religious Belief', in Basil Mitchell (ed.), *The Philosophy of Religion*, London: Oxford University Press, pp. 72–91.

16 Ludwig Wittgenstein, 1953, *Philosophical Investigations*, trans. G. E. M. Anscombe, Oxford: Blackwell, pp. 197–80.

17 Something similar also applies to illocutionary acts. These too are constituted by

presuppositions about the nature of the world. Thus, I logically cannot make a promise without presupposing that I will be able to fulfil my promise, and I logically cannot request someone else to do something while denying that the other has the ability to do what I ask. See my paper on 'Speech Acts', included in *Brümmer on Meaning*.

18 R. W. Hepburn, 'Poetry and Religious Belief', in A. MacIntyre (ed.), 1957, *Metaphysical Beliefs*, London: SCM Press, p. 148, emphasis in original.

19 For an extended analysis of the nature of such realism-claims in religion, see my paper on 'Does God really exist?', in *Brümmer on Meaning*.

20 For an extended explanation of this statement, see chapter 6 of my *What are We Doing when We Pray?*, London: SCM Press, 1984.

21 Origen, *Treatise on Prayer*, trans. and introduced by E. G. Jay, London: SPCK, 1954, XII.2.

22 I. T. Ramsey, 1971, *Our Understanding of Prayer*, London: SPCK, p. 22.

23 O. C. Quick, 1916, *Essays in Orthodoxy*, London: Macmillan, p. 289.

24 A. Alhonsaari, 1973, *Prayer: Analysis of Theological Terminology*, Helsinki: Luther-Agricola Society, pp. 47–8.

25 John Drury, 1972, *Angels and Dirt: An Enquiry into Theology and Prayer*, London: Darton, Longman & Todd, chapter 1.

26 Quoted in J. Neville Ward, 1976, *The Use of Praying*, London: Epworth Press, p. 30.

15

Unbound Hair and Ointmented Feet
An Ecofeminist Reading of Luke 7.36–50

ELAINE WAINWRIGHT

A strong case can be made for the fact that environmental degradation is the greatest threat and challenge we face as we look into the future.[1]

[W]e Western Christians . . . need to free ourselves from both our chauvinism and our escapism to be able to play with the insightful aspects of our Jewish, Greek, and Christian legacies, as well as critically appraising their problems, letting go of both the need to inflate them as the one true way, or repudiate them as total toxic waste.[2]

The ecofeminist perspective does not cast the Bible aside; it merely works with it from a different perspective.[3]

Currently, biblical scholars are seeking to read biblical texts in many and varied ways in the face of widespread devastation of the earth and an anthropocentrism that ignores or elides the other of the earth community.[4] At the same time, some feminists and other liberationists aim to 'rethink alternative and radical ways of transformation in our present world' through a 'profound questioning into the ways of love in our lives as individuals and as society, and the things love can do in our world' with a particular focus on 'the sexual construction of theology'.[5] In this paper I propose to read one biblical text, namely Luke 7.36–50, the story of the woman who pours perfumed ointment over the feet of Jesus and wipes them dry with her hair, from an ecofeminist perspective informed also by the 'queerer' end of that hermeneutic.[6] I will give attention to the materiality of the other-than-human and of human bodies and to the material spaces in which these interact. I will also seek to demonstrate how such interaction can be characterized as transgression.[7] This, in its turn, will throw new light on the construction of gender and sexuality[8] in the text and its relationship to the agency and subjectivity of the human and other-than-human. The biblical methodology used will be sociorhetorical.

I undertake this paper with pleasure to honour Ann Loades, whose scholarly career has been devoted to doing theology and shaping spiritualities that engage with the most pressing issues of contemporary society in order to enliven liberation, especially for women but also for all oppressed and all denied fullness of being within the entire earth community.[9]

Behold a Woman

The Lucan story (7.36–50) begins with Jesus having been invited to the house (*oikon*) of a Pharisee for a meal where he reclined in his place at table (v. 36). The opening words of the story take the reader immediately into the space of the *triclinium*, which is predominantly male-gendered: that of public men with their associates, a place of contestation of honour and of *convivia*.[10] This cultural space is, as the second half of verse 36 makes clear, grounded in the materiality of a first-century Palestinian house evoked by the explicit use of the word *oikon*.[11] It is the stone walls of the house, the stone or wood of tables and benches in the *triclinium*, the earthen or wooden floors that give context to this story and in which hair is let down, tears pour out and fragrant ointment is lavishly spent. These earth-given materials provide the ambiance of the designated spaces in which culture is negotiated, in which gender and sexuality are constructed and enacted. In contrast to the materiality of house, these latter two categories of gender and sexuality are considered in my analysis as 'heuristic etic designation[s], not emic one[s]'.[12] They belong to the language and conceptual framework of contemporary interpreters rather than to the Lucan text or its Graeco-Roman world. The opening verse of the text, however, does more than simply construct conceptual categories. It evokes materiality, reminding readers that culture, which includes the theologizing operative in the gospel text, is always located in the material.

The scene shifts rapidly, however, to the emphatic introduction of a woman (*idou gynē*: Look! A Woman!) who arrives on the scene of what seems to have been set up as a male *deipnon* or meal, how we are not told. She is, however, described immediately with the associative phrase 'in the city', which, like the house, is doubly evocative. It is generally assumed that the house was associated with the private and was the space of women while the city was that of public men. Such gendering and cultural construction was, however, being challenged and continually negotiated, especially during the first century of the Common Era when women were taking up roles that took them into the public arena of the city. The explicit placing of the woman 'in the city' could, however, be suggesting that she was transgressing the generally accepted gendering of space.

The materiality of the city rises up before the interpreter in all its complexity with this associative phrase: massive stones giving shape to houses, public buildings and streets; wooden and other material structures in alley ways and on the periphery; varieties of smells from open drains, from street vendors and from the incense of temple worship. And it is this space that was discursively/culturally constructed as male in the first-century Roman Empire.[13] The woman is out of place according to this construction and hence may have been seen as threatening to the sexual and gender politics of the Lucan community. Is it this transgression of male space, one is led to ask, that gives meaning to the second descriptor at the end of the opening phrase of verse 37, namely that she is a sinner?[14]

There has been much discussion and disagreement among scholars about whether the woman is characterized as a prostitute.[15] Considered from the perspective of the inner texture of the text, the phrase 'in the city' seems to be an unnecessarily obscure way of referring to a woman who was a prostitute when Luke has no hesitation in using the word *pornē* in 15.30. The woman is, however, not explicitly linked to a household as daughter or wife or mother-in-law as are a number of other women in the Lucan narrative (4.38; 8.3, 42), and she arrives on the scene of the male *deipnon* virtually off the streets and seemingly uninvited. She is named in relation to the *polis* or city, the public material and cultural space that is male-designated space, but that very naming means that she violates both the public space by her presence and the private space of the Pharisee's meal to which he as host could invite his guests.[16] Transgression is a key characteristic of the sociocultural texture of the opening verses of this text, a transgression associated with gender and sexuality as constructed by the dominant paradigms operative in the first-century world.[17] It opens up possibilities for a transgressive theology to emerge in front of the text as this interpretive task unfolds. Such theologizing will seek to avoid the 'in/decent' dualism in relation to gender and sexuality as brought to our attention by Marcella Althaus-Reid,[18] as well as in relation to the material and cultural or the material and spiritual. I will also dialogue with the work of Avaren Ipsen, whose book, *Sex Working and the Bible*, proposes a reading with contemporary sex workers who are seeking 'a sex positive reading of biblical prostitution'.[19]

A Woman of Action

The description of the woman begins with a series of participles (four, in fact, piled up one on the other):

1 *Knowing* that Jesus was reclining in the house of the Pharisee renders the woman at least an observer of Jesus, a woman watching male behaviour in the public arena, the material space of the city (7.37). She may also have been seen to transgress what was set up in the opening verse as male space, drawing attention to the way in which the cultural seeks to control access to the material.

2 *Acquiring* an alabaster jar of perfume/*myron* (7.37) may evoke intertextually for the implied reader Athenaeus' *Deipnosophistae*.[20] Chapter 15 of that text is set in a *symposium* and the matter under discussion is *myron* or perfume, the discussion beginning with the phrase 'when the slaves passed round perfumes in alabaster bottles' (*en alabastois . . . myra*). It would generally have been female or male slaves or *hetairai* who would have administered the *myron*. The woman is thus rendered even more ambiguous culturally but she is intimately connected to the transluscent marble of the *alabastron* and the perfumed ointment that is gift of the earth.[21]

3 *Standing or setting herself* behind Jesus at his feet (7.38) places the woman in the role of the servant or slave in this meal setting. Ipsen demonstrates convincingly that, in antiquity, there was often a blurring of the role of the prostitute or courtesan and the slave. Women became slaves, and in many instances prostitutes, as a result of being the booty of war, of families incurring debt and selling the female child/ren into slavery, and of exposure as infants.[22] Corley likewise emphasizes this link, stating that '[c]entral to Greco-Roman meal ideology was the continued association of sexuality, slavery, and prostitution'.[23] The woman's placing of herself within the material space of the *triclinium*, behind the reclining Jesus, constructs her within the gender and sexual politics of antiquity. From a narrative perspective, however, the reader of the inner texture might read her action as an explicit blurring of these constructed boundaries.

4 *Weeping* tears (7.38) turns attention to other intertexts. In the
   Hebrew and Greek Scriptures, tears as bodily fluid belong to women
   and men and are often directed to God in supplication and recognition of failure or transgression (2 Kings 20.5; 2 Macc. 11.6; 3 Macc.
   1.16; Ps. 6.6; 42.3; Mal. 2.13; Isa. 25.8; 38.5; Jer. 9.1), the material
   being the vehicle of relationship with the divine but also linking the
   woman with her designation as 'sinner'. In 3 Maccabees 1.4, however, Arsinoe goes to the troops of her brother to entreat them to fight
   to win, with tears but also with her hair unbound. Gendered ideology
   and the sexual politics of women's influence on men by virtue of their
   sexuality seeps through this text.

The initial description of the woman by way of four participles reveals
quite a complex scene in which the woman's interconnectedness with
the material functions to construct a scene fraught with gender and
sexual politics. This focus continues through the four active verbs that
dominate the conclusion of verse 38, three of which are in the imperfect,
the tense of continuity. It will be these same actions that Jesus will use at
the end of the narrative to reflect back upon Simon's behaviour toward
him in contrast to the woman's.

   She begins to wet Jesus' feet with her tears. Scott Spencer has pointed
out that the verb *brechō* can mean much more than just 'wet'. Since it
often designates rain, the woman could be seen as raining on or flooding Jesus with her tears.[24] She uses her body and its fluids to connect
with the body of Jesus, to touch that body, initially with tears but also
in a more intimate way as her actions pile up on one another.[25] The
woman is characterized by an embodiment that is relational, that is
erotic. The verb *brechō* and its association with rain also evokes the
Creator, who in Genesis 2.5 is the one who in good time will 'cause it to
rain upon the earth' (see also Joel 2.23; Matt. 5.45). Like the woman
who rains erotic tears down upon the body of Jesus, so too the Creator
rains down rain upon the earth. The body of Jesus is paralleled with
earth in a way that transgresses western dualisms that generally associate woman's body with earth. More than that, the erotic and the ecological merge to create new meaning that is itself transgressive. This play
between texts and meanings that the action of the woman's raining
down of tears has set in motion might draw the reader to another place
where female Wisdom plays/rejoices in the Creator's 'inhabited world'
(Prov. 8.31) having been present when the Creator assigned the waters
to their designated places, from which they would rain forth only at the
Creator's command (Prov. 8.27–9).

Transgression continues into the next of the piled up actions – the woman wipes the feet of Jesus with her hair, an action in which again the material and the cultural struggle against one another. It has been almost indisputably demonstrated that culturally Graeco-Roman women, including Jewish women, wore their hair bound up either with pins if they were wealthy or with a cap if poorer.[26] By implication, however, this woman's hair is lavishly unbound, otherwise she could not have wiped Jesus' feet with it. Charles Cosgrove provides a range of intertextual possibilities for a woman having her hair unbound: sexual connotations, veneration and participation in religious ritual, grief and others.[27] At this point in the Lucan story, literary and sociocultural intertexture would certainly confirm the sexual connotations inherent in the woman's action.

Judith K. Applegate draws attention to the fact that the imperfect form of the verb *ekmassō* renders this extraordinary action continuous.[28] She is not just wiping but massaging the feet of Jesus, who does not draw away from her but rather gives his body to her ministrations and plays them back to Simon later in the story. Her action is erotic in a way that social construction of gender would connote as transgressive – it is not within the private sector of the house, nor is it between husband and wife. And as in so many of the other actions of the woman, it is the material, her hair, that is culturally laden with codes that she transgresses. The erotic and the ecological continue to play in this new space of transgression.

In the final two actions, the woman kisses the feet of Jesus and anoints them with *myron* or ointment. She now touches with her own body, her lips, the feet of Jesus, which are a particular focus in this text (the word *pous* will, in fact, appear seven times in the story). Feet already have strong phallic implications intertextually.[29] The erotic imagery of the embodied language is further emphasized by the woman's kissing of Jesus' feet, especially when the Song of Songs 1.2 – 'Let him kiss me with the kisses of his mouth' – echoes through the text.

Athenaeus' *Deipnosophistae* provides further intertexts for exploring the import of anointing with *myron* or perfumed ointment. It is an action performed by either slaves or free-born (*Deipn.* 15.686) and is associated with a life of luxury, is significantly gendered and carries strong sexual connotations: '(you should have seen me) lying at ease in the bed-chamber! And all about me luxuriant demoiselles, very voluptuous and mincing, will rub my foot with unguents [*myrois*] of amaracus' (*Deipn.* 12.553). In this same context, Athenaeus cites *The Man from Zante*, in which the protagonist questions his right to be a *philo-*

gynēs (one fond of women) and 'to take delight in keeping . . . mistresses [*hetairas*]'. To his own question he gives the reply: 'Why, just to enjoy the very thing you are doing now, and have my feet rubbed with fair soft hands, isn't it magnificent?' (*Deipn.* 12.553). It seems that the *Deipnosophistae* is very explicit in relation to the imagery evoked by the anointing of feet with *myron*. It is a luxury that is highly charged with sexual or erotic overtones. This cultural aspect, however, is constructed around the *myron*.

Within the three opening verses of this narrative (vv. 36–8), a woman acts in a highly erotic and excessive manner in relation to the body of Jesus,[30] taking the initiative, doing actions intended to give pleasure to Jesus – sexual pleasure – not just once but continuously. Intimately woven into and through her actions is the materiality of the human body, its substances and fluids, and the material of earth, its substances and fluids. Jesus in no way interrupts her actions that catch him up in the interplay of bodies, earth, fluids and substances. Rather he receives her ministrations. Her actions transgress both the physical space of the house of the Pharisee and the culturally gendered politics encoded in the text in and through the material that the text evokes.

Examined through the lens of Jean-Louis Chrétien, the embodied material touch of the woman has profound implications for an eco-feminist reading. He suggests that 'Tactile experiencing of the other is simultaneously self-experiencing' and that this belongs not just to the human but also to the other-than-human world.[31] In her very action of touching, the woman is touched by Jesus and a relationship is established: the 'experiential price', Chrétien calls it, of touch.[32] The radical and embodied subjectivity and interrelationship of each is confirmed.

Into this material interconnection established by touch is introduced the *myron* with which the woman anoints the feet of Jesus. Jesus is touched or smeared with it; the *myron* effects the touch of Jesus; and it is the woman who sinks her hands into the ointment in order to massage Jesus' feet with it. Perfumed ointment, the woman and Jesus are brought into intimate relationship with *myron* having its own unique significance in the web of interconnections established by the woman's actions.[33] Both the materiality of human touch and of perfumed ointment effect a call and a response in Jesus, in the woman and in the *myron* – each being called into the web of interconnection and each responding. Verses 37–8 invite readers into a profound intimacy of the erotic and the ecological, whose meaning unfolds with the story.

Making Meaning of the Woman's Action

The Pharisee's interpretation of the woman's action aligns with that of the narrator: she is a sinner, verse 39 echoing verse 37. The woman and her action, however, are made pawns by the Pharisee in his critical evaluation of Jesus as prophet. If he were a prophet he would have recognized her actions as transgressive within the highly charged sexual politics that the narrative evokes. One must assume in this regard that the woman is not wearing the regalia of a prostitute otherwise Jesus would have recognized her immediately as such rather than having to be prophetic.[34]

Jesus, turning toward the woman but addressing Simon, interprets her actions, reflecting back to Simon the same verbs that the narrator used in verse 38. Jesus receives the woman's flooding of his feet with her tears (in place of the water Simon failed to provide); her kissing of those feet (in place of the kiss of welcome Simon failed to give) and her anointing them with ointment (in place of the anointing oil Simon failed to pour over the head of Jesus). Engaging intimately with the materiality of body and earth, she has shown the hospitality that Simon failed to show to Jesus, who is a prophet. Jesus demonstrates his prophetic insight not by stereotyping the woman but by recognizing, in this woman of outrageous love expressed in and through powerfully erotic materiality, the great love of one who has been forgiven (as the twice-repeated perfect passive of *aphiēmi* (*apheōntai*) implies (vv. 47, 48)).[35] She knows herself forgiven before she acts. She has not waited for the men in this context to tell her that she was forgiven whatever her sins were that have been hidden from the readers of this text. She has a relationship with the Loving Forgiving One quite separate from that affirmed or denied by either the designated legal entrepeneur, the Pharisee, or the one whom the gospel names as Teacher. Having been drawn into the intimate and erotic experience of the forgiven woman, Jesus the prophet recognizes in her great act of love that Loving Forgiving One whom she acclaims through all that we have seen caught up in her actions. The permeating *myron* infuses and is infused by the radical incarnationality manifest in the woman, in Jesus, in the *myron* and in the erotic intimacy of their encounter, which is caught up into divinity.

Conclusion

Turning the lens of sexual and ecological politics on this Lucan text, gendered female love expressed through the meeting of bodies as tears flow down on feet, and as loosened hair is used to massage those wet feet while hands rub on perfumed ointment and lips kiss, is stereotyped sinful or reclaimed as hospitality and the love that has known forgiveness. Taking up a reading position at the queerer end of feminist and ecological hermeneutics, this text speaks of a woman whose transgression of gender and sexual boundaries in and through the material radically embodies incarnation. Such a reading opens up space, within the ongoing unfolding of the gospel story, for those who are sex workers,[36] for those whose sexual orientation and expression is marginalized or ostracized, and for sexuality and the material as vehicles of relationship with the divine and the living out of the gospel. The transgression that is at the heart of this gospel story and through which the material continually played, invites its readers to be attentive to transgression as a site of radical relationship with divinity and among the human and other-than-human of the earth community. And finally, salvation belongs to this woman of great love and is manifest through loving sexual expression and sexual relations in which the material of earth and the intimate touch of body on body manifest the love that has been forgiven and that loves much.

Notes

1 Rita M. Gross, 2001, 'Sustainability and Spiritual Discipline', in Rita M. Gross and Rosemary Radford Ruether (eds), 2001, *Religious Feminism and the Future of the Planet: A Buddhist–Christian Conversation*, London: Continuum, p. 207.

2 Rosemary Radford Ruether, 2003, 'Ecofeminism', in Janet Martin Soskice and Diana Lipton (eds), 2003, *Feminism and Theology*, Oxford Readings in Feminism, Oxford: Oxford University Press, p. 31.

3 Ivone Gebara, 1999, *Longing for Running Water: Ecofeminism and Liberation*, Minneapolis, MN: Fortress, p. 131.

4 Gebara, *Longing for Running Water*, pp. 131–2, critically evaluates the authority that has been given to the Bible over against life experience; but she goes on to indicate that ecofeminists in her native Brazil as well as elsewhere are seeking 'to reread the biblical scriptures and rediscover in them the integrity of creation and respect for women'. The five volumes of the Earth Bible project edited by Norman Habel and the Ecological Hermeneutics Consultation of the Society of Biblical Literature chaired by him also provide a forum for such explorations of ways to read the Bible from an ecological perspective.

5 Lisa Isherwood and Marcella Althaus-Reid, 2004, 'Queering Theology', in Marcella Althaus-Reid and Lisa Isherwood (eds), 2004, *The Sexual Theologian: Essays on Sex, God and Politics*, London: T & T Clark, pp. 2–5. See this volume generally for more extensive discussion of the queer perspective and also Marcella Althaus-Reid (ed.), 2006, *Liberation Theology and Sexuality*, Aldershot: Ashgate.

6 Queer theology, with its roots in queer theory, questions the sexual construction of theology. In this paper, I do not intend to take up the 'genre' of queer theology but rather to be attentive to queer theology's focus on sexuality and embodiment or incarnation as this can be read as a central aspect of the text of Luke 7.36–50.

7 For a more extensive development of a hermeneutic that combines an ecological and feminist perspective, see Elaine M. Wainwright, 2006, *Women Healing/Healing Women: The Genderization of Healing in Early Christianity*, London: Equinox, pp. 7–32. Teresa Hornsby, 2004, 'The Woman is a Sinner/The Sinner is a Woman', in Amy Jill Levine and Marianne Blickenstaff (eds), 2004, *A Feminist Companion to Luke*, Cleveland, OH: Pilgrim Press, pp. 121–32, addresses both the transgression contained within this story and the ways in which the woman has been read as transgressive.

8 In general terms, gender will be understood as the sociocultural and discursive construction of the differences between the sexes, whereas sexuality will be considered as more performative although there is a strong recognition that such a distinction is difficult to maintain.

9 By way of example, see Ann Loades (ed.), 1990, *Feminist Theology: A Reader*, London: SPCK; Jeff Astley, David Brown and Ann Loades (eds), 2003, *Creation: A Selection of Key Readings*, Problems in Theology 1, Edinburgh: T & T Clark; and Ann Loades, 2001, *Feminist Theology: Voices from the Past*, Cambridge: Polity Press.

10 Jorunn Oakland, 2004, *Women in Their Place: Paul and the Corinthian Discourse of Gender and Sanctuary Space*, Journal for the Study of New Testament Supplement Series 269, London: T & T Clark International, p. 66, who says of the house, as 'a place for men's work', that it was 'important for bonding and business'. See also Jerome H. Neyrey, 2003, 'Jesus, Gender, and the Gospel of Matthew', in Stephen D. Moore and Janice Capel Anderson (eds), *New Testament Masculinities*, Semeia Studies 45, Atlanta, GA: Society of Biblical Literature, pp. 43–66. The house was, however, also the space associated with women, who could function as patrons and leaders of house churches according to the research of Carolyn Osiek and Margaret Y. Macdonald with Janet H. Tulloch, 2006, *A Woman's Place: House Churches in Earliest Christianity*, Minneapolis, MN: Fortress. Also, Kathleen E. Corley, 1993, *Private Women, Public Meals: Social Conflict in the Synoptic Tradition*, Peabody: Hendrickson, indicates that the gendering of the *triclinium* was changing, even if only so slightly, during the Roman period in which the Lucan Gospel was written. There is also at issue here the question of how significantly practice needs to change before there is a shift in the sociocultural construction of gender.

11 While the word 'house'/*oikos* occurs in 31 verses of Luke's Gospel, there are only 4 explicit occasions when Jesus clearly enters a house: 7.36 is the first; 8.41, 51 (the house of Jairus), 14.1, when he dines again in the house of Pharisee; and 19.5–6, when he sojourns in the house of Zacchaeus.

12 Økland, *Women in Their Place*, p. 40. Økland goes on to say that 'the concept [her referent is to gender but the queer perspective would also see sexuality as being constructed] helps us to gather under one umbrella a variety of ancient assumptions and views of the origins of the world, cosmos, women, men, and to analyze their relation to each other and to the divine'.

13 See Neyrey, 'Jesus'.

14 The designation of 'sinner' is not new in the Lucan text. Peter calls himself a sinner following the great catch of fish (5.8) and there are a number of references to sinners: Jesus eats and drinks with them (5.30); they are the ones he has come to call (5.32); their behaviour is described negatively over against that required of those listening to the Sermon on the Plain (6.32, 33, 34); and Jesus cites the label given to him by the crowd, 'friend of tax collectors and sinners', just prior to this text (7.34). It is, therefore, an ambivalent category, designating relationship with and yet also distance from Jesus and will, therefore, function ambiguously for readers of this text. This is, however, the first time the label is laid upon an individual by the narrator and it is qualified by the phrase 'in the city'.

15 Corley, *Private Women, Public Meals*, p. 124, says that the combination of terms 'makes it more than likely that Luke intends for his readers to identify her as a prostitute, or more colloquially, a "streetwalker" or "public woman"'. Similarly Luise Schottroff, 1991, *Let the Oppressed Go Free: Feminist Perspectives on the New Testament*, Gender and the Biblical Tradition, Louisville, KY: Westminster/John Knox, pp. 150–5, considers the woman a prostitute and explores the implications of this for interpretation. Barbara E. Reid, 1996, *Choosing the Better Part? Women in the Gospel of Luke*, Collegeville, PA: Michael Glazier, pp. 116–21, questions too easy an acceptance of this designation, demonstrating that readers cannot simply assume that her sins known to others in the city are those of prostitution.

16 Oakland, *Women in Their Place*, pp. 39–75, who offers a very nuanced discussion of gender and space that is not possible here.

17 Corley, *Private Women, Public Meals*, pp. 60–1, discusses Cicero's portrayal of Clodia, the well-born woman from a Republican family, in his defence of M. Caelius Rufus with whom she was in a relationship for two years after her husband's death. She is depicted by Cicero as leading 'the life of a courtesan' and 'attending dinner parties with men who are perfect strangers . . . in the city, in the park' (Cicero, *Cael.* 44–9). Corley concludes that '[h]er behavior betrays that her true vocation is prostitution'.

18 Marcella Althaus-Reid, 2000, *Indecent Theology: Theological Perversions in Sex, Gender and Politics*, London: Routledge.

19 Avaren Ipsen, 2008, *Sex Working and the Bible*, London: Equinox, and '"In Memory of Her", the Prequel: Prostitutes, Aphrodite, and the Anointing of Jesus', Paper at the annual meeting of the Society of Biblical Literature, Washington DC (2006), p. 2.

20 This is a second-century CE text but is in the form of a collection of quotations from a wide range of much earlier Greek literature and hence points to practices and cultural constructions of that earlier time.

21 For a more extensive exploration of the materiality of the 'alabaster jar of perfumed ointment', see my article, 'Healing Ointment/Healing Bodies: Gift and Identification in an EcoFeminist Reading of Mark 14:3–9', in Norman Habel and Peter Trudinger (eds), 2008, *Exploring Ecological Hermeneutics*, Symposium Series 31, Atlanta, GA: Society of Biblical Literature.

22 Ipsen, *Sex Working and the Bible*, pp. 162–3.

23 Corley, *Private Women, Public Meals*, p. 78.

24 F. Scott Spencer, 2004, *Dancing Girls, Loose Ladies, and Women of the Cloth: The Women in Jesus' Life*, New York: Continuum, p. 112.

25 Elizabeth Grosz, 1994, *Volatile Bodies: Toward a Corporeal Feminism*, St Leonards: Allen & Unwin, p. 194, who says of bodily fluids that 'they seep, they infiltrate . . . they betray a certain irreducible materiality . . . assert[ing] the priority of

the body over subjectivity'. She goes on, however, to distinguish between bodily fluids, noting that 'tears take on a different psychological and sociological status than the polluting fluids that dirty the body'. Tears, which are commonly culturally associated with women and femininity, point to cleansing and purifying rather than polluting. This is significant in terms of the meaning that will emerge as this story unfolds.

26 S. E. Wood, 1999, *Imperial Women: A Study in Public Images, 40 B.C.–A.D. 68*, Mnemosyne: Bibliotheca Classica Batava, Leiden: Brill, especially the plates at the back; and C. L. Thompson, 'Hairstyles, Head-coverings, and St. Paul: Portraits from Roman Corinth', *Biblical Archaeologist*, 51 (1988), 99–115, who includes a depiction of a poorer woman with her hair bound up in a cap.

27 Charles H. Cosgrove, 'A Woman's Unbound Hair in the Greco-Roman World, with Special Reference to the Story of the "Sinful Woman" in Luke 7:36–50', *Journal of Biblical Literature*, 124 (2005), pp. 675–92.

28 Judith K. Applegate, 1988, '"And She Wet His Feet with Her Tears": A Feminist Interpretation of Luke 7.36–50', in Harold C. Washington, Susan Lochrie Graham and Pamela Thimmes (eds), *Escaping Eden*, The Biblical Seminar 65, Sheffield: Sheffield Academic Press, p. 80.

29 Ruth 3.4, 7 and 14 set up a play between feet and genitals that is evoked in the Lucan text by the sexual nature of the woman's actions. In this regard see Ellen van Wolde, 1997, 'Intertextuality: Ruth in Dialogue with Tamar', in Athalya Brenner and Carole Fontaine (eds), *A Feminist Companion to Reading the Bible: Approaches, Methods and Strategies*, Sheffield: Sheffield Academic Press, pp. 445–6; and Illano Rashkow, 1993, 'Ruth: The Discourse of Power and the Power of Discourse', in Athalya Brenner (ed.), *A Feminist Companion to Ruth*, Sheffield: Sheffield Academic Press, pp. 37–8, who cites Ex. 4.25; Judg. 3.24 and 1 Sam. 24.4 as evidence for the use of the term 'foot' as a euphemism for 'penis'.

30 'Erotic' is used here to connote love generally, together with the most typical implication being sexual love.

31 Jean-Louis Chrétien, 2004, *The Call and the Response*, trans. Anne A. Davenport, New York: Fordham University Press, pp. 84–5.

32 Chrétien, *Call and Response*, p. 85.

33 For a much more extensive exploration of the 'gift' aspect of this interaction, see my article, 'Healing Ointment/Healing Bodies'.

34 Bruce W. Winter, 2003, *Roman Wives, Roman Widows: The Appearance of New Women and the Pauline Communities*, Grand Rapids, MI: Eerdmans, p. 43.

35 This very significant insight for the interpretation of Luke 7.36–50 is discussed in detail in Evelyn R. Thibeaux, '"Known to be a Sinner": The Narrative Rhetoric of Luke 7:36–50', *Biblical Theology Bulletin*, 23 (1993), pp. 151–60. On the basis of the perfect passive of the verb, Thibeaux skillfully demonstrates (p. 152) that 'the woman's sins have been forgiven before she performs the loving actions in vv. 37–38' and that the words of Jesus are simply 'his offering her *assurance* (sure knowledge) that God has forgiven her sins and salvation is hers'.

36 See Ipsen, *Sex Working and the Bible*, whose work has this goal.

PART 3

The Dance of Grace: A Sacramental World

Chapters in this section reflect Ann's consistent concern with the possibility – and costs – of the embodied generosity that can result from a sacramental imagination. The result has been a serious engagement not only with the Christian tradition but also with the wider world, which is also viewed as a vitally important arena of divine activity and so justifiably labelled 'sacramental'.

16

An Experiment in Creativity

ALAN SUGGATE

The Arts and Recreation Chaplaincy, on whose management committee Ann for long served, was set up in 1968. It grew out of an idea for ministry that the Revd Bill Hall shared with Bishop George Snow of Whitby, who secured the support of Archbishop Donald Coggan of York and Bishop Ian Ramsey of Durham. Since 1974, it has been sponsored regionally by the Dioceses of York, Durham and Newcastle. Canon Hall was Senior Chaplain (mostly full time) right through to his retirement in 2005, and there have been a number of part-time Chaplains, including the Revd Robert Cooper. The Chaplaincy recognizes the creative gifts in all people and the integrity of the skills and insights of artists. It is also committed to the integrity of the Christian vision and story, and works on behalf of the Church, as part of its mission, to develop creative relationships between artists and Church. Its huge range of practical work has included pastoral ministry to travelling artists, commissions and exhibitions, and the monitoring of government proposals affecting the arts and culture. It stimulates a deeper theological exploration of the role of creativity in human life.[1]

The Releasing Creativity group sprang from a workshop on creativity run by Robert Cooper and Ellie Bowen at a half-day conference in the Durham Diocese in late 2003. Its first four meetings, held in mid 2004, were seminal.

It is not the intention of the group to attain practical proficiency in a range of creative activities, but rather to appreciate by encounter and activity, and to reflect on the experience. Christopher Leith is a renowned master of every aspect of puppetry, including the creation and animation of his own puppets. We were startled by a yapping dog: in Christopher's hands the simplicity of the material – no more than a mop head – conveyed a scottie to perfection, and we could readily suspend our disbelief. Then a beautiful girl moved through the group, greeting each one of us with a graceful curtsey. This was surely not manipulation: Christopher respectfully let her be, and she radiated a life of her own.

Christopher believes that the best puppetry is a perfect synthesis of sculpture and theatre. He encourages the quality of attention more usually associated with the enjoyment of painting, sculpture and music. The very simplicity and naivety of puppets can be highly expressive quite naturalistically. They appeal to the child in each of us, inviting a playfulness of imagination. Puppetry is often seen as a dogsbody art, yet Christopher demonstrated in moments that it scales the heights of human life. His work is indeed part of a wider movement towards the reawakening of the spiritual in western art, and he also draws on oriental theatre, especially the Japanese Noh tradition.

We were invited to pay respectful attention to quite humdrum things that we possessed. We were struck by the multiple associations they evoked. Thus my own watch evoked my childhood love of watches, the modern skills of the Swiss maker, Charles de Gaulle airport (where I bought it), Japanese friends, the gift of time, the fact of our mortality. This suggests a knowledge built of chains of association and diversely personal to each of us; it is quite different from the prevalent paradigm of knowledge as objective information.

Later in the day we worked individually on a mandala, and then collaboratively in groups of four. In silence various objects were laid in turn and the members modified the pattern until the mandala was agreed. We became keenly aware of the diverse sensibilities of the members.

We also tackled 'the critic on the shoulder'. Many members had crippling memories of art at school. Drawing had meant strict representation and our efforts had often been met with 'That's not very good, is it?' The task was to get on terms with the critic and transmute its negative mantra into positive creative energy.

The second session was with Ellie Bowen, who trained as a painter and has a special enthusiasm for and expertise in drawing. She developed several of the motifs of the first session. We were asked to handle a natural object with our eyes shut, thus forcing us to pay attention with our other senses. We were then given a vast range of materials with which to respond to that experience. Thus we became very conscious of the importance of a variety of media for expression. Later we were allowed to see the object and we shared with the group our feelings and thoughts during the experience. This sharing was to become a very important dimension of our work, since it enabled us to appreciate and accept not only our own reactions but the rich diversity among us.

The third session, 'Enjoying the World', was led by Robert Cooper himself. He has a deep interest in calligraphy but is primarily a photographer, with a particular interest in rhythms, patterns and line. Paul Klee once described drawing as 'taking a line for a walk'. Robert thinks of the photographer as responding to lines and patterns in nature, so many of his photographs are like being taken for a walk by a line. I have seen a Japanese man prepare himself for calligraphy by meditation. So too for photography. Robert quoted the Buddhist monk Thich Nhat Hanh: 'Nothing wonderful can happen to us unless we first stop.' We needed to match our breath to our steps, to enjoy the rhythm of our walking and breathing. We should say with our inward breath 'Here', with our outward breath 'Now', (in) 'Present moment', (out) 'Wonderful moment'. We should also be observant of whatever catches our attention, impose no particular expectations and allow ourselves to be surprised.

Then we entered into a meditation by Thomas Traherne, to the accompaniment of sacred music by Gerald Finzi. Traherne was gifted with the vision of the world as a 'mirror of infinite beauty', a beauty that elicited great joy. His was a 'reverent esteem' for the Creator. Moreover, he saw that everyone was heir to this vision, so that one should love all people so as to desire their happiness. The emphasis was on blessing God for the here and now and treasuring it in its very contingency. We surely touch here on the gratuitous.

Only then did we venture into the city of Durham with our cameras to look with fresh eyes and try to record on film whatever presented itself to us. Once again we were attending to the present fleeting moment, respecting and rejoicing in it. Then we returned to discuss our developed work. We speak of exposing the film, but we were conscious that it was we who had been exposed. It was not only that we had received several quizzical looks from bystanders. What we had seen was recorded on our hearts; it had become our treasure. We also speak of taking a picture, or capturing a scene, but it was rather that things had captured us. We were reminded that the monk Thomas Merton had spoken of being present to oneself and one's surroundings as spiritually vital for our humanity. It was good to do something for its own sake, to open one's eyes to live in the fulness of time, knowing that it is God's time. This contrasted so sharply with the prevalent view of time in modern society as a scarce commodity to be frantically used in utilitarian fashion for future goals.

Quite fortuitously the fourth session was suddenly left without its intended leader and the group spontaneously turned it into a review where all could speak for themselves. Overwhelmingly members expressed delight at the atmosphere created in the group. Many came from churches where imagination was sadly lacking. Here, however, they felt at home; affirmed and liberated to be themselves in their uniqueness and develop their creative potential. 'I maybe came here to learn about God; I'm now learning about me', said one member. That was in reality a recognition that her understanding of God was being re-imagined. We all felt that we had long been embarked on a journey. God alone knew us through and through and knew what our role was. The hawk may know its business by nature, but our journey was more unpredictable. As T. S. Eliot said, 'For us, there is only the trying. The rest is not our business.'[2] In our finitude we are vulnerable to the contingencies of nature and to the violence of humans (this was in the wake of the Beslan massacre); but creativity could transform destructive forces. Moreover, the journey was not only growth towards inward self-knowledge: it was also a journey together. Several of us had seen in Durham Cathedral Fenwick Lawson's sculpture *The Journey*, with six monks, all with different postures, moving along bearing the body of St Cuthbert.

We were thus able to determine our own forward movement as a group. From then on we welcomed several visiting artists: Simon Airey (a storyteller); Barbara Vellacott (who works with poetry); Ewan Clayton (a calligrapher, on whose AIDS icon we also later meditated); and Geoffrey Stevenson (a mime artist). However, several members felt so released by the sessions that they offered to take the risk and contribute their own skills and insights. So there were sessions on play, textiles, writing, mathematics, banner-making, dance, painting/chalks/collage and piano music. In almost all cases we combined exposure to creative practice with reflection. At regular intervals we conducted a review. This included a check not only on our own bearings, but also on our emerging spirituality; for example we made a study of Matthew Fox's *Creativity*.

The group also related itself to the region, supporting various creative activities. One of our members published a booklet distilling 20 years of experience of teaching in her parish church, and the group gave some advice beforehand and later considered her theology and its possible implications for the future practice of the group.[3] Also the Diocese held a conference in 2005 entitled 'Imagine', and the group took a leading role in a follow-up day that offered many avenues of expression. Moreover, in May 2006, several members took part in a retreat on Holy Island, led by Robert Cooper and Ellie Bowen, where about 16 people explored 'Being the Moment'.

As a member of the group I will attempt to convey some of the main insights of this diverse and growing process. I will also look beyond by drawing in my own reading and reflection. My conclusion is that our experience has strong affinities with some of the finest writing in the past and the present.

Creativity occurs in a responsive interplay between us humans and our environment. So who are we? I mean all human beings, of course, not just professional artists. More than any other creature, we humans have the capacity to apprehend the universe to which we are integral. To do so we need to be willing to stop and attend, to respect, to contemplate, to delight, to be surprised. This entails an investment of the whole person, with all the senses. If we do so, we are captivated, perhaps by the vastness and complexity of the whole, perhaps by the tiniest and simplest fragment, its pattern or line. And if we allow our imaginations to be stretched, then we find that we have a freedom to be more fully ourselves. We are empowered with a vital energy and it is from this that creative works spring.

Now, unless creative works are pure subjective fantasy, this carries crucial assumptions about the nature of the universe. It is surely a universe of great fascination and elicits an awe reminiscent of Traherne's. At any moment even the smallest thing seems capable of a huge variety of responses. Our session on painting/chalks/collage opened up three possible responses to an apple, saving us from the myopic tyranny of strict representation. Our mathematician also dispelled the critic, installed on our shoulder through unimaginative teaching in school, by encouraging us to play, to visualize in different ways, to be surprised and ask why. And our expert in textiles underlined the infinite variety of textures in nature and in cultures round the world to delight our sight and touch and trigger our efforts playfully to respond.

It is also surely a universe of amazing dynamism and diversity. It is continually evolving new forms and making itself other. There seems here to be a baffling blend of order and serendipity. Surely there is here a consonance with the picture given to us by the sciences – from the immense vistas of cosmology to the complex evolution of forms of life on our planet, and eventually human culture, brilliantly presented, for example, by David Attenborough in *Life on Earth*.[4]

This in turn raises questions about the kinds of knowledge entailed in creativity. Both in mathematics and in the sciences the most memorable moments are the great creative breakthroughs – the imaginative paradigm shifts that Thomas Kuhn highlighted decades ago. They are the lifeblood of the deductive and inductive methods. They refute the idea of a neutral objective world out there waiting to be charted by rational minds; for they clearly entail a form of profound personal engagement in the quest for truth.[5]

Rowan Williams develops Douglas R. Hofstadter's observation that consciousness is fugal: the following of one set of clues or triggers sets off another trajectory, generates another set of moves.[6] Williams claims that the whole human system of knowing is a 'spiral of self-extending symbolic activity; its relation to its environment is inescapably mobile, time-related'. One cannot abstract from the passage of time a set of objective stimuli and a correct reception of them by an inner free subject. Truthfulness unfolds in time. Basic here is 'a sense of the real as active rather than static, a mobile pattern whose best analogy is indeed musical, not mechanical'. What is enacted and seen in one place is lived again in another, so knowing involves more the re-enacting of a performance than the labelling of an object.

Art is an acute case of knowing in general, says Williams. The artist responds to the generative capacity of the world by creating a work that both has a life of its own and in turn generates more responses. (An example from the group might be a work by Chopin generating innumerable interpretations.) There seems to be gratuitous excess here, which forever escapes our control. The modern world is prone to take instrumental thinking as its paradigm, manipulating objects to solve practical problems. No wonder that the play involved in art then seems to be idle or arbitrary, an expression of will or emotion. In fact, artists testify to the hard work involved in creating, as they struggle with the logic of what is there and seek to bring into being a particular concrete work. To ensure the work's own integrity, the creator often needs to obey, to experience a drivenness, even a self-dispossession. There is a kind of necessity in the thing being made, underlying the contingency of a world that has been truthfully imagined. Respecting this integrity can be said to be the mode of the artist's love.

This has two further implications. First, creative work has its own integrity and should not be used to promote something external to it, whether some ideology or dogma, or to change the world for the better. Nor may one abstract from a work some philosophical concept or Christian 'message'. Conversely, religious art is corrupted if it merely illustrates a pre-existing theology.

Yet of course, second, genuine creative work does communicate, for it always occurs within a shared universe and our shared humanity. Barbara Vellacott led us to ponder Romeo's enchanted meeting at night with Juliet, and Simon Airey told us the story of the firebird. Stories engage teller and audience together in our common experience of good and evil. Moreover, they resist conversion into moral exhortation or religious dogma, often challenging us with questions and defying closure. The group was particularly conscious of the depth of our shared experiences as we respected each other's diverse perceptions and worked collaboratively in small groups, sharing each other's puzzlement and delight.

How then might creativity relate to God? There can certainly be no question of using human creativity to prove the existence of God. It is clear that creativity is a capacity of humans as such and their creative works have an integrity of their own. Yet surely by now we can at least see several consonances between creativity and the Christian faith. Moreover, it is very common for artists to reach for the word 'spiritual' to characterize their work. Christopher Leith is a good example. Their respectfulness for their materials, for the universe, and their sense of discipline, drivenness and even dispossession are at least akin to religious attitudes. It is a tragedy that such voices are often drowned out by aggressive Christians conducting a war on modernism and post-modernism, as if a wholly benighted modern culture should be replaced by a Christian counter-culture. The truth is that modern culture is ambiguous, and Christian orthodoxy ever a task of exploration. As Bernard Lonergan once said, dogmas are not battlements to be defended but large estates that await the full exploration of their hospitality. In particular, the relationship between faith and creativity remains sadly underdeveloped. For lack of space I will comment on two areas only among many.

The group's own search led to a study of Matthew Fox's *Creativity*, which is subtitled *Where the Divine and Human Meet*.[7] We agreed with much of his critique of modern culture: the reign of 'muzak', passive consumerism, unimaginative education. We agreed with him when he wrote, 'In place of fear and addiction to control, we need trust', and when he emphasized the necessity of taking risks. However, we were less impressed with his blanket condemnations of modernity, his rather romantic view of nature, and his simplistic antithesizing in a world of complexity: for example, rational is pitted against pre-rational, transcendence ditched in favour of immanence. True, God does not impose control on a chaotic universe, so warranting a host of dualisms and patriarchal dominance, but that does not justify pure immanence.

In his critique of Fox and others, Rowan Williams goes back to the classic doctrine of 'creation out of nothing'.[8] It is not an exercise of power, because it is not exercised *on* anything. As Aquinas said, 'creation' simply points you to existing reality in relation to a Creator. It is necessarily a status of dependence. But, unlike the insecure exchanges of creatures who need affirmation but fear manipulation, God has no needs and is free to be God without the process of struggle. 'Properly understood, this is the most liberating affirmation we could ever hear. I cannot be functional to God's being.' Creation is pure gift, and warrants our wholehearted trust.

So God desires to be God for what is not God – desires its pleasure and flourishing. This desire is groundless, in the sense that nothing other than God causes it. But it is not arbitrary, because there is nothing random in God. This leads us to think of God's own self as eternal identity in otherness, a self-affirming in giving away. Belief in creation from nothing is one reflective path towards understanding God as Trinity, intrinsic self-love and self-gift. Not everyone in the group may wish or be able to go this far, but it is surely consonant with our emerging spirituality.

Second, another path comes to mind, which picks up on our group's engagement with dance. There is a long tradition that holds together the created order, the incarnation and the sacraments. David Brown and Ann Loades entitle their introduction to their jointly edited book *The Sense of the Sacramental*, 'The Dance of Grace'.[9] They stress that the sacramental is often thought of as static: a changeless God in episodic relationship to a constantly changing world. They show that this is belied by our human experience. The sacraments are rather movements of grace in space and time towards our growth and transformation into closer conformity to Christ within the divine life. By the end of the introduction they are writing of the perichoresis within the Trinity as a dance of divine love. 'The freedom and exhilaration of the divine dance can be sacramentally experienced by us all.'

Sadly, the post of the Senior Chaplain lapsed on Canon Hall's retirement, as did that of the Assistant Chaplain in York Diocese, Francis Minay. Moreover, the post held by Robert Cooper in Durham Diocese was terminated from mid 2008. Under financial pressure, the Diocese decided that the Chaplaincy did not sufficiently fit into its priorities, and in any case the style of the Chaplaincy was deemed to be under debate. There are surely profound theological issues here, centring on forms of knowing and the relationship of the world, the arts and the faith. At least a group of ordinary Christians has meanwhile been developing a practice that is fully consonant with some of the finest spirituality and theology of the Christian tradition, past and present. Happily, the Episcopal Church of Scotland is deeply committed to chaplaincy to the arts, so we are searching for a way of uniting whatever continues based in the North-East of England with the new life evident in developments north of the border. It remains our hope that the Church of England will also perceive the vital importance of the arts for the faith and make a sustained supportive response.

Notes

1 For more details see the Chaplaincy's website: www.artschaplaincy.org.uk.

2 T. S. Eliot, 'East Coker', v, 18, in T. S. Eliot, *The Complete Poems and Plays of T. S. Eliot*, London: Faber & Faber, 1969, p. 182.

3 Meg Orr, 2005, *Creative Learning in the Local Church*, Spirituality Series S94, Cambridge: Grove Books Ltd.

4 David Attenborough, 1979, *Life on Earth*, London: Collins.

5 Thomas S. Kuhn, 1962, *The Structure of Scientific Revolutions*, Chicago, IL: University of Chicago Press. Michael Polanyi, 1958, *Personal Knowledge*, London: Routledge and Kegan Paul.

6 Rowan Williams, 2005, *Grace and Necessity: Reflections on Art and Love*, Harrisburg, PA and London: Morehouse-Continuum, pp. 135ff. On symbols, see James Hollis, 2000, *The Archtypal Imagination*, College Station: Texas A&M University Press. On music and life, see Daniel Barenboim's Reith Lectures for 2006.

7 New York: Tarcher-Penguin, 2004.

8 Rowan Williams, 2000, *On Christian Theology*, Oxford: Blackwell, chapter 5.

9 David Brown and Ann Loades (eds), 1995, *The Sense of the Sacramental: Movement and Measure in Art and Music, Place and Time*, London: SPCK, pp. 2–16. See also Michael Mayne, 2001, *Learning to Dance*, London: Darton, Longman and Todd; Michael Austin, 2005, *Explorations in Art, Theology and Imagination*, London: Equinox Publishing.

17

Giving Voice to the Ordinary

Theological Listening and the Mother Tongue

JEFF ASTLEY

Speaking in Tongues

In her powerful 1986 Commencement Address to the female students of Bryn Mawr College, the novelist Ursula Le Guin distinguished between two types of discourse.[1] On the one hand, she argued, there is the 'mother tongue' of the home: the conversational language mode that we learned from our mothers and speak to our children, 'the language stories are told in'. It is native to us, as the medium of the mutually empowering intercourse of communication and relationships. On the other hand, there is the 'father tongue', which is native to no one: an 'excellent dialect', 'immensely noble and indispensably useful', that we have to go to college to learn fully. This is the distancing language of the objectivity of scholarship; but it is also the discourse of social power and success (and self-gratification). This latter tongue is said neither to expect nor to hear any 'answer', for it is the one-way communication of the lecture, in contrast to the dialogical form of the mother tongue. Le Guin does not say that the father tongue alone uses the language of rational thought, but that it employs that species of reason (there are wider ones) that creates a space between the subject and the other.

It may seem odd that an audience of bright, high-achieving women should be told that the mother tongue is 'the language spoken by all children and most women'; that many men 'learn not to speak it at all'; and that it appears, from the standpoint of the father tongue, and its schools and colleges (which teach us not to listen to it), to be 'inaccurate, unclear, coarse, limited, trivial, banal . . . repetitive . . . earthbound, housebound'. It is the vulgar tongue of connections, of human communication and exchange; the language of relationship and conversation. In using such language, people are not striving to get something done but to maintain a relationship and to express what it means to its participants.

On average, women display more of the language that sustains associations (and therefore cultures), while men are more likely to utilize – and to prefer – the cooler medium of 'talking at' the other person, preferably about a topic that is deliberately analysed at arm's length and often to impart information or prove a point. Is that why women and girls routinely speak more than men and boys (except in public)? The sociolinguist Deborah Tannen distinguishes the *rapport-talk* of this female voice from the *report-talk* more common among men. In the former, 'emphasis is placed on displaying similarities and matching experiences'; whereas 'for most men, talk is primarily a means to preserve independence and negotiate and maintain status . . . by exhibiting knowledge and skill . . . more like giving a report than establishing rapport'.[2]

In developmental psychology, Carol Gilligan's critique of Laurence Kohlberg's theory of the development of moral judgement (initially based on interviews with males) employs the metaphor of a 'different voice'. This may be heard when females are allowed to speak about their moral decision-making and express a less separative and independent 'ethic of care'.[3] Mary Belenky and colleagues make much of this figure of speech, contrasting it with visual metaphors such as 'a point of view'. In their in-depth interviews with 135 women, 'women repeatedly used the metaphor of voice to depict their intellectual and ethical development . . . the development of voice, mind, and self were intricately intertwined'. They found a style of knowing that they labelled 'procedural', which engages in systematic analysis and evaluation of the views of others and exists in two distinct types. *Separate knowing* is the stereotypical academic mode of thinking, involving critical, impersonal argument that separates the knower from the object of her knowledge. By contrast, *connected knowing*, a voice that is 'harder to hear', is less adversarial in its epistemological stance; more empathetic, patient and particular; and grounded in personal experience. When connected knowers ask, 'Why do you think that?', they do not mean 'What were the steps in your reasoning?' but 'What circumstances led to that perception?' – an invitation to tell one's own story.[4] Although neither voice is exclusive to one particular sex, and most of the women interviewed could employ them both, a college education particularly favoured the separate voice and its more doubting and distanced critical accent.

Nicola Slee's reflections on women's faith development were based on interviews with over 30 female graduates, many of whom were highly theologically educated. Her summary of the general features of these women's 'faithing strategies' is of considerable interest.

> First, there is a dominance of concrete, visual, narrative and em-bodied forms of thinking over propositional, abstract or analytical thought. Whilst conceptual thought was not absent from the inter-views, there was a marked preference amongst the majority of the [women] for a more concrete language of metaphor, story or exem-plar as the vehicle for the expression of their faith experience. This seems particularly significant, given that the women in my study were an educational 'elite' and had ready access to more conceptual and analytical discourses, but nevertheless chose, on the whole, not to employ them. Second, there is a dominance of personalised and rela-tional forms of appropriating faith over abstract and impersonal means: faith was worked out in relation to the other, and this is demonstrated in the preference for metaphors emerging from personal life and relationship, the use of exemplars drawn from per-sonal life and narratives centred around issues of inclusion and exclu-sion from communities of belonging, as well as in the conversational nature of the interview itself . . . Third, each of the faithing strategies is rooted in a dynamic context of meaning-making in which the *process* of the interaction between interviewer and interviewee is as significant as the content. It was not only *what* was said, but the *way* in which it was said, and the para-linguistic features that surrounded and supported the narrative, which indicated the nature and style of the women's faith.[5]

Ordinary Theology

These accounts closely match my general portrait of 'ordinary the-ology', the reflective God-talk characteristic of those who have received no scholarly theological education.[6] With Rowan Williams, I acknow-ledge that men and women alike employ both of Le Guin's modes of speech, but add that the ordinary theology of both sexes tends to be voiced in the style of a mother tongue. (Men's ordinary theology some-times inclines to be more impersonal and abstract than that of women, but not to the same extent as the theology of the academy.) Ordinary theology employs non-combative, expressive, self-involved, essentially

conversational, warm words. It, too, is 'not dominated . . . by considerations of power and advantage'; what matters here is 'not victory but
keeping the exchange going'.[7] In such ways, ordinary theology lies
closer to the primary religious language of prayer and worship than to
the secondary articulations of academic theology; it is talk about God
that is only a knee away from talk with God.[8]

Some psychologists have researched the dimensions of human personality that society generally sees as distinguishing 'masculinity' and
'femininity'. These are aspects of a person, differences of psychological
type rather than biology, and may be present in varying degrees in both
men and women, as Ann Loades insists.[9] According to Sandra Bem's
gender orientation theory, masculinity and femininity are orthogonal
constructs, in that our position on one dimension is independent of our
position on the other; although men record higher *mean* scores on
masculinity and women on femininity. Bem's femininity scale includes
descriptives such as 'sympathetic', 'sensitive to the needs of others',
'understanding', 'compassionate' and 'warm'. These clearly relate to a
nurturing and helping disposition – the so-called 'three Cs' of care, concern and connection. Interestingly, quantitative studies have shown that
being religious is a function of (this reading of) gender orientation rather
than of being male or female, at least for adolescent and adult females.[10]

Can the theology that we first learn, while still beyond the influence of
the academy, be said to be in a similar way more 'feminine' in its
configuration, concerns and content, even for males?[11] It is certainly
more of a personal reflection and orientation; less technical, certain and
systematic; richer in story (including autobiography) and metaphor;
and more affective and conversational in tone. Its form is personal
anecdotal theology.[12] The term '*ordinary* theology' intends no dispar-
agement, connoting only that it is normal, regular, prevalent and general, in a way that academic theology is not.[13] Designating it as 'feminine'
is also not a criticism. It certainly does not imply that women are less
likely to succeed at academic theology. Material from women writers is
among the best academic theology, philosophy and ethics that I have
read. But I have also found that, in doing academic theology, women are
often more open to – and skilled at – drawing on their own and other
people's ordinary theology, their 'graced responses . . . however
inchoate and incoherent', as Ann has put it.[14] Yet men can do this too,
and some women do not attempt it.

What is the relationship between ordinary theology and its academic
cousin? I agree with those, including Karl Barth,[15] who hold that ordinary theology has a chronological priority over academic theology but

also continues alongside it. The relationship between the two can be traced in social communication across a church. One might think of ripples radiating across the water of a pond from a disturbance in the water, with the unruly, vigorous disturbances (metaphors) of ordinary theology merging into more constrained undulations (concepts and arguments) of systematics. But we may also understand the preposition 'alongside' to mark the relationship between these two theologies within an individual. The analogy of a tree is preferable here, where the visible outer layers of bark and branches are sustained and supported by the different tissues that lie hidden within. Similarly, inside every academic theologian there is an ordinary theologian: one that he or she is often trying to keep in. Is that task more difficult for the more strongly feminine female (or male) academic theologians, who must do their theology in the relatively alien tongue that Le Guin describes as the discourse of the academy? I don't know. What I would suggest is that many of the positive contributions of feminist theology result from a melding of the two voices, drawing on the strengths, resources and contexts of more ordinary theology.

Certainly, some have argued persuasively for less masculine ('phallic'?) styles of theological thinking and argumentation: less 'hardness' and 'strength', fewer 'penetrating points'. And many would claim as one gift of feminist theology 'its accentuation of the importance of theology as an embodied and passionate process, rather than one that is purely cerebral and logical'.[16] This includes a form of reasoning that is less authoritarian, abstract, rationalistic, objective and individualistic; and more tentative, holistic, social, particular (and therefore incarnational) – very like ordinary theology. Even philosophy of religion has lately turned from classic Enlightenment concerns for public evidence and universalizability towards

> more subtle and contestable categories of experience, trust, affectivity, subjectivity, interiority and mystical theology. Such categories are often, either implicitly or explicitly, founded in *women's* narratives of transformation; but even if they are not, they bear much of the freight of stereotypical femininity.[17]

Many feminist theologians argue that women's experience celebrates such 'ordinary' experiences as friendship, love, sex, embodiment, childbirth and nurture.[18] Prioritizing these emphases promotes a theology that is more inclusive, humane and integrated than is much academic theology. Mary Grey proposes the phrase 'sapiential yearnings' as a metaphor for feminist theological education, where the pattern is 'not of separation from the chaos and messiness of ordinary living, but of *immersion in it*.[19]

There is a strong affective dimension to many of these concerns. And religion is best understood through its affective, self-involving, passionate and committed side. It is visceral, a 'thinking with the blood'.[20] Jonathan Edwards held that 'true religion lies much in the affections', since the things of religion take hold of human souls 'no further than they affect them'.[21] To embrace a religion is to fall in love with it, in a personal, passionate embrace.[22] While men can do that too, it is the feminine side of human nature that is stereotypically associated with the more tender, compassionate, connecting emotions. This may be another partial explanation for the preponderance of female – and 'feminine' male? – churchgoers.

Theological Listening

There are several reasons for engaging in the study of ordinary theology.[23] Pragmatically, ministers' understanding of the actual beliefs and modes of thinking and believing of those in their care is important for their practice of Christian pastoral work, preaching and teaching. Clergy need to listen, and this should include a dimension of *theological* listening that acknowledges that people's often halting, unsystematic and poorly expressed words about their faith constitute a form of theology.

But there may be a more theological justification for engaging in this study, if a better understanding of the nature of ordinary theology can help us discover what it is about any theology that *works* for people. Theology must chime in with human experience, and ordinary theology includes insights and convictions that have been tested out in a wide range of circumstances by a very wide variety of people. The results of this testing process will only be available to the student of ordinary theology. It might help to earth our more 'extraordinary' academic theology.

A third reason for swallowing our contempt for ordinary theology is that much ordinary theology remains inside academic theologians. And just as a knowledge of children can teach adults about themselves, so a knowledge of another's ordinary theology can help those who engage in academic theology from a position of religious commitment better to understand some of the more hidden dimensions, motivations and connections of their own, more articulate theology.

In these different ways, it may be to our advantage to listen out for ordinary theology.

Learning Theology

How do these concerns impact on the practice of Christian theological education, including its broadest redaction as 'Christian formation', nurture or education, or 'education for Christian discipleship'?

Some reflections first on theological education in the academy. In a collection subtitled *The Vocation of the Theological Teacher*, Susan Simonaitis addresses the problem of teachers dominating the thinking of their students by her promotion of 'genuine conversation', in which teachers risk themselves, as a paradigm of teaching.[24] This classroom conversation is part of a greater conversation with the theological and religious tradition: the given, articulate content of the Christian faith. It is now commonplace to treat theological education and theological reflection as hermeneutical processes of dialogue or correlation. The two elements brought together in this relationship are the learner's reflections on her or his present life experience and the Christian heritage of faith: 'deliberately connecting our reflection on life to our religious heritage'.[25]

Parker Palmer portrays teachers as introducing their academic subject to the student as one introduces a friend, bestowing on the student the graceful blessing of sharing that friendship. He writes of one mentor:

> The passion with which he lectured was not only for his subject but also for us to know his subject. He wanted us to meet and learn from the constant companions of his intellect and imagination.[26]

Both conversations – with the tradition and with the learner – require an attentive and respectful listening. Paul Wadell writes:

> [W]e want students to listen to us because we want to share our truth with them; but students have their truth to share too, and perhaps the greatest respect we can extend to them is to take their truth seriously.[27]

In this context, we should note that the mother tongue is the discourse of conversation, and that sincere listening is particularly important if we are to unearth the depths of the ordinary theology of the newcomer to academic theological conversation, just as it is for uncovering the profundities of religious texts and arguments. Theology and ethics are subjects where 'students have their truth' as well. The (religiously agnostic) ethicist, Robert Nash, puts this point strongly:

> Each student's search for a usable and sustainable set of truths is always and everywhere an unpredictable, difficult, and challenging process. All students need our wise and sympathetic assistance, not our omniscient interference, in this demanding endeavor. Just the way we do, they, too, need to form their own sets of values in order to inform their own lives in their own best ways. . . .
>
> All of us, students and teachers alike, are genuine seekers in the realm of values, ethics, and religion. Few of us have made up our minds once and for all on these topics, and few of us ever will. Therefore, we need to treat each other with exquisite respect and sensitivity. Critique and feedback, when appropriate, ought always to come out of a framework of generosity and compassion, and always with an intention to make the other look good. Spirited and candid conversations aimed at getting to the heart of some sustainable truths are more likely to occur when students and teachers feel safe and supported enough to speak their truths-in-process to others . . . [T]he receptive mode of listening and responding in a seminar is far more effective than the attack mode of adversarial discourse.

He adds, 'all students need to tell their stories, not because their stories are right, but because they have a right to tell those stories'.[28] Because these others are human beings like ourselves, we have a duty to listen to their account of themselves. Their stories are (in Richard Rorty's categories) not epistemologically but *morally* privileged. In theology, I would hold, this extends to a duty to take seriously their theological accounts of themselves and their faith, however 'ordinary'. With such an attitude one may attain the pastoral ideal of teaching, whose 'energizing force should be that of love' for 'education should be an interaction of love'.[29]

Outside the seminar room, these rules apply most strongly. As Francis Oakley argues, we should pay more attention to 'the religious thinking of the broad masses of ordinary believers in society at large beyond the intellectual ramparts of the academy'.[30] It would be my contention that listening out for, and learning to hear and to respect, the reflective mother tongue of believers – their ordinary theology – is one significant way of doing this.

One last, different point. Galatians 3.28 is often quoted for its insight that the Church should transcend gender discriminations, since 'there is no longer male and female; for all of you are one in Christ Jesus' (NRSV). But the rest of the verse extends beyond this to forbid superficial judgements based on divisions of race, class or religion – 'no longer Jew or Greek . . . slave or free'. The disregarding of ordinary Christians and their ordinary theology, excommunicating them from doing theology on the grounds of their lack of academic prowess, is another form of the discrimination that women suffer. In all such cases, the basic sin is that of despising another as a consequence of judging their merit by irrelevant externals – equating intrinsic human or religious worth with some form of status or rank, nature or achievement.

Those who dare to follow Christ should know better.

Notes

1 Ursula K. Le Guin, 1989, *Dancing at the Edge of the World: Thoughts on Words, Women, Places*, New York: Grove, pp. 147–60.

2 Deborah Tannen, 1990, *You Just Don't Understand: Women and Men in Conversation*, London: Virago, p. 77.

3 Carol Gilligan, 1982, *In a Different Voice: Psychological Theory and Women's Development*, Cambridge, MA: Harvard University Press.

4 Mary Field Belenky, Blythe McVicker Clinchy, Nancy Rule Goldberger and Jill Mattuck Tarule, 1986, *Women's Ways of Knowing: The Development of Self, Voice and Mind*, New York: Basic Books, pp. 14–15, 18, chapter 6.

5 Nicola Slee, 2004, *Women's Faith Development: Patterns and Processes*, Aldershot: Ashgate, pp. 79–80, emphasis in original.

6 Jeff Astley, 2002, *Ordinary Theology: Looking, Listening and Learning in Theology*, Aldershot: Ashgate, pp. 57–86.

7 Rowan Williams, 2000, *Lost Icons: Reflections on Cultural Bereavement*, Edinburgh: T & T Clark, pp. 74–5.

8 Abby Day assesses the informal chatting at a weekly women's prayer group as a potent medium for theological work ('Doing Theology: An Empirical Study of a Women's Prayer Group', *Journal of Contemporary Religion*, 20 (2005), 343–56).

9 Ann Loades, 1987, *Searching for Lost Coins: Explorations in Christianity and Feminism*, London: SPCK, p. 99.

10 S. L. Bem, 1993, *The Lenses of Gender: Transforming the Debate on Sexual Inequality*, London: Yale University Press; Edward H. Thompson, 'Beyond the Status Characteristics: Gender Variations in Religiousness', *Journal for the Scientific Study of Religion*, 30 (1991), 381–94; Leslie J. Francis and Carolyn Wilcox, 'Religiosity and Femininity: Do Women Really Hold a More Positive Attitude Toward Christianity?', *Journal for the Scientific Study of Religion*, 37 (1998), 462–9. The use of Bem here is not invalidated by criticisms of her (early) appeal to 'androgyny' as an ideal (cf. Elaine Graham, 1995, *Making the Difference: Gender, Personhood and Theology*, London: Mowbray, pp. 19–22).

11 For both sexes, the mother has a greater influence on a child's attitude to Christianity than the father: William K. Kay and Leslie J. Francis, 1996, *Drift from the Churches: Attitude toward Christianity during Childhood and Adolescence*, Cardiff: University of Wales Press, chapter 6.

12 Jeff Astley, 2007, *Christ of the Everyday*, London: SPCK, p. xiii.

13 Astley, *Ordinary Theology*, pp. 47–52.

14 Ann Loades, 2004, 'Finding New Sense in the "Sacramental"', in Geoffrey Rowell and Christine Hall (eds), *The Gestures of God*, London: Continuum, p. 169.

15 Barth writes of a fragmentary, aphoristic, 'free' or 'irregular' dogmatics, which contrasts with the systematic enquiry of 'regular' or academic dogmatics. See Karl Barth, 1975, *Church Dogmatics*, 1/1, ET, Edinburgh: T & T Clark, pp. 277–8.

16 Ellen Clark-King, 2004, *Theology By Heart: Women, the Church and God*, Peterborough: Epworth, p. 24.

17 Sarah Coakley, 2005, 'Feminism and Analytic Philosophy of Religion', in William J. Wainwright (ed.), *The Oxford Handbook of Philosophy of Religion*, Oxford: Oxford University Press, p. 518, emphasis in original.

18 Elisabeth Moltmann-Wendel, 1994, *I am My Body: New Ways of Embodiment*, London: SCM Press.

19 Mary Grey, 1996, 'Sapiential Yearnings: The Challenge of Feminist Theology to Religious Education', in Jeff Astley and Leslie J. Francis (eds), *Christian Theology and Religious Education: Connections and Contradictions*, London: SPCK, pp. 78–94, emphasis added.

20 Don Cupitt, 2006, *The Old Creed and the New*, London: SCM Press, chapter 13.

21 Jonathan Edwards, 1961 [1746], *Select Works, Volume III: Treatise Concerning the Religious Affections*, London: Banner of Faith, pp. 27–53.

22 Astley, *Ordinary Theology*, pp. 27–36; John Cottingham, 2005, *The Spiritual Dimension: Religion, Philosophy and Human Value*, Cambridge: Cambridge University Press, pp. 8–13, 80–8.

23 Astley, *Ordinary Theology*, pp. 143–62; Clark-King, *Theology by Heart*, pp. 23–5.

24 Susan M. Simonaitis, 2002, 'Teaching as Conversation', in L. Gregory Jones and Stephanie Paulsell (eds), *The Scope of Our Art: The Vocation of the Theological Teacher*, Grand Rapids, MI: Eerdmans, pp. 104–6.

25 Patricia O'Connell Killen and John De Beer, 1995, *The Art of Theological Reflection*, New York: Crossroad, p. 68. See also Thomas H. Groome, 1980, *Christian Religious Education: Sharing Our Story and Vision*, San Francisco, CA: Harper and Row, part IV; David Durston, 1989, 'Theological Reflection: Definitions, Criteria', *British Journal of Theological Education*, pp. 3, 32–9; Laurie Green, 1990, *Let's Do Theology: A Pastoral Cycle Resource Book*, London: Mowbray, chapter 5; Don S. Browning, 1991, *A Fundamental Practical Theology: Descriptive and Strategic Proposals*, Minneapolis, MN: Fortress, chapters 2, 3, 9.

26 Parker J. Palmer, 1998, *The Courage to Teach: Exploring the Inner Landscape of a Teacher's Life*, San Francisco, CA: Jossey-Bass, p. 137.

27 Paul J. Wadell, 2002, 'Teaching as a Ministry of Hope', in Jones and Paulsell, *Scope*, p. 132.

28 Robert J. Nash, 2002, *Spirituality, Ethics, Religion, and Teaching: A Professor's Journey*, New York: Peter Lang, pp. 98–9, 189.

29 Nicholas P. Wolterstorff, 2002, *Educating for Life: Reflections on Christian Teaching and Learning*, Grand Rapids, MI: Baker Book House, p. 105; see also Jeff

Astley, 2005, 'Christian Teaching, Learning and Love: Education as Christian Ministry and Spiritual Discipline', in Jeff Astley, Leslie J. Francis, John Sullivan and Andrew Walker (eds), *The Idea of a Christian University: Essays in Theology and Higher Education*, Carlisle: Paternoster, pp. 132–46.

30 Francis Oakley, 'Concluding Reflections on the Lilly Seminar', in Andrea Sterk (ed.), 2002, *Religion, Scholarship, and Higher Education: Perspectives, Models, and Future Prospects*, Notre Dame, IN: University of Notre Dame Press, p. 244.

18

The Eucharistic Body in Art and Literature

DAVID JASPER

At each new celebration of the Eucharist, and in obedience to the divine command, the body is displayed, eaten and consumed. The words are unequivocal – *this* is my body, *this* is my blood in the species of bread and wine, though there is a clear reference to the physical body of Jesus present before his disciples at their last supper together, now to be ingested by them as an act of remembrance. It is a performance and a display, the materials shockingly held up for all to see. Tertullian's sarcasm against the naivety of pagan critics cannot reduce the shocking fact:

> No doubt [the Christian] would say, 'You must get a child still very young who does not know what it means to die, and can smile under your knife; and bread to collect the gushing blood . . . Come, plunge your knife into the infant . . . Or, if that is someone else's job, simply stand before a human being dying before it has really lived . . . Take the fresh young blood, saturate your bread with it, and eat freely.'[1]

At the heart of the mystery there is an irreducible violence and a necessary scandal of the flesh, an insistent reminder that the body cannot be removed from thought, and that human history, red in tooth and claw, swims in the river of blood from its torn and shredded victims, torn by hatred and torn by desire. In *The Ideology of the Aesthetic*, Terry Eagleton remarks that 'Few literary texts are likely to make it nowadays into the new-historicist canon unless they contain at least one mutilated body. A recovery of the importance of the body has been one of the most precious achievements of recent radical thought.'[2] But there has to be more to mutilation than that, perhaps especially in an age of bodily dismemberment from the singular to the genocidal. To move from the

Passion to the eucharistic is to enact a transfer of the broken body from the meaningless to the mythic, the ritualized and the liturgical – no less scandalous or terrible but at least, and at the very least, a gesture towards wholeness.

Christianity, perhaps inevitably given its focus on the cross, has always been ambivalent in its attitude towards the body. As Ippolit, a character in Dostoevsky's *The Idiot* (1869), contemplates Holbein the Younger's painting *The Body of the Dead Christ in the Tomb*, he reflects that 'if, on the eve of the crucifixion, the Master could have seen what he would look like when taken from the cross, would he have mounted the cross and died as he did?'[3] Could even Christ himself have born to look upon the cadaver, or asked this of his disciples? From the body, which suffers such corruption, there is the temptation to flee to the bliss of the disembodied soul, but always and ever a return to that deep, elusive claim that 'in my flesh shall I see God' and an insistence upon the scandalous physicality of the word made flesh. Even within the deepest recesses of the practice of contemplative prayer the body is acknowledged, though tranquil and not on display, but held in balance and ready to acknowledge its fleshly integrity with the soul. In George Eliot's *Adam Bede* (1859), the Methodist preacher Dinah Morris sits by her bedroom window as she prepares to leave the community to whom she has ministered.

> And the pressure of this thought soon became too strong for her to enjoy the unresponding stillness of the moonlit fields. She closed her eyes, that she might feel more intensely the presence of a Love and Sympathy deeper and more tender than was breathed from the earth and sky. This was Dinah's mode of praying in solitude. Simply to close her eyes, and to feel herself enclosed by the Divine Presence; then gradually her fears, yearning anxieties for others, melted away like ice-crystals in a warm ocean.[4]

The description of Dinah in contemplation is profoundly physical, albeit still and silent, a movement not away from the body but rather into it and into a sense of feeling that remains responsive to the physical metaphors of warmth and cold. It involves a movement towards presence so that within her flesh Dinah comes to 'see God', though never experiences merely a thought, never abstract or abstracted. If James Joyce's Mr Duffy always 'lived at a little distance from his body', the very opposite is true of Dinah Morris and all true contemplatives. They live entirely within them. Professor Loades herself, of course, has clearly pointed out the limitations of my proposal in her description of what she calls a 'deadly form of Christianity' in the anorexic body of someone like Simone Weil, her (self) sacrifice a problem for theology in her devouring of her own flesh, a problem in Christian asceticism for women 'so far as women can imitate a male saviour':

> The problem is that whilst in one sense as no-males they cannot be *in persona Christi*, they can be *'in persona Christi'* all too successfully if the Christ they imitate is the dead or dying Christ, rather than the Christ of the resurrection.[5]

Now while I take this entirely seriously, at the same time I want to suggest a possible way beyond (even for a Simone Weil), for this deepest eucharistic presence is always, at the same time, also an absence, the displayed body – *Corpus Domini nostri* – too much to bear, crossing the boundaries of body and spirit. Graham Greene catches this quixotic limit most movingly in the final pages of *Monsignor Quixote* (1982), in which the holy fool of a priest, approaching death, celebrates the sacrament without bread and wine:

> and with no hesitation at all he took from the invisible paten the invisible Host and his fingers laid the nothing on his tongue. Then he raised the invisible chalice and seemed to drink from it. The Mayor could see the movement of his throat as he swallowed.[6]

Can we ever do more than this even with the fragment of bread and the drop of wine, touching for a moment the deepest interiority of the body – our bodies – with the divine absent presence in an act of pure remembrance? And Greene's crazy, dying priest passes on from this life, like Walter Pater's Marius in the peace of a 'kind of candid discontent',[7] with the mystic bread on his lips, the awful and necessary opposite being the suffering flesh of Holman Hunt's *Scapegoat* (1854), hovering between life and death in the salt flats of the Dead Sea, the bedraggled image of the scandalous flesh that sees things to their bitter end. The scapegoat is the harsh reality, the reverse side, of the body removed; that which slips down Monsignor Quixote's throat unseen, brings him to puzzlement, his candid discontent, and becomes both his end and his consummation.

The scandalous body removed and devoured – a body so terrible that we wonder if Christ himself would have asked us to endure the sight of it had he known – is also the body remembered in its 'unaccountable darkness'.[8] And thus to remember is no passive thing, but a recreation in the whole of, and at the depths of, our being, a presencing as in Dinah Morris and her body's call to prayer. Not only the liturgy of the Eucharist, or the Passover festival, but all literature echoes with the hauntings of anamnesis, of the eternal presence of that which is most deeply absent. The most deeply sensuous art is the most interior, almost nothing on the surface but that tingling to the touch, unforgettable and almost forgotten.

> Every four days she washes his black body, beginning at the destroyed feet. She wets a washcloth and holding it above his ankles squeezes the water onto him, looking up as he murmurs, seeing his smile. Above the shins the burns are worst. Beyond purple. Bone.
>
> She has nursed him for months and she knows the body well, the penis sleeping like a sea horse, the thin tight hips. The hipbones of Christ, she thinks. He is her despairing saint. He lies flat on his back, no pillow, looking up at the foliage painted onto the ceiling, its canopy of branches, and above that, blue sky.[9]

The body in Ondaatje's *The English Patient*, unknown and unrecognizable is half-brother to Holbein's *Dead Christ*, but for the smile. It is a body remembered and still known in its sexual potential as the woman, like those who washed the body of their dead Master, nurses her 'despairing saint'. But at the same time it is a body almost entirely interior. Is not sainthood a condition of despair? The man murmurs and smiles, and his weakness and its mystery, after he fell burning into the desert, is the still centre of Ondaatje's narrative. Even he does not know who he is, but his weakness, like every genuine weakness, proves to be above all strength as he draws the woman's care down upon him.[10] Ondaatje's later novel, *Anil's Ghost* (2000), continues the theme of embodied haunting, the stretching out of the forgotten and half-remembered, in our own lives and in the lives of others both known and unknown, and the insistence of 'this sweet touch from the world'.[11] And so the scandalous, exhibited body – *this* is my body – is interiorized, removed and remembered and always present. It is the very opposite of kitsch, whose objects and themes are instantly recognizable and identifiable,[12] and the very opposite of the obscene – for its terrible beauty, as in Grünewald's great image of the crucifixion, finally draws us to its deepest consolations. Even in its scandal it effects a transfiguration that is the obverse of the transformation of the beautiful and debauched body of Zola's Nana, finally a Venus decomposing and for whom there is no kind nurse and only utter solitude: '"Ah, she's changed, she's changed," murmured Rose Mignon, the last to leave.'[13] But there is more than one way to change.

Why transfiguration – a world-changing in this show of fractured body and blood? It is precisely because, at this very deepest moment of embodied, human suffering in absolute pain of body and spirit, it is possible to go no further and this alone guarantees – something – within the utter despair uncontaminated by false hope or the consolation of illusions. Art and literature continue to touch upon a barely conscious depth that Christian consciousness, nursed by theology, can barely comprehend in its narratives of resurrection and ascension, for it is only in a radical reversal of such consciousness, in an acknowledgement of the utter scandal of the body, that sacramental presence can begin.[14] Truly, the celebration of the sacrament is a descent into hell whose darkness cannot comprehend the light that shines in the flesh. The body displayed is a broken body, a mutilation that is at the same time a regaining of the mythic and the ritual. But it begins only in true despair and a necessary deconstruction of all that is dearly and most desperately preserved. Think only of the dismantling of the patterns of faith in the poetry of Wilfred Owen with its piercing slants of light shed upon the bodies of young soldiers mangled by war. Here is not the dismemberment that is celebrated in our consumerist entertainment culture, the easy body counts of popular cinema that dull to extinction our *anagnorisis*, our shock of recognition, our possibility of reversal.[15] On 4 July 1918, Owen wrote to Osbert Sitwell of his experience as an officer training young men to fight at the front:

> For 14 hours yesterday I was at work – teaching Christ to lift his cross by numbers, and how to adjust his crown; and not to imagine his thirst till after the last halt. I attended his Supper to see that there were not complaints; and inspected his feet that they should be worthy of the nails. I see to it that he is dumb, and stands at attention before his accusers. With a piece of silver I buy him every day, and with maps I make him familiar with the topography of Golgotha. [16]

The effect of one narrative placed upon another is almost unbearable – the Passion narrative already overlaid by millennia of ritual and theology, its outcome celebrated in the guarantees of Easter symbolism: the narrative of the young troops another story entirely, conveyed through Owen's heavy irony in his role as Judas, a national hero. Or are the narratives so very different? What makes these bodies of young men, separated by nearly 2,000 years of bloodshed, and eucharistic celebration, so different? At least Owen takes us back to the shock of recognition and the insistent presence of the body, so that even in its absence, in the 'mock' Eucharist of Monsignor Quixote, it makes his beating heart cease. Into every Eucharist we die. And the suffering of the mutilated body can never be justified. In Pat Barker's novel *Regeneration* (1991), the first of her trilogy of novels on World War One, the army psychologist W. H. R. Rivers witnesses the total breakdown of a young man, of no particular virtue, who has come back utterly shell-shocked from the Front, his mind and body in a state of complete collapse.

> His body felt like a stone. Rivers got hold of him and held him, coaxing, rocking. He looked up at the tower that loomed squat and menacing above them, and thought, *Nothing justifies this. Nothing, nothing, nothing.* Burns' body remained rigid in his arms. Rivers was aware that if it came to a fight he might not win. Burns was terribly emaciated, but he was also thirty years younger. His surrender, when it came, was almost shocking. Suddenly his body had the rag-doll floppiness of the newborn. He collapsed against Rivers and started to shake, and from there it was possible to half lead, half push him out of the moat and up on to the relative safety of the path.[17]

It is another scene of nurturing, almost reminiscent of a *Pietà*, but yet a moment of utter negativity. No great cause, no national security, *nothing* justifies the sufferings of this ordinary young man: what then of the sufferings of another young man who died at about the age of 30 in the most ghastly way imaginable? What justifies such mutilation of body and soul: the salvation of the world? Perhaps it is only that at this meeting point of all realities, where alone true ritual is born and where every narrative is deconstructed, and only thereby is any gesture of wholeness possible.

But every saint is a despairing soul. R. S. Thomas, in his early poem 'The Priest', picks his way through an uncaring, uncomprehending, superficial parish.

> 'Crippled soul', do you say? Looking at him
> From the mind's height; 'limping through life
> On his prayers. There are other people
> In the world, sitting at table
> Contented, though the broken body
> And the shed blood are not on the menu.'
>
> 'Let it be so', I say. 'Amen and amen.'[18]

Thomas' poem is another pattern placed upon the eucharistic narrative, a further realization of human identity with the broken, present body, unbearable save for the insight of St Athanasius, developed in the theology of St Maximus the Confessor, that Christ became like us in order that we might become like him in the deified flesh.[19] But the suffering and the scandal remain – absolutely.

And perhaps there is a further scandal that we have barely even touched upon as yet. For this scandalous body – so blatantly displayed in the insistent 'this is my body', and in the 'wildly counter-evidential, counter-cultural claim'[20] that 'in my flesh I shall see God' – is also a gendered, decaying body, endlessly unsettled by its own eroticism and its ageing processes and the differences between male and female. If excess and the exploitation of the differences offer endless possibilities to the darker elements in human nature, even sheer frankness can be hard to contemplate in *this* body in all its disturbing qualities. D. H. Lawrence's *Lady Chatterley's Lover* (1928), described by Richard Hoggart in the Introduction to the Penguin edition as *not* a dirty book, but as 'clean, serious and beautiful',[21] may seem almost unreadable and even turgid, but at least there is a certain honesty in its attempt to unravel the language of sex from its late Romantic and Edwardian pseudo-mysticism and to 'represent sexuality as a cognitive activity'.[22] Lawrence does not deflect our gaze. Much later, John Updike, in his novel *Seek My Face* (2002), offers an uncompromising image of ageing flesh in the central character of Hope Chafetz, sitting alone in her underwear and wondering at the decay of her own body, hardly able to own it: 'The swelling of arthritis in a number of joints has caused the top segments of her fingers to deviate from the straight. She marvels that this gnarled crone's hand is hers.'[23] The contemplation of even our own bodies can be unbearable, because of what they signify, because of their reality. Or it might be simply the difficulty of deviation from a norm into which a gendered element has been introduced, a shift away from accepted cultural or social patterns. Thus Eric Gill's 1922 woodcut, *The Nuptials of God*, shows what appears to be a haloed female form pressing herself upon the crucified Christ, thereby herself crucified even as she appears to kiss the figure before her. This suggestive and elusive image sets up counter-currents in its bodily display, its intrusion into our established patterns of response to the image of the cross. The confusion to such established patterns has been taken in a different direction by Margaret Miles in her essay 'The Virgin's One Bare Breast: Female Nudity and Religious Meaning in Tuscan Early Renaissance Culture'.[24] She studies a theme in fourteenth-century Tuscan paintings of the Virgin Mary with one breast exposed, feeding the infant Jesus, arguing that the messages conveyed by the image have a complex history beyond, but never wholly distinct from, bodily exposure. Clearly the theme of the nurturing and sustaining mother is predominant, and Miles argues that the image was not associated with eroticism in the mind of the medieval viewer.

However, and with further reference to Leo Steinberg's now classic text *The Sexuality of Christ in Renaissance Art and Modern Oblivion* (second edition, 1996), it is clear that such images are actually rarely unambiguous or entirely innocent, as is suggested by the Renaissance convention of portraying the covered side of Mary as entirely flat and the exposed breast as a rather artificial cone that appears as an appendage rather than as part of the woman's actual body.[25] At best there seems to be a certain coyness here. The point is that, however much theology and its themes intervene (and one may add further curious images in western art of a nurturing and lactating Jesus and paintings of Mary squirting life-giving milk from her breast into the mouths of St Jerome and other skinny, isolated and ascetic saints), images of the body are invariably complex and have the power to disturb in more ways than one. However removed, interiorized, remembered, the displayed body remains insistently *there*, its consumption in the Eucharist a scandal, albeit a necessary and even salvific one, in more ways than one.

Let us pursue Margaret Miles' theme a little further in the context of two disturbing though rather beautiful moments in modern fiction. At the end of John Steinbeck's novel *The Grapes of Wrath* (1939), Rose of Sharon, having given birth to a stillborn child, feeds a dying man with her milk, the man awed by what is offered to him. The final scene is another and complex *Pietà*.

> She moved slowly to the corner and stood looking down at the wasted face, into the wide, frightened eyes. Then slowly she lay down beside him. He shook his head slowly from side to side. Rose of Sharon loosened one side of the blanket and bared her breast. 'You got to,' she said. She squirmed closer and pulled his head close. 'There!' she said. 'There.' Her hand moved behind his head and supported it. Her fingers moved gently in his hair. She looked up and across the barn, and her lips came together and smiled mysteriously.[26]

There are elements of seduction as well as nurturing, reminiscent of George Herbert's great eucharistic poem 'Love Bade Me Welcome'. Above all there is a showing and a feeding on the body of the girl – an eating and a drinking. The same image is explored more scandalously, but no less movingly in Guy de Maupassant's short story 'Idyll', in which a wet nurse, trapped on a train with breasts strained to the full with milk, feeds a poor peasant man in her carriage. She thanks him for the relief he has given her, but her gift to him is even greater, even life itself: 'And he gratefully replied: "It's me as has to thank you, Madame. I hadn't had a thing to eat for two days."'[27] And yet there is something deliberately illicit in de Maupassant's telling of the story. The young man remarks that 'That's put new life into me', and somehow this ingesting of forbidden yet freely offered nutrition has a knowing complexity that is at once deeply sacred and utterly scandalous, even blasphemous.

Strangely, however, the literary readings allow for the human freedom proposed by Professor Loades in her reading of Kant's 'authentic theodicy', embracing a truthfulness which is 'a sought-for quality of mind exposed to temptations, entailing many a sacrifice, to be guarded and cultivated earlier than any other virtue'.[28] But they also prompt what Ann has called in her description of feminist theology, a 'challenge [to the Christian tradition] from within', and a recognition that often the most radical challenges are from that deep, interior place within the faith.[29]

'This is my body . . . this is my blood.' The words remain insistently, showing and inviting to the even deeper horror of consuming the elements, thus becoming one with the flesh incarnate, dismembered and resurrected. Some critical focus has been given in recent years on the eucharistic presence in the writings of poets within the English tradition from John Donne through Gerard Manley Hopkins and up to Geoffrey Hill and R. S. Thomas.[30] But the study remains resolutely *wordy*, forgetting the power of the image and the real presence of a body that is infinitely complex, incorporating and transgressing modes of discourse, offering itself as food to the eyes and to the mouth, and that remains present (as bodies do) even and perhaps especially in its physical absence. In his now standard work, *The Power of Images* (1989), David Freedberg reviews the history of both idolatry and iconoclasm, examining the power of images to disturb so that we frantically embrace them and equally frantically destroy them before they destroy us. But at the heart of the Eucharist is more than an image. It is the word made flesh, a shift towards an infinitely complex territory of embodiment that we share with the incarnate Word. When Jesus showed his disciples his body in the simple forms of bread and wine, he showed them not less than everything, and the cost, which was all. But turn the image around, into the notion of the flesh made word.[31] Is that not what we more often do, and it is a move both more simple and ultimately infinitely more dangerous. For to trap the body in words and to designate the flesh in a word is to define and limit it, to hold it for our own purposes and within the limits of our own definitions: bodies become the slaves of the words ascribed to them – defining both our moral response and the roles expected of them. The body is clad in the voluminous folds of language, for good and usually for ill, and becomes the victim of its defining rhetoric. Bodies are granted stability – true – but framed as metaphors of power and enslavement. But to show the body of the word made flesh, however, and to invite its ingestion, is to enter a far more complex and liturgical world of presence and absence, of the unity of body and soul beyond the mere constructions of language, and yet still capable of utterance in a language that is strange and even violent beyond all collective intolerances and mysterious beyond all comprehension – but entirely familiar and inwardly known, yet always as if for the first time.

Notes

1 Tertullian, *Apology*, 8. Quoted in Elaine Pagels, 2003, *Beyond Belief: The Secret Gospel of Thomas*, London: Macmillan, p. 18.

2 Terry Eagleton, 1990, *The Ideology of the Aesthetic*. Quoted in Robert Detweiler, 1990, 'Torn by Desire: Sparagmos in Greek Tragedy and Recent Fiction', in David Jasper (ed.), 1993, *Postmodernism, Literature and the Future of Theology*, London: Macmillan, p. 60.

3 Quoted in Julia Kristeva, 1989, *Black Sun: Depression and Melancholia*, trans. Leon S. Roudiez, New York: Columbia University Press, p. 109.

4 George Eliot, 1859, *Adam Bede*. Quoted in Martin Laird, 2006, *Into a Silent Land: The Practice of Contemplation*, London: Darton, Longman and Todd, p. 31.

5 Ann Loades, 1987, *Searching for Lost Coins: Explorations in Christianity and Feminism*, London: SPCK, p. 43. See also, Ann Loades, 1984, 'Simone Weil – Sacrifice: A Problem for Theology', in David Jasper (ed.), 1984, *Images of Belief in Literature*, London: Macmillan, pp. 122–37.

6 Graham Greene, 1983, *Monsignor Quixote*, London: Penguin, p. 250.

7 Walter Pater, 1885, *Marius the Epicurean*, New York: New American Library, p. 283.

8 Geoffrey Hill, 1959, 'Canticle for Good Friday', in *For the Unfallen*, London: Andre Deutsch, p. 39.

9 Michael Ondaatje, 1993, *The English Patient*, London: Picador, pp. 3–4.

10 Compare Austin Farrer's sermon for Christmas Day, 'A Grasp of the Hand': 'We will not lift our hands to pull the love of God down to us, but he lifts his hands to pull human compassion down upon his cradle.' *Said or Sung*, London: The Faith Press, 1960, p. 35. The comparison with Ondaatje's novel is intended to be disturbing.

11 Michael Ondaatje, 2002, *Anil's Ghost*, London: Picador, p. 307.

12 See Tomas Kulka, 1996, *Kitsch and Art*, University Park, PA: Pennsylvania State University Press, p. 33.

13 Emile Zola, 1871, *Nana*, trans. George Holden, London: Penguin Classics, 1972, p. 469.

14 See, Thomas J. J. Altizer, 1970, *The Descent into Hell: A Study of the Radical Reversal of the Christian Consciousness*, Philadephia and New York: J. B. Lippincott Company.

15 See Detweiler, *Torn by Desire*, p. 75.

16 From the Introduction to *The Collected Poems of Wilfred Owen*, by C. Day Lewis, 1963, London: Chatto & Windus, p. 23.

17 Pat Barker, 1992, *Regeneration*, London: Penguin, p. 180.

18 R. S. Thomas, 1986, *Selected Poems, 1946–1986*, Newcastle: Bloodaxe Books. Used by permission.

19 See, Adam G. Cooper, 2005, *The Body in St. Maximus the Confessor: Holy Flesh, Wholly Deified*, Oxford: Oxford University Press.

20 Margaret R. Miles, 2005, *The Word Made Flesh: A History of Christian Thought*, Oxford: Blackwell, p. 391.

21 Richard Hoggart, Introduction to D. H. Lawrence, 1961, *Lady Chatterley's Lover*, London: Penguin, p. v.

22 Peter Brooks, 1993, *Body Work: Objects of Desire in Modern Narrative*, Cambridge, MA: Harvard University Press, p. 261.

23 John Updike, 2003, *Seek My Face*, London: Penguin, p. 272.

24 In Susan Rubin Suleiman (ed.), 1985, *The Female Body in Western Culture: Contemporary Perspectives*, Cambridge, MA: Harvard University Press, pp. 193–208.

25 Miles, 'The Virgin's One Bare Breast', p. 204.

26 John Steinbeck, 1951, *The Grapes of Wrath*, London: Penguin, p. 416.

27 Guy de Maupassant, 1971, *Selected Short Stories*, trans. Roger Colet, London: Penguin Classics, p. 264.

28 A. L. Loades, 1985, *Kant and Job's Comforters*, Newcastle-upon-Tyne: Avero, p. 149.

29 Ann Loades, 1990, *Feminist Theology: A Reader*, London: SPCK, p. 8.

30 See, for example, Eleanor J. McNees, 1992, *Eucharistic Poetry: The Search for Presence in the Writings of John Donne, Gerard Manley Hopkins, Dylan Thomas and Geoffrey Hill*, Lewisburg, PA: Bucknell University Press.

31 See Helena Michie, 1987, *The Flesh Made Word: Female Figures and Women's Bodies*, New York and Oxford: Oxford University Press.

19

Grace Dances
Liturgy and Embodiment

STEPHEN BURNS

Liturgists have not always been sensitive to what sacramental theologian Louis-Marie Chauvet calls 'the concreteness of the body', through which, he claims, 'the truest things in our faith occur'.[1] This is despite the way in which worship might, if we echo James F. White, be described as 'speaking and *touching* in Christ's name':[2] washing the body in baptism, laying on hands in prayer for healing or in confirmation or ordination, and not least eating and ingesting into the body the elements of Holy Communion – each in their own way make the point. Yet much liturgical study remains preoccupied with words, and especially with texts: a problem to which Ann Loades has herself pointed.[3] She highlights the need for greater concern than what Robert Hovda castigates as textual critics 'dissecting, reducing, analyzing, [and] abstracting'[4] texts, and at the very least points to the importance of looking at both words *and* gestures, and the possibilities of their interplay and alliance. My purpose in this essay is to highlight some trajectories in Ann's work that I think can help liturgists expand their attention to embodiment in liturgical celebration, and to honour Ann in doing so. In the first part of the chapter, I look at how some of Ann's feminist convictions play out in worship, making an important contribution to feminist reflection on Christian assembly. In the second part, I explore Ann's expansive understanding of sacramentality.

Since the mid 1990s and the publication of the companion volumes co-edited with David Brown,[5] Ann has written a considerable amount about aspects of worship.[6] Most of this writing approaches worship, as does Chauvet, through the optic of sacramental theology,[7] although, as Siobhàn Garrigan reminds us, Chauvet has been criticized for neglecting women's experience.[8] This cannot be said of Ann, although, as we shall see, the feminist perspectives she advocates are sometimes distinctive and in addition to those of many feminist liturgists. This notwithstanding, her sacramental focus is at times strongly engaged with liturgical concerns – an engagement no doubt motivated by her 'assumption' 'that worship is the root of theology'.[9]

Feminist Perspectives

In the WCC publication *Worship Today*, Gail Ramshaw (whom Ann cites with approval in her *Feminist Theology* Reader[10]) makes the following claim:

> Much of what the 20th-century liturgical movement advocates corresponds to feminist concerns. Both movements value many of the same goals: circular rather than rectangular space; participatory rituals rather than passive attention to leaders; a re-evaluation of the role of the clergy; multiplicity of voices in the assembly . . . In fact it can be argued, not that feminists have been influenced by the liturgical renewal movement, but the opposite: that the ecumenical liturgical renewal movement is yet another demonstration of the rise of feminist consciousness.[11]

Yet, mirroring liturgists' preoccupation with words, as yet the main area of revision called for by feminists has been language. This itself relates to embodiment at least in so far as Christian liturgical language is riddled with notions of a 'gendered God'. A lively critique of the centrality of images of male embodiment in Christian theology is offered by James Nelson, who traces alliances between patriarchal values and what he calls 'phallic meanings'.[12] He makes the following connections: patriarchy shapes the priorities that

> bigger is better (in bodily height, in paychecks, in the size of one's corporation or farm); hardness is superior to softness (in one's muscles, in one's facts, in one's foreign policy positions); upness is better than downness (in one's career path, in one's computer, in one's approach to life's problems). In a 'man's world', small, soft and down pale beside big, hard and up.[13]

When these priorities shape images of the divine, as they often do, God turns out as 'omniscient, omnipresent, and controlling the world by divine fiat . . . built on the same sexual dualism that split spirit from body'.[14] Hence numerous feminist theologians demand an inclusive or expansive revision of this language[15] – although, interestingly, this is a concern with which Ann has shown much less direct interest than many other feminists. At least with regard to the image of God as 'mother', this may reflect her sense, following A. J. Ayer, that

> someone tells us that God loves us as a father loves his children. We are reassured. But then we see a child dying of inoperable cancer of the throat. His earthly father is driven frantic in his efforts to help, but his Heavenly Father reveals no obvious signs of concern. Substitute 'mother' all the way through, and the child will still die of inoperable cancer of the throat, just as one singer of Psalm 22 died on the cross.[16]

So rather than engaging in the kind of metaphorical circumlocutions that have preoccupied some other feminist theologians,[17] as we shall see, Ann has favoured an emphasis on tracking human enactment and interaction for its sacramental capacity. The force of her point is that, whatever language is chosen to depict the divine, human concern needs to be expressed beyond words in actions; with regard to 'mother' metaphors, for example, they can only help *if* there are emphatic and 'genuine' attempts to try to repair the damage to women'.[18]

In light of this conviction Ann has often seemed to draw her own resources from reconsideration of deeply 'traditional' verbal prayer – creeds and 'prayers we have in common' – turning to these prayers to 'declare loyalty to and dependence upon God, and put even the best of the "lords" of this world in their places'.[19] This statement of intent reveals that she believes that they can still to some extent be critically turned on patriarchy and, in so far as this may be the case, Ann Loades holds to some options about feminist use of liturgical language that might quite starkly remind others that *in and of itself* language change apart from enacted concern bears little promise.

For some feminist theologians, however, it has not been only the language of liturgy that is seen as deficient, but inherited rituals and postures have also been deemed to be grossly inappropriate. A notable early collection of early feminist worship resources, *Women-Church* by the 'exceptionally important . . . splendidly subversive'[20] Rosemary Radford Ruether, imaged the feminist Christian assembly gathering in a 'celebration center' in which the 'conversation circle' was a primary spatial arrangement, an antidote to hierarchical arrangements of space.[21] And Janet Walton sketches the wide-ranging impact of feminist sensitivity on the gesture and ceremonial that may or may not be employed:

she affirms 'horizontal gestures' suggesting 'equality and interdependence', with obvious implications for styles of presiding, space and ceremonial. 'Generally we do not look up to find God.' Furthermore, 'we
pray with our eyes open and without bowing our heads'. Bowing
gestures the body into a 'non-reciprocal action' that reinforces male
domination, just as kneeling may yield to misplaced power. And 'clos-
ing one's eyes is dangerous in an unjust society'. In short, 'feminist liturgies intend to provide occasions to practice resistance and expressions
of shared power'.[22]

As Susan White points out, 'enforcing' particular places for standing
and sitting during services has long been a 'highly effective means of
controlling women's behaviour',[23] and Walton's remarks, just cited,
may at the very least be read as contest to this lengthy history of relegation and inferiority. One of White's examples of such relegation is
Durham Cathedral's 'line of blue marble set into the floor at the
entrance of the chancel serv[ing] as a permanent reminder to women of
their exclusion from the area around the altar'.[24] Ann was (notably) the
first female Lay Member of Chapter at that cathedral from 2001 to
2007, and ranked pews were never shaped into circles. However, one of
the ways in which Ann perhaps worked to 'gesture resistance' in at least
aspects of this particular space – which through its 900-year history
has, like other sacred spaces, been 'invariably designed, erected, and
furnished by men and regulated by male-dominated institutional structures'[25] – was to play a particular role in cultivating the arts, and especially those which introduced female presence. For instance, Ann was
involved in bringing to the cathedral Paula Rego's 'Margaret and
David', a painting of Queen Margaret of Scotland (1046–93) and her
son, which 'speaks of a woman whose spirituality is wise, tough, discerning and far-sighted',[26] a comment that might be made of Ann herself. While this painting of Margaret of Scotland portrays her in her role
as mother, she is also one among a now-expanded list of female saints in
the Church of England's calendar who are recognized for the exercise of
grace beyond the domestic realm, a development in the Church of
England's *Common Worship* that Ann herself helped to foster.[27] In
doing so, Ann can be seen to have contributed to the creation of space
for women in the church's worship and spirituality[28] that parallels her
call for attention in the academy to the undervalued, even neglected,
contributions of such women as Mary Wollstonecraft, Josephine Butler,
Dorothy L. Sayers and Evelyn Underhill.[29] The recognition of female
saints is entirely consistent with her emphasis on enacted concern
apparent in her comments on God as 'mother', cited earlier. It might

well also be related to what she considers to be the main problem hindering the appointment of women as bishops in the Church of England, namely the prevalence of a view that 'women are always "at fault" unless they are subordinate to males' (which for her 'remains one of the points at which both Scripture and tradition must be criticised not just for being ambiguous, but for being most profoundly mistaken'[30]). Lifting up images of powerful and self-determining women, embodying their concern so as to effect public change, is a key contribution that Ann Loades has made to feminist reflection on worship.

The Sense of the Sacramental

Alongside the particular female voices from the past to which Ann attended in her *Feminist Theology* monograph and in her book on Evelyn Underhill, another key figure in her writing has been Simone Weil. Ann critiques Weil as one representative of a larger problem of 'holy anorexia', the root of which Ann diagnoses as an '[i]nab[ility] to explore the alliance of matter and emotion'.[31] Weil became 'tested to destruction' by denial of the body's basic needs of sustenance – a disturbing expression of desire to be 'consumed' by the divine. Ann's explorations of Weil's afflictions shape very strong caution about 'morbid over-identification with Christ as suffering victim',[32] and are a vivid example of 'the last kind of Christianity that women are likely to need'.[33] Her reserve about the playing out of this tradition in an inversion of 'eucharistic' living is of major importance to the theme of 'liturgy and embodiment'. At the very least, it helps to define what 'paschal mystery' – that much-used notion in liturgical theology – is *not*. Also important is Ann's long-standing concern with theological reflection on the care and harm of children,[34] dual foci all too rare in feminist theology, let alone in wider theological circles. Across the breadth of Ann's writings, study of child sexual abuse and concern about the kind of theologies that might entrench its dynamics can be set alongside her convictions about the spirituality of bodily bearing and rearing 'smelly, spotty, runny-nosed, crying, cross and sleepless' children,[35] so that a connection with worship is made in her image of the young flourishing as 'living prayers'[36] of those in whose care they are raised.

Childcare is one important expression of 'sacramentality' as Ann understands it, and a poignant one in light of her use of Ayer, quoted above. She has consistently placed emphasis on the importance of diverse expressions of what she, following Rowan Williams, has called 'the body's grace'. As her example of childcare suggests, this is by no means found only in sexual intimacy, and indeed she argues that it may come to expression in many forms of public life, retreat from which is an 'evasion', not least of the responsibility that can be learned in the liturgy to make common the holy and to sanctify the common.[37] We might note that this insistence on the public dimension of sacramentality is an important contribution to feminist reflection on the sacraments – scant as it is – which has often accented if not the two or seven sacraments then the context of (albeit sometimes re-imagined) rites and ministries in more or less churchly mode[38] (understandable as this of course is in ecclesial environments where women's access to the sacraments has largely been circumscribed by men). Still, a wider view of sacramentality preoccupies many of Ann's writings to emerge through the last 15 years of her teaching career and clearly embraces what liturgical theologians might call 'the liturgy of the world'. Pointing to this wider view, she writes:

> By sacramentalism I do not mean simply the seven or two sacraments, but recovering or imagining or experiencing what it is to be embodied persons in relation to space, time, rhythm, dance, buildings and all that we see, hear, smell, taste, touch, eat, celebrate, make ceremonies of, decorate, make jokes about – joie de vivre, grace, conviviality – living with others.[39]

Within this perspective, liturgical celebration, *as so many other aspects of human life*, might celebrate the sacramentality of the body, edging at a sense of 'holy and glorious flesh', to quote Dante's Solomon in Canto 14 of *Paradise*, as Ann herself likes to.[40] For within, as beyond, the rites of Christian worship, human beings may become 'body of Christ' as they mediate grace in relationships and 'in . . . freedom and love both honour one another and generously exchange places with each other'.[41] At the very least, the capacity to see oneself in such a light represents resistance to Weil's desire to 'be deprived of all the senses':[42] indeed, it invites the possibility of human persons becoming their best selves through mutually vulnerable interdependence.[43] Conversely, the same kind of sacramental spirituality leads her to insist that

> we cannot become 'body' of Christ if, for instance, starvation, deep-seated poverty, the displacement and decimation of populations in war, racism, the resort to violence and the provocation of hatred remain characteristic of the dealings human beings have with one another,[44]

a point of major and obvious import in relation to her stress on enacted concern, discussed earlier. With respect to worship, so much turns on whether or not

> in the course of engagement with a certain kind of ceremonious activity . . . we are enabled to say 'God', and having learned to say 'God' may be able to discern God beyond the framework of liturgy.[45]

In terms of sacramentality, engaging the metaphor of the body of Christ is especially important to what might be learned.

If we follow through an example, we are able to see more clearly the lead that Ann offers to liturgists. For liturgy, like Scripture, employs the metaphor of the body in many and varied ways such that 'body' is one of the most multivalent terms put to use in Christian worship.[46] The 'body of Christ' may refer to Jesus' body, to sacramental matter in the Eucharist and/or to the people of the Church.[47] Also, in the latter case, the singular 'body' is a corporate entity, comprised of a diverse and plural multitude. There are different levels of meaning, often interacting, perhaps especially in the primary liturgical expression of an 'exchange of grace' in the Christian tradition, the sharing of communion. It is precisely this interaction that Ann's thought engages, elaborates and celebrates in the wide thinking into which she spirals but which is rarely the focus of the limited interests of liturgists 'proper'. The 'body of Christ' may refer participants to bread being given and received. However, the exchange is also itself the referent of the statement: the action of giving and receiving is that of the body of Christ. Further, alongside the speaker and hearer, giver and receiver, others who may be surrounding them are also the body of Christ. The entire eucharistic assembly is the body of Christ. And in part, what is meant and what is understood by the exchange depends on how the words 'the body of Christ' are related to accompanying gestures. As Jan Michael Joncas notes,

> connotations depend on how the minister and recipient make eye contact, what tone of voice the minister uses, how the recipient articulates 'Amen', and whether or not the host is placed on the hand or the tongue.[48]

Because the texts of the liturgy considered apart from their alliance to such gestures cannot themselves so readily stretch into the range of connotations needed to enable worshippers to learn the sense of the sacramental – of the sacramentality *of their own embodied persons* – attention to the non-verbal dimensions of liturgy is of the highest importance. Ann herself enriches this conviction with her dazzling insight that divine presence being associated with the very matter of the sacraments means that it may be 'fleeting, contingent, here today and gone tomorrow' as the signs themselves are 'fluid, or consumable, transient, except in their immediate or longer term effects on the persons concerned, themselves the pilgrims'.[49] By stressing the very momentariness of ceremonial scenes in the liturgy, she invites attention to the fragile beauty of the sacramental celebration of sacramental selves and in doing so quite emphatically pushes away from the kind of restricted, inadequate attention to texts that has characterized so much liturgical study, and this apart from questioning any assumption that bodiliness and 'concreteness' (in Chauvet's word) can easily be equated.

One of the key things then that liturgists might learn from Ann's work is that their looking beyond the texts of their rites must be oriented on the task of enabling participants and presiders to 'learn to say "God"' – in the exchange around the altar, 'body of Christ' – in the alliance of words and gesture employed. Here greater attention than is sometimes given to the role of rubrics may be crucial, although something like Robert Hovda's exciting talk of presiders yearning to 'create a kingdom scene' that 'relax[es] the status quo, so that people can move and breathe and envision alternatives'[50] may emphatically be needed to prevent rubrics shrivelling down into 'dried out tradition'.[51] In my view, both the metaphorical circumlocution of some feminist liturgists and moving the furniture with others might have important, even crucial, parts to play in envisioning such alternatives. For if liturgy is to facilitate, enable or serve 'body of Christ' (or, as Hovda might put it, for the assembly to understand *itself* as the primary symbol of the liturgy) certain juxtapositions must be kept alive.[52] By freeing up attention to action and environment in the liturgy, Ann's thought can animate in fresh ways the juxtapositions that are central to liturgical-theological method[53] and, more than that, nurture worshippers in manifesting the mystery they praise.[54]

Notes

1 Louis-Marie Chauvet, 1995, *Symbol and Sacrament: A Sacramental Reinterpretation of Christian Existence*, Collegeville, MN: Liturgical Press, p. 141.

2 E.g. James F. White, 1997, 'Coming Together in Christ's Name', in Blair Gilmer Meeks (ed.), *The Landscape of Praise: Readings in Liturgical Renewal*, Valley Forge, PA: Trinity Press International, p. 253 (emphasis added).

3 'Too text-bound by half, to put it mildly': Ann Loades, 'Why Worship?', *In Illo Tempore* 16 (2000), 34–42, p. 34.

4 Robert Hovda, 1994, 'Response to the Berakah Award', in John F. Baldovin, (ed.), *Robert Hovda: The Amen Corner*, Collegeville, MN: Liturgical Press, pp. 241–53, p. 249.

5 David Brown and Ann Loades (eds), 1995, *The Sense of the Sacramental*, London: SPCK; David Brown and Ann Loades (eds), 1996, *Christ: The Sacramental Word*, London: SPCK.

6 There have been no full-length monographs on this subject, but rather a cluster of dictionary and journal articles, not all of which are readily or widely available in the UK, sometimes either because they were published 'locally', such as in the *Ushaw College Liturgy Bulletin* and the Sunderland University produced collection *Art and the Spiritual*, or outside Britain as with her contribution to the Australian compendium *Faith in the Public Forum*. Please see bibliography for details.

7 E.g. Ann Loades, 2004, 'Finding New Sense in the Sacramental', in Geoffrey Rowell and Christine Hall (eds), *The Gestures of God*, London: Continuum, pp. 161–72; Ann Loades, 2005, 'Sacramentality and Christian Spirituality', in Arthur G Holder (ed.), *The Blackwell Companion to Christian Spirituality*, Oxford: Blackwell, pp. 254–68.

8 Siobhán Garrigan, 2004, *Beyond Ritual: Sacramental Theology after Habermas*, Aldershot: Ashgate, p. 144. Ann Loades was one of the examiners of the doctoral thesis on which this work is based.

9 Ann Loades, 2005, 'On Music's Grace: Trying to Think Theologically about Music', in Julias Lipner (ed.), *Truth, Religious Dialogue and Dynamic Orthodoxy*, London: SCM Press, pp. 25–38, p. 25.

10 Ann Loades, 1990, *Feminist Theology: A Reader*, London: SPCK, p. 165.

11 Gail Ramshaw, 2004, 'Christian Worship from a Feminist Perspective', in Thomas Best and Dagmar Heller (eds), *Worship Today: Understanding, Practice, Ecumenical Implications*, Geneva: World Council of Churches, pp. 208–13, p. 212.

12 James Nelson, 1992, *The Intimate Connection: Male Sexuality and Spirituality*, London: SPCK, pp. 94–5.

13 Nelson, *Intimate Connection*, pp. 94–5. Ronald Grimes traces some related liturgical concerns in 'Liturgical Supinity, Liturgical Erectitude: On the Embodiment of Ritual Authority', *Studia Liturgica* 23 (1993), pp. 51–69.

14 Nelson, *Intimate Connection*, p. 101.

15 See Marjorie Procter-Smith's distinctions between non-sexist, inclusive and emancipatory language in her *In Her Own Rite: Constructing Feminist Liturgical Tradition*, Akron: OSL, second edition 2000, pp. 66–7.

16 For example, Ann Loades, 1987, *Searching for Lost Coins: Explorations in Christianity and Feminism*, London: SPCK, pp. 96–7.

17 Cf. Gail Ramshaw, 1996, *Liturgical Language: Keeping it Metaphoric, Making it Inclusive*, Collegeville, MN: Liturgical Press, pp. 36–8.

18 Loades, *Lost Coins*, p. 98.

19 E.g. Loades, 'Finding New Sense', p. 171.

20 Loades, *Feminist Theology: A Reader*, pp. 135, 137.

21 Rosemary Radford Ruether, 1985, *Women-Church: Theology and Practice*, San Francisco, CA: HarperCollins.

22 Janet Walton, 2000, *Feminist Liturgy: A Matter of Justice*, Collegeville, MN: Liturgical Press, pp. 37–8.

23 Susan J. White, 'Finding Their Place: Women and the Environment for Worship', *International Journal for the Study of the Christian Church* 4 (2004), 235–48, p. 240. This particular edition of the journal was edited by Ann Loades: see her editorial 'Women in the Church', pp. 189–93.

24 White, 'Finding their Place', p. 237.

25 White, 'Finding their Place', p. 235.

26 Dean and Chapter's descriptor standing beside the painting in Durham Cathedral.

27 See, for example, her editorial in *Theology* 786 (1995), 417–18, in which she makes that point that Josephine Butler is the one British woman, as well the only woman to have lived since the Reformation, to be included in the ASB santorale. Note also her contributions to Robert Atwell (ed.), 2004, *Celebrating the Saints*, Norwich: Canterbury Press, second edition, acknowledged on p. 836. As part of her contribution to reflection on the communion of saints, Ann has offered a number of reflections on Mary: see 'The Virgin Mary in the Feminist Quest', in Janet Martin Soskice (ed.), 1991, *After Eve*, London: Marshall Pickering, pp. 156–78; 'Feminist Theology: A View of Mary', in William McLoughlin and Sarah Pinnock (eds), 1997, *Mary is for Everyone*, Leominster: Gracewing, pp. 32–40, and 'The Position of the Anglican Communion Regarding the Trinity and Mary', *New Blackfriars* 82 (2001), 363–74.

28 Note also the inclusion (among six persons in total) of three living women – Helen Oppenheimer, Margaret Spufford and Janet Martin Soskice – featured in Ann Loades (ed.), 1995, *Spiritual Classics from the Late Twentieth Century*, London: CHP.

29 Ann Loades, 2001, *Feminist Theology: Voices from the Past*, Oxford: Polity Press; also, on Sayers, Ann Loades (ed.), 1993, *Dorothy L. Sayers*, London: SPCK, and on Underhill, Ann Loades, 1997, *Evelyn Underhill*, London: Fount.

30 Ann Loades, 'Women in the Episcopate?', *Anvil* 21 (2004), 113–19, pp. 114–15. Ann was herself a member of the working party that produced the Church of England report *Women in the Episcopate*, London: CHP, 2004.

31 Loades, *Lost Coins*, chapter 3; Ann Loades, 1991, 'Eucharistic Sacrifice: The Problem of How to Use a Liturgical Metaphor, with Special Reference to Simone Weil', in Stephen W. Sykes (ed.), *Sacrifice and Redemption*, Cambridge: Cambridge University Press, pp. 247–61.

32 Loades, *Lost Coins*, p. 41.

33 Loades, *Lost Coins*, p. 57.

34 E.g. Ann Loades, 1994, *Thinking About Child Sexual Abuse*, London: University of London; Ann Loades, 1996, 'Dympna Revisited: Thinking About the Sexual Abuse of Children', in Stephen C. Barton (ed.), *The Family in Theological Perspective*, Edinburgh: T & T Clark, pp. 253–72; Loades, *Voices from the Past*, chapter 4.

35 Loades, 'Sacramentality', p. 259.

36 Ann Loades, 'Death and Disvalue: Some Reflections on "Sick" Children', *Hospital Chaplain* 93 (1985), 5–11, p. 11.

37 Loades, 'Sacramentality', p. 261.

38 Note the work of Susan A. Ross, 1998, *Extravagant Affections: A Feminist Sacramental Theology*, New York: Continuum, written from a Roman Catholic perspective, which, while suggesting the 'experiential' broadening of the meaning of sacramentality, continues to stress 'the parish' as context for sacramental expression (pp. 210–31).

39 Ann Loades, 'Introductory Address', *Feminist Theology* 3 (1993), 12–22, p. 20.

40 E.g. Loades, 'On Music's Grace', p. 35.

41 Ann Loades, 1995, 'Creativity, Embodiment and Mutuality: Dorothy L Sayers on Dante, Love and Freedom', in Colin N. Gunton (ed.), *God and Freedom: Essays in Historical and Systematic Theology*, Edinburgh: T & T Clark, pp. 103–18, p. 118.

42 Loades, *Lost Coins*, p. 48.

43 Ann Loades, 2005, 'Sacramentality and Spirituality', in Philip Sheldrake (ed.), *The New SCM Dictionary of Christian Spirituality*, London: SCM Press, pp. 553–5, p. 554.

44 Ann Loades, 2005, 'Eucharistic Spirituality', in Sheldrake, *SCM Dictionary of Christian Spirituality*, pp. 286–9, p. 288.

45 Loades, 'Finding New Sense', p. 167.

46 See Bruce T. Morrill (ed.), 1999, *Bodies of Worship: Explorations in Theory and Practice*, Collegeville, MN: Liturgical Press.

47 For recent discussions, see Judith Kubicki, 2006, *The Presence of Christ in the Assembly*, New York, NY: Continuum; and Samuel Wells, 2005, *God's Companions: Reimagining Christian Ethics*, Oxford: Blackwell. As Wells relates in his Foreword, he imagines this book as being in continuity with the doctoral thesis that he undertook under Ann Loades' supervision.

48 Jan Michael Joncas, 2003, 'Toward Ritual Transformation', in Gabe Huck (ed.), *Toward Ritual Transformation: Remembering Robert Hovda*, Collegeville, MN: Liturgical Press, pp. 49–69, pp. 51–2.

49 Ann Loades, 1999, 'Word and Sacrament: Recovering Integrity', in Robert Gasgoine and Nicholas Brown (eds), *Faith in the Public Forum*, Adelaide: Open Books, pp. 28–46, pp. 33–4.

50 Robert Hovda, 1976, *Strong, Loving and Wise: Presiding in Liturgy*, Collegeville, MN: Liturgical Press, p. 18.

51 Elaine Ramshaw, 1987, *Ritual and Pastoral Care*, Minneapolis, MN: Fortress Press, p. 22.

52 See Benjamin M. Stewart, 'Facing the Assembly: The Legacy of Robert Hovda', *Worship* 78 (2004), 421–44.

53 For a strong, highly regarded recent statement of the importance of juxtaposition in liturgical-theological method, see Gordon W. Lathrop, 1993, *Holy Things: A Liturgical Theology*, Minneapolis, MN: Fortress Press; on Lathrop, see Stephen Burns, 2006, *Worship in Context: Liturgical Theology, Children and the City*, Peterborough: Epworth Press, chapter 5.

54 I am grateful to Nicola Slee and Natalie K. Watson for their comments on an earlier draft of this chapter.

20

Vision and Vulnerability

The Significance of Sacramentality and the Woman Priest for Feminist Theology

TINA BEATTIE

My introduction to feminist theology was by way of the collection edited by Ann Loades, *Feminist Theology: A Reader*,[1] when I was a mature student doing Ursula King's course on 'Feminist Theology in a Global Context' at the University of Bristol in the early 1990s. As a mother of four young children juggling the demands of family life and studying for a degree, feminism immediately struck a chord with me. I began to reflect for the first time on the significance of gender in the formation of my own identity and on the ways in which my religious and social positioning had to some extent been dictated by an uncritical attitude to stereotypes of maternal femininity. From then on, all my academic research has been viewed through the 'lens of gender',[2] although I remain ambivalent with regard to many of the claims and arguments of feminist theology and theory.

Loades' writings on sacramentality and spirituality[3] touch on many of my own theological concerns in struggling to negotiate a feminist path between the appeal to women's experience that risks a naïve literalism and lack of critical analysis, and a cultural linguistic approach that risks adopting an esoteric form of critical theory at the expense of engagement with the experienced realities of women's lives.[4] In reflecting on these methodological problems, I have discovered a rich resource in sacramental theology for exploring the performative and narrative dimensions of the Christian life, in which experience and language are woven together in a conscious quest to incarnate one's own life story within the story of Christ and the Church.

In what follows, I reflect on the potential of sacramental theology for women seeking a holistic ethos beyond both the spiritually impoverished discourse of much secular feminist theory and the sexual dualisms and hierarchies that continue to shape much mainstream sacramental theology, particularly in the Roman Catholic tradition to which I belong. I begin by considering in more detail the tension between experiential and cultural-linguistic approaches, in order to suggest why a sacramental approach can allow for a creative feminist negotiation between the two. Next, I illustrate my argument by drawing on two recent doctoral theses by Anglican women priests – Gillian Hill's 'Birthright or Misconception? An Investigation of the Pastoral Care of Parents in Relation to Baptismal Enquiries in the Church of England',[5] and Alison Green's 'The Priest, the Body, the Bride and the Whore: Towards a Theology of Women's Priesthood'.[6] By considering these research projects, which draw their inspiration from feminist theology and from the sacramental experiences of women priests, I ask if the Anglican ordination of women is effecting a quiet revolution in liturgical and sacramental symbolism.

Language, Experience and Feminist Theology

Feminist thinkers often appeal to women's experience to challenge the pervasive androcentrism of the theological tradition. They seek to demonstrate that Christian theology and therefore the Christian understanding of God, the human and creation have been informed by an unacknowledged dependence upon male experience, so that the articulation of women's experience can provide a potent unmasking of and corrective to this one-sidedness.

However, this appeal to experience has been criticized for what has been perceived as its privileging of white, middle-class women's experience in a way that silences voices of difference based on race, class, sexuality, disability and other such factors that contribute towards the subordination and marginalization of women. In responding to this criticism, feminist theology has become a burgeoning textual landscape of plurality, multivocity and global diversity, as more and more women have added their voices to the debate. This entails continually negotiating a position between a postmodernist perspective that is resistant to any universal claims based on shared values and meanings and that therefore lacks a common foundation from which the feminist enterprise can be justified, and a universalism that risks the elimination of difference and diversity through an essentialist understanding of 'woman' and her discontents.

In questioning the scholarly legitimacy of the appeal to experience, I do not want to suggest that the demand for academic rigour should deafen feminist scholars to the often inchoate and unsystematic cries that emanate from the distressed, excluded and impoverished female body from her positioning in a variety of cultural, religious and economic contexts. But, as Mary McClintock Fulkerson points out, there is a disguising of power in feminist appeals to women's experience because these experiences are evaluated according to the highly selective criteria of feminist scholars who are often remote from the sites of struggle and suffering that they nevertheless cite for authentication of their theories. To quote Fulkerson,

> the institutional capacity to host the discussion and provide chairs at the table – or to shut down the building altogether, so to speak – is the site where real authorizing power is located . . . [T]hose without the skills required to participate in the table discussion will . . . not have their experience of the divine articulated, or will have it articulated by 'experts' who represent them.[7]

By its very nature, feminism validates some voices and discredits others because it filters women's experiences through a grid of values and criteria that are too rarely examined for their assumptions and exclusions. Only those women whose experiences conform to feminist expectations are likely to be granted a hearing and recognized as authentic and/or authoritative. So, for example, the growing number of women who find significance in conservative and even fundamentalist versions of religion are written out of the script of most feminist theological enquiries, while those who are adept at interpreting their experiences in terms acceptable to feminist scholars are granted a privileged hearing with considerable influence to shape feminist discourse.

Recognizing these subtle dynamics of interpretation, exclusion and authorization, since the 1980s a growing number of feminist theologians have turned to psycholinguistics and critical theory as a methodological approach that shifts attention away from experience *per se*, in order to focus on the linguistic and cultural narratives through which experience is interpreted and mediated.[8] This approach is informed by the argument that the experiencing body is a text, mapped by values not of its making, so that we read our own bodies through the meanings imparted to us by our linguistic habitats. To break free of the oppressive influences of those habitats we must attend to language itself and explore the contours of a new way of speaking about bodiliness – a morphology – that would allow for a remapping of the female body according to more life-giving criteria. In particular, this means recognizing the negative inheritance of a hierarchy of religious values that privileges sacrifice over desire, suffering over joy, spirituality over sexuality, culture over nature and masculine rationality and transcendence over feminine relationality and immanence. The female body is thus squeezed into linguistic meanings that deny the legitimacy of experiences such as female sexual desire, menstruation, pregnancy, childbirth and motherhood,[9] and other psychosexual differences in such a way that 'woman' constitutes the excluded other from the scene of representation, focused as it is on the normative male. From theology and philosophy to psychoanalysis and critical theory, this exclusion has been a persistent theme in the western intellectual tradition, although it has taken different forms and been argued in different ways through history.

To shift the focus of feminist theological analysis from women's experience to the symbolic and cultural significance of gender can give rise to new linguistic possibilities for the construction of feminist subjectivities, but the turn to language brings with it two significant risks. First, it can entail an Irigarayan approach in which sexual difference becomes the most significant feature of the function of language, and this risks a form of essentialism that refuses to allow either woman or man any space of transsexual mobility or discursive fluidity with regard to the symbols of sexual identity. It also privileges sexual difference over other forms of difference that function as markers to exclude or marginalize some groups in relation to others.[10] Second, an attempt to resist sexual essentialism can produce the kind of rhetorical performances adopted by Judith Butler and other radical postmodernists, in which all corporeal realities and gendered identities are dissolved in a parodic appropriation of multiple identities and performative sexual *personae*, where any attempts to appeal to fundamental criteria of justice arising out of the body's vulnerabilities and sexual 'givens' dissolve in the play of apparently infinite discursive possibilities.[11] In this respect, if much feminist theology still tends to privilege the raw material of women's experience over the high discursive gloss of critical theory, it may be for good reason. To quote Janet Soskice,

> Feminist theology is sometimes attacked by others in feminist fields as a theoretical backwater. If this is true, it may be part of the price paid for keeping an ear to the ground. 'A theologian', goes a Christian Orthodox adage, 'is one who prays' – and on this reckoning there are

many theologians who have minimal access to education of any sort, much less to theological education. Feminism in theology may lack the theoretical frameworks of some of its sister subjects, but its prospect for reaching millions of lives, including those of the world's poorest women, is immense.[12]

Notwithstanding this important caveat, those of us who work as academic theologians have a dual responsibility to the methods and standards of academia as well as to the political and domestic realities of those struggling on the margins of society. It is the need to negotiate a path between these different criteria that leads me to propose a sacramental and incarnational approach to language as a dynamic verbalizing of women's experiences through a conscious appropriation of the rituals, gestures and symbols of Christian faith and worship.

Sacramentality and the Female Body

Sacramental language is more accessible to those in Catholic forms of Christianity than in Protestant churches, but I argue that it offers feminist theologians access to a shared language that avoids the pitfalls of an unreflective appeal to experience on the one hand and a critical theoretical approach that sacrifices the experiencing body and nature to language and culture on the other. Sacramental language positions itself in the *aporia* between the body and language in order to explore the revelatory capacity of a natural world redeemed by Christ and suffused by grace. In this sense, the sacramental imagination is an expression of an all-encompassing way of being in the world. More narrowly, and for the purposes of this chapter, sacramentality refers to those forms of worship in which matter – the body's senses, gestures and linguistic performances, the nurturing elements of bread and wine, the elemental potency of earth, water and fire, the anointing significance of oil – becomes consecrated and incorporated into Christian worship so that nature itself is caught up in the life of grace. The sacramental life thus provides a common point of reference by which human experience is mediated and interpreted according to the meanings and possibilities inherent in the Christian story of creation, incarnation, crucifixion, resurrection and redemption, creating a graceful elliptical flow between language and the body, a sense of meaning in motion and life in becoming through a process of ongoing mutual transformation between the experiencing body and the liturgical narrative.

For women, this is a challenging interpretative task because the language of sacramentality immediately available to us is freighted with the projections, fantasies and fears of a history in which the female body has consistently been a sign of that which is beyond the limits of incarnate divinity and sacramental significance. Even today, in the Roman Catholic Church, the female body is always a sign of sacramental exclusion, never of sacramental inclusion.[13] These exclusionary functions mean that, when a woman speaks as a sacramental presence in the Church, when she enacts the dramatic performance of the liturgy in her own body, she sets in motion a new relationship between language and the body, reminding us that living symbols have a volatile and transgressive capacity to shatter the limits of meaning and to usher in new visions of grace.

With these suggestions in mind, let me turn now to consider Hill's and Green's research in more detail. Hill's thesis is based on a sociological investigation into infant baptism in two parishes in which she worked as an ordained minister – one an inner-city parish with a high level of urban deprivation and a large number of single mothers within the parish boundaries, and the other a more affluent parish where she ministered to a quite different socioeconomic group. Green's thesis is a theological and linguistic analysis of the Eucharistic Prayer, understood as a sacramental narrative enacted by the woman priest on the altar.

The Woman Priest and Baptism

Hill's research focuses on baptism in the context of parental motivation for seeking baptism for their children, encounters between parents and clergy prior to the baptism and the effects of gender on the understanding and experience of the baptismal process. She found that in the vast majority of cases it is the mother who initiates infant baptism, often because of an enduring Christian faith that no longer finds explicit expression through church attendance and that is poorly understood by some members of the clergy.

Part of the original motivation for the research was Hill's realization that, as a woman minister in an inner-city parish, she encountered an unprecedented number of single mothers bringing their children for baptism – a trend that did not continue when she was replaced by a male incumbent. Her research suggests that an imbalance of power and misogynistic tendencies on the part of some male clergy, combined with class differences between middle-class clergy and inner-city parishioners, makes it difficult for many mothers to communicate their reasons for seeking baptism. Although the interview sample was too small to draw any clear conclusions about differences in attitudes between male and female clergy, Hill tentatively proposes that 'male clergy appear to have a more didactic approach to baptism . . . The women on the other hand, focused more upon the family and making people feel comfortable with their environment' (p. 178).

Reflecting upon possible reasons for male antagonism towards women presenting their children for baptism, Hill suggests that an unacknowledged fear of sex that runs through the Christian tradition can translate into 'a view of women as possessing a dangerous sexuality and fecundity which must be controlled or subdued at all costs' (p. 274). Referring to 'structural misogyny within the Church' (p. 238), she draws on the insights of liberationist and feminist theologies to appeal for further research and a greater understanding of the ways in which encounters with clergy over baptism continue to be an alienating experience for many women, which has serious implications for the future of the Church given that women are the primary transmitters of faith to the next generation. This is particularly important with regard to single mothers who, although they constitute an increasingly significant parental grouping in modern society, are still generally viewed with veiled hostility and disapproval by many Christian clergy. In such situations, women are not '"better" as ministers than men, but . . . their gender speaks about the nature of God who is neither male nor female, and releases women to share their experiences so that the Church can be more whole' (p. 243).

Hill uses her sociological investigation to inform a theological analysis of the liturgy and symbolism of baptism. Citing early Christian texts, she draws attention to the shift during the fourth century from a model of baptism based on the baptism of Jesus in the river Jordan to a model based on the sacrifice of Jesus on Calvary. She suggests that 'this transition marked the demise of womb analogy to describe the baptism of Jesus which was present during the first three centuries' (p. 266). In one particularly vivid example of baptismal imagery, Hill quotes the third-century writings of Ephrem of Syria, who wrote:

The river in which Christ was baptised
conceived him again symbolically;
the moist womb of the water conceived him in purity,
bore him in chastity,
made him go up in glory. (pp. 266–7)[14]

This is by contrast with the modern Anglican baptismal liturgy, of which Hill observes, 'Given that parents have just been through the profound experience of childbirth, it seems extraordinary that there are just three references to birth, and none to the womb in the whole service' (p. 303). She argues:

> From a feminist perspective, the womb is a very powerful image, so the question must be asked at this point, is the disappearance of the womb as an image of baptism linked to the suppression of feminine imagery from the Church? Is what we have in essence a 'spiritual hysterectomy' where symbolism linked to women's procreative power has been excised in order to 'purify' the Christian faith? (p. 267)

In addition to appealing for a transformation in the interpretation of baptismal symbolism, Hill also questions why Anglican worship has become so exclusively focused on the church building rather than the domestic sphere. Citing examples from both Judaism and early Christianity of the significance of household worship, she asks if the shift to more institutionalized spaces of worship might be attributable to

> the exclusion of women from the sacred and a monopolisation of power by male leaders who have confined all processional activity, rituals and sacramental rites to church buildings, thus compounding a false division between secular and sacred by removing worship from the household to a sphere where they exercise power and control. (p. 279)

This leads her to suggest that 'Rediscovery of the household as a place of spiritual celebration could redefine the role of women and their importance as natural transmitters of a Christian faith earthed in their everyday experience' (p. 279).

Summing up her research, Hill points to the preference in contemporary society for people to describe themselves as spiritual rather than religious. She concludes that

> 'Spirituality' has become the defining word for today, and a challenge for the Church is how to demonstrate that at its heart is a profound spirituality which to a certain extent has become concealed, rather than revealed by the liturgy and structures of the Church. (p. 300)

The Woman Priest and the Eucharist

This quest to unearth the buried spirituality of the Christian liturgy also motivated Green's research. By way of a feminist refiguration of the Eucharistic Prayer (Prayer A, *Common Worship*), Green demonstrates how the symbolism of the Eucharist invites new interpretations informed by feminist insights, so that it becomes a potent and multivalent narrative of incarnation and cosmic redemption in which the female body, the poor and the marginalized, and the wounded creation are all gathered up in the inclusive drama of the liturgy. Drawing on the insights of psycholinguistic theory and feminist philosophy and theology, particularly the work of Luce Irigaray, Grace Jantzen and Paul Ricoeur, Green situates the woman priest as a mediating presence between the wisdom of tradition and the insights of feminism, so that liturgy performed by the woman celebrant becomes open to a range of interpretative possibilities that are masked or negated by an exclusively male priesthood. Green argues that the woman priest 'signifies the need to reinterpret ancient, polysemic Trinitarian symbols so as to "hear again" meanings that are true and appropriate to our time and place' (p. 154).

Green's thesis has a tripartite structure, with sections dealing with the human made in the image of God, the symbolic significance of bread in relation to God, the human and the natural environment, and the symbolism of blood in terms of the Eucharist, sacrifice and fertility. Each section includes chapters on 'The Received Wisdom of Classical Theology', 'Some Feminist Perspectives' and 'The Woman Priest', in which Green offers a summary of traditional teaching and sacramentality, followed by a critical feminist evaluation, and then offers a reinterpretation from the perspective of the woman priest.

The first three chapters take as their theme the quotation from the Eucharistic Prayer, 'Through him you have created all things from the beginning, and formed us in your own image'. Green argues that the Christian story so far has been 'the story of the same' (p. 84), insofar as sexual difference has been elided and the female body has been denied sacramental significance in a tradition that has identified God too narrowly with masculinity, as evidenced in 'The historic monopoly of men over holy spaces and rituals, and of male-dominated religious language and liturgy' (p. 85). The woman priest, signifying both Christ and the Church, represents a more inclusive and egalitarian model in which the priest makes present the reconciling action of Christ for all creation and represents all members of the Church regardless of any distinction, including gender. Such a reconciliation includes liberation from any state of presumed ontological impurity or inferiority arising from an essentialist interpretation of gender, race, class or other difference. (p. 86)

For this inclusive symbolism to be effective, the woman priest must signify not sexual neutrality (which functions as a mask for androcentrism) but sexual difference, in order to 'create a space for the female to be acknowledged, equally with the male, in *imago Dei*' (p. 86). This requires of the woman priest that, rather than seeking to mask the difference she represents, she must seek ways to incarnate that difference in the symbolic meanings and sacramental insights she brings to her performance of the liturgy. Although we cannot predict what the outcome of this symbolic transformation might be, maternal symbolism offers one potent way of introducing an alternative morphology into sacramental language. Drawing on Jantzen's privileging of a symbolics of natality and flourishing over and against the present Christian symbolics of sacrifice and mortality,[15] and on Irigaray's psychoanalytic restoration of the maternal body to the scene of representation, Green suggests that 'symbolic representation of the maternal (including the intra-uterine bond) . . . would help women to situate themselves within a female genealogy' insofar as 'the woman priest particularly represents the "birthing" role of priesthood in helping others to be "born" into the spiritual life and to mature as members of the Body of Christ' (pp. 91–2). Summarizing the transformative potential of such an affirmation of difference, Green suggests that

The woman priest . . . has begun to fill some of those lacunae left by the hitherto masculinist symbolic order, and demands the recognition of and respect for sexuate identity proper to each gender. The woman priest representing both God and the Body of Christ at the altar is a sign of the beginning of a transformation of human subjectivity away from repression and exclusion and towards acceptance and incorporation of the feminine/female as of sacramental significance, mediating the divine in the created world. (p. 89)

In the next three chapters, Green develops the ethical implications of this inclusive, creation-centred sacramentality. Taking as her key text the words, 'Take, eat; this is my body which is given for you', she argues that 'feminist theologies, earthed as they are in the concrete, broken world, make a major contribution to the way that Christians understand relationships with the divine, with one another and with creation' (p. 143). Again, she returns to the theme of natality to suggest how this sign of healed relationships might be manifest through the woman priest:

> The woman priest . . . facilitates that birth into redemption in which worshippers partake in sharing the sacrament at the Eucharist. The emphasis on mortality and escape from the mortal body evident through the history of a male-dominated Church is now counterbalanced by the presence of women priests, bringing a shift in the religious imaginary towards birth and the corporeal, nurture and the material, life in the here and now. (pp. 143–4)

Perhaps the most difficult obstacle to the woman priest seeking to incarnate difference is the long association in Christian nuptial imagery of the Church as a faithless bride whom Christ redeems from 'the fecklessness and concupiscence historically ascribed to women' (p. 148). Recognizing this requires challenging the traditional branding of women 'as lascivious seductresses and whores who tempt men to their doom' (p. 157).

With this in mind, the last section of Green's thesis focuses on blood symbolism associated with themes of sacrifice, sexuality and fertility, and evoked by the eucharistic injunction to 'Drink this, all of you; this is my blood of the New Covenant'. Here, the woman priest, associated as she is with the bloodshed of menstruation and childbirth, challenges deeply rooted taboos and fears in the masculine religious imaginary. Citing the anthropological studies of Nancy Jay,[16] Green explores the relationship between blood and sacrifice as a form of male bonding that elides the maternal role in giving birth, and establishes patrilinear descent through sacrificial bloodletting. In place of this, Green proposes

> a broadening of the symbolism of sacrifice to incorporate the nuances of sexual differences. By this means sacrifice can be interpreted not solely in terms of death and violence as a remedy for maternal birth, but also in terms of the feminine/female qualities of natality and nurturing, of gift and flourishing. (p. 192)

This involves the reclamation of the positive significance of female sexuality as well as maternity, and here Green refers to feminist appropriations of the figure of Mary Magdalene, not in the traditional image of 'a penitent whore, the type of contrite femininity' (p. 196) but as first witness to the resurrection, and authoritative preacher in the early Church. Referring to Irigaray's call for the development of a genealogy of women, Green suggests that

> As the first witness to the resurrection and Apostle to the Apostles, Mary initiates that female genealogy which can now be continued through the ordination of women. The figure of Mary Magdalene . . . offers an embodied model on which the woman priest can ground her vocation and ministry, particularly in terms of achieving subjectivity, valid discipleship and constructive self-sacrifice. (p. 197)

Green concludes her thesis with a photograph of Bishop Christina of the Lund Diocese, Sweden, dancing up the aisle with the Bishop of Bangor, the Rt Revd Tony Crockett, at the end of a Eucharist at Llandaff Cathedral to mark the tenth anniversary of the ordination of women in Wales. She observes that 'the image of those two bishops, moving in mutual esteem and harmony, sums up much of my contribution in this study towards a developing theology of women's priesthood' (p. 205).

The Vulnerability and Vision of the Woman Priest

Hill and Green both show how the language of sacramentality functions as a prism through which women's experience can be mediated in a way that is mutually transformative. The woman who seeks to articulate her experience through the sacramental symbolism of the Christian tradition has access to a neglected hinterland of linguistic meanings and symbolic gestures that are fluid and dynamic enough to accommodate the female body without doing violence to her difference or her desire. At the same time, the symbols are reactivated and become life-giving signs of hope and redemption to those who had previously been untouched by their promise. In Hill's case, this is linked to the experience of women who present their children for baptism and therefore it has a strong pastoral as well as liturgical focus. In Green's case, it is linked to the self-awareness of the woman priest as a potent symbol of difference, inclusivity and ethical transformation.

Yet the woman priest herself is particularly vulnerable, for her position is by no means assured, and she faces bitter enemies both within her own Anglican communion and through pressures from the Roman Catholic hierarchy, which continues to refuse even to contemplate the possibility of women priests. Green points out that

> As women collectively have suffered the pain of rejection and 'otherness', so the woman priest bears the print of this wound. She will be aware of the very short span of time which has elapsed since her calling has been recognised by the Anglican Church. She will know of the numbers of women whose priestly calling until very recently was ignored. She may well have been subject in her own early calling to being overlooked, misunderstood, even ridiculed. She may herself have suffered negative comments and attitudes in her search for affirmation of her calling. In her work she may find herself treated, in the male-dominated Church hierarchy, as an honorary man rather than as a real woman with a different way of knowing and her own particular feminine attributes and gifts. She will be aware, through her own experience, of other women's lives and ministries being painfully undervalued and possibly rejected. (p. 102)

In embracing the insights of feminism, a new generation of women priests is going beyond the pioneering work of those who came before them, who were often reluctant to identify themselves with feminism or to challenge patriarchal hierarchies and clerical norms in case it further compromised their already precarious standing in the Church of England.[17] But if the woman priest by her very presence poses a profound challenge to those structures, the feminist priest is, as the foregoing suggests, a more radical threat to the clerical status quo. She is as threatening as Christ himself was to established traditions, to religious authorities, to rules and regulations, bursting the wineskins and breaking open the jars that release an anointing fragrance within the Church. Like Christ, she has the capacity to challenge our understanding of God, ushering in a new vision of the sacramental significance of the human made in the image of God, and called as priest of God and of creation to consecrate the creation to its Creator, in whose womb we are nurtured and brought into the fullness of life.

Notes

1 Ann Loades (ed.), 1990, *Feminist Theology: A Reader*, London: SPCK, Louisville, KY: Westminster/John Knox Press.

2 Cf. Ursula King's reflection on the lens of gender in 'Introduction: Gender and the Study of Religion', in King (ed.), 1995, *Religion and Gender*, Oxford and Cambridge, MA: Blackwell, pp. 1–38.

3 Cf. Ann Loades, 2004, 'Finding New Sense in the "Sacramental"', in Geoffrey Rowell (ed.), *Gestures of God: Explorations in Sacramentality*, London and New York: Continuum International Publishing Group; Ann Loades, 2005, 'Sacramentality and Christian Spirituality', in Arthur G. Holder (ed.), 2005, *The Blackwell Companion to Christian Spirituality*, Oxford: Blackwell Publishing; as well as David Brown and Ann Loades, 1996, *Christ: The Sacramental Word – Incarnation, Sacrament and Poetry*, London: SPCK.

4 For further reading, see Tina Beattie, 2006, *New Catholic Feminism: Theology and Theory*, London and New York: Routledge. For the ongoing debate in feminist theology generated by this methodological conflict, see 'Roundtable Discussion: From Generation to Generation. Horizons in Feminist Theology or Reinventing the Wheel?', *Journal of Feminist Studies in Religion*, 15 (1999), 102–38.

5 Gillian Hill, 'Birthright or Misconception? An Investigation of the Pastoral Care of Parents in Relation to Baptismal Enquiries in the Church of England', unpublished PhD thesis, University of Portsmouth, 2006.

6 Alison Green, 2007, 'The Priest, the Body, the Bride and the Whore: Towards a Theology of Women's Priesthood', unpublished PhD thesis, Roehampton University, 2007. Please note that page numbers given in the text refer to the versions of these theses currently in my possession, but that they might not conform to upgraded or final versions.

7 Mary McClintock Fulkerson, 1994, *Changing the Subject: Women's Discourses and Feminist Theology*, Minneapolis, MN: Fortress Press, p. 16.

8 Cf. the collections of essays in Rebecca S. Chopp and Sheila Greeve Davaney (eds), 1997, *Horizons in Feminist Theology: Identity, Tradition, and Norms*, Minneapolis, MN: Fortress Press. See also Maggie C. W. Kim, Susan St. Ville and Susan M. Simonaitis (eds), 1993, *Transfigurations: Theology and the French Feminists*, Minneapolis, MN: Fortress Press.

9 There is of course a potent maternal dimension to Catholic forms of Christianity but, as many feminists have pointed out, the cult of the Virgin Mary has been overwhelmingly colonized by masculine theological projections and fantasies, so that it can be ineffectual or even oppressive in relation to women's spirituality and desire.

10 For an insightful critique of this aspect of Irigaray's theory, see Hanneke Canters and Grace M. Jantzen, 2005, *Forever Fluid: A Reading of Luce Irigaray's* Elemental Passions, *Manchester Studies in Religion, Culture and Gender*, Manchester and New York: Manchester University Press, chapter 6, 'Multiple Subjects and Fluid Boundaries'.

11 Cf. Beattie, *New Catholic Feminism*, chapter 2, 'Feminist Bodies and Feminist Selves'.

12 Janet Martin Soskice and Diana Lipton (eds), 2003, *Feminism and Theology* Oxford: Oxford University Press, pp. 7–8.

13 For a more detailed exploration of these arguments, see Tina Beattie, 2002, *God's Mother, Eve's Advocate: A Marian Narrative of Women's Salvation*, London and New York: Continuum, and Beattie, *New Catholic Feminism*.

14 Quoting Ephrem of Syria, *Hymns on the Church* 36:3–6, in Kilian McDonnell, 1996, *The Baptism of Jesus in the Jordan: The Trinitarian and Cosmic Order of Salvation*, Collegeville, MN: Liturgical Press, p. 104.

15 See Grace Jantzen, 1998, *Becoming Divine: Towards a Feminist Philosophy of*

Religion, Manchester: Manchester University Press, where she develops Hannah Arendt's theme of natality in the context of a pantheistic religious imaginary.

16 Nancy Jay, 1992, *Throughout Your Generations Forever: Sacrifice, Religion and Paternity*, Chicago and London: University of Chicago Press.

17 Cf. Helen Thorne, 2000, *Journey into Priesthood: An In-depth Study of the First Women Priests in the Church of England*, Bristol: Centre for Comparative Studies in Religion and Gender, University of Bristol.

21

Exchanges of Nature
Worship, Liturgy and Formation

BRIDGET NICHOLS

In her recent writing and lecturing, Ann Loades has made it a particular concern 'to rediscover a way of thinking, imagining, Christianly something of the character of God's relation to the world'.[1] The project has been pursued in relation to the sacraments, to music and to the nature of worship itself. For a conviction that worship is the necessary and obvious medium in which human beings discover and develop their relationship with God in a world that is not theirs, but that they are generously invited to enjoy, has been one of its dominant themes.[2] This relational account of worship is pursued still more ambitiously, towards a proposal that it is not only a duty of gratitude, and therefore to be offered at all times and in all places, sometimes in the most testing and unholy of circumstances,[3] but also that it is 'integral to becoming a fully human person', or indeed, 'a normal human person'.[4]

The confrontational and contentious nature of this claim for anyone encountering it from outside a tradition of worship can only be acknowledged in this chapter. Yet, even within that framework, a strong degree of persuasion may be necessary. Speaking of worship in its own right often provokes negative reactions, ranging from frank boredom, to misgivings about the capacity of something so apparently self-indulgent and self-regarding to engage seriously with the condition of being, and being Christian, in the world. The confidence and the passion of Ann Loades' approach are therefore especially admirable and especially urgent at a time when worship is most likely to find itself tied to subjects with practical application and measurable outcomes such as ethics, mission or the environment.

This pre-emptive conscription of worship to the advancement of particular programmes, I will argue, fails to grasp something essential to its nature. As Jeff Astley has insisted, 'it has no ulterior point or purpose, least of all an educational one'.[5] It is not *for* anything in a strategically instrumental sense. Outwardly directed, corporately performed and responsive as much to pain and disorder as to beauty, it is *for* everything that can be received with gratitude and praise, lamented over or held up in intercession. The ringing imperative, 'O all ye Works of the Lord, bless ye the Lord', in the opening verse of what the Christian tradition knows as the Benedicite, though its origins are much earlier, makes fitting acknowledgement of the joyful obligation implicit in this invitation.[6]

The instrumental view should not be completely rejected, however, even though we might be critical of a tendency to emphasize the aims and consequences of worship over the activity. Worship may not be for the achievement of particular results, but neither is it an end in itself. And if we are to pursue the claim that its purpose has something to do with the development of human persons, then it is not enough to propose that it will foster the virtues that build, guarantee and dignify the relationships of human beings with one another or with God, or promote proper forms of concern and attitudes of responsibility, simply by being performed. A great deal of this development will be related to the quality of performance, not in any narrowly aesthetic sense (though aesthetic considerations are immensely important) but in a sense that encompasses attentiveness, reflection and the involvement of the whole person.

Practical questions immediately arise. How does something that exists properly only as activity maintain vigilance over itself? How do its participants stand back to observe their own practice from a distance? What standards can be applied to determine whether it is good enough? There is always an obligation to re-examine what is done under the name of 'worship' if its practitioners are to avoid the dangers of sentimentality, introspection, complacency, carelessness and laziness. It is these concerns, rooted for the most part in the ordinariness of worship, that this chapter will explore.

Some reflections on precise use of language are appropriate before proceeding. So far, I have used 'worship' as a general term for the activity of public prayer, which implies certain general assumptions about the people who might participate and the traditions to which they might belong. It has conventionally been the task of 'liturgy' to study and comment on the texts and ceremonial instructions that are the deposit of the activity called 'worship' and to confirm the integrity of contemporary practice by remembering how that practice evolved.

Keeping the two terms distinct and free from unhelpful associations, however, is less easy than one might expect. Both in popular and in scholarly usage, they are increasingly interchangeable and may be used to name both the academic discipline and the performance of corporate prayer, especially where this follows an established rite.[7] That is the practice that will be followed here. At the same time, there is a tendency in some quarters to use 'liturgy' in a caricaturing way, as a name for the dessicated, fossilized and rarefied antithesis of 'worship', which encompasses all that is spontaneous, authentic, sincere and unconfined by rules. The obverse of this is equally pernicious. Here, 'liturgy' comes to denote the orderly and well-informed practice of the Church's rites, while 'worship' stands for a casual disregard of the heritage and tradition of the Church and for general bad taste in the conduct of public prayer. There is a need to reclaim both words into healthy currency in giving an account of a response to God that employs and develops human capacity – body, mind and soul – to its fullest. In other words, there is a need to be liturgical about the activity of worship on the one hand and worshipful about the study and development of liturgy on the other.

The proposition is neither new nor radical. A commitment to providing worshippers with the resources to join in corporate prayer with a surer understanding of what they are doing and why has been forcefully articulated as an aspiration in the Roman Catholic Church since the Second Vatican Council, under the banner of 'liturgical formation'. In more recent times, this has become an important part of the thinking of other Churches.

Much of the work that is done in the name of formation seems to concentrate on raising awareness of the shape and pattern of liturgical rites. Although its announced mission has been to foster the full, active participation of those who attend acts of worship,[8] its method has often been severely textual and structural, assuming a reasonably sophisticated level of literacy. Thus, for example, congregations at the Eucharist may be encouraged by subheadings in their orders of service to take note of transitions within the whole action from greeting to the proclamation of Scripture to sacramental action to dismissal. Additionally, they may be taught, either through preaching or through programmes that operate beyond the confines of the act of worship, how to place themselves within the tradition of the Church at large. Instruction in the historical and theological background of worship would be part of this amplification.

A great deal of ambition and idealism about the power of education to create better worshippers and better worship (whatever these danger-

ous value judgements may mean) undergirds the formational programme. What has not been sufficiently emphasized, however, is that it
is possible to be liturgical about worship in an organic way, approaching the subject from the inside as well as from the outside. In other
words, if – and the conditional is important if the temptation to invent
the ideal congregation or the ideal worshipper is to be resisted – those
who join reverently and absorbedly in public prayer are attentive to
what they hear and see, responsive to the presence of their fellow-
worshippers and, above all, open to being moved and amazed, no
matter how often they may have participated in the same rite, then they
have already begun to reflect formationally on the action of which they
are part.

This is necessarily a contextual reflection and for that reason there
may be no obvious starting points, for worship is a form of what Hubert
Dreyfus has called 'practical understanding'. Distinguishing it from
'theoretical understanding', Dreyfus explains that

> Although practical understanding – everyday coping with things and
> people – involves explicit beliefs and hypotheses, these can only be
> meaningful in specific contexts and against a background of shared
> practices. And just as we can learn to swim without consciously or
> unconsciously acquiring a theory of swimming, we acquire these
> social background practices by being brought up in them, not by
> forming beliefs and learning rules.[9]

In a similar way, worship involves a number of techniques learned
routinely in the course of its performance. Worshippers discover when
to stand, sit or kneel, when to join in responses, when to be silent, and
how to acknowledge other people, mainly through imitation and repetition. By associating certain words with corresponding actions, they
may come to recognize standing as an appropriate posture for praise
and thanksgiving, sitting for attentive listening to Scripture and preaching, and kneeling for contrition and adoration. Conventions will vary in
different traditions and communities and prescriptivism is unhelpful.
Of greater significance is the fact that worship requires conventional
gestures and postures at all.

The French Benedictine liturgist Patrick Prétot, summarizing the prin-
cipal anthropological models for human participation in the liturgy,
makes clear the crucial difference between mere technique and technique that is essential to the activity of worship:

Gestures and postures reveal to men and women that they are before God, and what they are before God. It is by means of the body that human beings discover the true meaning of their being 'before God'.[10]

Prétot's concern with the role of the body, and especially of gesture, in public worship is a concern for what makes public worship possible. Liturgical gestures, he reminds us, belong to their own grammatical system, calling the assembly of parts of bodies into relationship with God and with the gathered assembly. For that reason, he expresses anxiety about an increasing formational deficit, in that the 'physical "know-how" [savoir-être corporel] which the liturgy fosters is no longer osmotically passed on as it once was'.[11] This, he points out, poses a serious question for today, which we might diagnose as the loss of a common memory, general uncertainty about how to behave in gatherings for public prayer and the lack of any sort of gestural vocabulary that marks the transition from everyday life to a setting that requires concentration on the presence of God.

The question is a complex one and requires the expertise of anthropologists as much as liturgists.[12] A very brief and practical exploration of one of its immediately obvious dimensions – the matter of how, without the dependable transmission of the 'know-how' of worship, alert and inquiring participants are to make embodied sense of their prayers – must serve here as an indication of what deserves far more exhaustive treatment.

Liturgical rites produce their own stage directions, in addition to the conventional postures that gather around particular words. The interpretation of these directions takes place at the literal but also at the metaphorical level. If, for example, the congregation at Holy Communion according to the Book of Common Prayer continues to sit, having been invited to confess their sins, 'meekly kneeling upon [their] knees',[13] or if those present at a eucharistic celebration kneel or sit while the president thanks God for 'counting [the assembly] worthy to stand in [God's] presence and serve [him]',[14] then words and actions have become uncoupled. The rite, from an observer's point of view, would seem contradictory.

Just as important, though, is the metaphorical and imaginative dimension. While the elderly, the infirm and children might not be able to comply physically with the demands of ritual action, the instructions that I have noted invite all worshippers to contemplate meekness and humility as the proper attitude for confession, and upright confidence as legitimate in the case of those who have been assured that they are worthy to take their place in the presence of God. As a correlative to this, the frequent anthropomorphism of appeals to God as a responsive participant in worship (for example, 'Let thy merciful ears, O Lord, be open to the prayers of thy humble servants';[15] 'Look with favour on your people, gather us in your loving arms and bring us . . . to feast at your table in heaven'[16]) describes the dynamic commerce between worshippers and God in the larger compass of liturgical rites with their own distinctive shape and rhythm.

A great deal is lost, however, if we treat this constant striving to get to the heart of what is taking place principally as a series of metaphors that adorn the experience of worship. Beautiful language and dignified gestures are not only very practical; they are also vocational, in that they call worshippers to enter into the complex fullness of human identity before God, as honoured guests who are sincerely sorry for their mistreatment of the world and of each other but glad all the same to be able to depend on forgiveness and lay claim to the privileges that they name in their prayers. In the case of Anglican usage, an arguable tendency to dwell more on contrition and unworthiness than on confidence in the promises of redemption has been redressed in the recovery of the post-communion prayer in modern revisions, the anguish of confession now balanced against the victory of the resurrection, the joyful completion of the earthly pilgrimage and the vision of the heavenly banquet.

This gives a further clue to the development of an understanding of the integrity of physical involvement in worship, namely that this involvement should have real, even ethical content, extending well beyond the terms of acts of worship into engagement with the world. Prétot follows his warning about the dangers inherent in the loss of gesture by noting that

> physical practices engage with an ethic of respect and not only with a code of propriety interior to the liturgy. And this ethic is at the service of a living together, not only in the liturgy but also outside the liturgy.[17]

Worshippers, then, are not only called to behave well because they are in the presence of God but are also called to ordinary courtesy. As well as connecting the assembly to its eschatological hope, the image-laden language of welcome, contrition, generosity and hospitality carries the toughly resilient expectation of real welcome, real contrition, real generosity and real hospitality. What the worshipping community does when it assembles is not an idealization of human existence; it *is* human existence. Assisting newcomers to find places in church, apologizing to those we have hurt, being serious about gifts of money and offering eucharistic hospitality with genuine longing for the unity, love and restoration of all people, give substance, texture and reality to the language of heaven.

It is particularly important to prevent romantic or sentimental notes from entering into the discussion because these are in some senses quite everyday virtues. They are also virtues that are difficult to practise with sincerity and love, since they are challenged again and again by personal resistances. Evelyn Underhill remarked with wonderfully wry honesty that 'the very circumstances of common worship can do much to mortify fastidiousness and religious self-regard',[18] astutely capturing the frustrating lack of system, the untidiness and the obstacles of human imperfection that are part of contextual, physical liturgical formation.

Her observation is also a well-earthed safeguard against the temptation to treat participation in common worship as a 'technology of the self'. This term, adopted from Michel Foucault's work towards documenting the history of the ways, embedded within our culture, by which human beings acquire knowledge about themselves, has found liturgical application in the writing of Talal Asad and Nathan Mitchell.[19] Mitchell supplies Foucault's own definition: technologies of the self

> permit individuals to effect by their own means or with the help of others a certain number of operations on their own bodies and souls, thoughts, conduct, and way of being, so as to transform themselves in order to attain a certain state of happiness, purity, wisdom, perfection, or immortality.[20]

Not surprisingly, much of the discussion of technologies of the self in relation to Christian religious ritual has concentrated on monastic and ascetic practice, though there is more than a hint in Mitchell's work that the same concepts might be extendable to the practices of other worshipping communities. In particular, his conviction that in the Rule of St Benedict '[r]itual's role is to teach the body how to develop spiritual values by material means'[21] colours his wider reflection on the way 'Christians negotiate their access to the Sacred'.

Here worship, understood as the involvement of all human capacities, slides towards another kind of instrumental definition, this time with an extreme perspective on the self. Ritual, he says, is the means that Christians use for

editing experience, 'rewriting' personal history, and appropriating a
new identity. Inescapably, such activity will pose a substantial degree
of danger and discomfort. For ultimately, the performance of ritual is
the way we discover how and what we think.[22]

Such a brief summary can do no more than point to obvious pitfalls
in any view that emphasizes self-fashioning as the primary objective of
corporate worship and the practices associated with it. Against such a
view, however, the continual affirmation of individuals in the texture of
liturgical rites deserves closer attention. The reading of scriptural texts
recalls that God's dealings with human beings have repeatedly depended
upon a personal summons, and narratives of the patriarchs, prophets
and apostles offer numerous examples. Uprooted from their context
and appropriated into the language of worship, these promises gain new
significance. The words from Isaiah, spoken to candidates for confirmation in the Church of England's rite, translate God's faithfulness to a
chosen people into a personal address to those who are being encouraged to imagine their relationship to God and to the worshipping community in similar terms: 'God has called you by name and made you his
own' (Isa. 43.1).[23] A well-loved post-communion prayer chooses the
parable of the Prodigal Son as a governing motif for articulating the
pattern of fall and redemption, and making it specific to each member of
a particular gathering at a particular time: 'Father of all, we give you
thanks and praise, that when we were still far off, you met us in your
Son and brought us home.'[24] The invitation to Communion, 'Jesus is the
Lamb of God who takes away the sins of the world. Blessed are those
who are called to his supper', and the congregational response, 'Lord, I
am not worthy to receive you, but only say the word, and I shall be
healed', juxtapose the apocalyptic description of the wedding feast of
the Lamb with the dauntingly personal words of the grateful centurion
who sought Jesus' healing for his sick servant but would not hear of him
entering his unworthy house.[25] (Revision has neutralized the impact of
the earlier formulation: 'Lord, I am not worthy that you should come
under my roof.')

Beyond that summons lies a further horizon of formational activity,
this time transferring emphasis from the process of forming worshippers
through their physical, intellectual and spiritual involvement in worship, to the part played by God. Christopher Irvine finds this described
in a particular category of the 'formational language' of the liturgy – the
language 'of our being formed and remade after Christ's likeness'.[26]
This receives its ultimate expression in the prayer 'at the heart of the

Western Roman rite' that God '"may fashion us for himself"'.[27] How that fashioning might take place is variously and frequently depicted in the traditions of prayer and hymnody, and involves every aspect of the human person. It is the creation of 'new and contrite hearts', the inculcation of 'good desires', the transformation by grace of impoverished human nature and the strengthening of hands that have taken holy things for service in the world.[28]

Some reserve is necessary, though, in the face of Irvine's claim that corporate worship is implicitly understood as 'the performative act in which the worshipper, in community with others, is transformed into the likeness of Christ'.[29] Formation is a *process* inscribed in the regular repetition of actions and words, as well as in the longer cycles of liturgical life – the seasons of penitence, preparation and rejoicing, not neglecting the important tracts of 'ordinary time'.

Built into this process is a continuing reflection on what it means to be before God, and a liturgical approach to worship will use the resources of scholarship to sharpen this encounter and to nurture a greater awareness of context, tradition and content. Being worshipful about liturgy will draw on the body as the primary place of encounter with God and with other worshippers and, from that point, derive the logic of some of our liturgical language, as it governs both what is done now and what participants might become.

I cannot claim that this will create better worship or better worshippers in any sense that would at the same time satisfy critical observers and those who participate – only that it would sustain a quality of attention whose consequences for grace, dignity and generosity in liturgical action and in everyday life might be a surprisingly effective schooling for those who accept the invitation to share in a created world that expresses what Ann Loades so memorably characterizes as the 'exchange of love at the heart of the divine'.[30]

Notes

1 Ann Loades, 2004, 'Finding New Sense in the "Sacramental"', in Geoffrey Rowell and Christine Hall (eds), *The Gestures of God*, London: Continuum, pp. 161–72, p. 161.

2 Ann Loades, 2000, 'Why Worship?', *In Illo Tempore: Ushaw Library Bulletin and Liturgical Review* 16, pp. 34–42; 'Finding New Sense' and 'On Music's Grace: Trying to Think Theologically about Music', in Julius J. Lipner (ed.), 2005, *Truth, Religious Dialogue and Dynamic Orthodoxy: Reflections on the Works of Brian Hebblethwaite*. London: SCM Press, pp. 25–38.

3 Loades, 'On Music's Grace', pp. 36–7.

4 Loades, 'Why Worship?'

5 Jeff Astley, 1996, 'The Role of Worship in Christian Learning', in Jeff Astley, Leslie J. Francis and Colin Crowder (eds), *Theological Perspectives on Christian Formation*, Leominster: Gracewing and Grand Rapids, MI: Eerdmans, pp. 245–51, p. 245.

6 F. E. Brightman, 1915, *The English Rite*, London: Rivingtons, vol. 1, p. 139 (Mattins).

7 The Orthodox East refers to its eucharistic rite as the Liturgy.

8 Holy See, 1963, 'The Constitution on the Sacred Liturgy' (*Sacrosanctum Concilium*), in Austin Flannery OP (ed.), 1996, *The Basic Sixteen Documents: Vatican Council II: Constitutions, Decrees, Declarations*, Northport, NY: Costello Publishing Co. and Dublin: Dominican Publications, pp. 117–61 (see esp. Section II.14.). Concern for 'full, active participation' predates Vatican II by many years and was an important topic for the Liturgical Movement.

9 Hubert L. Dreyfus, 1985, 'Holism and Hermeneutics', in Robert Hollinger (ed.), *Hermeneutics and Praxis*, Notre Dame, IN: University of Notre Dame Press, pp. 227–47, p. 231.

10 Patrick Prétot, 2006, 'La Liturgie: Une expérience corporelle', *La Maison-Dieu* 247, pp. 7–36, pp. 18–19 (my translation).

11 Prétot, 'La Liturgie', p. 29.

12 The field is potentially vast but the following are particularly relevant: Marcel Mauss, 1979, 'Techniques of the Body', in *Sociology and Psychology: Essays*, trans. Ben Brewster, London: Routledge and Kegan Paul; Marcel Mauss, 2003, *On Prayer*, ed. W. S. F. Pickering, New York and Oxford: Berghahn; Catherine Bell, 1992, *Ritual Theory, Ritual Practice*, Oxford and New York: Oxford University Press.

13 Brightman, *The English Rite*, vol. 1, p. 681.

14 Archbishops' Council of the Church of England, 2000, *Common Worship: Services and Prayers for the Church of England*, p. 190.

15 Brightman, *The English Rite*, vol. 2, p. 495 (Collect for Trinity X).

16 *Common Worship: Services and Prayers*, p. 197 (Eucharistic Prayer E).

17 Prétot, 'La Liturgie', p. 33.

18 Evelyn Underhill, 1936, *Worship*, London: Nisbet & Co, p. 98.

19 See particularly Talal Asad, 1993, *Genealogies of Religion*, Baltimore, MD: Johns Hopkins University Press, chapters 2 and 4; and Nathan Mitchell, 1999, *Liturgy and the Social Sciences*, Collegeville, MN: Liturgical Press, pp. 64ff.

20 Mitchell, *Liturgy*, p. 65, quoting Luther H. Martin, Huck Gutman and Patrick H. Hutton (eds), 1988, *Technologies of the Self: A Seminar with Michel Foucault*, Amherst, MA: University of Massachusetts Press, p. 18.

21 Mitchell, *Liturgy*, p. 73.

22 Mitchell, *Liturgy*, pp. 75–6.

23 The Central Board of Finance of the Church of England, 1998, *Common Worship: Initiation Services*, p. 112.

24 *Common Worship: Services and Prayers*, p. 182.

25 *Common Worship: Services and Prayers*, p. 180.

26 Christopher Irvine, 2005, *The Art of God: The Making of Christians and the Meaning of Worship*, London: SPCK, p. 71.

27 Irvine, *The Art of God*, p. 77.

28 *Common Worship: Services and Prayers*, pp. 392, 402, 384 (Collect for Ash Wednesday; Collect for Easter V; Collect for Epiphany II); C. W. Humphrey and Percy

Dearmer (trans.), 'Strengthen for service, Lord, the hands', in The English Hymnal Company, 1986, *The New English Hymnal*, Norwich: Canterbury Press, p. 315 (no. 306).

29 Irvine, *The Art of God*, p. 72.

30 Loades, 'Finding New Sense', pp. 161–2.

22

'Faith, Hope and Loveliness'

JANET MARTIN SOSKICE

'Hope' is not an even, or an obvious, concept. Recently in the course of writing a book about two doughty Scottish ladies, travellers in the Middle East in the nineteenth century who became scholars of Arabic and Syriac Christian manuscripts, I visited the home that they had built for themselves in the 1890s. It is now a residence for university students and, as the custodian took me around, we noted a plaque over the front door bearing the motto 'Spes' – Hope. The custodian then surprised me by saying 'Hope, that's such a sad, sad word'. Why, I asked, did he think so? 'Because if you have to hope', he replied, 'it means things have gone wrong. It means someone is sick, or dying, or lost their job and you have to hope they will get better.' How different, I thought, from the view of the robustly Presbyterian ladies who built this house, and the difference was that for them hope was a theological virtue, whereas for the custodian, a bluntly secular Englishman, hope was escapism or a psychological mood that might be useful for someone in trouble. To explain that difference requires some work in the hinterland of Christian thought.

The title of this chapter, 'Faith, hope and loveliness', is an allusion to Saint Paul in 1 Corinthians 13 where, in summary of his famous exposition of love, he concludes that 'Faith, hope, and love abide, these three'. Saint Paul is fond of this trio and often puts them together. The slight twist is not of my devising – in St Paul's Chapel in Damascus, reportedly built at the place where the saint was lowered in a basket over the walls of the city to escape an enraged mob, a bronze plaque over a lintel bears these words: 'Faith, hope and loveliness: God bless this temple'. I thought it an apt title for what I have to say about the Christian life in this chapter in honour of Ann Loades.

The French philosopher Gabriel Marcel wrote, in 1942–3, essays on the topic of hope against the dark background of the occupation of his country. He wrote, as he said, in a time of universal sacrilege when some of the most vigorous minds which have been known in France for the last twenty years really seem to imagine that blasphemy . . . can become the corner-stone of philosophy and politics.[1]

He always said that it was the experience of the war years that forged his philosophy of hope, but not just those of World War Two.

In World War One, as a young man who had already studied philosophy, Marcel worked for the French Red Cross. Initially the plan was that he should direct a little service whose task was to send information about the hospitalized soldiers to their families back home. They soon discovered that there was no need for this: the men themselves or the nurses wrote to the families. Where there was a need concerned those missing in action. With the disastrous battles in Belgium of 1914, an endless stream of people wrote to enquire after a missing son or brother or husband whose letters home had stopped arriving. With the help of file cards, one for each man, Marcel and his co-workers searched among the wounded and those listed in German prisoner-of-war camps to try to find the fate of these young men – all too often a hopeless quest.[2] It caused a philosophical conversion in Marcel, who before the war had been a Hegelian, interested in devising world-embracing explanatory systems. Dealing each day with these cards and these families, each one utterly unique, created in him a great distaste for philosophical systems that swallowed up the individual and the particular in a universalizing, analytic scheme. This was intensified during World War Two by his revulsion at the technocratic thinking of Nazism, which deliberately defaced its victims and made them numbers in an administrative system.

Marcel moved away from system and instead his mature philosophy emphasizes the *particularity* of human existence and the contingency, fragility and limitations of our knowledge at any given time. His rambling philosophical style, initially irritating to readers used to a concise analytic style of philosophical writing, exemplifies his dislike of system and his preference for that which 'appears' before one.

To hope, for Marcel, was not to have all the answers or even to think you had them – that was the province of optimism. To hope was always to be open to that which was only glimpsed – it was a matter of moving from darkness towards the light without necessarily knowing what that end would be. To hope one had to surrender the presumption of knowing, a presumption dear to the philosopher. Instead one had to stand, with openness, before the other whose need came before me. Hope was always at the level, not of the 'I' but of the us. Solitary hopes, 'I hopes', were usually optimism – 'I hope it will rain tomorrow', 'I hope the stock market will go up'. Real hope was always the province of the 'us' – I hope, in Thou, for you. But above all to hope was to know oneself to be on the way, *en route*. The title of Marcel's book of essays on hope was, accordingly, *Homo Viator*, reflecting his view that 'a stable order can only be established on earth if man always remains acutely conscious that his condition is that of a traveller'.[3] Absolute hope, like the absolute faith from which it is inseparable, is for Marcel a response. Absolute hope 'appears as a response of the creature to the infinite Being to whom it is conscious of owing everything that it has and upon whom it cannot impose any condition whatever without scandal'. From the moment that I find myself before the 'absolute Thou who has brought me forth out of nothingness', he wrote, then despair – the opposite of hope in Marcel's scheme – is effectively impossible, for 'what is the meaning of despair if not a declaration that God has withdrawn himself from me?'[4] This declaration, for the believer, is impossible.

For Marcel, as for Paul Ricoeur whom he deeply influenced, hope involves giving up the will to mastery, autonomy and self-founding. To hope is to know oneself before the absolute Thou. Hope is not passive, however, but involves choice – most fundamentally the choice of hope over despair and of life over death.

There are clear similarities between Marcel's thought and that of his Jewish contemporary Martin Buber, who also stressed the contingent and the particular, and the need to make oneself available to the other person who, by whatever accident, came my way. Buber, too, spoke of a conversion in his thought from the general to the particular, although in his case it was not from Idealism but from a religious mysticism that he later thought actually hid from him the immediate face of the other. And, as with Marcel, the template for every human other for Buber was the Divine Other, the Thou who is God, the holy mystery or Shekinah.

Gabriel Marcel, by introducing this Divine Other as the 'Thou who brought me forth from nothingness', has of course introduced a theological ingredient to his philosophical essay, and I want to make this theological move even more explicit by identifying it with the Jewish, Christian and Muslim doctrine of *creation ex nihilo*. I want to argue that this teaching of religious metaphysics, while initially seemingly remote from our topic, is at the foundation of hope in these three traditions.

Creatio ex nihilo is a central teaching of all three faiths – Moses Maimonides believed it was the only one that they all three shared. It is not the same as the Big Bang Cosmology with which it is often confused.

Rather it is the teaching that God made everything, all that is, including space and time, and made it from nothing – no pre-existing matter as Plato seemed to think, no pre-existing void. God, moreover, made all that is freely – volitionally. This is by contrast to Aristotle's God who is a metaphysical corollary of the universe: for Aristotle one could not have the Universe without God, but equally one could not have God without the Universe. Not so for the God of Scripture.

The God of the Jewish, Christian and Muslim faiths need not create but freely chooses to do so. It follows that all that is, only is, not only because God has created it but because God sustains it in being at every instant. It also follows that 'all that is', including our own being, is Gift and, at the deepest level, good.

Creation *ex nihilo*, a consensus of faith, is not directly stated in the Bible. Genesis at least is susceptible to various readings as to whether God created from nothing or from some pre-existent matter. But it seems that, as Jews and Christians had increased contact with Platonic philosophers, they were forced to refine their ideas in order to preserve what they felt to be the Bible's teaching about the God of Israel. An interesting exchange from the end of the first century CE between Rabbi Gamaliel and a philosopher clarifies what was at stake. The Rabbi says that God made a beautiful world . . . And the philosopher replies that God had good colours to make it with – to which the Rabbi responds that God made the colours, too.[5]

From very early on the prime scriptural text for this teaching on creation was not from Genesis but Exodus 3, the story of the encounter of Moses with God at the burning bush. There, in response to Moses' request for a name, God says 'I AM WHO I AM', God also said to Moses,

> Say this to the people of Israel: 'The LORD, the God of your fathers, the God of Abraham, the God of Isaac, and the God of Jacob, has sent me to you': this is my name forever, and thus I am to be remembered throughout all generations. (RSV, Ex. 3.15)

'I Am Who I Am', especially as translated into Latin (*ego sum qui sum*) or Greek (*ego eimi ho on*), seemed a profound metaphysical claim to the early Christian Fathers, who read it to mean that God alone is the source of being. In Aquinas this becomes 'God is being itself'.

There is a disagreement here between Jews and Christians that I think we can largely lay to rest and it arises from the Hebrew phrase that is translated *I Am who I Am*. In the Exodus text, it seems clearly to be wordplay on the Holy Name, *YHWH*, which strictly speaking does not have a meaning but greatly resembles the Hebrew verb 'to be'. But the phrase that we render in English *I Am who I Am* in the Hebrew means something more like: 'I am the one who is with you and who will be with you'. Metaphysics, we can say, was alien to Moses or whoever edited the Pentateuch.

Martin Buber and Franz Rosenzweig made much of this largely Christian, metaphysical mistranslation. The God of Exodus, they said, is not a metaphysical notion but the God who promises Moses, and through Moses the people of Israel, that he is with them and *will* be with them. This is not a God of philosophy but a God of intimate presence – wherever you go, I will be with you.[6]

But this of course is also what was intended by those thinkers, Christian and Jewish, who favoured a metaphysical interpretation of this verse. So, for example, Moses Mendelssohn, writing at the end of the eighteenth century, says that, at the burning bush, God spoke to Moses and said 'I am the being that is eternal . . . Say to the children of Israel, "The eternal being . . . has sent me to you".'[7] But he quickly follows with an explanation drawing on a cluster of Jewish sages: because past and future are all present to the creator, God is the one who was and is now and will be – and thus God is the God of providence who will be with the children of men. So to say that 'God is eternal', and the eternal source of being is not to say that God is a philosophical spectre but that God, as creator of all, including time, is always already present to us, at any time in our need. This belief suffuses Jewish, Christian and Muslim understandings of Hope.

Related to this is the strong scriptural connection between creation and redemption. The God who is powerful to create can redeem. We find this in the Psalms, thus Psalm 121

> My help comes from the Lord,
> who made heaven and Earth.

and Psalm 124

> Our help is in the name of the Lord,
> Who made heaven and earth.

Creation as understood by Jews, Christians and Muslims is not a *change* – not a transition from one state to another. To be a 'change' is to be an event in an already existing chain of events, but there is no prior state, no space, no vacuum, into which Creation comes. It is 'supernatural' in the strict sense of the term. (Here, by the way, there is no conflict with science. Science does not address the question 'why is there something rather than nothing?')

That God creates all that is from nothing is central to another teaching of hope shared by Christians, Muslims and some Jews – the hope for the resurrection of the dead. 'Brothers, I am a Pharisee and the son of Pharisees. It is for our *hope in the resurrection of the dead* that I am on trial' (RSV, Acts 23.6, emphasis added), says Paul before the Sanhedrin, causing a dispute between the Pharisees, who accepted this teaching, and the Sadducees, who did not, and allowing Paul to slip away.

It is a matter of some debate as to when the idea of resurrection appears in Judaism. The belief is not stated clearly in Torah and its first explicit reference is late, in Daniel (12.1–3). Even today Jews differ on the matter. Jon Levenson, an Orthodox Jew, in his *Resurrection and the Restoration of Israel*, pushes hard for the centrality of belief in resurrection to Jewish faith.[8] It is not clearly stated in Torah, Levenson admits, but on the other hand belief in resurrection is a central plank of rabbinic teaching. It arises not from convictions about who we are but about who God is: as in Christianity and Islam, God is a God of loving faithfulness. God will not see the just go to destruction and, if God is powerful to create, then God is powerful to redeem. This is not a compelling proof of course but neither is it incoherent. Indeed the faithful must ask themselves that, if they find it hard to believe that God could raise the dead to new life, do they find it hard to believe that God is the Creator of the world? I suspect a curious inconsistency in those who are quite willing to believe that God made space and time but who hesitate over the raising of the dead.

My point is not here to mount a defence of the doctrine of resurrection but only to indicate that here is a metaphysics behind this hope, and then to draw out some similarities between Jewish, Christian and Muslim teaching. Consider this attempt from the Mishnah (c.70–200 CE) to prove, from Torah, the resurrection of the dead:

> Rabbi Simai says: How do you know that the resurrection of the dead can be derived from Torah? From the verse, 'I also established My covenant with them (that is, with Abraham, Isaac, and Jacob), to give them the land of Canaan' (Exod. 6:4). 'To you' is not written but 'to them.' Hence, resurrection of the dead can be derived from the Torah. (b.Sanh. 90b)[9]

The argument is that, since the promise of the land was made to Abraham, Isaac and Jacob, they must be alive – somehow – to receive it, even after they are dead. This is the same kind of argument that we find on the lips of Jesus in Mark 12. There the Sadducees, who do not believe in the resurrection, tell Jesus the story of one woman who has been married to seven brothers in succession, each one dying and the next taking her for his wife. Whose wife will she be in heaven? It is a trick question of course, and Jesus answers by bringing things back to Moses and the burning bush, 'Have you not read', he asks his questioner, 'how God said to Moses "I am the God of Abraham, and the God of Isaac, and the God of Jacob"? He is not the God of the dead, but of the living' (RSV, Mark 12.26–7).

There are two assertions here – the first that, since God is the God of the living, then Abraham, Isaac and Jacob must yet somehow be alive, and the second, that *God is the God of the living.* Whatever one's views on the resurrection of the dead, we have arrived at a central teaching of Judaism, Christianity and Islam which might be summarized as – choose life!

I now want to voice a concern about Gabriel Marcel's philosophy of hope as it stands up to scriptural teaching. Marcel, he himself stressed, devised his philosophy of hope in a time of war. Hope, in his philosophy, is always accompanied by the possibility of despair, life is chosen in the face of death. Marcel seems to allow no possibility for a pure untrammelled hope. Indeed he says that 'The truth is that there can strictly speaking be no hope except when the temptation to despair exists'.[10]

Although hope and despair may often be paired in this way in worldy reasoning, within Christian thought it can only be a mistake to elevate despair to the same ontological level as hope. The theological reason for this is similar to that which Augustine gave for saying that evil is not an equivalent and co-existing force to good. The world is good because it is God's creation. Evil, though altogether and horribly present, is not a self-existent counter-reality but the absence of good. Faith, hope and charity abide, but not always as harnessed to doubt, despair and hatred.

The place where we can see this most clearly – a hope unaccompanied by attendant despair – is in pregnancy and the birth of a child. The hope of pregnancy is not characteristically coupled with a temptation to despair, and with every child comes a new and initially uncompromised hope. Gabriel Marcel, writing in a time of war, saw death as the great existential horizon of life, but it is only one. Birth is another. If mortality demands our attention as a frame for human existing, then so does natality, a point made by Hannah Arendt, who thought of birth as the continual saving irruption of newness into human affairs.

We are neglectful of the powerful symbolism of gestation and new birth present within our sacred texts and traditions. The people of Israel wandered for 40 years in Sinai, Jesus after his baptism spends 40 days in the desert, Christians fast for the 40 days of Lent, and celebrate 40 days between Easter and Ascension. One is told that 40 is a Hebraism for 'a long time' but it is also the number of weeks of human gestation – a point that I have never seen anywhere mentioned in works of theology. All these scriptural and liturgical 'forties' – the 40 years in the wilderness, the 40 days in the desert, are times of gestation and growth, times of anticipation of what is promised but not yet delivered. As a friend of mine said when his wife was expecting their first child – 'it is like knowing you're going to get married, but not knowing quite when, or to whom!'

Pregnancy, too, is a journey of hope. It was the particular genius of Julian of Norwich to seize upon Paul's language of new birth and the gospel imagery of second birth and bring them together.[11] 'Kind' and 'kin' are the same in Middle English and, for Julian, Christ, becoming one of us through the incarnation – that is, one of 'our kind' – makes us the kin of God.

But the work of Christ is not complete at Bethlehem. Julian sees Christ as continually 'in travail', labouring to give birth to humankind in the fullness of its intended being. Our human mothers, she says, bear us to pain and death, but Christ – true Mother – bears us to joy and eternal life. 'So he carries us within him in love and travail, until the full time when he wanted to suffer the sharpest thorns and cruel pains that ever were or will be, and at the last he dies.'[12]

The full range of meanings of 'divine travail' is lost in the modern translation. In Julian's Middle English, Christ 'travails' has three concurrent senses. Christ is in labour with us (travail), sorrowing with us (sharing our travails) and, in doing both and a third meaning, 'travelling' with us on our way. We sorrow and stumble but in this Christ is our fellow traveller, always leading us amidst the changes and chances of this mortal life.

One is reminded of Augustine's *de Trinitate*, to which Julian whether directly or indirectly is surely indebted.[13] For Augustine as for Julian this life is a matter of 'travelling' with God – '*Through him we travel to Him* (*per ipsum pergimus ad ipsum*)' (XIII.24). Julian's embrace of the body and the polysemy of her native English allows her to see this travelling God as daily bearing us into new life, life more glorious than we could imagine.

Gabriel Marcel thinks that hope (and here he means religious hope,

hope in the Thou) always involves a connection between a return and something completely new, always involves elements both of preservation and of restoration; it is the 'as before, but differently and better than before'. It is never a return to the simple status quo but somehow an 'undreamed of promotion, a transfiguration'.[14] The fatalistic custodian of the student residence with whose remarks I began this chapter could only see hope as a sad thing because his world lacked the transcendent. For him, those in need of hope had a cup that was half empty, and even at best their cup would only return to being full – only return, that is, to Marcel's status quo. But hope in God, the creator who made heaven and earth, holds out the promise of more than this, 'undreamed of promotion, a transfiguration'. Grace, beauty, loveliness.

Bernard of Clairvaux in his Sermons on the Song of Songs has a reflection on the post-resurrection appearances of Jesus that bears considering in both an ecumenical and an interfaith setting. Bernard asks, how was it, if God is one and always that same, that Mary Magdalene mistook the risen Christ for a gardener, and that the disciples did not recognize him on the road to Emmaus until he broke the bread? The shortcoming, according to Bernard, is ours. For we cannot – yet – see God as God truly is. We are still being *conformed* to his image. To bear out his point, Bernard invokes 1 John 3.2: 'Beloved' (the Greek is plural so the Italian 'carissimi' has a better feel, or perhaps the Arabic 'habibi'), 'Beloved, we are God's children now; what we will be has not yet been revealed. What we do know is this: when he is revealed, we will be like him, for we will see him as he is (1 Jn. 3.2).'[15] There is a wonderful double uncertainty here – we do not yet know who we are, because we do not yet know the fullness of the glory of God in whose image we are made.

We moderns expect too little of God. Embarrassed by the bold expectations of the New Testament writers and crippled by an indifference to the metaphysics of creation in which the patristic and medieval theologians unfolded the cogency of these expectations, we become shy about resurrection and new life. 'God is good', might be 'our motto', but 'perhaps not as good as all that.'

The words of a seventeenth-century hymn say otherwise:

My song is love unknown, my Saviour's love to me;
Love to the loveless shown, that they might lovely be.[16]

I suspect that a modern hymnist, reworking the same theme, would write something like 'love to the loveless shown, that they may be loved'. But Samuel Crossan does not say that. He says 'Love to the love-ness shown that they *may be lovely*'. Of course our calling is to be not just loved, but lovely, because 'we will be like him' who is loveliness itself, the image of the invisible God (1 John 3.2).

We are travellers on the way to what we do not know, but we walk with confidence that it will be more than a matter of making the half-empty cup full. It will be, in Marcel's terms, surplus, gift, transfigura-tion: faith, hope and loveliness. In the meantime, we keep journeying. Walking, apparently, is really only controlled falling. The child learns to walk by learning to fall. Perhaps this is how the journey of faith must be, always a controlled falling. But we must risk the fall if we are to con-tinue on the way, if we are to learn in the end – to dance.

Notes

1 Gabriel Marcel, 1951, *Homo Viator: Introduction to the Metaphysics of Hope*, trans. Emma Craufurd, London: Victor Gollanz, p. 12.

2 Gabriel Marcel, 1984, 'An Autobiographical Essay', in Paul Schilpp and Lewis Hahn (eds), 1984, *The Philosophy of Gabriel Marcel*, Library of Living Philosophers, vol. 17, La Salle, IL: Open Court, pp. 20–1.

3 Marcel, *Homo Viator*, Preface, p. 7.

4 Marcel, 'The Metaphysics of Hope', in *Homo Viator*, p. 47.

5 Gerhard May, 1994, *Creatio ex Nihilo: The Doctrine of 'Creation out of Nothing' in Early Christian Thought*, Edinburgh: T & T Clark, p. 23.

6 Martin Buber, Martin and Franz Rosenzweig, 1994, *Scripture and Translation*, trans. Lawrence Rosenwald with Everett Fox, Bloomington, IN: Indiana University Press.

7 Cited by Rosenzweig in his essay '"The Eternal": Moses Mendelssohn and the Name of God', in Buber and Rosenzweig, *Scripture and Translation*, p. 101.

8 Jon Levenson, 2006, *Resurrection and the Restoration of Israel: The Ultimate Victory of the God of Life*, New Haven, CT: Yale University Press.

9 Quoted in Levenson, *Resurrection*, p. 28.

10 Marcel, *Homo Viator*, p. 36.

11 On the first, see Romans 8.29 where Christ is firstborn among many brethren, but also Colossians 3.15, and elsewhere, and on the second see especially the Gospel of John.

12 Julian of Norwich, *Showings, Long Text*, §60, ed. Edmund Colledge and James Walsh, Classics of Western Spirituality, New York: Paulist Press, 1978.

13 These arguments are developed in my book, *The Kindness of God*, Oxford: Oxford University Press, 2007, as are many of the themes that inform this chapter.

14 Marcel, *Homo Viator*, p. 65.

15 Bernard of Clairvaux, *On the Song of Songs, 1 (The Works of Bernard of Clairvaux, Volume 2)*, Cistercian Fathers Series, Kalamazoo: Cistercian Publications, 2005.

16 Samuel Crossan, 1624–83.

Biographical Epilogue

DAVID W. BROWN

Ann was born in September 1938 in the Cheshire town of Stockport. It was to a boarding school at Bowden in the same county that she was sent at the early age of three, while her mother earned her living, nursing in Manchester. Despite the undoubted drawbacks of being deprived of a normal home life so early, one major contribution that Bowden did make to Ann's future was encouragement of her passion for ballet, an interest that has continued throughout her life. Using the Cecchetti Method, she has taught adult classes in Newcastle for many years, and she also served for a while on the Management Committee for degree awards at the Royal Academy of Dancing.[1]

Thereafter secondary education continued at Hulme Grammar School for Girls at Oldham, near Manchester. Although her interests in music and history were also strong, the influence of her Scripture mistress, Miss G. P. Pestle, proved decisive. Not only had her two brothers (who were Anglican priests) read theology at Durham, so too had Miss Pestle, though at a time when women were still not allowed formally to take Durham degrees in theology.[2] So Ann first arrived in that great cathedral city in the autumn of 1957. Until the time of Michael Ramsey as Van Mildert Canon Professor, the Faculty (as it then was) had been exclusively Anglican. It was still predominantly so in Ann's day. It was, however, three Nonconformists who were to exercise the greatest influence on her and indeed become firm friends: Kingsley Barrett, Charles Cranfield and Alec Whitehouse. Courses in modern theology were open only to ordinands, but a special subject on 'Philosophy and the Christian Religion' taught by Alec Whitehouse caught Ann's imagination and was to lead eventually to her first publishing ventures on Coleridge and Kant. Alec was also a consummate preacher, much sought after by the BBC. This may have been one of the factors that led to his admiration for Austin Farrer, and for what might seem to some the rather puzzling equal valuing of Barth and Farrer on his bookshelves. If Ann was able only to follow him fully in respect of his enthusiasm for Farrer (attested both in her regular attendance at Farrer conferences and in numerous publications), she did also decide to mark her former tutor's retirement by editing a collection of his more important essays.[3]

Initially, it looked as though Ann's life was not marked for an academic career. She took a teaching diploma and went to teach for two years at Newbury Grammar School. However, in 1963 a scholarship to MacMaster University in Canada became available, and this led to an invitation for further study at the University of Chicago. However, her old university beckoned with the offer of a Resident Tutorship at her former college of St Mary's, then a much more significant post than it is in contemporary Durham life.[4] In a pattern that was repeated on a number of subsequent occasions, Ann then threw herself, body and soul, into the life of the institution, reorganizing the library, reforming the admissions process and so on. At the same time she began work on a doctorate. This she had hoped would be supervised by Alec Whitehouse but in the meantime he had been appointed to the new University of Kent at Canterbury. Perhaps it was her own experience of struggling to produce a doctorate under less than ideal conditions that led her in due course to take such pains with her own research students, a number of whom have contributed chapters to this volume.[5]

Of course, it is not always the most important elements in someone's life that are most remembered. So, just as a generation of St Mary's students have recalled Ann's rescuing of stray cats, the author Catherine Fox chose to pick out her erstwhile supervisor's cultivation of indoor hyacinths in her first novel, *Angels and Men*.[6] Yet there is something indicative here after all of Ann's character: not only her delight in religious examples drawn from nature but also in the way in which they can sanctify our own lives.[7] Cats might even contribute towards a 'mutual grace of salvation'.[8]

Ann's doctorate helped to secure her appointment as a University Lecturer in 1975. Hers was Durham's first full-time appointment in philosophical theology, and it was to that area of expertise that she was to devote her attention over the next decade, through essays on eighteenth- and nineteenth-century thought and in her important study on Kant's approach to the problem of evil in her first major book, *Kant and Job's Comforters* (1985). It was an interest that continued throughout her career in a form that would have pleased Austin Farrer, in the careful integration of philosophical and theological concerns, as can be witnessed in as recent an essay as her 2005 article on 'Philosophy of

Religion: Its Relation to Theology'.[9] Even Kant himself never entirely slipped from her sights, as she continued to defend him on his approach to theodicy as a good balance between naïve optimism and a pessimism that left no room for faith.[10]

However, an unexpected invitation in the mid 1980s to deliver the Scott Holland Lectures did result in a significant change of direction. The relevant trust requires the appointed lecturer to focus upon the social and political implications of the religion of the incarnation, phraseology intended to reflect Henry Scott Holland's view that insufficient attention had been given to the material side of Christology: that God taking a body must have implications for other bodies as well. Ann chose to take up that challenge through discussion of the issues raised by feminist theology, giving her work the intriguing title *Searching for Lost Coins* (1987). While severely critical of world-denying approaches to the Christian faith such as that of Simone Weil, there were already signs of a concern that was to become much more prominent in the later and much longer work, *Feminist Theology: Voices from the Past* (2001): that the movement in securing rights for the most vocal might also unintentionally mariginalize others such as children, mothers and indeed any who found self-assertion difficult. Her refusal to toe any one particular party line ensured that her *Feminist Theology: A Reader* (1990) was widely praised and advocated for its balanced approach.

Headship of the department came along with some major surgery in 1989, but fortunately with it the appointment of some new colleagues, which made it possible for her to branch out in some other new directions, as she relaxed into her new role as Professor of Divinity, Durham's first ever award (in 1995) of a personal chair to a woman.[11] Now teaching some more central areas of the syllabus, she was determined to draw discussion of Christian doctrine away from more cerebral approaches to one firmly anchored in spirituality and life more generally. In particular, her extensive experience in the 1980s of the problems involved in attempting to communicate religious issues on television led her to the conviction that theologians had to treat the arts much more seriously. Both undergraduates and research students benefited as novels, poetry and art were gradually introduced into the classroom. Students were encouraged to find a graced world well beyond any narrow biblical dispensation, with Dorothy L. Sayers and Evelyn Underhill among others called upon to help disclose such a sacramental world.

Although Eric Heaton had been a reforming Dean of the Cathedral whom Ann had admired, it remained true in the early 1990s that Durham was still liturgically far behind most other cathedrals in England. However, as things began to change more rapidly, so this aspect began to take on a larger role in her life. Beginning with the modest task of operating what was initially called being a No. 4 (leading the intercessions and announcing the hymns), by the end of the decade Ann had become an obvious person to be one of the first two laity (apart from the Chapter Clerk) to serve on the Cathedral Chapter. Not only did she throw herself into the task wholeheartedly, not least on the issue of 'development', she also added to her already heavy academic commitments in both the university and beyond by accepting appointment to various national church bodies, among them the Doctrine Commission of the Church of England, the Working Party on Women in the Episcopate and the Christian–Muslim Forum.

Contemporary academics often criticize the government's obsession with statistics and with certain kinds of output like those required for the RAE (Research Assessment Exercise), but they can sometimes be just as narrow themselves, though for different reasons. Despite her service on the AHRC (Arts and Humanities Research Council) and other such bodies, however, Ann consistently refused to be bound by the culture of only the heavy monograph counting. So, while she did contribute her own, at the same time she demonstrated an equal concern to reach a much wider readership with her various collections, among them *Spiritual Classics from the Late Twentieth Century*.[12] Likewise, her editing of the *Modern Churchman* (1982–91) and in due course of *Theology* (1991–7) was marked by the desire to ensure that these journals should reach a wide audience and not just the professional academic. So when she was duly honoured by being made President of SST (Society for the Study of Theology) for two years (2005–6), she used the occasion of her presidential address to insist that her professional colleagues face up to the deleterious consequences of the all-too-common modern narrowing of theological horizons.

That broad compass of interest in, and of service to, theology in the widest sense was rewarded in 2001 with the award of a CBE. It was a rare honour. The only other example of which I am aware was in the case of C. F. D. Moule. Charlie Moule's influence and friendships across the generations was legendary. So it is not without relevance that Ann chose as her three guests for the ceremony at Buckingham Palace someone in their 90s, one in their 50s and a third still in his 20s. Retirement in 2003 might have brought a slackening of pace but that is not in Ann's character. Among other things she embarked on chairing the Durham

Cathedral Choir Association and on the exhausting task of reorganizing and fundraising for the Meissen Library at Durham, a large library of theology in German gifted to the Church of England by Evangelische Kirche in Deutschland. It is therefore fitting that, in the same year as this book honours her academic achievements, Ann was instituted as an Honorary Canon of Durham Cathedral. It has been a life without compartments, in which worship and service have underpinned academic rigour. But even that is to put matters too negatively. The *joie de vivre* that so often characterizes her first passion – ballet – also reflects her more general infectious enthusiasm for theology anchored in life and in the wider world that she succeeded in communicating to so many, and to which this book bears ample witness.

Notes

1 Managed from Durham despite its location in London.

2 Degrees in other subjects first became available to women in 1895, in theology not until well into the twentieth century.

3 W. A. Whitehouse, 1981, ed. Ann Loades, *The Authority of Grace: Essays in Response to Karl Barth*, Edinburgh: T & T Clark.

4 More like 'College Officer' in today's jargon.

5 Fortunately in Ann's case the Old Testament scholar John Rogerson did what he could by way of encouragement and support in reading her work.

6 Catherine Fox, 1996, *Angels and Men*, London: Hamish Hamilton.

7 See, for example, Ann Loades, 1997, *Evelyn Underhill*, London: Fount, pp. 27, 57.

8 Words from a poem by Dorothy Sayers ('For Timothy, in the Coherence') and as such far from being as sentimental as it may sound out of context: see Ann Loades (ed.), *Dorothy L. Sayers: Spiritual Writings*, London: SPCK, pp. 3, 176–7.

9 Ann Loades, 2005, 'Philosophy of Religion: Its Relation to Theology', in Harriet A. Harris and Chris Insole (eds), *Faith and Philosophical Analysis: The Impact of Analytic Philosophy on the Philosophy of Religion*, Aldershot: Ashgate, pp. 136–47.

10 For the former, in critique of Francis Fukuyama, see Ann Loades, 2004, 'From Kant to Fukuyama and beyond', in William F. Storrar and Andrew R. Morton (eds), *Public Theology for the 21st Century: Essays in Honour of Duncan B. Forrester*, London: T & T Clark, pp. 143–57; for the latter, in critique of John Kekes, see Ann Loades, 1996, 'On Tearing the Darkness to Tatters: Hope for the World?', in David F. Ford and Dennis Stamps (eds), *Essentials of Christian Community: Essays in Honour of Daniel W. Hardy*, Edinburgh: T & T Clark, pp. 296–304.

11 In the centenary year of women's first admission to university degrees.

12 Ann Loades (ed.), 1995, *Spiritual Classics from the Late Twentieth Century*, London: National Society/Church House Publishing. The selections are nicely balanced not only in the most obvious sense of three contributions from women and three from men but also in the range of topics (from generosity to justice, from suffering to the reading of Scripture).

Ann Loades: bibliography

1975

- 'Kant's Concern with Theodicy', *Journal of Theological Studies* 27, pp. 361–76.

1978

- 'Coleridge as Theologian: Some Comments on His Reading of Kant', *Journal of Theological Studies* 29, pp. 410–26.

1979

- 'Analogy and the Indictment of the Deity', *Studia Theologica* 33, pp. 25–43.

1980

- 'Kant and Job's Comforters', *New Studies in Theology* 1, pp. 119–38.

1981

- (with Sheriden W. Gilley), 'Thomas Henry Huxley: The War Between Victorian Science and Religion', *Journal of Religion* 61, pp. 285–308.
- 'Immanuel Kant's Humanism', in K. Robbins (ed.), *Religion and Humanism*, Studies in Church History 17, Oxford: Blackwell, pp. 297–310.
- 'Moral Sentiment and Belief in God', *Studia Theologica*, pp. 73–83.
- Edited, W. A. Whitehouse, *The Authority of Grace: Essays in Response to Karl Barth*, Edinburgh: T & T Clark (US title: *Creation, Science and Theology: Essays in Response to Barth*, Grand Rapids: Eerdmans).

1982–1991

- Edited (with Anthony O. Dyson and others), *Modern Churchman*, Modern Churchman/Modern Churchpeople's Union.

1983

- 'No Consoling Vision: Coleridge's Discovery of Kant's Authentic Theodicy', in J. R. Watson (ed.), *An Infinite Complexity: Essays in Romanticism*, Edinburgh: Edinburgh University Press, pp. 95–124.
- Edited (with Jeffrey C. Eaton), *For God and Clarity: New Essays in Honor of Austin Farrer*, Alison Park, PA: Pickwick Publications; including: 'Austin Farrer on *Love Almighty*', pp. 93–110.

1984

- 'Sacrifice: A Problem for Theology', in David Jasper (ed.), *Images of Belief in Literature*, Basingstoke: Macmillan, pp. 122–37.

1985

- 'Death and Disvalue: Some Reflections on "Sick" Children', *Hospital Chaplain* 93, pp. 5–11.
- *Kant and Job's Comforters*, Newcastle-Upon-Tyne: Avero Publications.

1987

- *Searching for Lost Coins: Explorations in Christianity and Feminism*, London: SPCK.

1989

- 'C. S. Lewis: Grief Observed, Rationality Abandoned, Faith Regained', *Journal of Literature and Theology* 3, pp. 107–21.
- 'Feminist Theology', in David F. Ford (ed.), *The Modern Theologians: An Introduction to Christian Theology in the Twentieth Century*, Oxford: Blackwell, volume 2, pp. 235–52.
- 'The Grief of C. S. Lewis', *Theology Today* 46, pp. 269–76.

1990

- Edited, *Feminist Theology: A Reader*, London: SPCK/Louisville, KY: Westminster John Knox Press.
- 'The Virgin Mary in the Feminist Quest', in Janet Martin Soskice (ed.), *After Eve: Women, Theology and the Christian Tradition*, London: Marshall Pickering, 156–78.
- Edited, *History of European Ideas* 12.1 (on Kierkegaard).

1991

- 'Beyond God the Father: An Introduction to Mary Daly's View of Christian Tradition', in Andrew Linzey and Peter Wexley (eds),

Fundamentalism and Tolerance: An Agenda for Theology and Society, London: Bellow, pp. 113–27.

- Edited (with Loyal D. Rue), *Contemporary Classics in Philosophy of Religion*, La Salle, IL: Open Court.
- 'Eucharistic Sacrifice: The Problem of How to Use a Liturgical Metaphor, with Special Reference to Simone Weil', in Stephen W. Sykes (ed.), *Sacrifice and Redemption: Durham Essays in Theology*, Cambridge: Cambridge University Press, pp. 247–61.
- 'A Feminist Perspective on the Morality of the New Right', in Michael Northcott (ed.), *Vision and Prophecy: The Tasks of Social Theology Today*, Edinburgh: Centre for Theology and Public Issues, pp. 49–61.
- 'Neighbourly Benevolence or Arrogant Manipulation: On Artificially Assisted Human Reproduction', in Daniel W. Hardy and Peter H. Sedgwick (eds), *The Weight of Glory: A Vision and Practice for Christian Faith: The Future of Liberal Theology: Essays for Peter Baelz*, Edinbugh: T & T Clark, pp. 155–68.
- 'Some Reflections on C. S. Lewis's *A Grief Observed*', in Cynthia Marshall (ed.), *Essays on C. S. Lewis and George MacDonald*, Ceredigion: Mellen, pp. 31–51.

1991–1997

- Edited, *Theology,* SPCK.

1992

- Edited (with Michael McLain), *Hermeneutics, the Bible and Literary Criticism*, Basingstoke: Macmillan.

1993

- 'Dorothy L. Sayers and Dante's Beatrice', *Seven: An Anglo-American Literary Review* 10, pp. 97–110.
- Edited, *Dorothy L Sayers: Spiritual Writings*, London: SPCK.
- 'Feminist Theology and the Trinity', in James Byrne (ed.), *The Christian Understanding of God Today*, Dublin: Columbia, pp. 76–80.
- 'Introductory Address', *Feminist Theology* 3, pp. 12–22.
- 'Kierkegaard's Views on Art and Aesthetics', in David Cooper (ed.), *A Companion to Aesthetics*, Oxford: Blackwell, pp. 254–6.
- 'Simone Weil and Antigone: Innocence and Affliction', in Richard Hill (ed.), *Simone Weil's Philosophy of Culture: Readings Towards a Divine Humanity*, Cambridge: Cambridge University Press, pp. 277–94.

- 'Van Mildert – The Educationalist', in Charles Yeats (ed.), *A Christian Heritage*, Bangor: Headstart History, pp. 75–80.

1994

- 'The Face of Christ', in Heather Walton and Susan Durber (eds), *Silence in Heaven: A Book of Women's Preaching*, London: SCM Press, pp. 9–13.
- 'Mary of Magdala', in Heather Walton and Susan Durber (eds), *Silence in Heaven: A Book of Women's Preaching*, London: SCM Press, pp. 130–5.
- 'A Feminist Perspective', in Charles Yeats, *Veritatis Splendor: A Response*, Norwich: Canterbury Press, pp. 76–82.
- 'Foreword', in Catherine Wilcox, *Women in Early Quakerism*, Ceredigion: Mellen, pp. i–vii.
- 'On Mary: Constructive Ambivalence', *The Way: A Journal of Contemporary Spirituality Published by the British Jesuits* 34, pp. 138–46.
- *Thinking About Child Sexual Abuse: The John Coffin Memorial Lecture*, London: University of London.

1995

- 'Are Women Human? Dorothy L. Sayers as a Feminist Reader of Dante's Beatrice', *Feminist Theology* 8, pp. 21–38.
- 'Creativity, Embodiment and Mutuality: Dorothy L. Sayers on Dante, Love and Freedom', in Colin N. Gunton (ed.), *God and Freedom: Essays in Historical and Systematic Theology*, Edinburgh: T & T Clark, pp. 103–18.
- 'Creativity, Embodiment and Mutuality: Dorothy L. Sayers on Dante, Love and Freedom', *Proceedings of the Dorothy L. Sayers' Society*, pp. 24–31.
- Edited (with David W. Brown), *The Sense of the Sacramental: Movement and Measure in Art and Music, Place and Time*, London: SPCK; including (with David W. Brown): 'Introduction: The Dance of Grace', pp. 1–16.
- Edited, *Spiritual Classics from the Late Twentieth Century*, London: National Society/Church House Publishing.

1996

- 'Are Women Human? Dorothy L Sayers as a Feminist Reader of Dante's Beatrice', in Alison E. Jasper and Alistair G. Hunter (eds), *Talking It Over: Reflections on Women and Feminism in Religion*, Glasgow: Trinity St Mungo, pp. 150–66.

- Edited (with David W. Brown), *Christ the Sacramental Word: Incarnation, Sacrament and Poetry*, London: SPCK; including (with David W. Brown): 'Introduction: The Divine Poet', pp. 1–25.
- 'Consider Catherine', *New Blackfriars: The Monthly Review of the English Dominicans* 77, pp. 164–70.
- 'Domestic Violence', in Paul B. Clarke and Andrew Linzey (eds), *Dictionary of Ethics, Theology and Society*, London: Routledge, pp. 253–5.
- 'Prostitution', in Paul B. Clarke and Andrew Linzey (eds), *Dictionary of Ethics, Theology and Society*, London: Routledge, pp. 693–4.
- 'Dympna Revisited: Thinking About the Sexual Abuse of Children', in Stephen C. Barton (ed.), *The Family in Theological Perspective*, Edinburgh: T & T Clark, pp. 253–72.
- 'Mary', in Lisa Isherwood and Dorothea McEwan (eds), *A–Z of Feminist Theology*, Sheffield: Sheffield Academic Press, pp. 128–9.
- 'Trinity', in Lisa Isherwood and Dorothea McEwan (eds), *A–Z of Feminist Theology*, Sheffield: Sheffield Academic Press, pp. 227–8.
- 'On Tearing the Darkness to Tatters: Hope for This World?', in David F. Ford and Dennis Stamps (eds), *Essentials of Christian Community: Essays in Honour of Daniel W. Hardy*, Edinbugh: T & T Clark, pp. 296–304.
- 'Word and Sacrament: Recovering Integrity', *See Link*, pp. 3–15.

1997

- 'Anselm, Dante and Dorothy L. Sayers' *The Just Vengeance*', *Proceedings of the Dorothy L. Sayers Society*, pp. 29–40.
- *Evelyn Underhill*, London: Fount.
- 'Feminist Theology', in F. L. Cross and E. A. Livingstone (eds), *The Oxford Dictionary of the Christian Church*, Oxford: Oxford University Press, pp. 604–5.
- 'Feminist Theology: Transregional Movements', in David F. Ford (ed.), *The Modern Theologians: An Introduction to Christian Theology in the Twentieth Century*, 2nd edn, Oxford: Blackwell, pp. 575–84.
- 'Feminist Theology: A View of Mary', in William McLoughlin and Jill Pinnock (eds), *Mary is for Everyone: Essays on Mary and Ecumenism*, Leominster: Gracewing, pp. 32–40.
- 'Word and Sacrament: Recovering Integrity', *Forum* 4, pp. 1–16.

1998

- 'Austin Marsden Farrer', in Alister McGrath (ed.), *The SPCK Handbook of Anglican Theologians*, London: SPCK, pp. 120–3.

- 'Evelyn Underhill', in Alister McGrath (ed.), *The SPCK Handbook of Anglican Theologians*, London: SPCK, pp. 223–6.
- 'Dympna Revisited: Thinking About the Sexual Abuse of Children', in Kathleen O'Grady, Ann L Gilroy and Janette Gray (eds), *Bodies, Lives, Voices: Gender in Theology*, Sheffield: Sheffield Academic Press, pp. 40–58.
- 'Feminist Interpretation', in John Barton (ed.), *The Cambridge Companion to Biblical Interpretation*, Cambridge: Cambridge University Press, pp. 81–94.
- 'Feminist Theology: A New Direction in Christian Studies', *Farmington Papers: Modern Theology* 10.
- 'St Martin of Tours', *Actors' Church Union Report*, pp. 9–15.
- 'Theologie Feministe', in Jean-Yves Lacoste (ed.), *Dictionnaire de Théologie*, Paris: Presses Universitaires de France, pp. 463–4.

1999

- 'Feminist Theology', in Alan Bullock and Stephen Trombley (eds), *New Fontana Dictionary of Modern Thought*, London: HarperCollins, pp. 317–18.
- 'Mission, Inculturation and the Liberation of Genders: The Contribution of Feminist Theology', *Feminist Theology* 20, pp. 87–98.
- 'Schwangerschaftsabbruch: Ethisch', *Theologische Realenzyklopaedie* 30, pp. 633–40.
- 'The Politics of Grace and the Pain of Difference', *Religion in Public Life: Conference Proceedings*, Cape Town: University of Cape Town, pp. 35–75.
- 'Word and Sacrament: Recovering Integrity', in Neil Brown and Robert Gasgoine (eds), *Faith in the Public Forum*, Adelaide: Openbooks, pp. 28–46.

2000

- 'Abortion: A Feminist and Theological View', in Mark Thiessen Nation and Samuel Wells (eds), *Faithfulness and Fortitude: In Conversation with the Theological Ethics of Stanley Hauerwas*, London: T & T Clark, pp. 233–56.
- 'Creed', *The Women's Studies Encyclopedia*, Brighton: Harvester Press.
- *Feminist Theology: Voices from the Past*, Oxford: Polity Press.
- 'Feminst Theology', in Trevor A. Hart (ed.), *Dictionary of Historical Theology*, Grand Rapids, MI: Eerdmans, pp. 210–13.

- 'Simone Weil', in Trevor A. Hart (ed.), *Dictionary of Historical Theology*, Grand Rapids, MI: Eerdmans, p. 568.
- 'Sacrament', in Adrian Hastings et al. (eds), *The Oxford Companion to Christian Thought*, Oxford: Oxford University Press, pp. 634–7.

2001

- 'Music: The Sense of the Sacramental', *Church Music Quarterly* December, pp. 13–14.
- 'The Liberation of Genders: Feminist Theology as a Challenge to Inculturation', in Simon Barrow and Graeme Smith (eds), *Christian Mission in Western Society*, London: Churches Together in Britain and Ireland, pp. 198–211.
- 'The Position of the Anglican Communion Regarding the Trinity and Mary', *New Blackfriars: The Monthly Review of the English Dominicans* 82, pp. 364–74.
- 'Why Worship?', *In Illo Tempore: Ushaw Library Bulletin and Liturgical Review* 16, pp. 34–42.

2003

- (Doctrine Commission member), *Being Human: A Christian Understanding of Personhood Illustrated with Reference to Power, Money, Sex and Time*, London: Church House Publishing.
- 'From Kant to Fukuyama and Beyond: Some Reflections', in William F. Storrar and Andrew R. Morton (eds), *Public Theology for the 21st Century: Essays in Honour of Duncan B. Forrester*, London: T & T Clark, pp. 143–58.
- 'Theological Reflection', in Bill Hall and David Jasper (eds), *Art and the Spiritual*, Sunderland: University of Sunderland Press, pp. 53–5.

2004

- 'Christian Spirituality and Sacramentality', *Search* 27, pp. 89–96.
- Edited (with Jeff Astley and David W. Brown), *Creation: A Reader*, Problems in Theology, London: Continuum.
- Edited (with Jeff Astley and David W. Brown), *Evil: A Reader*, Problems in Theology, London: Continuum.
- Edited (with Jeff Astley and David W. Brown), *War and Peace: A Reader*, Problems in Theology, London: Continuum.
- 'Finding New Sense in the Sacramental', in Geoffrey Rowell and Christine Hall (eds), *The Gestures of God: Explorations in Sacramentality*, London: Continuum, pp. 161–72.

- 'Pubbliciste, In Verita "Teologhe"', in Cettina Militello (ed.), *Donna e Teologia*, Bologna: Edizioni Dehoniane, pp. 95–115.
- 'The Vitality of Tradition: Austin Farrer and Friends', in David Hein and Edward Hugh Henderson (eds), *Captured by the Crucified: The Practical Theology of Austin Farrer*, London: Continuum, pp. 15–46.
- (Working Party member), *Women Bishops in the Church of England?* (London: Church House Publishing).
- 'Women in the Episcopate?', *Anvil: An Anglican Evangelical Journal of Theology and Mission* 21, pp. 113–19.

2005

- 'Eucharistic Spirituality', in Philip Sheldrake (ed.), *The New SCM Dictionary of Christian Spirituality*, London: SCM Press, pp. 286–9.
- 'Sacramentality and Spirituality', in Philip Sheldrake (ed.), *The New SCM Dictionary of Christian Spirituality*, London: SCM Press, pp. 553–5.
- 'Feminist Theology', in F. L. Cross and E. A. Livingstone (eds), *Oxford Dictionary of the Christian Church*, Oxford: Oxford University Press, pp. 67–8.
- Edited (with Jeff Astley and David W. Brown), *God in Action: A Reader*, Problems in Theology, London: Continuum.
- Edited (with Jeff Astley and David W. Brown), *Science and Religion: A Reader*, Problems in Theology, London: Continuum.
- 'Sacramentality and Christian Spirituality', in Arthur G. Holder (ed.), *The Blackwell Companion to Christian Spirituality*, Oxford: Blackwell, pp. 254–68.
- 'On Music's Grace: Trying to Think Theologically about Music', in Julias Lipner (ed.), *Truth, Religious Dialogue and Dynamic Orthodoxy: Essays in Honour of Brian Hebblethwaite*, London: SCM Press, pp. 25–38.
- 'Philosophy of Religion: Its Relation to Theology', in Harriet A. Harris and Christopher Insole (eds), *Faith and Philosophical Analysis: The Impact of Analytical Philosophy on the Philosophy of Religion*, Aldershot: Ashgate, 2005, pp. 136–47.

2006

- 'Josephine Butler', *Borderlands* 5, pp. 27–30.
- (with David W. Brown), 'Learning from the Arts', in Jonathan Baker and William Davage (eds), *Who is This Man? Christ in the Renewal of the Church*, London: Continuum, pp. 67–102.

- Edited (with Robert MacSwain), *The Truth-Seeking Heart: An Austin Farrer Reader*, Norwich: Canterbury Press.
- 'Whither Theology and Religious Studies in Ireland and the UK?', *Discourse: Learning and Teaching in Philosophical and Religious Studies* 5, pp. 29–47.

2008

- 'Table: Sacramental Spirituality', in Stephen Burns (ed.), *Renewing the Eucharist: A Fourfold Journey*, Norwich: Canterbury Press.